THE
HEAVYWEIGHTS
THE DEFINITIVE HISTORY
OF THE HEAVYWEIGHT
FIGHTERS

THE
HEAVYWEIGHTS
THE DEFINITIVE HISTORY OF THE HEAVYWEIGHT FIGHTERS

BOB MEE

TEMPUS

First published 2006

Tempus Publishing Limited
The Mill, Brimscombe Port,
Stroud, Gloucestershire, GL5 2QG
www.tempus-publishing.com

British Library Cataloguing in Publication Data.
A catalogue record for this book is available from the British Library.

ISBN 0 7524 3426 8

Typesetting and origination by Tempus Publishing Limited
Printed in Great Britain

CONTENTS

INTRODUCTION

Since the days of James Figg, heavyweight boxers have had a special appeal.

Sometimes we have to forgive them their weaknesses: technically, it's a different game for heavyweights – what a lightweight or a middleweight can do, a 6ft 4in, 230lbs man can only dream of. In spite of that, the old saying that in the health of the heavyweight division lies the health of the sport still applies.

Purists, or those who would investigate beneath boxing's most obvious surfaces, will find more to admire in the speed, ferocity and craftsmanship of lighter fighters, but if the general sports fan in the street can't name the heavyweight champion of the world, then usually boxing has an identity crisis. It's well used to that, of course. This is not a sport, or business if you will, that has ever run smoothly for long. Every so often there is a superstar: a Jack Dempsey, a Joe Louis or a Muhammad Ali. And there are lulls, too, where it seems the old game will never be as good again. Somehow boxing has kept itself going, firstly in the bare-knuckle times, then through the transition to the use of gloves and on into the relatively well-regulated sport we know today.

What follows here is a tribute to the heavyweights since gloves were first used for world championship purposes. Dozens of books have been written about the champions, but I believe this is the first time the doings, and sometimes undo-ings, of the main men of the heavyweight division, champions, challengers and pretenders alike, have been placed side by side in one book. For those who don't know, a potted history may help place the achievements of these men in context.

The first heavyweight championship bout with gloves was in New Orleans in September 1892, during a three-day festival of boxing, when James J. Corbett knocked out John L. Sullivan, who had been champion without gloves for the previous ten years. Corbett won in the twenty-first round. In those days there were no set rules about the distance of a fight, although three-minute rounds had been introduced by the rules attributed in Britain to the Marquess of Queensberry and adopted in the United States. The distance was usually agreed on when the contract for the fight was drawn up.

Corbett lost the championship to Cornish-born Bob Fitzsimmons, whom he hated, in 1897. Fitzsimmons also held world titles at middle and light-heavyweight in an extraordinary career. James J. Jeffries, born in Ohio and based in California, took over from Fitzsimmons in 1899 and retired undefeated in 1905.

As so often happens there was a lull in interest after this because the public had no one they could believe in with Jeffries gone. His immediate successor was Marvin Hart from Kentucky, but he was quickly beaten by the diminutive Canadian Tommy Burns, who at 5ft 7in tall remains the shortest of the champions in history. Burns was busy – and took his title around the world, defending in London, Paris and then taking off for Australia, where on Boxing Day 1908 he finally lost to the masterful Jack Johnson, a Texan who was also the first black world heavyweight champion. The reaction to Johnson's victory was incredible: 'White America' in particular was outraged, and gradually a 'White Hope' campaign gathered force and peaked in Reno, Nevada, in July 1910 when public opinion virtually forced the long-retired Jeffries back into the ring. Johnson enjoyed himself hugely and won a one-sided fight in fifteen rounds when Jeffries' seconds climbed into the ring to prevent a count-out.

Johnson's win provoked race riots, lynchings and murders. He was a provocative individual who seemed to write his own rules – and eventually his taste for white women was too much for the authorities to bear. He was charged with taking a woman across a state line for immoral purposes and, under threat of jail, fled to Canada and on to Europe. Of course, he took his title with him. After the Jeffries fight he declined but it was not until 1915 that he lost the title to Jess Willard in Havana.

Willard was simply the man in the right place at the right time, a big, strong man who outlasted the tired, old, out-of-shape Texan. For a long time the tallest of all the champions at 6ft 6¼in, Willard was a giant. He preferred to cash in on his title without defending it by playing the entertainment circuit, helped by the eventual American involvement in the First World War. Then, in July 1919 near Toledo, Ohio, Willard was smashed to a three-round defeat by a ferocious assault from Jack Dempsey, who became one of the heroes of those post-war years. F. Scott Fitzgerald's novels identified this period as the Jazz Age – and Dempsey fitted perfectly the mould of the American hero, the man who emerged from the hobo jungles, overcame initial suspicion and unpopularity to become the greatest prize-fighter of his time. He was the first man to draw a million-dollar gate in world sport, when more than 80,000 people crammed into a specially constructed arena in Jersey City in 1921 to watch him destroy the French war hero Georges Carpentier.

In time, inactivity, Hollywood and the good life diminished Dempsey, and in 1926 before an amazing crowd of 120,757, on a rainy night in Philadelphia, he lost to Gene Tunney, a one-time Marine who had a literary streak. He corresponded with George Bernard Shaw and was at one time found by journalists at his training camp reading Shakespeare. He eventually married a society heiress and retired undefeated.

The Wall Street Crash of 1929 changed American life and heralded the years of the Depression that all but brought ordinary men and women to their knees. As it had been with Jeffries in 1905, Tunney's departure without losing in the ring left uncertainty. Things did not improve when Max Schmeling succeeded him in 1930 by becoming the first man to win the championship on a foul, a low blow from Jack Sharkey paralysing him in round four. Sharkey beat Schmeling in the return on a controversial points decision, then lost in six rounds to Primo Carnera, an enormous Italian who weighed 260lbs and more. Some suspected Sharkey took a dive because Carnera was backed by the Mob. Carnera was treated to a horrible beating by Max Baer in 1934, but Baer refused to take life as a champion seriously and clowned his way to defeat against the Cinderella Man, James J. Braddock, who only a short time before had been so broke he had claimed social relief to feed his family. Braddock, an organised, disciplined fighter who, unlike Baer, made the most of his talent and good fortune, lost the championship in 1937 to the great Joe Louis, but still managed to negotiate a deal whereby he had a percentage of Louis' ring earnings from future title fights. As Louis held the title through twenty-five defences and retired undefeated in 1949, that contract helped set up the frugal Braddock for life.

Louis was the first black fighter to be allowed to box for the championship since Johnson lost it in 1915. The reluctance of promoters to work with African-Americans cost a whole string of talented men opportunities. It was the same in other sports, in other jobs across the western world, of course, but Louis, along with the Olympic hero Jesse Owens and the baseball star Jackie Robinson, really did change public opinion and reduce prejudice.

The United States Government did not share the increased goodwill. The Internal Revenue Service decided Louis owed them a fortune, which forced him back into the ring. The quiet, gentle Ezzard Charles had won the vacant championship against Jersey Joe Walcott, a veteran who was actually older than Louis, but who had given him frights in two title challenges. Charles was in Louis's shadow, but at least had the chance to do something about that: the badly faded, broke ex-champ came back and challenged him in 1950. Charles won a one-sided fight on points.

Amazingly, Charles lost in 1951 when thirty-seven-year-old Walcott became the oldest man to win the title courtesy one of the sweetest, cleanest punches one could wish to see: a left hook that put Charles down and out in the seventh round in Pittsburgh. Walcott was infinitely more skilled than Rocky Marciano, but as he had done in his second fight with Louis, after scoring an early knockdown, he lost concentration and was knocked out, this time by a single, devastating right hand in the thirteenth round in Philadelphia in 1952. Marciano was a throwback to the Dempsey years, a sensational slugger who didn't worry about the niceties. He did modify his technique, but in essence remained a relentless pressure fighter who didn't mind taking a shot or three on the way in from slicker fighters. He retired undefeated in 1956.

He was replaced by twenty-one-year-old Floyd Patterson, a fast, hard-punching and clever youngster whose main weakness was a suspect chin. He was also a political pawn, the protégé of Cus D'Amato, an independent character who refused to bow to the requirements of the International Boxing Club that, to all intents and purposes, had run the sport since it came to power after the Second World War. The IBC eventually collapsed in scandalous circumstances, which helped lend D'Amato legendary status. His stand, however, was convenient in that he refused to have anything to do with the most dangerous contenders: Eddie Machen, Zora Folley and Nino Valdes were just three who should have had a title fight and didn't.

Patterson lost in three rounds to the big-hitting Swede, Ingemar Johansson, in 1959. Johansson floored him seven times. The following year Patterson became the first man to regain the championship, with a fifth-round knockout of Johansson, and then won the decider too, but that all took two years to sort out. Other contenders went stale waiting around. Patterson, embarrassed by D'Amato's insistence on avoiding the leading contenders, took some control himself in 1962 when, apparently after meeting President John F. Kennedy, he agreed to fight Sonny Liston, who destroyed him in 126 seconds. A rematch lasted four seconds longer. The uneducated, uncomplicated Liston was a character America did not especially want to acknowledge: a representative of the underbelly of society. He had served time for robbery and for assaulting a police officer and there were rumours that his career was controlled by the Mob. He had been required to give evidence at the US government investigation into boxing led by Senator Esteves Kefauver. Liston naively believed he would be accepted as a hero once he beat Patterson. He wasn't.

Even so, some preferred Liston to the loud-mouthed twenty-two-year-old Cassius Clay, who challenged him in Miami in 1964. Clay had won a gold medal at light-heavyweight in the Rome Olympics and grabbed headlines ever since with his brash, bright-eyed, media-conscious manner. Most felt Liston would knock him out quickly but, after six extraordinary rounds, the formidable champion stayed put on his stool, claiming a shoulder injury. In doing so, he became the first titleholder to retire in his corner since Jess Willard almost half a century before – and Willard had taken a pounding from Jack Dempsey and was semi-conscious.

More controversy followed when Clay changed his name to Muhammad Ali and announced his allegiance to Islam. These were volatile times: John F. Kennedy had been assassinated only months before Clay beat Liston. Martin Luther King and Robert Kennedy would be dead in similar circumstances within five years. American involvement in Vietnam accelerated during the decade and, of course, Ali came to symbolise the combination of the resistance to the draft and the energetic protest of the civil rights movement with his one-line protest: 'No Vietcong ever called me nigger!' Ali was outlawed from boxing for refusing to join the Vietnam war, his title taken away by politicians who denied him a licence in 1967.

In his three-year absence Joe Frazier emerged as the best of his replacements and then, after Ali came back, with public opinion at last beginning to swing, they met in their magnificent fifteen-rounder at Madison Square Garden in 1971. Frazier's career peaked in that sensational points win. He lost to the unbeaten, bludgeoning George Foreman in two rounds in Kingston, Jamaica, in 1973, and then the astonishing Ali regained the championship with that demonstration of his genius in the 'Rumble in the Jungle' in Zaire in 1974. That fight also announced to the boxing world the arrival of promoter Don King, who would dominate the heavyweight division, for good and bad, during the 1980s.

Ali boxed too long and lost a split decision to Olympic gold medallist and professional novice Leon Spinks in 1978. Spinks was too naive and inexperienced to understand the full significance of the hour, lost his way – and lost his title back to Ali later that year. By then the tradition of handing the title on from fist to fist had fallen prey to the rules of the sanctioning bodies who, in the 1980s and 1990s, would proliferate to the point where they would be collectively known as The Alphabet Boys. The World Boxing Association had been formed out of the old National Boxing Association in 1962 in an attempt to provide an organisation to oversee the sport and so, supposedly, keep it free from the corruption that had almost brought it down at the end of the 1950s. It was typical of the sport, however, that within six months those countries and US states not wanting to be a part of the WBA had formed the World Boxing Council, so denying boxing the opportunity of having a single body that would bring unity rather than disharmony and division.

The actions of the WBA and WBC didn't really affect the heavyweight division too much – the WBA had at one point refused to recognise Ali in the 1960s but had been ignored – but in 1978 that changed. Spinks signed for a rematch with Ali instead of meeting his official WBC contender Ken Norton. Therefore, in an astonishing move that had no sensitivity whatsoever for the sport's traditions and no appreciation of what it might mean long-term, the WBC, led by Jose Sulaiman, installed Norton as an alternative world champion to Spinks. Over the next decade Sulaiman would be repeatedly criticised for his close working relationship with Don King and boxing, being the rogue sport that it is, pretty much accepted that as the way things were to be. Nothing was done to control the situation and Sulaiman, who consistently proclaimed himself a humble servant of boxing, assumed an undue degree of power. The general perception was that the WBC, whose members included the British Boxing Board of Control, usually did what he wanted.

Norton lost his WBC title in an epic fifteen-rounder with Larry Holmes, who went on to be the moral if not entirely logical successor to Ali. Ali regained the WBA belt from Spinks, then retired. Holmes gradually established himself as the best heavyweight in the world with a string of twenty-one defences over the next seven years. One of those was over Ali, who made an ill-advised comeback at the age of thirty-eight. Along the way Holmes also fell out with the WBC and switched his allegiance to the International Boxing Federation, an offshoot from the WBA, led by the American Bobby Lee. The IBF was the first of the 'private' governing bodies, that is, one not formed by administrative federations and boards from around the world. It was, in essence, a private business. It would not have survived if it were not for the support of Holmes, whose fights drew television support. By 1985, Holmes was the world champion, recognised by most as the number one but only backed by the IBF. The WBA belt had, after Ali's retirement in 1979, passed from John Tate to Mike Weaver to Michael Dokes to Gerrie Coetzee of South Africa.

After Holmes' defection from the WBC in 1984 Tim Witherspoon out-pointed Greg Page, who was then switched to become WBA champion instead by defeating Coetzee. The situation became so ludicrous that even dedicated boxing fans and writers had trouble sorting out who was what. Witherspoon lost his WBC belt to Pinklon Thomas, who lost that to Trevor Berbick. Meanwhile, Page lost to Tony Tubbs, who in turn was beaten by Witherspoon, who so became WBA champion. It was all nonsense, but of course it lined the pockets of the sanctioning bodies and King, who by then controlled both versions of the championship. Holmes, who had tried to strike out on his own, lost two points decisions to Michael Spinks in 1985 and 1986. He argued vehemently that both were unjust.

The situation became even more of a mess when the IBF stripped Spinks for ignoring their instructions to box their number one contender and instead taking a big payday against Gerry Cooney, a New York-Irishman with a big following who had given Holmes one of his hardest fights. Spinks beat Cooney but suddenly found himself on the outside. Perhaps the entire mess had become too complicated for anyone to care any more.

Then twenty-year-old Mike Tyson exploded onto the heavyweight scene. Controlled by the contrasting individualists Jim Jacobs and Bill Cayton, he had been coached by Cus D'Amato, who died before Tyson's WBC title destruction of Berbick. Significantly, Tyson was not with King. A month later a disaffected Witherspoon lost the WBA belt to outsider James 'Bonecrusher' Smith in one round. After only three months as WBA champion Smith was beaten in a twelve-round maul by Tyson. The IBF matched James 'Buster' Douglas, one of King's fighters, with Tony Tucker. The latter won, but in August 1987, Tyson out-pointed Tucker to unify the division for the first time since the WBC stripped Leon Spinks almost a decade earlier. Tyson removed all doubts as to his supremacy with a first-round knockout of Michael Spinks in 1988. However, Jim Jacobs died young, and King in time signed Tyson to a promotional contract, eventually removing Cayton and the entire backroom team that had brought Tyson to his peak.

In February 1990 Buster Douglas pulled off one of the biggest shocks in boxing history by knocking out twenty-three-year-old Tyson in ten rounds in Tokyo. Douglas fought for independence, signing not for a rematch with Tyson but to box the number one contender Evander Holyfield at the Mirage Hotel in Las Vegas, run by Steve Wynn. King was paid off, but Wynn paid Douglas such a fortune that he still took home a life-changing sum of money. Douglas also folded inside three rounds. Holyfield, promoted by the Duva family's company, Main Events, was the undisputed champion – and King was out of the heavyweight picture. Holyfield lost to Riddick Bowe in a wonderfully intense twelve-round fight in Las Vegas in 1992.

Then the WBC interfered again. Bowe ignored their instructions to box Lennox Lewis and gave them their title back. The WBC, in a move that echoed their installation of Norton as champion in 1978, made Lewis the champion and Sulaiman travelled to London to present him with the belt in January 1993. Bowe went on as WBA and IBF champion, but lost them back to Holyfield in November 1993. Holyfield lost them to Michael Moorer in April 1994. In September 1994 Lewis was beaten in two rounds by Oliver McCall and, two months later, the sport descended into something of a farce when forty-five-year-old George Foreman knocked out Moorer for WBA and IBF recognition.

Foreman ignored the demands of the two organisations and was stripped by both of them. He was the legitimate heir to Tyson, Douglas, Bowe and Holyfield, but more or less drifted into the backwaters. He eventually retired after losing a decision to Shannon Briggs, but nobody recognised Briggs as the man-who-beat-the-man.

McCall lost the WBC belt to Frank Bruno, who was then overpowered in three rounds by Tyson in March 1996. Meanwhile, the IBF recognised Michael Moorer and the WBA saw Bruce Seldon as champion. Tyson and Seldon were with King. As the entire thing became unmanageable, Tyson gave up the WBC belt rather than box Lennox Lewis, who was not connected to King and who had resorted to legal action to establish his right to box for the WBC title after winning an official eliminator. Instead, Tyson knocked out Bruce Seldon to become WBA champion, but then lost it in another upset to Holyfield, who was by then with King as well. Lewis won the vacant WBC title against McCall and gradually, steadily accumulated defences while remaining independent.

Holyfield beat Moorer to become WBA and IBF champion and then, in 1999, Lewis and Holyfield met in their infamous unification fight at Madison Square Garden. Lewis appeared to win clearly only to be given a draw that prompted a governmental investigation. In a rematch in November 1999, Lewis out-pointed Holyfield to unify the division. He remained champion until his retirement in 2004, although predictably the sanctioning bodies interfered yet again. Lewis kept WBC recognition but lost the backing of the WBA and IBF. By now most boxing fans had become sick of the whole 'Alphabet Boy' process, especially as, although it had not affected the heavyweight division too much, the arrival of all kinds of other private businesses purporting to be world authorities had brought the entire sport into ridicule. Sports editors no longer bothered to cover anything beyond the basics of boxing. We had the WBO, IBO, IBC, IBA, WBF, WBBB, WAA, and more or less any other combination you could come up with.

The WBA preferred not to recognise Lewis, even to the point of recognising Holyfield again at one point. Their dominant figure was the King-promoted John Ruiz. The IBF recognised a southpaw from Michigan, Chris Byrd.

When Lewis retired, the WBC sanctioned a vacant championship bout between Vitali Klitschko, who had been ahead against Lewis before cuts had ruled him out in 2003, and a veteran South African, Corrie Sanders. Klitschko won to earn general recognition as the world number one. However, Klitschko, a 6ft 7½in Ukrainian with a doctorate in sports science from the University of Kiev, had an injury-affected start to his reign. He also refused to deal with King, who still had most of the leading contenders. This prevented, for the foreseeable future, any more unification bouts.

Boxing is far from a perfectly run sport – the IBF, for example, almost disintegrated in 2000 following the public disgrace of its founder, Bobby Lee, who was eventually jailed, and the WBC was almost put out of business by a court case when it was found to have wrongly stripped a light-heavyweight, Graciano Rocchigiani, of his belt. However, in spite of all the nonsense, the fighters all have their stories to tell. By and large their dreams remain the same. They want financial security… and they want what is still, for all the chaos that surrounds it, the biggest prize in sport. The title 'heavyweight champion of the world' is still something to dream of, chase and, for a fortunate few, cherish. This book is intended as a tribute to them all.

Bob Mee
Warwickshire, England, 2005

PICTURE ACKNOWLEDGEMENTS
All images supplied by Empics.

A

HENRY AKINWANDE

Born: 12 October 1965, Dulwich, London
Height: 6ft 7in   **Weight at peak:** 224lbs (16st)
Fights: 48   **Won:** 45   **Lost:** 2   **Drawn:** 1
KO percentage: 60
Rounds boxed: 272
World title fights: 1
Career span: 1989-2004 (15 years)
KO wins: 29
KO defeats: 1

'When I started boxing a lot of people said I was wasting my time,' said Henry Akinwande, before his world heavyweight title challenge against Lennox Lewis in 1997. 'They put me down, said I wasn't good enough. Even so-called friends said that.' Perhaps the knockers had a longer lasting effect than they can ever have imagined.

Akinwande probably can't explain what makes a good fighter freeze in his moment of destiny, but it happened to him against Lewis. He was disqualified in the fifth round after spending most of the fight mauling and clinching. In spite of landing a solid overhand right on the inside that made Lewis dip at the knees and touch the canvas, Akinwande fought as if haunted by uncertainty and doubt. Eventually referee Mills Lane threw him out. A fortnight earlier Lane had disqualified Mike Tyson for biting the ears of Evander Holyfield.

Akinwande, born in London, raised in Nigeria and by the mid-1990s living in Florida, had won recognition from the minor, Puerto Rican-based WBO. To earn that he had knocked out Jeremy Williams in three rounds in a native American casino in Indio, California, in June 1996. Successful defences over the Russian, Alexander Zolkin, and the hesitant Englishman Scott Welch took Akinwande's record to thirty-three fights without defeat – thirty-two wins and an unlucky draw in Germany against Axel Schulz, later avenged.

As an amateur Henry had won back-to-back ABA championships and boxed for Britain at the 1988 Olympics in Seoul. His boxing skills were plentiful. However, maybe tellingly, after losing to the experienced Dutchman Arnold Vanderlijde on a 3-2 split decision in the Olympics, he said, 'I didn't believe in myself... what can I do?' And way back in the final of the 1986 ABA championships, Akinwande had been disqualified for repeated holding against a man he should have beaten, Eric Cardouza from Northampton. Perhaps he grew up but didn't change.

After losing to Lewis, Akinwande out-boxed Orlin Norris in a WBA eliminator, then developed hepatitis and was out for more than a year. His last high-profile fight brought a tenth-round knockout to Oliver McCall at the Mandalay Bay in Las Vegas. Akinwande was way in front on points in the last round when he was flattened by a long right hand.

MUHAMMAD ALI

Born: 17 January 1942, Louisville, Kentucky
Full name: Cassius Marcellus Clay jnr
Height: 6ft 3in   **Weight at peak:** 210-216lbs (15st-15st 6lbs)
Fights: 61   **Won:** 56   **Lost:** 5
KO percentage: 60
Rounds boxed: 551
World champion: 1964-67, 1974-78, 1978-79
World title fights: 25
Career span: 1960-81 (21 years)
KO wins: 37
KO defeats: 1

Muhammad Ali, once acknowledged as the most recognisable man on the planet, transcended sport. Even in illness-restricted retirement, his appeal was his humanity, the presence of an all-too identifiable frailty at the core of his greatness.

Ali wasn't always the humble man of peace he became in his middle years. There are those who would testify now that in his eagerness to embrace the black Muslim movement he had a long spell of naivety that amounted to racism. Black was right, white was wrong. Inside the ring he was also capable of a vicious cruelty, as when he tortured Ernie Terrell in their fifteen-round unification fight in 1967. Screaming 'What's my name?' at Terrell was ugly but part of the showbiz. Putting Terrell in a headlock and scraping his face and eye along the ropes was not. People rightly enjoyed the mischievous humour of his put-downs of Floyd Patterson and Joe Frazier but beneath it lay a hard, political edge. Patterson and Frazier represented the old guard, the traditional and therefore subservient behavioural patterns.

The polarities in his character also made him the genius he was inside the ring. He was capable of extraordinary gambles, none greater than his rope-a-dope strategy against George Foreman in Zaire in 1974 when he allowed one of the biggest hitters in history to punch himself out by whacking his arms, his body... and, yes, too often his head. Then with timing that might even have surprised himself, he opened up and took out Foreman in a few, blurring seconds in the eighth round.

Ali was born Cassius Marcellus Clay Jnr in Louisville, Kentucky and famously took up boxing when his new bicycle was stolen and he was invited to put his frustration and anger to good use by a policeman, Joe Martin, who ran a boxing gym. At only eighteen he won the Olympic light-heavyweight gold medal in the 1960 Olympics in Rome, and quickly made his presence felt in a professional sport that was suffering major image problems. Sonny Liston, the heavyweight champion, had a criminal past and was linked by management association to the Mob. The International Boxing Club, which had more or less run boxing in the 1950s, had been exposed as corrupt, its leaders prosecuted.

As if that were not enough, in 1962 on national television, world welterweight champion Benny Paret was killed in a fight with Emile Griffith. Paret effectively died in the ring, slumped in a corner, unable to fall as Griffith unleashed a terrible barrage of punches with referee Ruby Goldstein waiting too long to stop the fight. A year later, in March 1963, featherweight champion Davey Moore lost his life in a world title bout with Sugar Ramos in Los Angeles. Boxing had little or nothing to recommend it.

Against this backdrop, Cassius Clay was busy telling the world in which round he would beat his opponents, often with the help of excruciating rhymes. His victims included the forty-nine-year-old Archie Moore, who had been light-heavyweight champion for a decade. He had unexpected problems in winning a ten-round decision over Doug Jones in New York, and had to recover from a shocking knockdown against Henry Cooper at Wembley Stadium in 1963 to win on cuts in the fifth round. Cooper exposed a vulnerability to a left hook that had been masked by his speed and reflexes. In a previous fight Clay had been floored by Sonny Banks before winning in round four. Years later Joe Frazier would nail him repeatedly with left hooks, put him down and take away his unbeaten record.

What nobody realised in 1963 was the terrific chin Clay had, allied to the heart of a champion. Yet, because of the Jones and Cooper fights, he was given little chance when he challenged Liston for the title at Miami in February 1964. It was a toss-up as to which of them was more unpopular: Liston with his brooding, bitter scowl and dubious connections, or Clay with his boastfulness... allied to darker rumours that he was about to join the intimidating black Muslim movement known as the Nation of Islam. This was only three months after the assassination of John F. Kennedy and America was in turmoil. The McCarthy purges of a decade earlier were gone but not forgotten. The war against Communism in Vietnam was escalating. Ordinary folk suspected the presence of dangerous revolutionaries and subversives behind every curtain of society.

Clay overcame a bad patch when a substance got into his eyes – an old Mob trick – perhaps from a towel, a substance in a water bucket that got onto Liston's gloves – which meant he couldn't see the most dangerous heavyweight in the world. Apart from that session he out-boxed, out-sped and demoralised Liston, who seemed to age ten years in twenty minutes. At the end of the sixth Liston quit with a damaged left shoulder. While sports fans were still getting used to the shock result, Clay became Muhammad Ali and officially embraced the Nation of Islam.

He knocked out Liston in one round of an equally controversial rematch before a tiny crowd in Lewiston, Maine; he toyed with the former champion, Floyd Patterson, before a one-sided fight was stopped in the twelfth, and then – so soon – his quarrels with the US government over the Vietnam War began to affect his career. In an interview he let slip the sentence that became a testament to a heroic defence of a principle, and illustrated perfectly the racism prevalent in American society. 'I ain't got no quarrel with them Vietcong,' he said. 'No Vietcong ever called me nigger.' The effect on a nation that believed it was involved in a justified war was dramatic. Ali took the world championship out of America to continue earning a living: he out-pointed George Chuvalo in Toronto, stopped Henry Cooper and Brian London in London and Karl Mildenberger in Frankfurt.

He was persuaded to defend in the United States against Cleveland Williams in Houston, Texas, in November 1966 and responded with perhaps the most lethal performance of his life, a four-knockdown, three-round demolition of an old but still dangerous opponent. That, above any other, convinced hardened fight watchers that Ali was one of the best heavyweights in history.

The World Boxing Association had withdrawn recognition from Ali and installed Ernie Terrell as their champion in 1965. This was a ludicrous decision, and a forerunner of the way boxing would be all but ruined in the latter part of the century by self-seeking administrators, but it provided Ali with another opponent. Terrell refused to acknowledge Ali's Muslim name and continued to refer to him – as did many, including *Ring* magazine – as Clay. Ali gave Terrell a pounding for fifteen rounds, a prolonged, nasty, one-sided beating that endeared him to no one beyond his immediate circle.

In March 1967 Ali knocked out veteran contender Zora Folley with ease in seven rounds, but then refused to take the symbolic step forward before the US Draft Board. For this he was stripped of his world championship – as if that honour belonged to the United States of America! – and forced to tour the lecture circuit to earn a living. He lost millions of dollars, but his critics, and those Americans who lost sons, brothers and fathers in Vietnam felt he should have lost his liberty. He was sentenced to a jail term but never served it because of the long-winded appeal system. Eventually, in October 1970, he returned in Atlanta, Georgia, stopped Jerry Quarry after three rounds on a cut eye, and resumed his career. New York followed Georgia's lead and gave him a licence – and he stopped Oscar Bonavena in the fifteenth round in the Garden to set up a huge fight with his successor as champion, Joe Frazier, in March 1971. With hindsight he had not given himself enough time to prepare, but against that Frazier hit a wonderful peak in that fight, reached his own moment of destiny and, given the ferocity and speed of his left hooks, might have won anyway. Ali fought well but was knocked down in the last round and out-pointed.

Ali's bravery in defeat and his post-fight honesty and humility won over a new generation of fans. The tide of public opinion was changing over Vietnam, too. Ali won ten in a row after losing to Frazier, then took Ken Norton too lightly in San Diego in March 1973, had his jaw broken and lost a split twelve-round decision. He would always have trouble with Norton's style. In a rematch in Los Angeles he edged out the former Marine on another split decision, and near the end of his career, in 1976, won a bitterly disputed unanimous verdict in New York with the title at stake.

In January 1974 Ali also avenged his defeat by Frazier, giving him a boxing lesson over twelve hard rounds in the Garden. Then came the magical rebirth against the supposedly invincible Foreman in the 'Rumble in the Jungle' in Zaire. Critics believed almost to a man that Foreman would pound Ali into retirement, but while everything went wrong for the one-dimensional champion in Zaire, including a cut eye that postponed the fight for three weeks, Ali responded to the experience of being in Africa. If it were possible for a man of his nature to grow in stature, he did it there, and by the time they entered the ring in Kinshasa, he was conducting the crowds to a chorus of 'Ali, bombaye!' – which translates as 'Ali, kill him!' As the world knows, he knocked out Foreman in the eighth round.

His last great performance was when he stopped Frazier at the end of the fourteenth round in their gruelling, horribly draining third fight, the 'Thrilla in Manila', in October 1975. Ali said afterwards he had gone into the Near Room in that fight, the place next to death. He could barely stand when a compassionate Eddie Futch pulled Frazier out.

Ali's training regime became increasingly erratic and he had trouble with the tricky Jimmy Young, who believed he was robbed over fifteen rounds in Maryland in 1976. Less than a month later Ali was in Munich stopping the willing but limited English southpaw Richard Dunn in five rounds. If he was fortunate to beat Norton, he did out-box the brutally heavy-handed Earnie Shavers over fifteen rounds in September 1977, but then failed to prepare for the novice Olympic champion Leon Spinks in Las Vegas in February 1978 and lost a split decision. He couldn't rest with that result hanging over him, and drilled himself into shape one last time to trounce Spinks over fifteen rounds in New Orleans in September 1978. Ali, at thirty-six, had become the first man to win the heavyweight championship three times.

Ali announced his retirement in June 1979, and began to show signs of illness. He took weight-reducing drugs to attempt one final miracle against his old sparring partner, the methodical but hugely talented Larry Holmes, in October 1980. Holmes exposed him as a shell, pounding him to defeat after ten horribly one-sided rounds. Still Ali would not stop. Fourteen months later he was back again, in Nassau in the Bahamas, losing over ten rounds to the Jamaican Trevor Berbick who wouldn't have hit him in his prime. Then came the illness, soon diagnosed as a form of Parkinson's Disease, but which many attributed to the thousands of punches he had taken in his career, including the poundings he admitted he had taken from sparring partners when out of shape.

Ali settled down with his fourth wife, Lonnie, confronted reality and, with his Muslim faith now acceptable in a more tolerant era, grew to be loved and revered. He admitted he was at peace with himself and God. There were those who criticised his appearance at the 1996 Olympic Games in Atlanta, when he lit the flame in the stadium with such a faltering hand there was serious concern that he might drop it, but most accepted his most public acknowledgement of his frailty as a positive statement.

As he moved into his sixties, Ali was a symbol of the costs sometimes involved in the toughest sport of all and in the price we sometimes pay for our mistakes, but also an iconic figure who rose above his plight. He remained the champion of the people of the world, loved and respected to an extent that simply would not have been believed in 1960s America. He really was The Greatest.

B

BUDDY BAER

Born: 11 June 1915, Denver, Colorado
Full name: Jacob Henry Baer
Died: 18 July 1986, Sacramento, California
Height: 6ft 6½in   **Weight at peak:** 245lbs (17st 7lbs)
Fights: 57   **Won:** 50   **Lost:** 7
KO percentage: 78
Rounds boxed: 178
World title fights: 2
Career span: 1934-42 (8 years)
KO wins: 45
KO defeats: 2

Buddy Baer, the big, hulking younger brother of world champion Max Baer, fought Joe Louis twice in title fights. In the first, in May 1941 at Griffith Stadium, Washington DC, the 6ft 6½in, challenger made it to the end of the sixth round. In the rematch, in January 1942 in Madison Square Garden, New York, Buddy lasted only two minutes fifty-six seconds – and never fought again.

Baer had his brief moment of glory in the opening round of their first fight when he charged Louis onto the ring apron. Louis was given a count but hauled himself back up at 'four'. Baer stuck to the job, even when out-punched, and cut Louis under the left eye in round five. In round six, however, the champion dropped Baer four times. The last time he hadn't heard the bell and the punch landed after it. Baer was carried to his corner by trainer Ray Arcel and manager Ancil Hoffman – and they wouldn't let him out for round seven, claiming a foul. Referee Arthur Donovan, however, opted for a bizarre course of action: he disqualified Baer!

Frankly, it was scandalous that Donovan controlled a total of twelve of Louis's twenty-five world title defences – he worked for Louis's promoter, Mike Jacobs. On this particular day, it was said Donovan had been drinking in a bar because he believed incessant rain would mean a postponement. However, the weather cleared and he had to make the best of it while, it was said, not exactly 100 per cent.

The rematch contained no such controversy. Louis contributed his entire purse, less training expenses, to the US Navy Relief Fund, while Baer offered up a percentage of his. In the ring Republican presidential nominee Wendell Wilkie paid tribute to the public-spiritedness of both boxers – although he couldn't pronounce the heavyweight champion's name and called Buddy Baer Max! Once the bell rang Baer, 13lbs heavier than in their first fight, was taken apart. He went down three times. Afterwards Louis paid $47,100 to the Navy, promoter Jacobs handed over $37,229 from the gate and Baer chipped in with $4,078. The following day, Louis joined the US Army and later in the year Buddy signed up too. 'The only way I could have beaten Joe that night was with a baseball bat,' said Baer. 'I never liked to hurt people – and I never liked to get hurt myself.'

Baer was born in Denver – first names Jacob Henry – and based in California from the age of seven. As a teenager he sparred with his brother in the Yosemite Gym in Oakland, California, and after one amateur fight he decided he might as well be paid for it and signed with Hoffman, who was Max's manager (Max was world champion at the time). In his first year Baer fought twenty-five times, including a first-round knockout of the flamboyant, fragile Irishman Jack Doyle in Madison Square Garden. On the Joe Louis-Tommy Farr undercard at Yankee Stadium, New York, in August 1937, Baer overcame a bad first round to stop Abe Simon in three. It was a seventh-round stoppage of 'Two Ton' Tony Galento in Washington DC in April 1941 that earned him the championship shot at Louis. He suffered a serious injury in the return and never boxed again.

In retirement Buddy worked for the California State Senate and was involved in the Church of Latter Day Saints in Sacramento. He sang at church functions, while his wife Vicki accompanied him on piano. He also took bit-parts in movies, including *Jack and the Beanstalk* (1952) *The Monster From Green Hell* (1957) and *Snow White and the Three Stooges* (1961).

Baer died at the age of seventy-one on 18 July 1986.

MAX BAER

Born: 11 Feb 1909, Omaha, Nebraska
Full name: Maximilian Adalbert Baer
Died: 21 Nov 1959, Los Angeles, aged 50
Height: 6ft 2½in   **Weight at peak:** 209lbs (14st 13lbs)
Fights: 83   **Won:** 70   **Lost:** 13
KO percentage: 62
Rounds boxed: 445
World champion: 1934-35
World title fights: 2
Career span: 1929-41 (12 years)
KO wins: 52
KO defeats: 3

Historians have tended to be unkind to Max Baer, making much of his careless-ness in losing his title to the underrated James J. Braddock in 1935. Contemporary critics also massacred him for not getting up when still conscious against Joe Louis, but he said, 'If people want to see the execution of Max Baer it will cost more than $50 a seat.'

His style was basic. He stood tall and could jab well enough but carried his left hand too low, didn't have quick hands and didn't move his head well enough to slip punches. He slung left hooks in too wide an arc, but his right was much straighter and far more effective. As he showed against former champion Max Schmeling in 1933, he knew how to finish a fight. After a gruelling struggle, he landed a terrific right cross in the tenth round and unleashed a barrage of twenty-nine unanswered punches – including two illegal back-handers – that put the German down. Schmeling got up and took ten more blows before it was stopped as he reeled along the ropes.

When Baer won the world title in 1934 with an eleventh-round stoppage of Primo Carnera, he toyed with the Italian, flooring him eleven times and playing shamelessly to the gallery. 'Last one up's a cissy!' he laughed when he tripped over Carnera's feet as the giant Ambling Alp was on one of his visits to the canvas.

Baer saw life as a huge adventure. 'I'm a ham at heart,' he said. 'I've got a million-dollar body and a ten-cent brain.' This was borne out by his achievement in selling 113 per cent of himself to a variety of sponsors – a situation it took his manager, Ancil Hoffman, four years to sort out. Baer was born in Omaha, Nebraska, and raised in Colorado and then, from the age of thirteen, in Livermore, California, about forty-five miles east of San Francisco. His father Jacob bred cattle and ran a butcher's business. Max worked for a dollar a day in the slaughterhouse and learned the basics of boxing in a gym at the family ranch. Eventually, he moved to Oakland and began fighting for money in 1929. There was no point in anyone try-ing to turn Baer into a boxing scientist. However, in a ball park in San Francisco in

August 1930 an opponent, Frankie Campbell, died a few hours after Baer knocked him out in the fifth round. A distraught, demoralised, still only twenty-one-year-old Max didn't want to box again, especially after he read newspaper headlines like 'Murderer' and 'Ban The Killer From The Ring For Life'. A court ruled the death an accident. When he returned to boxing, he struggled mentally. Tommy Loughran would probably have out-pointed him anyway but he also lost to Ernie Schaaf, Johnny Risko and Paolino Uzcudun.

In 1933, as well as beating Schmeling, he took a pleasant payday opposite Myrna Loy and Jean Harlow in *The Prizefighter and the Lady*. In a fight scene in that movie he starred with Primo Carnera, the man he was to beat for the world title the following year. The beating he handed Schaaf in a rematch might have contributed to Ernie's death after another fight with Carnera. Officially it was a points decision but Schaaf was on the floor at the final bell and was carried from the ring.

Baer brought much-needed flamboyance to what was, until the arrival of Joe Louis, a rather flat heavyweight division. Yet when he lost to Braddock in June 1935 after a year of exhibitions and public appearances, he drifted through the fight, allowing the quietly effective, underrated challenger to pile up points with accurate punches and take the title after fifteen low-key rounds. Max barely had time to get used to being a former champion when he lost to Louis in Yankee Stadium, New York, in September 1935. Louis was more or less punch-perfect in taking him out in four rounds.

Baer fought on until 1941 without getting another title shot, but few would have paid to see him fight Louis again anyway. He lost and won two distance fights with Tommy Farr, lost twice to Lou Nova but stopped 'Two Ton' Tony Galento. He retired after the second defeat by Nova when he broke a bone in his neck. Ancil Hoffman had insisted he invest almost all of his $215,000 purse for the Louis fight in a trust fund, for which he remained grateful. He did walk-on parts in movies, at one time had a nightclub act with the old light-heavyweight champion 'Slapsie' Maxie Rosenbloom, and occasionally picked up a payday as a boxing referee. He married twice – actress Dorothy Dunbar, in 1931, and then in 1935, just after he had lost the world title, Mary Ellen Sullivan, with whom he had three children. This marriage survived to Baer's premature, sudden death in a Los Angeles hotel room of a heart attack (his third) on 21 November 1959 at the age of fifty.

JOE BAKSI

Born: 14 January 1922, Kulpmont, Pennsylvania
Height: 6ft 1in   **Weight at peak:** 215lbs (15st 5lbs)
Fights: 72   **Won:** 59   **Lost:** 9   **Drawn:** 4
KO percentage: 38

Rounds boxed: 460
World title fights: 0
Career span: 1940-54 (14 years)
KO wins: 28
KO defeats: 1

A big, powerful heavyweight who was persistent and determined, if a touch slow and clumsy, Joe Baksi was very close to a world title shot in the second half of the 1940s – and is remembered in Britain for ruining the championship pretensions of Bruce Woodcock at Harringay Arena in April 1947. In more compassionate times the fight would have been over in round one when Woodcock took a terrible pounding and was knocked down heavily. However, Bruce was not rescued until round seven. The film of the fight is chilling. Woodcock said later, 'I couldn't see properly, the whole vast arena seemed to be swimming round me in a crazy whirlpool of lights and heads and white shirts... I lost all sense of balance and distance, all count of time. I don't remember going down but Tom says I was on my back, looking vaguely up at the roof.'

That was Baksi's second trip to London. In November 1946 he had beaten Freddie Mills, the leading British light-heavyweight, in six rounds. Mills, who was too small to trouble him, retired in his corner. He had five cuts over the eyes.

Trained by Ray Arcel and managed by Nate Wolfson, Baksi was originally a coalminer from Kulpmont, Pennsylvania. He left when his father was killed in a pit accident and took jobs as a dishwasher, fish cleaner, 'chucker-out' in bars and, most bizarrely, as minder to a troupe of midgets in a circus. He said the midgets gave him more trouble than anybody! By the time he was eighteen he was boxing in four-round preliminary bouts (without any amateur experience) and living in New York. He fought as often as he could on small shows and on the undercards of bigger ones and lost only one six-round decision in his first thirty-six fights.

In August 1945 he travelled to Camden, New Jersey, where Jersey Joe Walcott was at long last being given a break as a house fighter. Jersey Joe beat him on points over ten rounds. The wins in Britain over Mills and Woodcock increased his reputation but a surprise points defeat to Olle Tandberg in Sweden checked his rise and then he was beaten on an eleventh-round stoppage by Ezzard Charles in Madison Square Garden in December 1948. Baksi was led to his corner when he admitted to referee Ruby Goldstein that he could no longer see.

He won his next seven fights, but that took him until 1951 when he retired temporarily. After two years he came back, won once, then, when he lost a unanimous ten-round decision to Bob Baker in Brooklyn in May 1954, his manager Leon Feureisen collapsed at ringside and died in the dressing room. Baksi never boxed again.

NICK BARONE

Born: 12 June 1926, Syracuse, New York
Died: 12 March 2006, Syracuse, New York, aged 79
Height: 5ft 10in   Weight at peak: 175lbs (12st 7lbs)
Fights: 57   Won: 44   Lost: 12   Drawn: 1
KO percentage: 36
Rounds boxed: 409
World title fights: 1
Career span: 1946-51 (5 years)
KO wins: 21
KO defeats: 5

A light-heavyweight from Syracuse, Nick Barone was crude, wild but extremely resilient. He challenged Ezzard Charles for the title in Cincinnati Gardens arena in December 1950, and was game enough, but Charles knocked him out in the eleventh round. For his heavyweight chance, Barone still weighed only 178½lbs – 12st 10½lbs.

His real name was Carmine but he borrowed his elder brother's birth certificate – and name – in order to join the US Marines when he was sixteen. He saw active service in the South Pacific and was cited for bravery at Iwo Jima. While stationed in Hawaii he did a little boxing but after a three-year stint returned home to Syracuse and, apparently, a career in the steel mills. To supplement his income he decided to box professionally – and his strength and persistent aggression earned him a fanbase, along with the well-deserved nickname The Bull.

The erratic but dangerous Bob Satterfield out-pointed him in Chicago and he lost on points to Lee Oma in Buffalo, but two wins over middleweights Joe Taylor and Jimmy Beau earned him the chance against Charles. Afterwards he lost three of his next four, his final fight a three-knockdown, sixth-round knockout defeat by Don Cockell, the British light-heavyweight champion, before an amazing crowd of 50,000 at White City, London, on Jack Solomons' Festival of Champions show in June 1951.

TREVOR BERBICK

Born: 1 August 1952, Port Anthony, Jamaica
Height: 6ft 3in   Weight: 218lbs (15st 8lbs)
Fights: 62   Won: 50   Lost: 11   Drawn: 1
KO percentage: 53
Rounds boxed: 446
World champion: 1986
World title fights: 3
Career span: 1976-2000 (24 years)
KO wins: 33
KO defeats: 2

An erratic, difficult character, Trevor Berbick held the World Boxing Council belt for eight months before Mike Tyson demolished him in two rounds in Las Vegas. Berbick had won WBC recognition with a points victory over Pinklon Thomas at the Riviera in Las Vegas in March 1986. It was a close, unanimous decision with two scores of 115-113 and another of 115-114. By then, however, Tyson's meteoric rise was taking shape and in November 1986 Berbick defended against him at the Las Vegas Hilton. Expected to use his reach and move, instead he stood straight in front of Tyson, who took a round to find his range and then blew him away with two knockdowns in the second. Berbick's attempts to rise, staggering around the ring, as British commentator Reg Gutteridge said, 'like a baby in a playpen', remains one of the most dramatic pieces of film in heavyweight championship history.

Berbick was originally from Port Anthony, Jamaica. His age has been disputed, but way back when he had no reason to lie, in the Montreal Olympic Games in 1976 when as an eleven-fight novice he represented Jamaica, his date of birth was recorded as 1 August 1952. That made him twenty-four when he made his professional debut in Canada, where he stayed on after the Montreal games; twenty-eight when he lost a wide, unanimous decision to Larry Holmes for the WBC title at Caesars Palace in April 1981; thirty-three when he won the WBC belt against Thomas, and thirty-four when he lost it to Tyson.

The win that made him was a ninth-round knockout of John Tate, the for-mer WBA champion, on the first Roberto Duran-Ray Leonard promotion in Montreal in June 1980. Ten months later he challenged Holmes, didn't win a round on one card, four on the other two. He wasn't ready for Holmes. At the end of 1981, Berbick outworked the ill, thirty-nine-year-old Muhammad Ali over ten depressing rounds in Nassau in the Bahamas.

Berbick had an on-off promotional relationship with Don King and at one time allegedly knocked on the promoter's hotel room door in Las Vegas at 6.30 a.m. brandishing a Bible and wearing a large crucifix. 'The Lord is on your side,' he said. 'Only with thine eyes shalt thou behold and see the reward of the wicked.' Out of the ring his behaviour became increasingly unfathomable and dangerous. He had a street altercation with Holmes, allegedly put a gun into the mouth of an ex-manager – and in 1992 this self-proclaimed Soldier of the Cross was convicted of raping a babysitter, for which he was sentenced to four years. He served fifteen months.

His last fight in anything approaching the big-time was when he was floored in the first round and out-pointed by Hasim Rahman, then an unbeaten prospect, in a ten-rounder in Atlantic City in Ocober 1996. The following year he was deported to Jamaica from the United States, but fled to Canada where, after a long legal case, he was allowed to stay. When, at the age of forty-seven, he out-pointed Shane Sutcliffe over twelve rounds for the Canadian heavyweight title, a subsequent CAT scan revealed a tiny blood clot on his brain. He retired.

FREDDIE BESHORE

Born: 28 September 1922, Harrisburg, Pennsylvania
Died: 1 June 1981, aged 60
Height: 5ft 9in   **Weight at peak:** 185lbs (13st 3lbs)
Fights: 53   **Won:** 35   **Lost:** 15   **Drawn:** 3
KO percentage: 22
Rounds boxed: 383
World title fights: 1
Career span: 1942-54 (12 years)
KO wins: 12
KO defeats: 7

Freddie Beshore, from Pennsylvania, was a surprise choice as challenger for Ezzard Charles in Buffalo in August 1950 – a surprise not least on the grounds that he had lost three of his previous four fights, two of them to Lee Oma and one to the unheralded Bob Dunlap. Charles took time to wear him down. Beshore hung on until the fourteenth round before referee Barney Felix pulled him out, officially because of a severe gash on his ear.

Beshore was short at 5ft 9in and, like Charles, when in proper shape only just above 180lbs – when they fought the champion was 183¼lbs (13st 1¼lbs) and Beshore 184½lbs (13st 2½lbs). Beshore was born in Harrisburg, Pennsylvania, joined the US Navy at seventeen and served on USS *Wisconsin*, a battleship, in the South Pacific during the Second World War.

He plodded along for years as a crowd pleaser in Los Angeles, but beat nobody of consequence. After losing to Charles, he was used as a stepping stone. Joe Louis, slow and old at thirty-six, stopped him on cuts in four, Don Cockell out-pointed him in London, Harry Matthews beat him on cuts in seven and Rocky Marciano knocked him out in four in the Boston Garden.

DAVID BEY

Born: 11 March 1957, Philadelphia, Pennsylvania
Height: 6ft 3in   **Weight at peak:** 233lbs (16st 9lbs)
Fights: 30   **Won:** 18   **Lost:** 11   **Drawn:** 1
KO percentage: 46
Rounds boxed: 176
World title fights: 1
Career span: 1981-94 (13 years)
KO wins: 14
KO defeats: 8

David Bey fought Larry Holmes for the title in Las Vegas in March 1985 but was out of his depth. Holmes, though past his best, controlled the fight until Bey was rescued by referee Carlos Padilla two seconds from the end of round ten.

From Philadelphia, Bey knocked out James 'Buster' Douglas in two rounds of his professional debut in Pittsburgh in 1981 and earned his shot at Holmes by out-pointing former champion Greg Page in a twelve-rounder for the United States Boxing Association belt in August 1984. As the IBF, who recognised Holmes, ran the USBA title as well, it was natural for them to approve Bey as a challenger for the championship proper, even though he had only a 14-0 record at the time. Muhammad Ali saw him and called him 'Dark Gable', telling him with a laugh: 'You're the only one prettier than me.' He still carried his union card from his time as a pile-driver in the docks, where he worked for the same company that employed his father Joseph for thirty-eight years.

Bey said promoter Don King talked him out of going to South Africa to box the WBA champion Gerrie Coetzee because of the apartheid situation, and waited a few months longer to box Holmes instead. It turned out to be his only opportunity. Three months later he was stopped by Trevor Berbick and the following year was out-pointed by Bonecrusher Smith and, in Sydney, by a thirty-six-year-old Joe Bugner. After that, while he always seemed to try in the ring, he ran out of gas or desire after a few rounds and he gradually drifted along to retirement in 1994.

TYRELL BIGGS

Born: 22 December 1960, Philadelphia, Pennsylvania
Height: 6ft 5in   **Weight at peak:** 228lbs (16st 4lbs)
Fights: 40   **Won:** 30   **Lost:** 10
KO percentage: 50
Rounds boxed: 213
World title fights: 1
Career span: 1984-98 (14 years)
KO wins: 20
KO defeats: 7

They say Tyrell Biggs never really recovered from being booed in his professional debut in Madison Square Garden in November 1984. A beautifully sculpted, 6ft 5in heavyweight who had won the super-heavyweight gold medal in the Los Angeles Olympics, he was signed by Main Events, the Duva family business, and seemed to have it made. However, he laboured in his debut over a defensive journeyman, Mike Evans, and, it was said, took the boos to heart. A month later he checked into hospital in Orange, California, for a serious cocaine problem.

Born in Philadelphia, he was taken to fights as a boy by his father James, who was a regular at the Spectrum on Monday nights. When he was ten, he saw Ali fight Frazier on closed circuit and from that night on wanted to be a boxer. His father set up a heavy bag in the basement and he won 108 of 114 amateur bouts, including at the Olympics a quarter-final win over Lennox Lewis and a gold-medal performance against Francesco Damiani of Italy.

After his drug rehabilitation, he returned to the ring in April 1985, and gradually worked his way up. George Benton trained him. He beat James 'Quick' Tillis, Renaldo Snipes and David Bey. He also showed there was nothing wrong with his heart when he out-pointed Jeff Sims in Reno in spite of a broken right collarbone. After fifteen wins he was nowhere near ready for a peak Mike Tyson, but there was nowhere else to go with him. Tyson broke him up in seven rounds in Atlantic City in a world title fight in October 1987. 'When I hit him in the body, he squealed like a girl,' said the charmless young champion. With that defeat, Biggs's fragile temperament gave way – he didn't box for a year, then returned with a rematch of the Olympic final, but lost in five rounds to Damiani in Milan. Another year out was followed by a seventh-round knockout by Gary Mason in London.

The top two heavyweights of the 1988 Olympics, Lennox Lewis and Riddick Bowe, both stopped him. After that Biggs worked the circuit until his retirement in 1998, aged thirty-seven.

JIMMY BIVINS

Born: 6 December 1919, Dry Branch, Georgia
Full name: James Louis Bivins
Height: 5ft 11in   **Weight at peak:** 178lbs (12st 10lbs)
Fights: 112   **Won:** 86   **Lost:** 25   **Drawn:** 1
KO percentage: 27
Rounds boxed: 902
World title fights: 0
Career span: 1940-55 (15 years)
KO wins: 31
KO defeats: 5

Jimmy Bivins, one of the real craftsmen of the ring, should have at least had a shot at the world light-heavyweight title in his prime – and far worse fighters were given paydays against Joe Louis during the Brown Bomber's twelve-year heavyweight reign.

Between April 1942, when Bob Pastor out-sped him over ten rounds, and February 1946, when Jersey Joe Walcott beat him on a disputed split decision, Jimmy had an unbeaten run of twenty-six contests. *Ring* magazine ranked him the number one contender in both the heavyweight and light-heavyweight divisions. In that time he outscored Ezzard Charles, Joey Maxim, Tami Mauriello, Pastor in a rematch, Lee Savold and knocked out Archie Moore in six rounds in Cleveland in August 1945. While the freezing out of Bivins was a crime, it's also true that his prime came during the four years America was involved in the Second World War. He had time out to serve in the US Army and perhaps wasn't available when matches might have been made.

Bivins was born in Dry Branch, Georgia, but his parents, Allen and Fleda, moved the family, two-year-old Jimmy and his three sisters, to Cleveland in search of a better life, where Jimmy worked as a painter, carpenter and locksmith. He also reached the final of the 1939 National Golden Gloves. Olympic legend Jesse Owens advised him to turn professional, and so he began, managed by a Harvard-educated jeweller, Charles Shane jnr, in January 1940, a month after his twentieth birthday. One of his nineteen wins in that first year was a ten-round decision over the brilliant middleweight Charley Burley. Already *Ring* rated him number nine.

He remained a world-class operator for the next dozen years. When his career finally wound up he had boxed three heavyweight champions: Joe Louis (a points defeat in Baltimore in 1951), Jersey Joe Walcott and his old friend from his amateur days, Ezzard Charles (five times, Charles came out on top 4-1). Bivins believed he beat Walcott – 'The only thing he did was knock me down in the seventh round' – and thought he might have had the better of Louis too. In retirement he had eighteen years as a driver for a bakery in Cleveland, had a share in the Old Angle gym in the city and acted as a judge for the Ohio commission. He was married twice, but lost his son, Jimmy jnr, who died of carbon monoxide poisoning when he fell asleep in his car in Detroit, shortly before he was to be sent to Vietnam.

Bivins' achievements were eventually honoured when he was inducted into the boxing hall of fame in Canastota, New York, in 1998. A couple of years earlier he had been discovered, reduced to skin and bone, living in the attic room of a member of his family. He was rescued and the family member convicted of his neglect.

JURGEN BLIN

Born: 7 April 1943, Grossensee, Germany
Height: 6ft 2in   **Weight at peak:** 198lbs (14st 2lbs)
Fights: 48   **Won:** 31   **Lost:** 11   **Drawn:** 1
KO percentage: 18
Rounds boxed: 384
World title fights: 0
Career span: 1964-73 (9 years)
KO wins: 9
KO defeats: 3

Jurgen Blin made his name among German fans with his seventh-round defeat by Muhammad Ali in a non-title fight in Zurich on Boxing Day, 1971. Ali was between championship reigns at the time. Blin, by his own admission, had no chance. 'I didn't have the talent, I didn't have the size, I didn't have the punch,' he said in an endearing interview with Stephen Brunt, author of the fine book *Facing Ali*. After the New Year holiday, the modest, realistic German was back at the day job as a master butcher in a sausage factory.

Blin was born in the countryside near Grossensee in the north-west of Germany, the son of a farmhand, left school and home at fourteen and made his own living in Hamburg. He narrowly missed a place in the German Olympic team of 1964, so turned professional.

Maybe the Ali fight gave him some inspiration because the following June in Madrid he out-pointed the heavy-handed but wild Jose Urtain over fifteen rounds to become European champion. His reign lasted only four months. Joe Bugner, who had previously out-pointed him, knocked him out in eight rounds in October 1972.

After his last fight, when he lost in two rounds to Ron Lyle in his American debut in Denver, he quit his job and invested the money he had saved from his ring earnings to open a small snack bar at the railway station in Hamburg. He did well enough to expand the business but had to endure personal tragedy with the mental illness and eventual death of his son, Knut, who had also been a professional fighter.

JACK BODELL

Born: 11 August 1940, Swadlincote, England
Height: 6ft 1in   **Weight at peak:** 203lbs (14st 7lbs)
Fights: 71   **Won:** 58   **Lost:** 13
KO percentage: 43
Rounds boxed: 419
World title fights: 0
Career span: 1962-72 (10 years)
KO wins: 31
KO defeats: 11

The determinedly unfashionable Midlands southpaw Jack Bodell was one of the best heavyweights Britain had in the 1960s. Bodell hit a belated peak when he trounced twenty-one-year-old Joe Bugner for the British, Commonwealth and European championships at Wembley in September 1971.

He ignored most of the jibes of the London-based national press about his down-to-earth habits, old-fashioned clothes and hairstyle and thrifty ways. Bodell, from the Derbyshire town of Swadlincote, was an accomplished enough amateur to win a bronze medal in the 1961 European Championships in Belgrade. He showed his character by overcoming several early career defeats that would have demoralised a lesser man and his first British title bid against Henry Cooper lasted only a couple of rounds. But he out-pointed Johnny Prescott over ten rounds, stopped Brian London in nine – and his eighth-round hammering of Billy Walker at Wembley in March 1969 ended the career of the 'Blond Bomber' from West Ham. He also beat Joe Roman, the Puerto Rican who would go on to a ridiculous title challenge against George Foreman. When Cooper handed back the British title, Bodell won it with a fifteen-round decision over Carl Gizzi in Nottingham. Although he lost it back over fifteen bruising, untidy rounds to Cooper in March 1970, Bodell defied a shut eye to out-point Manuel Ramos, a Mexican who had fought Joe Frazier for the New York version of the world title. Unfortunately, manager George Biddles then matched him with Jerry Quarry two months later and Bodell was knocked out in the first round.

He was effectively finished and two rapid defeats by Jose Urtain and Danny McAlinden persuaded him to stop. Bodell was never afraid of a day's hard graft and prospered in retirement. By the 1980s he was running a fish and chip shop in Coventry.

OSCAR BONAVENA

Born: 25 September 1942, Buenos Aires, Argentina
Full name: Oscar Natalio Bonavena
Died: 22 May 1976, Nevada, USA, aged 33
Height: 6ft ½in   **Weight at peak:** 206lbs (14st 10lbs)
Fights: 68   Won: 58   Lost: 9   Drawn: 1
KO percentage: 64
Rounds boxed: 421
World title fights: 1
Career span: 1964-76 (12 years)
KO wins: 44
KO defeats: 1

Oscar Bonavena lived life with no apparent regrets – and died young.

Bonavena stood fairly square on and liked to counter-punch, especially with the left hook, though when the mood took him he could brawl with the best. Although he could punch, he wasn't the best finisher in the world; he let Joe Frazier off the hook in their first fight and had Karl Mildenberger down four times yet had to settle for a points win. His chin was solid – in sixty-eight fights spread over a dozen years, only Muhammad Ali stopped him, and that in the final round of a fifteen-round battle at Madison Square Garden in December 1970.

Originally from Buenos Aires, Bonavena made his name in New York where the Garden fans were always pleased to see him. And though by the time of his premature death he was living in a trailer park in Nevada, he was on a run of seven wins and still ranked seventh in the world. After his last fight, a points win over Billy Joiner in Reno in February 1976, he hooked up with Joe and Sally Conforte, who ran the Mustang Ranch brothel in Storey County, Nevada. Early in the morning of 22 May 1976 he arrived at the Mustang, irate because his home had been burgled. He was ready to blame Joe Conforte. It was said Bonavena had been sleeping with Sally. After an altercation at the gate, as he returned to his car he was shot dead by a guard, an ex-convict called Willard Brymer. Conforte, annoyed that the investigating police had crossed the county line, said, 'It's just a dead man... So we got a dead man here. So what?' After a strange trial Brymer plea-bargained his way to a sentence of two years for voluntary manslaughter.

As an amateur Bonavena was disqualified in the semi-final of the 1963 Pan-American Games against Lee Carr of the USA in Sao Paulo, Brazil. He bit Carr on the shoulder. In only his sixth pro fight Bonavena beat the former world title challenger Tom McNeeley in five rounds, although the stoppage was messy and the fans booed. His first defeat was when Zora Folley gave him a boxing lesson and knocked him down at the Garden in February 1965. That was hardly surprising: Bonavena was having only his ninth fight, while Folley had been a contender since the 1950s and was in fight number eighty of a fine career.

In New York in June 1966 he outslugged George Chuvalo on a majority ten-round decision, and then almost upset the young, unbeaten Frazier. In the second round Bonavena put Smokin' Joe down twice with heavy right hands. A third knockdown would have brought the automatic finish, but Oscar couldn't do it. Frazier took over and although Bonavena finished strongly he lost a split decision that, from the tape, looked fair.

After Ali had been stripped of the title, the WBA paired eight contenders in an elimination tournament. Bonavena travelled to Frankfurt to out-point the German southpaw Karl Mildenberger over twelve rounds. Three months later Jimmy Ellis, fighting in his home town of Louisville, Kentucky, was too slick for him and put him out of the tournament. Back in Argentina, he beat the declining Folley and another top contender, Leotis Martin. Those wins earned him a shot at the heavyweight championship as recognised by the New York State Athletic Commission against Frazier in front of a surprisingly small crowd of 7,500 in Joe's home town of Philadelphia in December 1968. This time Frazier won by clear unanimous decision over fifteen rounds – and Bonavena, whose eyes were swollen almost shut by the end, was so mad he wrecked his hotel suite.

His next big fight was two years later in the Garden against Ali. Going into the fifteenth round, Ali was ahead by ten, seven and three points. In the last, Bonavena was dropped three times and stopped with fifty-seven seconds left. Back in Buenos Aires, Bonavena beat Al 'Blue' Lewis of Detroit on a foul, but only after being knocked down three times, then returned to box the aged but still popular former champion Floyd Patterson. Between them they almost sold out the Garden. Bonavena put Patterson down with a flash left hook in round four and thought he had won, but over the full ten the judges and referee all had Floyd ahead.

Bonavena decided to live permanently in the USA. Ron Lyle beat him over twelve gruelling rounds in Denver in front of more than 10,000 fans in March 1974. 'You no chicken,' grinned the bruised, battered Argentine at the end.

RIDDICK BOWE

Born: 10 August 1967, Brooklyn, New York
Height: 6ft 5in   **Weight at peak:** 235lbs (16st 11lbs)
Fights: 44   **Won:** 42   **Lost:** 1   **No Contests:** 1
KO percentage: 75
Rounds boxed: 186
World champion: 1992-93
World title fights: 4
Career span: 1989-2005 (16 years)
KO wins: 33
KO defeats: 0

Riddick Bowe's supreme achievement was to out-fight Evander Holyfield in a classic twelve-round world title fight at the Thomas and Mack Center, Las Vegas, in November 1992. That night, perhaps for the only time in his life, Bowe touched greatness. Some of Bowe's technical work was of the highest order and the tenth and eleventh rounds were breathtakingly exciting, with both men in trouble and finding the resolve and skill to fire back. Bowe won clearly: 117-110 on two cards, 115-112 on the third. He won the undisputed championship – recognition from the three governing bodies that mattered: the WBC, WBA and IBF.

In the 1988 Seoul Olympic final Bowe had been stopped on his feet in the second round by Lennox Lewis. When he took over from Holyfield he inherited Lewis as the mandatory challenger of the WBC, but he wanted to make his own decisions and so gave that belt back. He believed, as 'the man who beat the man', he had the right to choose who to defend against and where.

The decision to avoid Lewis hung over him for the rest of his career. On the way up he had proved himself by beating former champions Pinklon Thomas and Tony Tubbs. He also stopped the 1984 Olympic super-heavyweight gold medallist Tyrell Biggs in eight and knocked out a future WBA champ, Bruce Seldon, in a round. His credentials were sound.

A quick-witted, genial family man with wife Judy and children usually in tow, he took a break for a world tour and met the Pope and Nelson Mandela. He also stopped off in London for a card headlined by future opponent Herbie Hide. He ate a pizza, yawned and said: 'He ain't exactly a Bengal Tiger, is he?' When he defended the WBA and IBF belts against Michael Dokes, three months after beating Holyfield, he had put on eight pounds. When asked if he thought he was in shape, he said: 'Good enough to beat Dokes.' He was right. The veteran from Ohio was washed up. It lasted

139 seconds. By then Lewis had been awarded the WBC title. Most critics hoped for a unification fight, so it was a major disappointment when Bowe selected the veteran journeyman Jesse Ferguson in what was billed as a homecoming in Washington DC in May 1993 (Though born and raised in Brooklyn, Bowe lived outside Washington over the Maryland stateline). Ferguson made it – just – into round two.

Then, in November 1993, Bowe lost the title back to Holyfield in the fight forever remembered for the arrival of a paraglider, James Miller, who descended into the arena and crashed into the ropes of the ring. The fight was put on hold at a time when Bowe seemed to be taking over. His manager, Rock Newman, should have thought on his feet and demanded a No Contest. After all, Bowe's pregnant wife had been overcome and taken away and his venerable trainer, Eddie Futch, was also ill. It was chaos. Eventually the fight restarted and Holyfield kept his mind together better than Bowe and rallied to win a majority decision: 115-114, 115-113, 114-114. There should have been an immediate rematch but Holyfield instead was allowed to defend against Michael Moorer and lost.

Newman saw the sense in making the Lewis fight for the latter's WBC title, but Oliver McCall scuppered that plan by upsetting the British star in September 1994. Six months on, Bowe beat Herbie Hide in six rounds for the irrelevant WBO belt. He beat the giant Cuban, Jorge Luis Gonzalez, also in six, then lost interest in the WBO. At last, he fought Holyfield for the third time – and once again these great warriors responded magnificently. It lacked the class of their epic first fight but its sways of fortune were even more extreme. By the fifth Holyfield looked so weary and hurt that George Foreman, commentating at ringside, jumped to his feet and called out to referee Joe Cortez to stop it. 'This guy's going to end up in a pine box!' he said. Yet in round six Holyfield suddenly produced a left hook that sent Bowe toppling onto his back. Bowe got up, stunned, and stood against the ropes, somehow managing to absorb the follow-up attack. Holyfield punched himself out and in the eighth Bowe knocked him down twice for a stoppage win. In fact, the fight took more from the winner than it did Holyfield, who would come back to earn millions more in two fights each against Mike Tyson and Lennox Lewis.

Bowe looked jaded as Andrew Golota twice out-fought him only to be disqualified for low punching. Afterwards the former champion seemed to be slurring his words. He suddenly seemed a lost soul. There was a strange incident when he announced he was joining the US Marines only to quit boot camp days later because he was missing his wife and children too much. At the time, they had a home so big in Maryland that the road had to be reconstructed to accommodate it. Yet the life of this once sharp, intelligent man unravelled. His marriage disintegrated and he was arrested and eventually jailed for kidnapping his wife and forcing her into his car against her will. At his trial, his lawyers pleaded that his ring career had left him brain-damaged. Then another brief marriage fell apart.

Amazingly, in 2004 he was given a licence to box in Oklahoma and he told anyone gullible enough to listen that he wanted to regain his championship. He won his first fight easily enough, then, surprisingly in view of the evidence at his trial, he passed medical tests in California. A slow, shambling, overweight figure, he edged a ten-round split decision over a Utah club fighter, Billy Zumbrun.

JAMES J. BRADDOCK

Born: 7 June 1906, New York City
Full name: James Walter Braddock
Died: 29 November 1974, North Bergen, New Jersey, aged 68
Height: 6ft 3in   **Weight at peak:** 193-197lbs (13st 11lbs-14st 1lb)
Fights: 86   **Won:** 51   **Lost:** 25   **Drawn:** 6
　　　　　　　　　　No Decisions: 2   **No Contests:** 2
KO percentage: 30
Rounds boxed: 597
World champion: 1935-37
World title fights: 2
Career span: 1926-38 (12 years)
KO wins: 26
KO defeats: 2

James J. Braddock was one of boxing's blue-collar champions, a workmanlike, organised professional who epitomised the hungry fighter. His story was popularised in 2005 by the release of the movie *Cinderella Man*, starring Russell Crowe.

Braddock won the world heavyweight championship because of his attributes, which contrasted with the lackadaisical attitude of the champion he had to beat, Max Baer. Braddock wasn't supposed to do more than give Baer a workout, twelve months after the big-punching Californian had thrashed Primo Carnera to become champion in the Madison Square Garden Bowl on Long Island. In the intervening period Baer had been distracted by out-of-the-ring pursuits and, it was felt, needed a fight to shrug off the rust. Braddock appeared to fit the bill perfectly. At one time a world-class light-heavyweight, he had drifted into life as a journeyman in the early 1930s. He worked in the New Jersey ports when he could – and when he couldn't, he was forced to provide for his wife and family by accepting $17 a week welfare relief. His fortunes changed in 1934 when he came in as a substitute and stopped Madison Square Garden's rising star Corn Griffin in three rounds. Points wins over John Henry Lewis, the future light-heavyweight champion, and the bigger, heavier Art Lasky, set him up for Baer.

Years later Braddock, who prepared with typical care, said, 'I was determined not to make a fool of myself.' He knew that if he could take Baer's punches he could box fifteen quick rounds. And he did just that, jabbing smartly, countering on the move and landing orthodox right hands. When Baer hit him cleanly a couple of times, Braddock absorbed the shock and said, 'Is that as hard as you can punch?'

Baer, who was known for taunting opponents, found himself on the other end of that as Braddock talked to him, then peppered him and won the decision.

Braddock, having known poverty, made the championship pay, first by hawking himself around the celebrity or vaudeville circuit as the Cinderella Man, and then when forced to box again, two years after the Baer fight, he made a financial deal that secured him for life. He agreed to give Joe Louis the opportunity that the Brown Bomber's talent thoroughly deserved, but only on condition that for the next ten years he was given ten per cent of Louis's gross purses, which he later estimated earned him a 'pension' of around $150,000.

James Walter Braddock was born in Hell's Kitchen, the sprawling warren that ran down to the docks on the west side of Manhattan. When he was a boy the family moved across the Hudson to New Jersey, where he lived for the rest of his life. When he began boxing he became James J., after the great champions Corbett and Jeffries, and learned the arts and tools of the craft from the old heavyweight contender Joe Jeannette. He had more than 100 amateur bouts but early in his pro career hand problems forced him to rely on skill rather than power. By the time he was in a position to challenge Tommy Loughran for the world light-heavyweight title in July 1929 he had lost only three of forty-six fights. Loughran, however, was one of the slickest boxers of his or any other time, and won fourteen of the fifteen rounds at Yankee Stadium.

The emphatic nature of the defeat demoralised Braddock: he won only one of his next six fights. He moved up to heavyweight, but drifted from fight to fight. He worked on the docks in Hoboken, picking up paydays in the ring but losing more fights than he won. Finally, he broke both hands against Abe Feldman in Mount Vernon in September 1933. He couldn't box – and he couldn't do his heavy manual work. The only alternative, in order to provide food for his wife Mae and three young children, Jay, Howard and Rose Marie, was welfare relief.

When he beat Baer, people rose to his honest approach. He was mobbed all the way to the dressing room. He made a point of repaying the money he had been given by the welfare service and agreed to box Max Schmeling only for wrangling to keep him out of the ring for two years. In the end it was not Schmeling but Joe Louis he met at Comiskey Park, Chicago, in June 1937. More than 45,000 fans turned out, paying a total of $715,470. Braddock made a great start, dropping the twenty-three-year-old challenger in the opening round, was in the fight after four, but then took a beating until he was knocked out in round eight. Afterwards he needed twenty-three stitches in his face, and his front teeth had been driven through his gumshield into his lip.

Braddock had one more fight, a ten-round decision over Tommy Farr in January 1938, but his legs were not what they had been and he retired. During the Second World War he served in the US Army transportation corps and until 1956 he had a business, dealing in marine equipment, before working for the Operating Engineers Union. He and his wife lived in the house in North Bergen that they bought when he was world champion. Braddock died, aged sixty-eight, in November 1974.

BILL BRENNAN

Born: 23 June 1893, Chicago, Illinois
Real name: William Schenck
Died: 15 June 1924, New York City, aged 30
Height: 6ft 1in   Weight at peak: 197lbs (14st 1lb)
Fights: 126   Won: 91   Lost: 18   Drawn: 7   No Decisions: 10
KO percentage: 53
Rounds boxed: 812
World title fights: 1
Career span: 1913-23 (10 years)
KO wins: 68
KO defeats: 5

Bill Brennan gave Jack Dempsey a decent argument for the world title in Madison Square Garden in December 1920. Promoter Tex Rickard had bought the Garden, which was deep in debt, and set out to make boxing a major attraction in New York with Dempsey, the colourful, controversial heavyweight champion, as his centrepiece.

To help sell tickets for the Brennan fight, Dempsey trained in the city. However, it was winter. While he did his gym work in tennis courts on the corner of 57th Street and Eighth Avenue, Central Park was frozen, which made roadwork tough, and by night time there was the noise and bright lights of Broadway. Dempsey enjoyed to the full the attractions of the city that never slept. The champion was also over-confident because he had beaten Brennan easily in six rounds in February 1918 when, after being knocked down several times Bill broke an ankle.

With the pre-Christmas fun at its height, around 14,000 people bought tickets. The fight was to be followed, twenty-four hours later, by a world heavyweight wrestling match. Ideas that Brennan would provide a gentle workout for the champion ended in round two when Dempsey was stunned by a right uppercut. Brennan boxed on the move behind the left lead – the classic tactic against the Manassa Mauler – and crossed his right over to keep the points piling up. In the tenth round, when a slashing right split Dempsey's left ear, it seemed the title might change hands. However, in the twelfth, Dempsey suddenly got through with body attacks and turned the fight around. A left to the body took the wind out of Brennan and a long right knocked him into the ropes and down. He just failed to beat the count. After the fight, when Dempsey's ear was being stitched in the dressing room, Brennan came in and laughed, 'I'll get you, you son of a gun!' They liked each other.

Bill was a decent fighter. He took on world light-heavyweight champ Battling Levinsky four times in non-title bouts and also faced legendary middleweight Harry Greb four times. After the Dempsey world title bout, Brennan went back to the circuit. Probably his best win was a fifteen-round decision over Fighting Bob Martin, a talented prospect, in the Garden in February 1921.

He ran a speakeasy on Broadway called the Tia Juana, but on the night of 15 June 1924 someone walked in and gunned him down. Brennan was thirty years old.

FRANK BRUNO

Born: 16 November 1961, London, England
Height: 6ft 3in   **Weight at peak:** 238lbs (17st)
Fights: 45   **Won:** 40   **Lost:** 5
KO percentage: 84
Rounds boxed: 170
World champion: 1995-96
World title fights: 5
Career span: 1982-96 (14 years)
KO wins: 38
KO defeats: 5

Frank Bruno's love affair with the British public has so far lasted more than two decades. The nation celebrated with him as Bruno finally won the World Boxing Council version of the championship in the open air of Wembley Stadium, London, in September 1995 when he outworked Oliver McCall over twelve rounds. Bruno wept tears of joy and relief as red, white and blue ticker tape cascaded down on the ring. After defeats in previous world title attempts against Lennox Lewis, Mike Tyson and Tim Witherspoon, he had finally fulfilled his dream. 'I've been trying for this for thirteen years,' he said. 'I know some of you wrote me off years ago, said I had no stamina, that I couldn't take a punch, I couldn't do this, I couldn't do that, but I'm just trying to say I was blessed by the man above. If I never walk again, get run over or get shot, it's down in history that I'm heavyweight champion.'

How different that was to Bruno's first title shot in that same arena, beneath the twin towers of the home of English football, nine years before when, after coping well for ten rounds, he was floored and stopped in the eleventh by Tim Witherspoon. He was taken to hospital that night to have his wounds tended and sat waiting for a doctor alongside a man who had watched the fight, but broken his leg falling down some steps. 'At least you got well paid for ending up in here,' said the disconsolate punter.

Bruno was British amateur champion at eighteen, then had to wait while a problem with short sight was cured by pioneering surgery in Colombia, before making his debut under manager Terry Lawless and his partners Harry Levene, Mickey Duff and Jarvis Astaire in 1982. They guided him expertly through potentially difficult early years and overcame a solitary setback when, way in front on points, he was knocked out in the tenth round by James 'Bonecrusher' Smith at Wembley Arena.

Although the policy of caution was criticised frequently, Bruno was allowed time to mature. In March 1986 he demolished the fading former champion Gerrie

Coetzee in one round and then, aged twenty-four, lost to Witherspoon for the WBA belt. When he challenged Mike Tyson at the Las Vegas Hilton in February 1989, Bruno was knocked down in the opening seconds, lost another point for holding, but rallied to shake Tyson with a left hook in a dramatic first round. He couldn't repeat that, but hung on until the fifth when Tyson overwhelmed him.

An eye injury almost finished his career but, after much debate, he was granted a licence by the British Board of Control and returned to the ring, but without Lawless as his manager. Levene had died, and Duff became the visible head of operations, with Bruno's partner (later wife) Laura taking on the official role of manager. Frank challenged Lennox Lewis for the WBC title on a rainy night at Cardiff Arms Park in October 1993. For six rounds Bruno boxed well behind his left lead, but then a left hook from the champion took everything out of him and he stood against the ropes, absorbing a bombardment of punches until it was stopped. After a facile first round win over the barely interested Jesse Ferguson in Birmingham, Bruno left Duff – and switched to Frank Warren at the start of 1995.

Warren, through his working relationship with American promoter Don King, secured Bruno the fourth world title bid against the erratic WBC champion Oliver McCall. Bruno won on workrate and commitment. In the final round McCall made a desperate attempt to turn it round, did manage to hurt Bruno for the first time, but at the final bell, was well adrift on points: two judges gave Bruno nine of the twelve rounds at 117-111, with the third scoring 115-113.

Bruno's first defence, and final fight, was a third-round stoppage by the revitalised Tyson in the MGM Grand, Las Vegas, in March 1996. Bruno was cut early on and was pummelled into defeat without really giving Tyson the kind of argument some believed he was capable of. It was a sad way to go, and several months later he announced his retirement after a medical had revealed a deterioration in his eye condition.

Always hugely popular in pantomime and with regular appearances on television as a boxing pundit, celebrity guest and in commercials, his financial future seemed assured. However, investment difficulties, the suicide of his long-time trainer George Francis and the breakdown of his marriage were followed by an alarming deterioration in his psychological condition, which led to a spell in hospital for depression in 2003. With the good wishes of the nation behind him, he recovered enough to work in pantomime again that winter.

JOE BUGNER

Born: 13 March 1950, Szoreg, Hungary
Height: 6ft 4in   **Weight at peak:** 230lbs (16st 6lbs)
Fights: 83   **Won:** 69   **Lost:** 13   **Drawn:** 1
KO percentage: 49
Rounds boxed: 572

World title fights: 1
Career span: 1967-99 (32 years)
KO wins: 41
KO defeats: 4

Far and away the best British heavyweight of his generation, Joe Bugner's reputation was harmed by his over-cautious approach to his world title bid against Muhammad Ali in Kuala Lumpur in 1975. Bugner could fight, though, as he showed when he stretched both Ali and Joe Frazier in 1973. He could also be said to have exploited boxing well enough by doing things his own way. That, by the way, is a compliment. Too many reckless, exciting fighters have ended up needing help after their time in the sport has finished that it was heartwarming to meet Bugner again in London at a Lennox Lewis press conference in 2000 as bright, sharp and friendly as he ever was. 'I came to no harm,' he said of his lucrative comebacks of the 1980s and 1990s. 'The guys I fought weren't good enough to hurt me and I earned decent money.'

Bugner learned perspective as a child. Following the 1956 Hungarian uprising, with his mother, sister and two brothers, they travelled by bus, then walked through forests to Yugoslavia, spent eighteen months in a refugee camp and eventually reached Britain, where they settled in St Ives in Cambridgeshire. Joe was a national schools discus champion but preferred boxing – and because he was big and good enough, turned professional at seventeen with local manager Andy Smith. Bugner ended the careers of Brian London and Johnny Prescott, two of the best British heavyweights of the previous generation, and then did the same to Henry Cooper on a disputed fifteen-round decision at Wembley in March 1971. At only twenty-one, Bugner learned what it was to depose an icon. With hindsight, the fight was a no-win situation: if he had lost, it would have been to an old man, but in winning, especially controversially, he upset the British public. The boos may well have taught him as much as Cooper did.

Six months later, he lost the British, Commonwealth and European titles he won against Cooper in a fifteen-round points defeat to Jack Bodell, but gradually re-established himself. He knocked out the German Jurgen Blin to regain the European title and was still only twenty-two when he boxed Muhammad Ali in a twelve-round non-title fight in Las Vegas. He acquitted himself well, was cut in round one but stayed calm, and eventually lost on points by margins of between three and five rounds on the cards. Ali was magnanimous: 'In two-and-a-half years, when I retire, he will be the champion of the world.'

Two-and-a-half years later, Ali did box Bugner again in Kuala Lumpur, this time in a title defence in July 1975. Bugner, who had previously lost on points to Joe Frazier in an exciting twelve-round fight at Earl's Court, London, was given a chance, especially in the sweltering Malaysian heat against a thirty-three-year-old champion who was not as quick as he used to be. Bugner had showed a lot of heart to climb off the floor and rock Frazier with a right hand in the tenth round but against Ali he fought conservatively.

Those close to him say his game plan was to wait until Ali tired, then press forward over the second half and wear him down, but unfortunately the heat got to Bugner too and he just couldn't get going. That may have been true, but it was perceived as the performance of a non-trier. This was not helped by Bugner splashing around merrily in the hotel pool later that day. Mickey Duff, who made the matches for the first part of his career, recalled their conversation. 'I suppose, Joe, at the end of the day, the name of the game is money,' he said. Bugner said, 'Yes – and being able to count it.'

Bugner retired, returned to blast out Richard Dunn in the first round at Wembley to regain the British, Commonwealth and European titles, but then laboured to a split-decision defeat in Las Vegas against Ron Lyle in a fight he was capable of winning. He retired to go into movies, had a brief British comeback when new promoter Frank Warren was making waves and eventually settled for good in Australia, where he ran a vineyard. He continued to box off and on, beat good veterans like Greg Page and James Tillis, then returned to London in 1987 and lost to Frank Bruno at White Hart Lane football ground in Tottenham. According to those around him, Bugner did not exactly exert himself in preparations – some cynics suggested that at 256lbs (18st 4lbs) he was heavier by fight time than when he arrived in the country. Bruno won in the eighth.

In the 1990s he came back again, won the Australian title, talked up bouts with George Foreman and Mike Tyson to keep the headlines coming in, then eventually acknowledged he shouldn't go on, following a ninth-round disqualification win over the competent American Levi Billups in 1999.

RED BURMAN

Born: 18 March 1915, Baltimore, Maryland
Real name: Clarence Burman
Height: 5ft 11in   **Weight at peak:** 188lbs (13st 6lbs)
Fights: 73   **Won:** 57   **Lost:** 14   **Drawn:** 2
KO percentage: 38
Rounds boxed: 493
World title fights: 1
Career span: 1933-42 (9 years)
Longest winning run: 14 (1936)
KO wins: 28
KO defeats: 5

Clarence Burman, known as Red, was advised by Jack Dempsey in the 1930s and fought Joe Louis for the championship at Madison Square Garden in January 1941. He wasn't big enough at 5ft 11in and 185lbs, but neither did he qualify as one of the bums of the month. Going into the Louis fight, he had won nineteen of his previous twenty contests. The exception was a twelve-round points defeat by

Tommy Farr in London in April 1939. Three months earlier he had beaten Farr on a majority decision in New York. Burman threw so many he punched himself out in the first fight with Farr, whose rally over the last two rounds swayed the crowd if not the judges. They booed long and loud – and were still complaining as the next bout got underway. The rematch was at Harringay Arena in front of 11,600 fans and this time there was no controversy – Farr won well behind his left lead.

Against Louis, Burman took the fight to the champion in spite of conceding 14½lbs as well as an immeasurable degree of talent. He also spent the rest of his life believing he knocked Louis down with a right hand in round three, though referee Arthur Donovan didn't call it. Louis knocked Burman out with body punches in the fifth. 'When I was in a ring I wasn't scared of nobody,' he said years later when he was working as a security guard. 'I always had the feeling I could beat anybody in the world. He changed my mind that night.'

Burman had turned professional at the age of seventeen and had a tough ring upbringing, which included over-ambitious matches against future middleweight champion Ken Overlin and reigning light-heavyweight champ John Henry Lewis. He knock out Corn Griffin in one round. Corn, who had been a prospect until he bumped into James J. Braddock two years earlier, was suspended by the Maryland Commission. In April 1937 he out-pointed Gus Dorazio over ten rounds in Philadelphia and although three months later he lost to the Olympic champion Alberto Lovell of Argentina, he continued improving, outscored the veteran Johnny Risko in Florida and, in the fight before he boxed Louis, he outscored Tony Musto in a bloody ten-round war in Baltimore in October 1940.

After Louis, Burman was never the same. He retired in 1942.

TOMMY BURNS

Born: 17 June 1881, Hanover, Ontario, Canada
Real name: Noah Brusso
Died: 10 May 1955, Vancouver, Canada, aged 73
Height: 5ft 7in   **Weight at peak:** 172-183lbs (12st 4lbs to 13st 1lb)
Fights: 61   **Won:** 46   **Lost:** 6   **Drawn:** 9
KO percentage: 60
Rounds boxed: 499
World champion: 1906-08
World title fights: 13
Career span: 1900-20 (20 years)
KO wins: 37
KO defeats: 2

It has become fashionable to dismiss Tommy Burns as an under-sized, bogus heavyweight who was champion of the world only because it took Jack Johnson two years to hunt him down. While Johnson's supporters have an argument and nobody could genuinely claim a place for the Canadian in the all-time top ten, Burns' ability should not be so easily dismissed. Anybody who was 5ft 7in tall and weighed about 180lbs had to be able to fight in order to reach the top, let alone hold the championship through eleven defences – even if some of his challengers were among the worst ever given a shot at the sport's biggest prize.

In his own time Burns was lightly regarded because he followed the hulking, talented James J. Jeffries, who had retired undefeated the year before. The memory of the 6ft 2½in, 220lbs Jeffries was simply too fresh in people's minds for a comparative midget like Burns to be readily accepted. However, Burns knew how to box, could punch extremely hard and accurately for his weight, and was unerringly brave. Even when Johnson picked him to pieces in Rushcutter's Bay outside Sydney on Boxing Day 1908, Burns complained angrily about the stoppage, declaring he could still have worn the big Texan down.

Burns was a tough, independent man from his early days in Ontario – he was born Noah Brusso in a log cabin near Hanover, about eighty miles north-west of Toronto. When he was twelve, by which time the family were in Chesley, he was sent to work in his uncle's saw mill. At fourteen, with his father now dead and his mother having remarried, he was thrown out of the house by his new stepfather for spending $80 on a suit. He worked as a wool-spinner, then as a baggage handler on a steamer. By 1900 he was in Detroit and although he had one spur-of-the-moment professional fight that year – he came out of the crowd to box as a substitute and won – he did not begin to box regularly until he was twenty years old in 1901. In his youth he was a good-class skater and lacrosse player, and in his early twenties he mixed his boxing with semi-professional ice hockey.

His early fights were under his real name but when an opponent almost died and he spent several days under arrest his mother pleaded with him to stop boxing. He promised her he would, but simply moved away from Detroit and used the name Tommy Burns. By 1905 he was boxing twenty-rounders against top middleweights like Jack (Twin) Sullivan, Dave Barry and Hugo Kelly. One marriage, to Irene Pepper, had been brief, but in 1906 he married Julia Keating – and the union lasted twenty years. He moved around the country, however, and while in Nevada in July 1905 he saw Marvin Hart win the world heavyweight title vacated by James J. Jeffries. He was convinced he could beat the big man from Kentucky, who in turn felt the tiny Canadian would provide a perfect opponent for a safe first defence. They met in the Naud Junction Pavilion, Los Angeles, on 23 February 1906.

Burns mocked Hart in the ring – and the ill-tempered, mediocre champion threw a punch before the first bell rang! The fight itself was a dull, lethargic affair, but Burns controlled it with his left lead and speed of hand and foot. Hart was hurt in the fourteen and fifteenth rounds. Burns won the twenty-round decision, but impressed few.

His first defence was a knockout of Fireman Jim Flynn in Los Angeles. Burns toyed with the former railroad worker, then opened up with heavy punches to drop him three times in the fifteenth round. In his second defence he boxed Philadelphia Jack O'Brien in a boring, listless battle over twenty rounds in which it is said neither man tried too hard. Referee Jim Jeffries, probably as fed up as the crowd, scored a draw. Six months later they met again in a tawdry episode. O'Brien offered Burns $3,500 to take a dive. Burns accepted, O'Brien barely trained, and then the champion reneged on the deal and gave his challenger a pounding over the full twenty rounds. Boshter Bill Squires came all the way from Australia to challenge Burns in Colma, just outside San Francisco, on 4 July 1907. Squires came forward with his chin exposed and Burns took him out with perfectly timed right hands in 129 seconds of the opening round. By then Jack Johnson was the leading contender and Burns had been an unimpressive champion. He was also Canadian and, although he was black, Johnson was American and therefore the big, talented Texan commanded some support from people who would not have bothered had Burns been an American.

Burns, ever the businessman, decided to take the championship on the road. He wasn't afraid of Johnson but wasn't in a rush to box him either. In December 1907 he fought the hulking, slow British heavyweight champion Gunner Moir at the National Sporting Club in London. The NSC were the self-imposed, autocratic rulers of British boxing at the time and were used to boxers doffing their caps. Consequently, when Burns demanded his £3,000 purse to be paid in cash they were furious. Burns destroyed Moir in ten rounds. Before he left London, Burns knocked out Jack Palmer in four at the Wonderland Arena, which at least enabled the ordinary British boxing fan to get a glimpse of the world champion. They, of course, were not allowed through the portals of the NSC. Again Burns upset the promoters, arriving early and padlocking every turnstile except one, then sitting close by until enough people had paid for him to collect his purse in cash in advance.

In Dublin on St Patrick's Day he destroyed Jem Roche in eighty-eight seconds. Jewey Smith lasted five rounds in Paris, a city that Burns appreciated so much that he stayed on to knock out Bill Squires in the eighth round of a rematch. He followed Squires home to Australia, organised a third fight and this time Boshter Bill lasted into round thirteen, though it was rumoured Burns had carried him. Nine days after beating Squires, Burns knocked out another Australian, Bill Lang, in six rounds, and finally agreed to box Johnson for $30,000. Promoter H.D. (nicknamed Huge Deal) McIntosh had an arena specially constructed in Rushcutter's Bay and staged the fight on 26 December 1908. McIntosh hated Johnson and was a little afraid of him – he took to carrying a lead pipe in case the American attacked him – but refereed the fight himself to ensure fair play. Johnson taunted Burns, toyed with him, and eventually knocked him down in round fourteen. The police, edgy and uncertain of their responsibilities on an afternoon of legalised violence, switched off the film cameras and jumped in to stop the fight.

Burns fought only rarely after that. He tried promoting, but that ended in tragedy when the heavyweight Luther McCarty died in the ring against Arthur Pelkey. He ran a health farm in California and worked as a physical training instructor in the Canadian Army at the end of the First World War. He moved to Britain, ran a pub in Newcastle, but in 1927 divorced his wife and returned to the USA, where he managed a fighter or two, ran a speakeasy during Prohibition, sold insurance and worked in a shipyard.

Amazingly in 1946 he married his childhood sweetheart Nellie Schweitzer, whose father had instructed her to break off their relationship because Tommy was a boxer. A year or so later Burns, suffering badly from arthritis, was ordained as an evangelical preacher. He died of a heart attack while visiting Vancouver in 1955.

JOE BYGRAVES

Born: 26 May 1931, Kingston, Jamaica
Height: 6ft 1in   **Weight at peak:** 195-200lbs (13st 13lbs-14st 4lbs)
Fights: 72   **Won:** 42   **Lost:** 29   **Drawn:** 1
KO percentage: 30
Rounds boxed: 491
World title fights: 0
Career span: 1953-67 (14 years)
KO wins: 22
KO defeats: 7

Joe Bygraves was a free-swinging heavyweight, originally from Kingston, Jamaica, who emigrated to England in the early 1950s. He became the first West Indian to hold a British Empire championship when he out-pointed Kitione Lave of Tonga over fifteen rounds at Wembley Pool in June 1956.

Once Britain began to settle down after the Second World War, the Government actively promoted immigration, with the result that people dreaming of a better life arrived from Africa and the West Indies at Liverpool Docks, including future world champions Hogan Bassey and Dick Tiger... and Bygraves. While earning regular wages as a ship's painter, the big Jamaican created a reputation as an amateur, but in May 1952 he was disqualified while boxing for England against Wales. The Welsh referee, ironically named Mr English, made the mistake of visiting the dressing room afterwards, where a still-fuming Bygraves knocked him out. That was the end of his amateur career: he turned pro with his trainer, Johnny Campbell, a local scrap metal dealer who had seen the great Jack Dempsey-Luis Firpo fight and ever since had dreamed of producing his own world champion.

In 1956 Bygraves took the future world heavyweight champion Ingemar Johansson the distance in Gothenburg, a ten-round bout that the Swede always remembered as one of his toughest. Bygraves also finished the career of the former British titleholder, Jack Gardner, in two rounds. The British Boxing Board of Control were so concerned at the way Gardner was being whacked around they withdrew the old champion's licence. After beating Lave for the vacant British Empire title, Bygraves tried his luck in New York but lost dismally to Wayne Bethea on a nationally televised show at the atmospheric St Nick's Arena in Brooklyn. Bygraves was exhausted by round four and retired himself after the fifth. Campbell said, 'He just ran out of gas. I don't know how to account for it, unless it was the change of climate.' At home, Bygraves ended the career of another former British champion, Johnny Williams who was pulled out, cut and tired, by his veteran manager Ted Broadribb, after six rounds in Manchester.

Most people tipped Henry Cooper to take away Bygraves's Empire crown at Earl's Court, London, in February 1957, but the Jamaican caused a surprise by cutting Cooper around both eyes and dominating with fast, swinging attacks. Body punches floored Cooper twice, the second time for the count, in round nine. In May 1957 Bygraves and Welsh slugger Dick Richardson abandoned any pretence of the niceties of the art and slugged and slogged away for fifteen rounds in Cardiff – and veteran referee Eugene Henderson scored a draw. Bygraves was disqualified in ridiculous circumstances in Dortmund only a month later. He floored Heinz Neuhaus for nine in the sixth, and when he followed up and knocked him out, Bygraves was disqualified for 'boxing on before being told to do so'. Joe was furious, shouting at the referee, 'You told me to box on – you told me to box on!' He was booed all the way to the dressing room.

His Empire title reign came to an end before 10,000 fans in Leicester in November 1957 when he was out-boxed comprehensively by Joe Erskine – Bygraves might have edged the first two rounds but after that the Welshman won everything. He attempted to rebuild against world-class Americans, but Willie Pastrano out-pointed him and Zora Folley stopped him in nine rounds, and then in a trip to Houston, Texas, in 1959 he lost over the full ten rounds to Roy Harris. He lost in seven rounds to Johansson in a rematch in 1962, when the Swede was near the end of his own career, and was out-pointed by Karl Mildenberger in Frankfurt, even though he attacked most of the way.

In January 1964 Bygraves was disqualified against Billy Walker but he slogged away to last ten rounds with the world number three, George Chuvalo at the Albert Hall. After losing clearly on points to Eduardo Corletti of Argentina at the Anglo-American Sporting Club, London, in March 1967, he retired to run a pig farm.

CHRIS BYRD

Born: 15 August 1970, Flint, Michigan
Height: 6ft 2in   **Weight at peak:** 214lbs (15st 4lbs)
Fights: 41   **Won:** 38   **Lost:** 2   **Drawn:** 1
KO percentage: 48

Rounds boxed: 309
World champion: 2002-05 (IBF)
World title fights: 4
Career span: 1993-2005 (12 years)
KO wins: 20
KO defeats: 1

Chris Byrd was skilful enough to hold the IBF version of the championship but his colourless, 'do-just-enough' style and his southpaw stance convinced few that he was the best heavyweight of his time. Byrd lost by huge margins on the cards to Wladimir Klitschko in October 2000 and six months earlier had been way behind against Vitali Klitschko when the Ukrainian retired unexpectedly because of a shoulder injury.

From Flint, Michigan, trained by his father Joe, Byrd he was the middleweight silver medallist in the Barcelona Olympics, and turned pro in 1993. Within two years he had grown heavier. He turned professional as a super-middleweight in January 1993 and two years later was a heavyweight. The best of his early wins was a twelve-round unanimous decision over former WBC title challenger Phil Jackson.

Byrd was derailed by the unbeaten Nigerian Ike Ibeabuchi, whose career ended in disgrace when he was jailed for an assault on a dancer. Ibeabuchi stopped Byrd in five rounds in Tacoma, Washington, in March 1999.

The fortuitous nine-round win over Vitali Klitschko earned Byrd the WBO belt, which he lost to Wladimir. He won the IBF belt by outscoring forty-year-old Evander Holyfield in December 2002. Holyfield was more or less one-armed because of a shoulder problem and Byrd out-boxed him at will: 117-111 on two cards, 116-112 on the third.

C

PRIMO CARNERA

Born: 26 Oct 1907, Sequals, Italy
Died: 29 Jun 1967, Sequals, Italy, aged 59
Height: 6ft 5¾in   **Weight at peak:** 260-270lbs (18st 8lbs-19st 4lbs)
Fights: 103   **Won:** 88   **Lost:** 14   **No Decisions:** 1
KO percentage: 66
Rounds boxed: 533

World champion: 1933-34
World title fights: 4
Career span: 1928-1946 (18 years)
KO wins: 69
KO defeats: 5

Primo Carnera became the mould for the stereotypical Mob-controlled heavy-weight of countless Hollywood movies, in particular the 1956 Budd Schulberg classic *The Harder They Fall*, starring Rod Steiger and Humphrey Bogart.

Between 1930 and 1937 his career was influenced by a pair of known gangsters, 'Big' Bill Duffy and Owney Madden, and one of his later managers, 'Good Time' Walter Friedman, admitted many of his early fights in the United States were fixed. What his word was worth is open to question, but Friedman claimed the night Carnera won the title against Jack Sharkey at Long Island Bowl in June 1933 nobody messed with the result: it was fair. Any ability Carnera possessed was hidden behind the fixes – and the poor man had neither the business acumen nor connections of his own to prevent his earnings being carved up. For example, when he won the championship against Sharkey in front of 40,000 fans with official receipts of $184,000, Carnera was promised just $10,000. Even then, his take home may been a fraction of that. A few days earlier he had filed for bankruptcy, protesting when a woman to whom he had proposed marriage sued him for breach of promise, 'I no got dough. Everybody wants dough, dough, dough. I no got dough.'

Apart from the woman, Emilia Tersini, the first creditor in line was one of his managers, Luigi Soresi, whose front was the vice-presidency of a bank. Soresi, to whom Carnera entrusted his financial well-being, claimed he was owed $6,300. His former manager Leon See chipped in with a claim for $3,779. His liabilities were listed as $59,829 – surely not an insurmountable problem if he had been paid properly – and his assets a pathetic $1,182. Soresi claimed in court that Carnera owed him almost $100,000 for two villas and a 1,000-acre farm in Italy that he had sold the fighter in 1931. They did not exist. Even when Primo was champion, the humiliation continued. They arranged a three-day exhibition in Atlantic City for a total purse, before deductions, of $4,500. The opponent was a kangaroo.

When Carnera returned to Europe in 1936 he had boxed in the United States sixty-three times, had won and defended the heavyweight championship of the world and had boxed Joe Louis in front of 62,000 people in Yankee Stadium and Max Baer in Long Island Bowl before an official attendance of 52,268. Yet he had just $7,000 in his bank account to provide for his family's future.

The man they called the Ambling Alp was from Sequals, a village in north-ern Italy. Originally apprenticed to a carpenter, he drifted to France and worked as a circus strongman, 'Juan the Unconquerable Spaniard'. An old fighter, Paul Journee, gave him lessons as a boxer. Journee persuaded Leon See to manage him and he began boxing in Paris in September 1928. On the back of two supposedly fixed fights with Young Stribling – a disqualification win each – in London and Paris at the end of 1929, See took him to the United States. Friedman and Duffy, and whoever they worked for, took over.

In 1930 they had Carnera in action twenty-six times. They fixed fights for him anywhere from Kansas City to Minneapolis. Sometimes they bent the opponent themselves, sometimes it was the cornerman who might put a doping substance on the towel. Not all of the fights were bent, but so many were that it was impossible to decipher real knockouts from fake. The talented heavyweight George Godfrey 'under-performed' when losing to Carnera on a foul in June 1930 in Philadelphia. So did the stocky Australian veteran George Cook, who was known for his durability. He was knocked out in two rounds in Cleveland in July 1930. However, Jimmy Maloney out-pointed the giant over ten rounds in Boston in October 1930. Carnera returned to Europe for a few months, out-pointed Paolino Uzcudun over ten rounds in Barcelona and knocked out the British heavyweight Reggie Meen in two. Both were probably fair fights.

In 1931 he out-pointed Maloney in Miami and Kingfish Levinsky in Chicago, among a total of eight wins, but found Jack Sharkey much too sharp for him over fifteen rounds in Brooklyn. Back in Europe he was given a boxing lesson by Larry Gains. His breakthrough came in February 1933 when he scored a tragic thirteenth-round knockout of Ernie Schaaf, Sharkey's protégé, and then in June 1933 he pulled out that terrific right uppercut to flatten Sharkey himself in the sixth round of their world title fight at the Long Island Bowl. Benito Mussolini sent him a telegram of congratulations.

He returned to Italy for his first defence, as thousands gathered in an outdoor square in Rome to watch him out-box Paolino Uzcudun over fifteen rounds. For publicity purposes, his managers allowed him to pose in the Fascist blackshirt uniform and agreed that he donate his purse to the party. Another idea came a cropper – he was installed as 'co-driver' with the legendary Tazio Nuvalari in a long-distance race only for the car to break down because it was not built for seating giants like Carnera!

In March 1934 he looked ridiculous in grinding out a points win over the 86lbs-lighter Tommy Loughran in Miami. His reign came to an end in New York in June 1934 when Max Baer pounded him to the canvas repeatedly for a stoppage in round eleven. During the fight Baer taunted him mercilessly. Carnera tore ligaments in his right ankle in one of the knockdowns and wept with disappointment in the dressing room. After he was savaged in six brutal rounds by Joe Louis in June 1935, on the way from the ring, Duffy berated him loudly, calling him 'stupid'. When he returned to Italy, he was rewarded for his defeat by being called up into the Italian Army – again as a propaganda tool. His passport was briefly withdrawn.

His career ground to a halt when Leroy Haynes, a talented prospect, stopped him in three rounds in March 1936. Duffy agreed a rematch in May and this time, when the fight was stopped in the ninth, Carnera's left leg was temporarily paralysed. He had kidney damage too – and one was eventually removed. When he returned to Italy this time he was walking with a stick. He needed money for his medical bills, so boxed in exhibitions, had a couple of real fights in Paris and Budapest, after the Second World War came out of retirement again, but had nothing. He returned to the USA to wrestle and although it was sad to see, he at least did earn well enough in a 'ham' world, where at least everybody knew the entertainment was fixed, to open a liquor store in California. By then he had married Giuseppina Kovacic, a Serbian woman who had been kind enough to fill out a form for him in a post office.

They became American citizens and one of their sons became a doctor of medicine. Carnera popped up in movies from time to time, including *On the Waterfront*, and lost a court case when he sued for defamation over *The Harder They Fall*. Eventually, liver disease wrecked his health and in 1967 he returned to Sequals to die. He passed away on 29 June 1967, thirty-four years to the day after he had knocked out Jack Sharkey to become heavyweight champion.

GEORGES CARPENTIER

Born: 12 January 1894, Lens, France
Died: 28 October 1975, Paris, France, aged 81
Height: 5ft 11½in   **Weight at peak:** 172lbs (12st 4lbs)
Fights: 109   **Won:** 88   **Lost:** 14   **Drawn:** 6   **No Decisions:** 1
KO percentage: 51
Rounds boxed: 852
World champion: (light-heavyweight champion 1920-22)
World title fights: 1
Career span: 1908-26 (18 years)
KO wins: 56
KO defeats: 8

The Orchid Man, Georges Carpentier, earned his place in heavyweight history when he boxed Jack Dempsey in the first ever million-dollar-gate fight at Boyle's Thirty Acres arena in Jersey City on 2 July 1921. Promoter Tex Rickard, well aware Carpentier wasn't big enough to trouble Dempsey, kept him under wraps and concentrated on the French war hero angle, shamelessly exploiting the notoriety that surrounded Dempsey's military history (He was labelled a slacker because he had been photographed wearing inappropriate shoes while supposedly working at an exempt job in a shipyard).

Carpentier was a smooth, slick boxer with a snappy, powerful right hand – but when he nailed Dempsey with his honey punch all he did was break his thumb. Any chance he might have had of causing an upset went in that split second – and once the Manassa Mauler got him in range the fight was over in round four. Still,

Rickard and the boxers made a fortune because it drew a crowd of more than 80,000 who paid an incredible $1,789,238. It was the birth of the era of million-dollar gates.

Carpentier was from Lens in northern France. He began boxing in 1908 as a fourteen-year-old boy, won the European welterweight, middle and light-heavyweight titles, and knocked out Bombardier Billy Wells in four rounds in Ghent to become European heavyweight champion in June 1913. In a rematch in London in December 1913 he polished off the big English soldier in the first round. On the way from the ring, the brilliant Welsh featherweight Jim Driscoll shouted at Wells that he was a coward.

Carpentier lost a fifteen-round decision to Joe Jeannette in Paris in March 1914, but beat Gunboat Smith on a foul in a return to London in July 1914. After the First World War, in which he was a debonair hero of the French air force, he resumed duties as European champion and then won the world light-heavyweight title with a fourth-round knockout of Battling Levinsky in Jersey City in October 1920. After losing to Dempsey, he knocked out the Australian heavyweight George Cook in four, retained his light-heavy title with a one-round knockout of Ted Kid Lewis but then under-trained for a film project against Battling Siki that was sup-posed to show off his talents for movie audiences. He lost, exhausted, in the sixth round in Paris in September 1922.

He cashed in on his career and became one of the extravagant personalities of that rather boisterous, live-for-today age. He knocked out Joe Beckett in the first round again, but was stopped in fifteen rounds by Gene Tunney in New York in July 1924. A ten-round points defeat by Tommy Loughran effectively finished him and his last competitive contest was in September 1926.

Carpentier remained a national hero until his death in Paris on 28 October 1975 at the age of eighty-one.

EZZARD CHARLES

Born: 7 July 1921, Lawrenceville, Georgia
Full name: Ezzard Mack Charles
Died: 27 May 1975, Chicago, aged 53
Height: 6ft   **Weight at peak:** 180-186lbs (12st 12lbs-13st 4lbs)
Fights: 122   **Won:** 96   **Lost:** 25   **Drawn:** 1
KO percentage: 47
Rounds boxed: 968
World champion: 1949-51
World title fights: 13
Career span: 1940-59 (19 years)
KO wins: 58
KO defeats: 7

One of the most underrated champions in world heavyweight history, Ezzard Charles' achievements deserve to be reassessed.

As Larry Holmes suffered from following Muhammad Ali, so Charles was over-shadowed by Joe Louis, who had dominated the division for a dozen years before his retirement in 1949. Charles, a slender, 6ft-tall stylist who in reality was little more than a light-heavyweight, had to prove himself by accumulating victories – all the while being downgraded by contemporary writers and critics, who simply could not accept him as a viable successor to Louis. Yet this modest, hard-working man won nine world title fights before losing the championship on a shock-ing defeat courtesy of a devastating left hook thrown by the ancient Jersey Joe Walcott in 1951. True, some of his challengers were poor, and Charles messed up an opportunity to regain the title from Walcott, but in 1954 he was still good enough to stretch Walcott's successor, Rocky Marciano, to the limit for fifteen torrid rounds. Altogether, Charles took part in thirteen world heavyweight championship bouts.

Part of the problem was the reaction of the doyen of boxing writers, the editor of *Ring* magazine Nat Fleischer, who called the heavyweights who were involved in the scramble to inherit Louis's crown 'about as seedy a lot as ever were assem-bled in quest for world honors'. When Ezzard beat Walcott for the vacant title, as recognised by the National Boxing Association but not by the extremely power-ful New York State Athletic Commission, the headline in *Ring* was 'Charles Not a Champion of Any Place'.

Charles was not given to chest-thumping and seems to have been content to let writers and the public come around to his side in their own time. It took too long. When he trounced the old light-heavyweight champion Gus Lesnevich in his first defence, the New York commission refused to allow the promoters to use the words 'world heavyweight championship' in the billing or even in the official souvenir programme. Perhaps as a result of that a crowd of only 16,630 – small enough to have been housed indoors at Madison Square Garden instead of the cavernous Yankee Stadium – turned out to watch him dissect Lesnevich in seven rounds. By his third defence, when he stopped Freddie Beshore in fourteen rounds in Buffalo, New York, tickets were virtually given away at an average of $5 a head to the 6,000 or so fans.

Charles's case was helped when Louis returned to the ring because of his finan-cial embarrassments and in September 1950 in Yankee Stadium, Ezzard gave the thirty-six-year-old legend a pounding over fifteen rounds to win a unanimous decision. Even Fleischer had to acknowledge he was the best heavyweight in the world – after predicting a Louis win. It was a sweet moment for the quiet man from Cincinnati, who said, 'I want to be a credit to the ring, just like the great champion I beat tonight.'

Charles was born in July 1921 in Lawrenceville, Georgia, but when he was nine his parents parted and his mother left for New York to work as a dressmaker. Ezzard, nick-named Snook, was sent to his grandmother, Maude Foster, and great-grandmother,

Belle Russell, in Cincinnati. They raised him as a churchgoing boy alongside seven of Maude's younger children, although his early education in Georgia had been minimal – he couldn't read when he arrived in Cincinnati, for example, and he was never really able to catch up. After a fine amateur career, he turned professional to add some money to the household as an eighteen-year-old middleweight in March 1940. It took him nine years to reach the top although long before that hardened fight traders knew how good he was. Ray Arcel, his trainer, said the extent of Charles's talent emerged when he twice beat the middleweight Charley Burley in Pittsburgh in back-to-back bouts in May and June 1942.

'You must understand that Charley Burley was the best fighter I ever saw who not only never won a title but never got any glory,' he said in an interview with the American writer Dave Anderson thirty years later. 'In those days if you were a good black fighter, nobody wanted to fight you… When Charles fought Burley the first time, Burley was a 1-3 favourite. I think Charles won eight of the ten rounds. Nobody could believe it. In the rematch Burley was still a 1-3 favourite but Charles got the decision again. That's how great a fighter Charles was.'

In the Second World War he served for three years in the US Army in Italy and north Africa. When he returned home, he found his investments made from his ring earnings were faltering. It took him years to pay off back-taxes. He knew, in spite of weighing only a few pounds above the light-heavyweight limit of 175lbs, he would have to fight heavyweights. From February 1946 until his victory over Walcott for the vacant NBA championship in June 1949, Charles crammed in more than thirty fights and lost only once, on a ten-round decision to big Elmer 'Violent' Ray in New York in July 1947. Against that, he twice knocked out Lloyd Marshall, twice out-pointed Jimmy Bivins, stopped Ray, beat Archie Moore three times, knocked out Joe Baksi (in eleven rounds in New York in December 1948) and then out-pointed Joey Maxim on a fifteen-round split decision to earn his shot at the championship.

It is true that sometimes his self-effacing character didn't encourage public confidence in him. When, after his win over the 32lbs-heavier Baksi, someone suggested he might box Louis next, he seemed alarmed. 'My goodness, not yet,' he said. Louis announced his retirement in March 1949, having survived two rocky defences against Walcott, and so the match between Charles and Jersey Joe, made for Chicago in June 1949, was entirely logical in spite of Fleischer's opposition. Some said Charles was not as positive as he might have been because of the death of an opponent, Sam Baroudi, in a bout in Chicago in 1948 but although he had to be persuaded to continue by a local clergyman the record does not bear out claims that he was less aggressive or decisive. In his very next fight he beat Elmer Ray in nine rounds (and gave a part of his purse to Baroudi's family) and before the year was out had also stopped Baksi.

The fact was he just wasn't big enough to trade punches with genuine heavyweights from the opening bell, and had to use his skills to wear them down.

When he fought Walcott he was only 181¾lbs – and boxed cautiously to out-point the veteran who had possessed enough power to put Louis on the floor in both of their fights. 'It was just another fight,' he said afterwards, which didn't help anybody who was even the slightest bit inclined to recognise the Cincinnati Cobra as the heavyweight champion of the world. After beating Lesnevich he knocked out Pat Valentino in eight in San Francisco's famous Cow Palace – the first heavyweight championship fight in the city since Jack Johnson knocked out Stanley Ketchel forty years earlier.

After queries about a heart abnormality kept him out of the ring for ten months, he stopped Freddie Beshore in fourteen, and six weeks later at last earned full recognition as champion by handing out a points drubbing to the elderly Louis before another disappointing crowd of 13,562 at Yankee Stadium. The gate suffered because of the sale of television rights to a brewery company who launched a huge campaign to entice fans to watch the fight on screens in bars instead of making the trip to the Bronx. Charles, weighing only 183½lbs to the former champion's 218lbs, dictated with his speed and precise left-hand work. Louis landed enough to cause swellings around both of Charles's eyes, but his own face was swollen and bloodied and at the end of fifteen rounds the margin was clear on all three scorecards: 10-5, 13-2, 12-3, all in rounds.

Suddenly, after being scorned, Charles was compared to Gene Tunney, another unfashionable stylist who had out-boxed Jack Dempsey for the title in 1926. Even Fleischer acknowledged his boxing skills as superb, while rightly allowing time to reflect on the decline of the Brown Bomber. In her Harlem flat, Charles's mother, by now Mrs Alberta Moss, prayed for the duration of the fight, unable to listen to the radio broadcast or watch the television pictures. Afterwards she promised to watch him in the future. 'If he's good enough to beat Joe Louis, he's good enough for me not to be scared to look at too.' Charles had what amounted to a home-coming celebration in Cincinnati by knocking out Nick Barone in eleven rounds, stopped Lee Oma in ten, out-pointed Walcott and then came through a fifteen-round defence over Joey Maxim in Chicago. Still newspaper critics hounded him though. Dan Parker, in the *New York Post*, dismissed him as a colourless mediocrity. After the Maxim fight, one paper reported it with a three-inch white space!

Then, in an upset that shattered his reputation, he was knocked out by as clean a left hook as you could wish to see, thrown by thirty-seven-year-old Jersey Joe Walcott in the seventh round in Pittsburgh in July 1951. He did his best to prove it was a freak result, stopping rising contender Rex Layne in eleven rounds, beating Maxim again – and in June 1952 he appeared to have out-boxed Walcott in a return in Philadelphia. The majority of ringside reporters thought he won but the scorecards, including that of the first black referee for a world heavyweight title fight, Zach Clayton, were in Walcott's favour: 8-7 twice and 9-6. The edge came off him after that but he dragged it back together one last time when he challenged Rocky Marciano for the title in Yankee Stadium in June 1954. He stayed on his feet, pressed Marciano hard but lost another unanimous decision. In a rematch three months later, though he opened a gory gash on the champion's nose, he was knocked out in eight.

He should have retired but carried on for another five years. He did quit after a pathetic two-round disqualification in London against Dick Richardson, but financial worries forced him back. His last fight was a small-time ten rounder in Oklahoma City in September 1959 when, aged thirty-eight, he lost on points to Alvin Green.

Two years later he was broke. Married with three children, he tried a little wrestling, was a doorman in a nightclub in Kentucky, sold cemetery lots and whisky, worked for a wine company and with young people on Chicago's South Side. In 1968 he was diagnosed as suffering from lateral sclerosis, a disease of the nervous system, and spent his last years in hospital. He died in Chicago on 28 May 1975, aged fifty-three.

JOE CHOYNSKI

Born: 8 November 1868, San Francisco, California
Died: 25 January 1943, Cincinnati, Ohio, aged 74
Height: 5ft 10½in   **Weight at peak:** 168lbs (12st)
Fights: 81   **Won:** 51   **Lost:** 17   **Drawn:** 7   **No Decisions:** 6
KO percentage: 35
Rounds boxed: 475
World title fights: 0
Career span: 1888-1904 (16 years)
KO wins: 29
KO defeats: 10

In another era Joe Choynski would probably have been an exceptional world middle or light-heavyweight champion but in the chaotic 1890s he had to make do with earning the respect of the best heavyweights in the world. James J. Jeffries, who was 6ft 2½in tall and more than 210lbs, said, 'Little Joe was the hardest hitter I ever tangled with. He hit me with a right high on my cheekbone and I figured that was the hardest punch I ever took.'

Jeffries drew a twenty-round war with Choynski when he was still a six-fight novice in November 1897. Choynski, 5ft 10½in and usually about 165lbs, was from the Golden Gate Avenue neighbourhood in the Hayes Valley area of San Francisco. He had minimal schooling, worked in the docks and by his late teens was boxing. He fought his great local rival James J. Corbett three times in six weeks in the summer of 1889, two years before Corbett took the world title from John L. Sullivan. When Corbett was an amateur and Choynski was a dock-fighter, according to Gentleman Jim, they had fought two private bouts, one in his father's stable and one in a quarry. Their first bout as professionals was in front of 100 people in a barn in Fairfax, ended prematurely in five rounds and was ruled a No Contest. Choynski had been floored for a count of five, but had rallied and was doing well, with Corbett in pain from a jarred thumb, when the police intervened.

Battle resumed six days later on a barge in Benicia Bay where the police had no official jurisdiction. Corbett, a thoughtful, scientific boxing master, cut Choynski's mouth early on but then his thumb, obviously not fully healed from the first bout, let him down again. Choynski slammed away and had Corbett almost out in round fourteen, but by the eighteenth his mouth was in such a state that he asked his second, the middleweight champion Jack 'Nonpareil' Dempsey, to cut the loose flesh from his lips. By round twenty, Dempsey was asking him to quit, but Choynski refused. Corbett had to knock him out to win – and eventually did that with a left hook in round twenty-seven. The fight was so brutal it knocked the rivalry out of them and turned them into lifelong friends. Corbett remembered they were carried onto the deck of a tug, shook hands and taken to a Turkish bath for seven hours to recover. Their third bout in San Francisco in July was little more than an exhibition, with Corbett winning on points after four rounds.

Choynski also boxed a three-round exhibition with world champion Sullivan in San Francisco on 20 December 1891. When he returned from a lucrative exhibition tour of Australia he fought the legendary black fighter, George 'Old Chocolate' Godfrey, who had been one of the great boxers of the time but by then was forty years old. Godfrey showed what he used to be when he put Choynski down heavily in round eight and again without a count in the thirteenth, but eventually he faded and Joe knocked him out with a right to the temple in round fifteen.

In Boston in June 1894 Choynski was given a five-round draw with Bob Fitzsimmons, who was world middleweight champion at the time. He knocked Fitzsimmons down, the bell rang – possibly early – and then the police entered the ring to stop it on the grounds that it no longer constituted the advertised 'exhibition'. Fitzsimmons, like Jeffries, acknowledged Choynski's power. 'I saw the blow coming,' he said. 'It was an overhand, snaky looking thing. I didn't think it packed much steam but when it struck my jaw I lost all sensation and my head filled with sparkling stars.'

Choynski helped Jeffries prepare for his world title-winning fight with Fitzsimmons in 1899, lost surprisingly in seven rounds to the future welterweight champion Joe Walcott in New York in 1900, but in February 1901 had far too much experience for a young Jack Johnson in Galveston, Texas, where a cyclone had recently ripped off the roof of the arena. A law banned blacks and whites boxing each other but to get around that it was announced as a public demonstration by Choynski with Johnson as the sparring partner. Choynski knocked out Johnson in the third round. He said, 'In the opening round we both did a lot of dancing. Johnson was awfully long and reachy and I had a hard time getting my punches to his face. He was a pretty clever boy.' In round three, he feinted himself an opening for a left hook that dropped Johnson heavily for the count. The police locked them both up for twenty-eight days.

Upon retirement in 1905, Choynski became a boxing and fitness instructor at the Pittsburg Athletic Club in California. He died in Cincinnati, Ohio, in 1943 at the age of seventy-four.

GEORGE CHUVALO

Born: 12 September 1937, Toronto, Canada
Height: 6ft 1in   **Weight at peak:** 213lbs (15st 3lbs)
Fights: 93   **Won:** 73   **Lost:** 18   **Drawn:** 2
KO percentage: 68
Rounds boxed: 493
World title fights: 2
Career span: 1956-78 (22 years)
KO wins: 64
KO defeats: 2

George Chuvalo once said, 'A caveman would understand boxing. He wouldn't understand golf.'

Chuvalo, one of the toughest, gamest heavyweights of all time, fought without pretence. He was, first, last and always, a slugger of the first order who traded on durability and cussed persistence. He didn't win a world title, but then he was around when Muhammad Ali and Joe Frazier were in their peak years, and he fought just about everybody there was to fight in a career than lasted more than two decades. His was also a story of terrible personal tragedy: he lost his wife and three of his sons to drug-related deaths and in his sixties was crusading diligently to attempt to save others from similar fates. He referred to it as 'my personal holocaust'.

The son of Croatian immigrant parents, Chuvalo was born in Toronto, began boxing at ten and worked in the slaughterhouses of his home city. He turned professional in 1956 when, as a raw eighteen-year-old, he won a novice heavyweight tournament sponsored by Jack Dempsey. He knocked out all four opponents in the first or second rounds. He forced his way into the world-class category: Zora Folley and former champion Floyd Patterson out-pointed him, but he knocked out Doug Jones in eleven rounds in New York in 1964.

Although most people knew Muhammad Ali was the genuine world champion, the three-year-old World Boxing Association stripped Ali and recognised the 6ft 6in Ernie Terrell instead from May 1965. Terrell's first defence of the 'paper title' was against Chuvalo before 12,500 fans at the Maple Leaf Gardens in Toronto in November 1965 – and George lost on points over fifteen rounds. Chuvalo finished strongly but by then was too far behind. One official had it close – in rounds, 7-5 with 3 even – but the others saw Terrell up 10-3 with 2 even. A disgruntled, unbroken Chuvalo grumbled, 'I won the fight and can't get a square deal in my own country', and in the dressing room complained angrily to his manager Irv Ungerman, 'I fight my guts out all my life. And you won't let me win.' The implication is obvious. His wife Lynne joined in, berating Ungerman in style: 'How can you let them do this to George? He was robbed. It's an outrage. There's something rotten going on here.'

After two fights in London, a win over Joe Bygraves and a points defeat to the clever Argentine Eduardo Corletti, Chuvalo was considered a drawcard opponent for Ali in another Maple Leaf Gardens fight in March 1966. Having lost two of his last three fights, he didn't deserve the opportunity, but as always he gave it everything he had. This time, though, there was no room for debate about the decision – the margins were eight, ten and eleven points. *Ring* editor Nat Fleischer wrote that Ali 'hamburgered' Chuvalo's face.

Amazingly, he was back in the ring six weeks later and won seven of eight more fights that year. The exception was a points defeat over ten rounds to Oscar Bonavena in New York. By the time he was matched with Joe Frazier in Madison Square Garden in July 1967, Chuvalo was on a winning streak of a dozen fights, all of them inside the distance. However, Frazier, the unbeaten Olympic gold medallist from the Tokyo Games, was magnificent that night – and for the first time in his life Chuvalo was stopped. When the fight was waved off in the fourth round his eyes were swollen to slits; he waved his arms in disarray and turned away by the ropes. 'It felt like my eyeball had exploded,' he said.

He always remembered his fifth-round knockout of the big Mexican, Manuel Ramos, in New York in September 1968 as one of his best performances, but fight fans will perhaps point to a seventh-round knockout of Jerry Quarry in December 1969 as his peak. Chuvalo had been out-punched in the first, cut in the fourth and after the sixth the ringside doctor examined his right eye, which had closed almost to a slit. Then in the closing stages of the seventh, a left hook to the temple from Chuvalo disorientated and dropped Quarry. He got up, dropped back to one knee – and was still there when referee Zach Clayton reached ten. Quarry argued that he couldn't hear the count, but Chuvalo grunted, 'If he couldn't tell nine from ten it must have been a good punch.' There would be no more world title fights. In August 1970 he was hammered in three one-sided rounds by twenty-one-year-old George Foreman and although yet again this incredibly strong man stayed on his feet, people began to suggest he might think about retiring.

He was out-pointed by Jimmy Ellis, the former WBA champion, in Toronto in 1971, but then travelled to Houston to outscore the veteran Texan, Cleveland Williams. In Vancouver in May 1972 he fought Ali, who was between championship reigns, and lasted twelve rounds for a payday of $65,000.

For a while life was good to him but then he lost his sons Jesse, Georgie Lee and Steven to drug-related deaths between 1985 and 1996. Days after the funeral of Georgie Lee, grief-stricken Lynne Chuvalo took a fatal overdose of prescribed

drugs. Their two other children, Vanessa and Mitchell, went on to get degrees.
Chuvalo, haunted and almost broken, came through it in part, eventually remarried and threw himself into giving talks to students, using the examples of his sons
and a documentary on the family (in which Steven was still alive) made by the
Canadian Broadcasting Corporation in 1995. Chuvalo had children, step-children
and grandchildren – and laughter again, but admitted in a newspaper interview
in the late 1990s, 'Once I stop, once things slow down, the TV's off, the lights are
out… I have a hard time. You don't want to be me after midnight.'

RANDALL COBB

Born: 10 December 1954, Bridge, Texas
Height: 6ft 3in   **Weight at peak:** 230lbs (16st 6lbs)
Fights: 52   **Won:** 43   **Lost:** 7   **Drawn:** 1   **No Contests:** 1
KO percentage: 69
Rounds boxed: 229
World title fights: 1
Career span: 1977-93 (16 years)
KO wins: 36
KO defeats: 1

Randy Cobb was a big, durable Texan who could punch… but whose preference
for partying to training was widely appreciated. Monastic, he was not.

Cobb had an independent spirit, a ready wit and a genuine toughness that
enabled him to survive in the highest company. When he challenged Larry Holmes
for the heavyweight title in November 1982, he didn't win a minute of the fight let
alone a round. Yet when the final bell rang, he leered out of his bloody, swollen face
at the champion and yelled, 'Let's party!' That was the night the rather pompous
ABC commentator Howard Cosell proclaimed that he was finished with boxing.
The hypocrisy and the sleaze, he said, had finally worn him out, and he wanted to
see no more of the kind of one-sided drubbings he had just witnessed. Cobb heard
this and declared, 'I can do my sport no greater service than this…'

Cobb was always a wonderful interview. He refused to take boxing seriously, saw
his promoter Don King for what he was but, like Holmes, chose to do business
with him when necessary. That didn't mean he was prepared to pay homage to the
most influential man in the business. When King moved the financial goalposts for
the Holmes fight, Cobb stood up at the post-fight press conference and reversed
the protocol by introducing the promoter. 'This,' he said, 'is the lying, thieving
mother who cut me to $500,000.' Cobb wasn't being particularly personal in this.
Another time he said, 'Don King is like everybody else in boxing. He's a liar, a
thief, a murderer and a racketeer. And a con man. But there ain't nobody as bad as
Bob Arum!' Arum was King's major promotional rival of the time.

Cobb believed fighting wasn't an art worth eulogising. 'All I want to do is hit somebody in the mouth,' he said in an interview with *Ring* magazine. 'Don't make anything noble out of what I do... Something like fighting is pretty ridiculous. What I do is hit people. I'm not promoting anything that's real or valuable.' Point taken.

Cobb did train hard when he had to, but resented it. 'Abstinence is for monks,' he said. 'This kind of life is really overrated.'

He was born in Bridge, a couple of hours from Houston, and was raised in the old wild west town of Abilene. His father died when he was six and from his youth he survived as best he could. He tried kick-boxing, then became a pro boxer in 1977. His style excited people and he crashed into the big time in August 1980 when he stopped Earnie Shavers in the eighth round. He said Shavers hit him hard every single time... but by then the man Muhammad Ali dubbed the Acorn was past his prime. He could still intimidate good heavyweights, but not Cobb. 'Here's big, bad Earnie Shavers, probably the baddest man God ever allowed to walk on two legs, and he got up there with his bald head and his Fu Manchu and his bulging muscles – and he stared at me. I cracked up. What did he think I was gonna do, leave?'

Three months later Cobb lost a split decision to Ken Norton and then was outsmarted by the unbeaten Michael Dokes. But wins over Harry Terrell, the dangerous but unpredictable Bernardo Mercado and Jeff Shelburg re-established him and his colourful personality and crowd-pleasing style, and of course his promotional deal with King, brought him to the title fight with Holmes at Houston Astrodome in November 1982. Cobb lost, in rounds, 15-0, 15-0, 14-1, on the scorecards. To some extent, Cosell was right.

Cobb, who at the time was training with George Benton in Joe Frazier's gym in Philadelphia, didn't get another chance. He could beat the second-rate heavyweights, but in November 1984 he lost a majority decision to another Don King fighter, Buster Douglas, and faded out of the title scene. He acted in movies, primarily alongside Jon Voight in *The Champ*, but didn't think much of Hollywood. 'Any man who's lived with a woman can act,' he said.

In 1988 Cobb put the name of Leon Spinks on his record when he out-pointed the washed-up former heavyweight champion over ten rounds in Memphis.

DON COCKELL

Born: 22 September 1928, Battersea, London, England
Died: 17 July 1983, London, England, aged 54
Height: 5ft 11in   **Weight at peak:** 205lbs (14st 9lbs)
Fights: 79   **Won:** 64   **Lost:** 14   **Drawn:** 1
KO percentage: 45
Rounds boxed: 501

World title fights: 1
Career span: 1946-56 (10 years)
KO wins: 36
KO defeats: 9

Don Cockell's reputation was made by his unforgettable courage in the face of a ruthless nine-round hammering by world heavyweight champion Rocky Marciano in the Kezar Stadium, San Francisco, on 16 May 1955. It was a brutal exhibition by Marciano who, alongside his usual marauding aggression, fouled repeatedly with little or no interruption from 'third man' Frankie Brown, whose $1,000 fee was the highest ever paid to a referee in California. Most observers shrugged, most of the purists from the old school shuddered. British radio commentator Eamonn Andrews was outraged. 'Marciano is one of the toughest champions who ever rubbed a foot in resin,' he said. 'But he never read the rule books. He played a different sport from the one Cockell was taught. He butted unmercifully… He hit Cockell with his elbows. He hit low. A British referee would have sent him to his corner after three rounds.' The old lightweight champion Willie Ritchie at ringside shook his head and called Cockell 'one of the gamest guys who ever trod this earth'.

   Before the fight Cockell's manager John Simpson publicly stated his fears about the champion's disregard for the rules and demanded the British Boxing Board of Control secretary Teddy Waltham see propriety was enforced. It was a pointless gesture. Cockell had watched films of the champion, knew he could not out-punch him toe-to-toe but believed he could win by countering and clever box-fighting. His fans were encouraged by the fact that Marciano had been knocked down in sparring. He might be fading, said some. However, a crowd of 15,235 saw Marciano batter those dreams into the canvas of the tiny 16½ft-square ring. Cockell edged the second round on the card of judge Jack Downey and shared it on those of referee Brown and judge John Bassenelli, continued to land sharp left hooks but was relentlessly worn down. Marciano, who said he had turned down a Mafia bribe to throw the fight, threw instead a hail of punches and followed through with forearms, elbows and shoulders. He hit Cockell with barrages of legitimate blows but also some that were horribly low. He forced the Englishman to abandon all ideas of boxing on the counter and stand and trade. After round three he hit him after the bell. In the fourth Cockell was cut from a butt and years later admitted the champion was no more than a blur after that. Marciano hit him three times after the bell to complete round six. At the end of the eighth Cockell went down and after two more knockdowns in the ninth it was stopped. 'I'm disappointed,' he said. 'I really thought I was going to win.'

   Cockell came home with a gross payday of around £23,000 but Marciano had knocked everything out of him. He bore no grudges though, and in September 1969, following Marciano's death in a plane crash, Don was one of the church ushers at a requiem mass in Hatton Garden, London.

From Battersea, Cockell boxed professionally from 1946 when he was seventeen. He also worked as a blacksmith. He won British and European titles at light-heavyweight and didn't move into the heavyweight division until he lost to Randolph Turpin in eleven rounds in June 1952. Some wrote that he was washed up.

Cockell ended the long career of Tommy Farr with a seventh-round stoppage at Nottingham and two months later won the British and Empire heavyweight championships by out-pointing Johnny Williams. He was still only twenty-four, but Solomons knew there was no point in allowing him to mature any further. He was already well past the sixty-fight mark. Consequently, Cockell made his American debut in Seattle in August 1953 with a ten-round decision over contender Harry Matthews. Roland LaStarza, the college kid who had given Marciano all the trouble he needed in two fights, came to London in March 1954 and went home on the wrong end of a ten-round decision. Then Cockell beat Matthews twice more, the second time in seven rounds in Seattle. He was never a big-punching heavyweight. He also carried excess baggage that some said was the result of a metabolic problem and others said was just fat. But when they made the match with Marciano, he had won ten out of ten as a heavyweight.

After losing to Rocky, Cockell returned to the ring in September 1955, but was blasted out in three rounds by the big, world-class Cuban Nino Valdes. The end came with a more surprising second-round knockout at the hands of the energetic, colourful Tongan, Kitione Lave, in April 1956. Cockell knew there was no point in going on, even at the relatively tender age of twenty-seven.

He died of cancer in on 17 July 1983. He was fifty-four.

GERRIE COETZEE

Born: 4 August 1955, Boksburg, Transvaal, South Africa
Height: 6ft 2½in   **Weight at peak:** 220lbs (15st 10lbs)
Fights: 40   **Won:** 33   **Lost:** 6   **Drawn:** 1
KO percentage: 50
Rounds boxed: 261
World champion: 1983-84 (WBA)
World title fights: 4
Career span: 1974-97 (23 years)
KO wins: 20
KO defeats: 4

The first African to win a version of the world heavyweight title, Gerrie Coetzee was a popular fighter in a volatile time. With South Africa ostracised because of its Apartheid policy, boxing was one of the few sports that provided even a modest platform for sportsmen from that country. Coetzee, from Boksburg, Johannesburg, had fans in the black and white communities in South Africa and his rise to the

World Boxing Association championship in 1983 was generally well-received in his home country.

When the American John Tate beat Coetzee's compatriot Kallie Knoetze in June 1979, black South Africans rejoiced because Knoetze, a former policeman, was a symbol of the repressive regime. However, an editorial in the *Johannesburg Post* was an open message to Tate about his forthcoming fight with Coetzee for the WBA title: 'If and when you meet Gerrie Coetzee, you'll find us different. You will find many of us switching our allegiance to him. Because he's human. He's warm. He's a gentleman. Above all he has publicly denounced racism. So if he eventually becomes world champion he will be a worthy holder. Someone our kids can look up to...'

Coetzee did box Tate before more than 80,000 fans in the Loftus Versveld Stadium, Pretoria, in October 1979 and lost a dreary fight on points. A year later in Sun City, Coetzee tried again but was stopped in thirteen rounds by Mike Weaver, who had knocked out Tate to win the WBA belt. Coetzee seemed on the way to victory when he dropped Weaver in round eight, but he failed to finish him off and gradually the American took control and won in round thirteen. Coetzee always said Weaver hurt him more than anyone else he faced: in the fight he broke his nose and cracked ribs on both sides.

It took three more years for the quietly spoken, shy South African to reach the top. In September 1983 Coetzee travelled to Richfield, Ohio, and knocked out defending WBA champion Michael Dokes in the tenth round. His 'bionic' right hand – it was broken so badly surgeons welded bone onto bone and set it in a fist shape – put Dokes down for the count. However, the knockout blow that made him a champion also led to frustration: the hand fractured, and then went again when he was preparing for a unificiation fight with Larry Holmes in the summer of 1984. He lost the belt controversially to Greg Page in Sun City in December 1984 when in the eighth round the timekeeper made a mistake, somehow missing a minute of the session. Three minutes and forty-eight seconds had elapsed when Page knocked him out. Coetzee complained but the WBA were not interested in ordering a return. They were bowing to pressure from the rest of the boxing world to join the clampdown on South Africa. Coetzee outscored James Tillis in Johannesburg but then in an eliminator for his old WBA belt he was overpowered in one round by Frank Bruno at Wembley in March 1986.

Coetzee was steeped in boxing from childhood. His father, Flip, was a car mechanic who ran an amateur boxing club. Gerrie, the eldest of his four children, won 185 of 192 amateur contests and went to college to learn to become a dental technician, but gave that up when his professional boxing career took over. Early in his pro career, which began in 1974, Coetzee out-pointed Knoetze over ten rounds, stopped the veteran former title challenger Ron Stander and overpowered Leon Spinks in one round in June 1979, only nine months after Spinks had lost the WBA title to Muhammad Ali. He also figured in one of the dirtiest heavyweight fights seen in South Africa against Mike Schutte. He won when Schutte kneed him in the groin in the sixth round.

Coetzee retired after the Bruno fight, had a couple of brief comebacks in the 1990s, and settled for a decade in California. He was involved with the career of Frans Botha and returned to South Africa with his wife Rina around the start of the new century.

BILLY CONN

Born: 8 October 1917, East Liberty, Pennsylvania
Full name: William David Conn jnr
Died: 29 May 1993, aged 75
Height: 6ft   **Weight at peak:** 174lbs (12st 6lbs)
Fights: 77   **Won:** 64   **Lost:** 12   **Drawn:** 1
KO percentage: 19
Rounds boxed: 651
World champion: (light-heavyweight champion 1939-41)
World title fights: 2
Career span: 1934-48 (14 years)
KO wins: 15
KO defeats: 3

Although Billy Conn was a light-heavyweight, he belongs in heavyweight history for his brilliantly flawed first attempt to wrest the world championship from Joe Louis at the Polo Grounds, New York, in June 1941. Frank Deford, writing for *Sports Illustrated*, put this magnificent, epic struggle into context: 'This was the best it had ever been and ever would be – the twelfth and thirteenth rounds of Louis and Conn on a warm night in New York, just before the world went to hell.'

Conn was a mesmeric, stylish boxer from Pittsburgh, Pennsylvania, who was twenty-three years old when he stepped into the ring with Louis – and proceeded to box rings around him for half an hour. Conn's quick combinations and neat footwork took him clear of the champion's heavier punches. After twelve rounds it seemed to most ringside critics and most in the 54,487 crowd, if not as it turned out the judges, that Conn only had to stand up for the final three sessions to win a shock decision. Louis, though, was typical of the extraordinary champions in this strange, compelling sport: even when a fight seemed lost, he had an instinct for finding a way to win. In round thirteen he drew Conn forward. Instead of boxing and moving, Conn, who had knocked Louis into the ropes in the previous round, traded punches and his entire future changed. Louis found the range, hurt him and knocked him down. Billy was counted out, still trying to wrench his gloves off the canvas and stand up, only two seconds from the end of the round. Louis said his trainers Jack Blackburn and Mannie Seamon had told him before round thirteen he needed a knockout. 'I knew they were right and I was waiting for him to lose his head,' he said. 'He's a real smart fighter and you got to admit he's faster than I am.' In fact, Conn had not been clear on the scorecards. After twelve rounds one official saw it 7-5 in rounds, another 7-4-1, both to the challenger, and the third had it level at 6-6. The chances are that if Louis had pressed the fight over the last three, without knocking Conn out, he would have retained his championship on a scandalously bad decision. Six months later the Japanese air force bombed Pearl Harbour and the United States joined the Second World War.

William David Conn jr was born in the East Liberty section of Pittsburgh. His ancestors came from County Down in Ireland, and his father worked as a steam-fitter in Pittsburgh. The eldest of five children, he was a precocious swimmer and a friendly, outgoing youngster who turned professional, without an amateur contest, at sixteen. He had already been in the gym of his trainer, Johnny Ray, for three years. 'Johnny was always drunk,' said Conn. 'But even drunk he knew more than most trainers do sober.' From 1936, when he out-pointed local rival and future wel-terweight champion Fritzie Zivic, Conn was world class. He won and lost against the former welterweight champ from Fresno, Young Corbett III, known to his mother as Raffaele Capabianca Giordano, and beat middleweight claimants Fred Apostoli and Solly Krieger, as well as contenders like Babe Risko, Vince Dundee and Teddy Yarosz. In July 1939, aged twenty-one, Conn out-pointed Melio Bettina from Connecticut for the vacant world light-heavyweight championship. He beat Bettina in a return, twice out-pointed Gus Lesnevich, then decided to go for the heavyweight title. He knocked out Bob Pastor in the thirteenth round and out-pointed Lee Savold, but blew the fight that really mattered, against Louis.

Three wins in 1942 included a twelve-round decision over Tony Zale, the great middleweight from Indiana but then he went to war. When it was all over and they made the long-overdue rematch with Louis, Conn had not boxed competi-tively for more than four years. Louis had made three title defences and had kept busy with a string of exhibitions. He was sharp enough and just about young enough at thirty-two, whereas Conn, while still only twenty-eight, had lost his speed and the excitement of youth. The Second World War made men wise, or just old, before their time.

Fans flocked to Yankee Stadium – 45,266 people shelled out $1,925,564, receipts topped at the time only by the second Dempsey-Tunney fight. Sadly, the spectacle couldn't live up to the expectation. Louis knocked Conn out in round eight of a one-sided fight. Years later Conn laughingly asked Louis why he couldn't have let him have the title in their rematch, so they could have made a fortune out of the decider. 'You could have sort of loaned me the crown for six months,' he said. Louis said, 'Billy, you had that title for twelve rounds...'

He settled in the Squirrel Hill district of Pittsburgh, invested his money in oil and real estate, and by the 1960s was a greeter at the Stardust Hotel in Las Vegas. He also refereed fights, most famously when he stopped a lightweight title fight in 1967 between Carlos Ortiz and Sugar Ramos in Mexico, awarding Ortiz the decision on a cut eye. Ramos and the Mexican-based World Boxing Council objected furiously but Conn stood his ground.

He died on 29 May 1993 at the age of seventy-five.

GERRY COONEY

Born: 4 August 1956, New York City
Height: 6ft 5in   **Weight at peak:** 225lbs (16st 1lb)
Fights: 31   **Won:** 28   **Lost:** 3
KO percentage: 77
Rounds boxed: 114
World title fights: 2
Career span: 1977-90 (13 years)
KO wins: 24
KO defeats: 3

Gerry Cooney could punch and he could fight. When his turn came to challenge for the world title, he was unfortunate enough to meet a Larry Holmes still somewhere near his peak – and he lost in the thirteenth round of a gruelling, engrossing fight.

Cooney came from a tough, loveless background, later developed alcohol problems and eventually, when a father and a retired fighter, ran a charity designed to help boxers who encountered hard times. 'I didn't have a peaceful existence,' he said of his upbringing as one of seven children of a steelworker. 'It was scary. The biggest emotion I experienced as a kid was fear...There was no love – and I wanted to be loved.' Cooney left home at seventeen, won two New York City Golden Gloves titles and lost only two of fifty-seven amateur bouts, then turned pro as a twenty-year-old – shortly after the death of his father Tony from lung cancer.

'I didn't understand my father,' he said. 'I couldn't understand why he was trying to break me... I was in bed every night at ten or eleven o'clock because my father said so...Two weeks after he was buried it hit me, the things I wanted to say to him and had never said, the things I still wanted to do with him.'

Under trainer and former fighter Victor Valle, he developed a reputation as a knockout puncher and by the end of 1979 had stacked up twenty-two wins, nineteen of them inside the distance. He was managed by a maverick combination who more than earned their nickname of the Whacko Twins, Dennis Rappaport and Mike Jones, two real estate brokers from New York City. One of their stunts was to try to have their 'who-needs-him?' middleweight, Ronnie Harris, fight a gorilla in Madison Square Garden. In May 1980 Cooney entered world class with a fourth-round stoppage of Jimmy Young, who was beginning to fade by then, then blasted out Ron Lyle in one round – and finally drew rave notices for a chilling fifty-four-second demolition of Ken Norton in Madison Square Garden in May 1981.

That earned him a huge, $10 million payday as challenger to Holmes for the WBC title in Caesars Palace, Las Vegas, in June 1982, which was one of the major boxing occasions of the decade. The champion felt, rightly, that Cooney hadn't been forced to pay his dues for chump-change the way a lot of black fighters from the inner cities had. However, the public wanted to see if Cooney could fight. Legend has it that President Ronald Reagan had a phone installed in Cooney's dressing room so that he could congratulate him if he won. However, in the fight – or more accurately in the tenth round when he took everything the champion had to offer and still fought back – the big New York Irishman earned Holmes's respect. Cooney had been dropped by a right hand in the second, but stayed with the champion until the thirteenth. Then, after he had gone down again, Valle jumped into the ring to save him. Technically it was a disqualification but it's now been accepted generally as a stoppage by Mills Lane. After twelve rounds, with three to go, surprisingly in view that he had lost points for low blows and seemed to be coming off second best, Cooney was behind by only two points on two cards, so at that point the fight was still winnable. He was six down on the third card.

The defeat shattered him – he felt, wrongly, that he let the people around him down – and his personal demons wrecked the rest of his career. He was out of the ring for two years after the Holmes fight, worked his way back gently with three wins in twenty months, which took him to the summer of 1986. Then he had another long absence, before returning without a warm-up for another big-money fight against Michael Spinks, who had dethroned Holmes. He lost in five rounds in Atlantic City in June 1987. He had one more fight, two-and-a-half years later, but was knocked out in two rounds by George Foreman.

'Ask me what happened with Cooney and I'm still at a loss,' said Larry Holmes in his autobiography. 'In the years that followed I'd get into arguments with people who would try to tell me Gerry Cooney was a bum. I really felt otherwise. That he never did get to be champion puzzled me.'

In 1998 Cooney, by then married with three children, launched FIST – Fighters Initiative for Support and Training – which helped boxers adjust to life in retirement. 'We help them with whatever they need,' he said, as he did the rounds of the fundraising circuit in 2003. 'Whether this is a substance abuse problem, or medical coverage, housing, job training... we just want to help them get on with their lives.'

Cooney was a world-class fighter – and has emerged as a top-quality man too.

BERT COOPER

Born: 10 January 1966, Sharon Hill, Pennsylvania
Height: 5ft 11½in   **Weight at peak:** 215lbs (15st 5lbs)
Fights: 59   **Won:** 36   **Lost:** 22   **No Contests:** 1
KO percentage: 50
Rounds boxed: 332

World title fights: 1
Career span: 1984-2002 (18 years)
KO wins: 30
KO defeats: 15

Bert Cooper's big night came when he challenged Evander Holyfield for the world heavyweight title in the champion's home town of Atlanta, Georgia, in November 1991. Cooper had been sitting at home minding his own business when the phone rang: Francesco Damiani had pulled out of the Holyfield fight and they needed a substitute. George Foreman and Riddick Bowe had both beaten Cooper in a couple of rounds and Bert had lost to Carl Williams, Ray Mercer, Nate Miller and Everett 'Big Foot' Martin. The promoters were that desperate. In front of his home fans, Holyfield just had to fight. Cooper, who wasn't doing much else that night, said yes. In the opening round at the Omni Arena, Cooper was on the floor, but he picked himself up, came back and in the third almost caused a sensation when he smashed a shocked Holyfield across the ring. The champion was prevented from falling only by the ropes and referee Mills Lane jumped in to impose the first official knockdown of Holyfield's career. The world champion regained control, pulled into a clear lead and by the seventh Cooper was out on his feet. The fight was stopped two seconds from the end of the session.

Nicknamed Smokin' Bert, Cooper was from Sharon Hill, Pennsylvania, and fought in the classic Philadelphia mould, tucking up, coming in low and hooking hard. Sadly, he was also distracted by a drug problem – during one spell of rehab one cynic relabelled him Non-Smokin' Bert. In 1986, only twenty and with plenty of ambition, he out-pointed Henry Tillman, the 1984 Olympic gold medallist, for the NABF cruiserweight title – and it was a four-knockdown, second-round stoppage of the former Olympic rep from Canada Willie DeWitt that suggested he might be a force.

However, after flooring Carl 'The Truth' Williams in the first round he faded and retired in eight. Defeats began to pile up, including the summary exits against Foreman and Bowe. Still, when he boxed Holyfield, he was coming off four wins in a row, all inside the distance. After doing well against Holyfield he lost a dramatic fight with the tall southpaw Michael Moorer for the vacant WBO belt in Atlantic City in May 1992. Both were floored in the first round, Moorer was down again in the third, but somehow rallied to stop Cooper in the fifth.

Although he fought on for another decade Cooper's half-hour in the spotlight against Holyfield was the night upon which his reputation was to rest.

HENRY COOPER

Born: 3 May 1934, London, England
Height: 6ft 2in　　　**Weight at peak:** 189lbs (13st 7lbs)
Fights: 55　　　**Won:** 40　　**Lost:** 14　　**Drawn:** 1
KO percentage: 49
Rounds boxed: 374
World title fights: 1
Career span: 1954-71 (17 years)
KO wins: 27
KO defeats: 8

By the end of his seventeen-year career Henry Cooper was firmly established as Britain's favourite sporting icon. His popularity continued in retirement, his friendly, down-to-earth sincerity enabling him to earn a living on the public engagement circuit and with a series of lucrative television advertisment appearances. He was also a long-time boxing analyst on BBC radio. Eventually, his achievements and the special place he enjoyed in the hearts of the British people were recognised by a knighthood.

One left hook altered Cooper's life. The punch that exploded against the exposed jaw of the twenty-one-year-old Cassius Clay at Wembley Stadium in 1963 so nearly changed boxing history – and his frustrating defeat only a round later because of an awful cut over the left eye left his fans believing he was foiled, not by the brilliance of the man who went on to become arguably the best heavyweight of all time, but by a freak of nature – fragile skin tissue. Cooper's left hook sent a glassy-eyed Clay toppling down the ropes to the canvas near the end of the fourth round. Clay got up, the bell rang and he veered unsteadily to his corner. No doubt had there been thirty seconds left in the round Henry, a good finisher, could have won the fight. In the interval, which was extended slightly by the discovery of a tear in Clay's glove, Clay's corner applied smelling salts to help bring him round. By the time the delayed round five started, with a board official having run off to the dressing room to find a replacement pair of gloves and a plan to fit them after the round had ended, Clay had recovered. Clay's long right hands and jabs opened the terrible cut that curtailed the fight – and allowed the young American to fulfil, by the unlikeliest of routes, his prophecy as to when the fight would end. It was sensational, controversial stuff. Clay went on to beat Sonny Liston for the championship and became Muhammad Ali.

He promised Henry a return – and in May 1966 at Highbury Stadium, home of Arsenal Football Club, he kept his word. This time there were no knockdowns but again with not too much between them Cooper was ruled out by another appalling gash over his eye in round six.

And so how good was Cooper? His manager, Jim Wicks, made no secret of the fact that he would have no part of Sonny Liston. Other champions of the era,

Floyd Patterson and Ingemar Johansson, both knocked him out. An attempt to box Jimmy Ellis for the World Boxing Association title late in his career was foiled by red tape applied by the British Boxing Board of Control, who were not affiliated to the WBA. Tickets were even printed for the fight before it was called off. If he couldn't quite beat the world champions, then Cooper was beyond dispute the best European heavyweight of his time. He held the British, Commonwealth and European titles in different spells that overall spanned the whole of the 1960s.

There was never any whiff of scandal around Cooper. Married to his Italian wife Albina from 1960, with children Henry and John, he was the epitome of the old-school, clean-living sportsman who earned his corn the honest way and did nobody a bad turn.

Henry and his twin brother George, who boxed as Jim Cooper, were born in hospital in Westminster and raised in Bellingham, south-east London. Their father worked on the London trams. Henry won the ABA light-heavyweight title twice and boxed in the Olympic Games in Helsinki in 1952. He lost his opening bout to a Russian, Anatoly Perov, on a split decision. Cooper turned professional in September 1954, lost early title fights against Joe Bygraves, Johansson and Joe Erskine, then in October 1958 moved up to world class with a shock ten-round points win over the world-rated Zora Folley at Wembley. Cooper made a bad start and in round three, already cut, he was knocked down. But Folley let him off the hook, went right-hand happy and Cooper out-boxed him to win over ten rounds.

Cooper won the British and Empire titles with a fifteen-round decision over Brian London, when his left-hand work got him home in spite of cuts around both eyes. He stopped the South African Gawie de Klerk and Joe Erskine in 1959, and the following year he scored two ten-round decisions over Roy Harris, a former world title challenger from Texas, and the Argentine tough guy Alex Miteff. After beating Erksine again, he was closing on a world title shot in 1961, but then in a rematch with Zora Folley lost inside two rounds. He won three Lonsdale Belts outright, turning back challenges from Erskine, Dick Richardson, Johnny Prescott, Billy Walker and Jack Bodell. Of course he was frustrated against Ali and in September 1966 was knocked out of the world title frame when Floyd Patterson beat him in four rounds at Wembley.

In 1968 he ended the career of the German Karl Mildenberger on an eight-round disqualification at Wembley in another European title fight. The rest of the year was spent struggling to overcome a knee injury, dealing with a greengrocery shop that was losing money and taking up offers to do television commercials. The TV marketing of Henry Cooper was taking shape. In 1969, again, he boxed only once, a fifth-round knockout of Piero Tomasoni in Rome. Tomasoni became famous for a low punch that put Cooper down in agony. Henry got up quickly... because the referee was counting! Then he knocked out the Italian with a left hook. In the dressing room he was still disgruntled as he showed reporters his buckled protector. He relinquished the European title because of injury and the proposed WBA fight with Jimmy Ellis fell apart. He was out of the ring for twelve months, then out-pointed an improved Bodell, who had won the British and by now Commonwealth (not Empire) titles in Cooper's absence. Henry's final win was a nine-rounds stoppage of the strong, big-hitting, colourful but crude Basque, Jose Urtain, at Wembley in November 1970.

Cooper was two months short of his thirty-seventh birthday when he lost all three titles on a bitterly disputed fifteen-round decision to Joe Bugner in what was largely a dull fight before a 10,000 crowd at Wembley. Henry told his wife before the fight he had already decided to retire and afterwards, even though he was convinced he had won, he stuck to his word.

JEAN-PIERRE COOPMAN

Born: 11 July 1946, Ingelmunster, Belgium
Height: 5ft 11½in   **Weight at peak:** 206lbs (14st 10lbs)
Fights: 54   **Won:** 36   **Lost:** 16   **Drawn:** 2
KO percentage: 37
Rounds boxed: 347
World title fights: 1
Career span: 1972-99 (27 years)
KO wins: 20
KO defeats: 6

Belgian stone-cutter Jean-Pierre Coopman had probably worked on more mobile statues than the figure he presented in his pathetic 'challenge' to Muhammad Ali in Puerto Rico in February 1976. Coopman's corner gave him champagne between rounds. One British writer suggested he might not have been the best title challenger in history, but he was probably the merriest.

Ali held him up for four rounds, allegedly checked with television executives whether or not their advertising breaks were 'away', and then proceeded to knock out the Belgian with the minimum of effort in the fifth. Ali, as was his custom, was charitable. In the build-up he had initially talked nasty in a bid to pump a bit of interest into the promotion but Coopman was just too pleased to be a part of it to take offence. He responded with a smile and a bow and Ali just gave up. 'What am I going to do with this guy?' he asked. It was said Coopman was given a pounding even by his hired sparring partners. He ignored it and persuaded himself he was about to become the heavyweight champion of the world. 'I believed it,' he said, 'until a few seconds after the bell rang!' Afterwards the champion said, 'I'm glad Coopman's not hurt. He is a gentleman. His wife is a nice lady.' Coopman, who toppled sideways to the canvas by the ropes from a right hand, said, 'I got hit. I tried to stay up but it felt like 500 pounds was falling on me.' The Puerto Ricans who had snapped up all 12,000 tickets to get a glimpse of even this thirty-four-year-old

Ali in the Roberto Clemente Stadium in Hato Rey filed out, and 'The Greatest' went on to his next defence against Jimmy Young two months later.

Coopman, whom they called The Lion of Flanders for his world championship bout, was born in Ingelmunster in the south-west of Belgium near the French border, and lived in Ghent. His first job was as a sculptor. With his stepfather, he helped restore the ancient St Nicholas's church in Ghent. Out of hours, he spent his time in bars – until someone suggested he try boxing after seeing him spar with a friend. Coopman gave up smoking and trained. He couldn't fight much but the Belgian people liked him for his strength and bravery.

He had beaten nobody of significance when he was picked as an opponent for Ali. Probably his best wins were a ten-round decision over a lanky German, Bernd August and a seven-round disqualification victory over Terry Daniels, who himself had been plucked from obscurity for a brief challenge to Joe Frazier in 1972. When he returned home Coopman found his popularity had risen and 7,500 turned out in Antwerp to see him pull out a right uppercut to knock out the overweight, over-the-hill Spaniard Jose Manuel Urtain in the fourth round to become European champion. His reign lasted two months. His first challenger, Lucien Rodriguez, had already beaten him in a ten-round non-title fight, and in Antwerp in May 1977 Coopman lost a fifteen-round decision to the Frenchman.

Six months later, the Spanish-domiciled Uruguayan, Alfredo Evangelista, was champion and knocked him out in one round in Brussels. Coopman retired in 1981 then, for reasons best known to himself, had one more fight, at the age of fifty-two in April 1999 when he drew an officially licensed six-round contest with another old-timer, Freddy De Kerpel, in Ghent.

JAMES J. CORBETT

Born: 1 September 1866 San Francisco, California
Full name: James John Corbett
Died: 18 February 1933, Bayside, New York, aged 66
Height: 6ft 1in   **Weight at peak:** 178-184lbs (12st 10lbs-13st 2lbs)
Fights: 23   **Won:** 14   **Lost:** 4   **Drawn:** 4   **No Contests:** 1
KO percentage: 30
Rounds boxed: 212
World champion: 1892-97
World title fights: 5
Career span: 1884-1903 (19 years)
KO wins: 7
KO defeats: 3

Gentleman Jim Corbett took boxing away from the time of the bare-knuckle bruisers who had traded on strength and endurance. There had been ring scientists in the old days too, of course – Jem Mace and Daniel Mendoza were prime examples – but Corbett was the first great general of the gloved era.

When he began boxing, everyone knew the heavyweight champion of the world: the brash, swashbuckling John L. Sullivan, who had won the title under London Prize Ring Rules by destroying big Paddy Ryan from upstate New York in nine rounds and ten minutes in Mississippi in 1882. Corbett was everything Sullivan was not: a bank clerk, an amateur boxer before he turned professional, a thoughtful boxer who had limitless patience, as precise as Sullivan was reckless. He was proud and aloof, no lover of the fans whose fickleness he well understood.

James John Corbett was born on the 'wrong side' of the San Francisco slot, the line on the map that divides the rich and the poor. He came from Hayes Valley, born of Irish immigrant parents on 1 September 1866. He boxed at the Olympic Athletic Club, picked up his first professional paydays in Utah and Wyoming under the name John Dillon while continuing his amateur career, and turned pro fully in 1889 with his three fights with San Francisco rival Joe Choynski. The first was interrupted by the local sheriff; the second, great battle was brutal and bloody – and was won by Corbett thanks to a left hook in the twenty-seventh round; the third a bloodless four-round decision victory for Corbett.

Marathon bouts, with or without gloves, were frequent. Corbett's great long-distance fight was against the greatest of the black boxers of the era, Peter Jackson, in San Francisco in May 1891. They were two patient, organised and essentially defensive-minded boxers and matched each other for skill. In the end they simply cancelled each other out, feinting, countering, waiting... and waiting, until the crowd grew so bored they were calling for something to happen. After warning both men to get on with it, and receiving no serious response, the referee ruled No Contest, which is a harsh ruling – a draw would be a more accurate reflection of what happened. Whatever the technicalities, they had boxed sixty-one three-minute rounds – the first time an automatic time-keeper was used. Corbett always acknowledged Jackson as one of the genuine greats. A month after that marathon, he had a far easier time of it in a four-round playaround with John L. Sullivan, in evening dress! It was no more than a light-hearted game for a theatre crowd but Corbett always said it gave him vital clues as to how the champion fought.

Corbett boxed nobody else of note until he answered an open invitation from Sullivan to the leading contenders. They set up the fight for New Orleans on 7 September 1892 on a three-day festival of boxing. At the age of twenty-five, Corbett systematically out-boxed the old champion before knocking him out in the twenty-first round. He said beforehand: 'Sullivan can't hit me in a week and he'll be the worst licked man you ever looked at.' Early on the impatient fans booed him and called for him to stop running, but he drew Sullivan's strength. His total self-confidence was justified. In spite of apparent efforts in training, Sullivan couldn't entirely get rid of his excess baggage about the belly – and his aura of invincibility just wasn't there any more. In round twenty-one a right hand dropped him for the full count.

'I was actually disgusted with the crowd and it left a lasting impression on me,' Corbett said in his autobiography. 'It struck me as sad to see all those thousands who had given him such a wonderful ovation when he entered the ring turning it to me now that he was down and out. I realised that someday too they would turn from me.'

Corbett was labelled a prima donna by some sections of the media. Not that he cared. He made the championship pay with public appearances, and in January 1894 knocked out the British challenger, Charley Mitchell, in three rounds in Jacksonville, Florida. In September 1894 he accepted the opportunity to feature in the first bout ever filmed by a moving camera, in Orange, New Jersey, against Peter Courtney, whom he knocked out in round six. It is not regarded as a championship contest. In 1895 he actually announced his retirement, but changed his mind when his old rival Bob Fitzsimmons, whom he disliked intensely, claimed the title. Eventually he agreed to defend against Fitzsimmons in Carson City, Nevada, on 17 March 1897 – and again a movie was produced. About a quarter of an hour of it still exists and shows a pedestrian bout. Corbett out-boxed the Cornishman easily early on and put him down on one knee in round six. However, Fitzsimmons got up, took everything he had to take and slowly in the mountain air it was Corbett who tired. Fitzsimmons worked the body in the time-honoured tradition. In round twelve Corbett flinched from one body shot and although he drew the blood from the challenger's nose again, in round fourteen Fitzsimmons drew him onto a perfect left hook to the stomach. Corbett went down, breathless and momentarily paralysed, for the full count.

Corbett lost on a foul to Tom Sharkey in New York and then, after an eighteen-month break, took on the new champion, James J. Jeffries, at Coney Island, New York, on 11 May 1900. He was in training camp for months, was in magnificent shape and with a few of the twenty-five rounds to go was a long way ahead. However, he tired and in round twenty-three he came off the ropes straight into the path of a brutal left hook. He was knocked out. He had done well enough to merit a rematch, but it took until 1903 to arrange, by which time he was almost thirty-seven years old. This time he lost in ten rounds and never boxed again.

Jeffries, late in his long life, said, 'Corbett was a master boxer. He knew every trick and angle. He was as game as he was scientific and, even though he was past his prime then, he cut a terrific pace while his stamina lasted.'

Corbett's personal life was not altogether smooth, and his second wife Vera had a rocky time keeping up with his antics. At one time she sued for divorce and said one of his late-career wins, over Charles 'Kid' McCoy, was fixed, but she later withdrew both the divorce suit and the allegation of corruption. One biographer suggests that among the old champion's dalliances, while on the vaudeville circuit, was Mae West. Corbett died of liver cancer in Bayside, New York, in 1933, aged sixty-six.

D

TERRY DANIELS

Born: 1 May 1946, Beaumont, Texas
Height: 6ft 1½in   **Weight at peak:** 195lbs (13st 13lbs)
Fights: 67   **Won:** 35   **Lost:** 31   **Drawn:** 1
KO percentage: 41
Rounds boxed: 393
World title fights: 1
Career span: 1969-81 (12 years)
KO wins: 28
KO defeats: 14

In one of the worst mismatches in the history of the championship, Terry Daniels, a one-time college kid from Beaumont, Texas, was butchered by a ring-rusty Joe Frazier in New Orleans in January 1972. Frazier had taken a ten-month layoff after his career-defining win over Muhammad Ali and this fight took the shape of a gentle reintroduction to ring activity for a champion who carried a rim of fat around his waist. Outweighed by 20lbs and outclassed by an incalculable distance, Daniels was knocked down five times before the dismal affair was stopped one minute and forty-five seconds into round four. The only surprise is that it drew a crowd of 7,800 curious fans who, presumably, paid in order to be able to say they saw the first world heavyweight title fight in New Orleans since James J. Corbett beat John L. Sullivan in 1892. When the show was in financial trouble, the champion also graciously agreed to take a $50,000 paycut from the agreed $250,000. Still, nobody could blame Daniels for taking the opportunity – or the payday of $30,000 including $5,000 to cover his expenses.

Daniels was managed by an insurance man, Doug Lord, and had been a football player in college. He had built a reputation as a decent puncher on the local club circuit, had lasted the full ten rounds with thirty-six-year-old Floyd Patterson and had beaten Manuel Ramos on points. Before he fought Frazier he knocked out Ted Gullick, who had briefly promised, only to fall short, in three in Cleveland. After the Frazier fight, Daniels lost five in a row, including points defeats by Cleveland Williams and Jose 'King' Roman and a seventh-round stoppage by John Conteh. Long before his last fight, against Alfredo Evangelista on the island of Ibiza in 1981, he was trading on his status as a one-time world title challenger just to get paydays.

JACK DEMPSEY

Born: 24 Jun 1895, Manassa, Colorado
Full name: William Harrison Dempsey
Died: 31 May 1983, New York, aged 87
Height: 6ft 1in   **Weight at peak:** 187-192lbs (13st 5lbs-13st 10lbs)
Fights: 83   **Won:** 66   **Lost:** 7   **Drawn:** 10
KO percentage: 61
Rounds boxed: 347
World champion: 1919-26
World title fights: 8
Career span: 1914-40 (26 years)
KO wins: 51
KO defeats: 1

Jack Dempsey was the great boxing hero of the Jazz Age, the fleeting years after World War One when the fantastic American Dream seemed obtainable, when poor men became rich, bought palatial homes in the sun, made movies, drove fast cars and dated faster women. If Dempsey could rise from the hobo camps of the Mid-West to be heavyweight champion of the world, then all men could be all things. Although he wasn't a giant in stature – a fraction less than 6ft 1in and at his peak less than 190lbs – he was larger than life. He was heavyweight champion for seven years, from 1919 until 1926, and if he boxed only half a dozen times in that time his inactivity merely added to his legend. He had a movie star wife, Estelle Taylor, whose every whim he indulged; they travelled to Europe, in particular to Paris; they did as they wished; and when he did box he drew million-dollar gates.

It speaks volumes for his character that, through it all, Dempsey remained a personable, down-to-earth man who could pass the time of day with rich and poor alike. He did not forget that his roots were among the ordinary people of Colorado, and in his middle years when he ran his restaurant on Broadway, he enjoyed nothing better than passing his time with working people who came in to enjoy a meal.

Dempsey was from the small town of Manassa in the flatlands of southern Colorado, near the border with New Mexico, where his father Hyrum and mother Celia raised eleven children on whatever work came along. They were Mormons: Hyrum's ancestors were Scottish and Irish, Celia's were Cherokee and Choktaw. When Jack, whose real name was William Harrison Dempsey, was ten, Hyrum took the family north-west to Cripple Creek and Leadville, where he shovelled ore in the mines. In 1966, the seventy-one-year-old Dempsey visited his birthplace and told the local sports writer, 'We were just working people, drifting around the west. I did everything to help make money. I thinned beets, pitched hay, worked a threshing machine. After we left Manassa, Dad and my older brothers were getting $1.50 to $2 a day shovelling ore. In a few years, so was I.'

In the gold towns he began to fight for coins for his supper. He was taught by his elder brother Bernie, and because of him used the old tricks of chewing pine resin to strengthen his jaw and soaking his face and hands in beef brine to harden them. His first known fight was in the Moose Hall in Montrose, Colorado, in 1912, a third-round knockout of Fred Wood, an old friend who was a local black-smith. They advertised the fight themselves, hired the hall and split the proceeds. It was a long journey from the Moose Hall to Madison Square Garden. Some say between 1912 and 1914 he had around 100 unrecorded battles in bar-rooms and saloons, or in the open air. He rode the rails, lived the hobo life, moving and working wherever he could. By the time he was twenty-one his career was offi-cial: he fought in Ogden, Utah, in Ely, Nevada, in Salida, Colorado... and in New York City, where he had three ten-round bouts in the summer of 1916. Usually he won, occasionally he didn't, but he found nobody who was too good for him until he bumped into the old contender Fireman Jim Flynn in Murray, Utah, in February 1917. Flynn, who had fought Tommy Burns and Jack Johnson in title fights, knocked him out in the first round.

Dempsey went on improving – and a year later, in Fort Sheridan, Illinois, he knocked out Flynn in one. He also flattened the former 'White Hope' Arthur Pelkey in one, then grabbed headlines by doing the same to the 6ft 6in Fred Fulton in Harrison, New Jersey, in July 1918. His manager Jack 'Doc' Kearns negotiated a world heavyweight title challenge to the giant Kansas cowboy Jess Willard, the man who had beaten Jack Johnson in 1915. Willard was 5½in taller than Dempsey, 58lbs heavier and had an inflated reputation as the conqueror of Johnson. Dempsey? Well, he was just a big punching kid who used to be a hobo. Tex Rickard, the promoter, admitted he didn't know whether Dempsey would cope but shelled out $100,000 to have a state-of-the-art, 80,000-seat arena built outside Toledo, Ohio, on the shores of Lake Erie. There was an enclosure, behind barbed wire, for ladies.

Independence Day 1919 was ferociously hot and Battling Nelson, the old lightweight champion, whose funds had not stretched to a room in a hotel, camped at the arena in a tent. He also took it upon himself to indulge in a rare bath in a conveniently situated vat of water. In fact, the 'water' was lemonade that was later served to thirsty and unsuspecting punters. The crowd of around 20,000 was a disappointment to Rickard, but the fight wasn't. Dempsey came off his stool for round one like a man on fire and whipped heavy hooks and swings at the uncertain, portly giant, who just couldn't get out of the way. Willard went down seven times in a brutal first round. It seemed referee Ollie Pecord had counted him out, but in the din nobody heard the bell ring. They hauled Jess to his stool, sloshed water on his face and shoved him up for round two. Dempsey and Kearns, thinking the fight over, had left the ring, then had to be recalled. Maybe the momentum or the adrenalin left him, but in rounds two and three Dempsey slowed and couldn't drop Willard again. The champion's fans pointed out a photograph that showed the seventh knockdown, with Jess sitting propped against the ropes, a dark object by his knee. Some speculated that it was a metal bolt that had fallen from Dempsey's glove. Others laughed and said it was a cigar. To the end of his days Willard said he felt there was something amiss, that no ordinary man could punch as hard as Dempsey hit him in that opening round. After three rounds he stayed on his stool. His cheekbone was broken in seven places. Two of his teeth were on the canvas. Kearns, in his own autobiography fifty years later, said he had soaked Dempsey's gloves in plaster of Paris. But as Don King once said, 'Everything you hear in boxing is a lie...'

Six months later Dempsey's popularity took a grotesque tumble. In 1916 he had married a Salt Lake City prostitute, Maxine Cates, after they had been together less than a year. Early in 1920 she wrote a letter to the *San Francisco Chronicle*, accusing the world champion of being a draft dodger. It blew into a huge story, and although a trial cleared him, his argument that he did essential war work in a Philadelphia shipyard was tempered by a publicity photograph that showed him toiling in the docks... in patent leather shoes.

In September 1920, Dempsey knocked out an old rival, friend and sparring partner, Billy Miske, in three rounds of his first defence in Benton Harbor, Michigan. Miske was in the initial stages of an illness that would kill him at the start of 1924 and was in debt. Eleven days before Christmas 1920, Dempsey knocked out another old rival, Bill Brennan, in twelve rounds in Madison Square Garden, the boxing mecca in the city of all-night speakeasies and jazz clubs.

In July 1921, Rickard staged the first of his amazing million-dollar gates in a sprawling arena at Boyle's Thirty Acres in Jersey City, just across the river from Manhattan. Dempsey, the so-called draft dodger champion, was matched with the French war hero Georges Carpentier. No matter that Dempsey was a strong, thunderous-punching heavyweight who had learned his lesson about preparations after the Brennan fight and that Carpentier, in spite of holding the light-heavyweight championship, was more of a blown-up middleweight who had to put on weight to come in at 172lbs. Rickard, sensibly, kept the elegant, charming Orchid Man under wraps until fight time. Ringside seats were occupied by Roosevelts, Rothschilds, Rockefellers and Astors. There were diplomats from Spain, Britain, Russia, the Netherlands, Peru and Romania. Dempsey marauded forward as he liked and dumped the Frenchman on the canvas for the count in round four.

Dempsey confined himself to movies and exhibitions in 1922, then Kearns and Rickard fell out, which led to the infamous defence against Tommy Gibbons in Shelby, Montana. Dempsey won on points over fifteen rounds, but the crowd was small. Kearns insisted on the champion being paid his entire purse and took Jack away on the first available train. Gibbons fought for nothing and, worse, the banks of Shelby, who had backed the 'investment', all went broke.

In September 1923, Kearns and Rickard worked together in an incredible promotion at New York's Polo Grounds and brought together a paying crowd of

88,228 to see Dempsey defend against Luis Firpo, the Wild Bull of the Pampas. In under four minutes of fighting mayhem one fan died of a heart attack. Dempsey was put down on to his knee by an uppercut in the opening ten seconds, and by the half-minute mark Firpo was down from a big right hand. He got up at nine. Dempsey slammed him to the canvas seven times, and then near the end of the most amazing round in heavyweight championship history was sent sprawling out of the ring by big, overhand rights. He clattered on to the ringside press desk, was pushed back in by reporters, and beat the count by a fraction. After nine knockdowns in round one, Dempsey recovered his senses in the interval – helped by a bucket of water from Kearns – and finished the job with two more knockdowns in round two. The whole drama lasted three minutes fifty-seven seconds!

In 1924 Dempsey married Estelle Taylor and embraced the celebrity lifestyle. He pampered his wife, went on tour, made movies, had an exhibition here and there... and went stale. It was three years from the Firpo fight to his next defence, against Gene Tunney in the Sesquicentennial Stadium, Philadelphia, in September 1926. By then Dempsey had parted with Kearns, who slapped a writ on him and managed to get his bank account frozen. Jack's marriage was under strain, he suffered some kind of stomach illness on the day of the fight and when the bell rang he was horribly ring-rusty. And before an astonishing official attendance of 120,757, who paid $1,895,733, on a rain-drenched night Tunney handed the champion a boxing lesson for ten rounds to take away his title after seven years and two months. Afterwards Estelle Taylor rang him. 'What happened, Ginsberg?' she said. 'Honey,' he said, 'I forgot to duck.'

Dempsey came back in July 1927 and for six rounds was losing to Jack Sharkey. In the seventh he hit Sharkey low. Sharkey turned to the referee to complain and Dempsey knocked him out with a left hook to the chin. That set up the rematch with Tunney at Soldier Field, Chicago, on 22 September 1927 before a crowd that Rickard put at 104,953, but which some reporters said was far, far higher. The gross live gate takings were $2,658,660, a record that stood until Muhammad Ali boxed Leon Spinks in 1978. This was the infamous Battle of the Long Count. Tunney controlled the fight until round seven when Dempsey drove him to the ropes and floored him heavily with a left hook. Referee Dave Barry delayed the count until Jack had retreated to a neutral corner – a new rule that he was unaccustomed to. That gave Tunney precious seconds of recovery time. At nine, after the clock later showed he had been down for almost fourteen seconds, he beat the count. Tunney ran, recuperated, began to fight back – and in the eighth put Dempsey down with his own left hook. At the end of ten, Tunney had won a clear decision. In February 1928 Dempsey announced his retirement. Like so many others, he lost a fortune in the 1929 Wall Street Crash.

He divorced Estelle Taylor in 1930, enjoyed himself with an exhibition tour in which some bouts were supposedly recognised as official contests – even when he boxed several men on the same night, and then gave up again. His last fights were at the age of forty-five in July 1940, but they didn't really count either. He married and divorced Hannah Williams, then in 1959 wed Deanna Piattelli, who survived him. He served with the US Coastguard in the Second World War, and his restaurant on Broadway was a mecca for fight people until it closed in 1974. He often took an early morning bicycle ride in Central Park, and was eighty-seven when he died of heart failure in May 1983.

MICHAEL DOKES

Born: 10 August 1958, Akron, Ohio
Height: 6ft 3in   **Weight at peak:** 216lbs (15st 6lbs)
Fights: 61   **Won:** 53   **Lost:** 6   **Drawn:** 2
KO percentage: 54
Rounds boxed: 366
World champion: 1982-83 (WBA)
World title fights: 4
Career span: 1976-97 (21 years)
KO wins: 33
KO defeats: 5

Michael Dokes was a talent gone to waste. So much of his life was spent battling cocaine abuse that it is hard to know how good he might have been.

Addiction is a hard burden for anyone to carry and in the end it beat him. He had two felony drug convictions and at the age of forty he beat and sexually assaulted his live-in girlfriend when she returned to their Las Vegas home late from a concert. It took a year for her to recover from her physical injuries. After pleading guilty to attempted murder, second-degree kidnap and battery with intent to commit sexual assault, the man who had once held the World Boxing Association heavyweight title with pride said, 'I am remorseful. There is no excuse for my action.' He was jailed, with a minimum term of four years and two months. His girlfriend said when he was sober and drug free Dokes was a good person. When he took drugs and drank, he became violent.

'Dynamite' Dokes was an exceptional amateur talent. He won the US Championships in 1975 and the National Golden Gloves in 1976 – and was still only eighteen when he turned pro in Hollywood, Florida. He signed for Don King. In his fifteenth fight and, still only twenty-one, he beat Jimmy Young on points at Caesars Palace, Las Vegas. Two fights later he outscored Lucien Rodriguez, the sturdy European champion from France. A draw with Ossie Ocasio was a blip – he was lucky – but in a rematch he knocked out the Puerto Rican in one round. A points win over Randy Cobb was followed by a fourth-round knockout of Britain's leading heavyweight John L. Gardner. In December 1981, when Don King was beaten up at the Trevor Berbick–Muhammad Ali fight in the Bahamas, it was Dokes who met him at Miami Airport and drove him to hospital.

He won the WBA title controversially in December 1982 when a fast start had defending champion Mike Weaver under systematic fire and only sixty-three seconds into the fight referee Joey Curtis decided Weaver couldn't defend himself and stopped it. The rematch was also steeped in controversy, with the Las Vegas judges producing a draw after fifteen rounds, when most seemed to feel Weaver had won. Two officials scored it level, while the third actually had Dokes ahead 145-141. Then, with his drug problems unseen but far from unheard, Dokes lost the title before his home state of Ohio's fans when Gerrie Coetzee knocked him out in the tenth round in September 1983. He later admitted he would have had cocaine in his bloodstream when he fought Coetzee. By round five he was exhausted. As Dokes lay on the canvas Don King, who had demanded options for the duration of Coetzee's world championship reign in the event of his winning and therefore taken over as his promoter from Cedric Kushner, stepped over the fallen loser in the rush to congratulate his new winner.

Dokes, who was young and impressionable when he began boxing under King's promotional wing, was upset when he asked King for a loan to pay taxes and was refused. King may have believed he was being cruel to be kind. Dokes came back with several wins, but in the summer of 1985 finally acknowledged his problems – 'I was in the fast lane, where the drugs go with the fast cars and the fast women' – and disappeared from view until the end of 1987 when, at twenty-nine, he set out to put his life on track. He tried hard, won eight in a row, but lost a war with Evander Holyfield on a tenth-round stoppage in Las Vegas in March 1989. He fought on but struggled with ordinary opponents, and then lost savagely in four rounds to Donovan 'Razor' Ruddock in Madison Square Garden in April 1990.

He was given a last world title chance against Riddick Bowe in Madison Square Garden in February 1993. It didn't even go a round. He boxed on for a few years for what amounted to chump-change, then committed the brutal attack on his girlfriend and by January 2000 he was behind bars. So very sad.

GUS DORAZIO

Born: 4 July 1916, Philadelphia, Pennsylvania
Real name: Justine Vincolota
Died: 19 May 1986, aged 69
Height: 6ft   **Weight at peak:** 193lbs (13st 11lbs)
Fights: 85   Won: 60   Lost: 23   Drawn: 1   No Contests: 1
KO percentage: 12
Rounds boxed: 694
World title fights: 1
Career span: 1936-46 (10 years)
KO wins: 11
KO defeats: 7

A Mob fighter from Philadelphia, Gus Dorazio was managed by the notorious Frank 'Blinky' Palermo. Dorazio was also known as Justine Vincolota. His only claim to fame was that he boxed Joe Louis for the championship during the Bum of the Month tour and lost on a knockout after ninety seconds of round two in February 1941. A notoriously light puncher, he stopped only nine of his eighty opponents, and had nothing to test Louis with.

His best wins were over Bob Pastor and Al McCoy, both of whom also lost to Louis in title fights, but he was beaten by Red Burman, cut to shreds in eight rounds by Billy Conn and lost to Arturo Godoy, Joe Baksi and Lee Savold. He was also disgraced when he was ruled out for not trying against Willie Reddish, who later trained Sonny Liston.

JAMES DOUGLAS

Born: 7 April 1960, Columbus, Ohio
Height: 6ft 4in   **Weight at peak:** 231lbs (16st 7lbs)
Fights: 46   **Won:** 38   **Lost:** 6   **Drawn:** 1   **No Contests:** 1
KO percentage: 54
Rounds boxed: 238
World champion: 1990
World title fights: 3
Career span: 1981-99 (18 years)
KO wins: 25
KO defeats: 5

If ever one performance made a man's life it was when James 'Buster' Douglas demolished 'Iron' Mike Tyson with a tenth-round knockout in Tokyo in February 1990. Tyson was twenty-three years old with a personal life in increasing turmoil and known to be losing his professional discipline. He had also walked away from his training team, led by Kevin Rooney, and brought in the inexperienced Aaron Snowell and an old friend, Jay Bright. The idea that he might lose soon was beginning to settle into the minds of critics... but nobody expected it to happen against Douglas.

The 6ft 4in, 230lbs challenger, from Columbus, Ohio, was not short of talent but his temperament was suspect. He had unravelled against Tony Tucker for the vacant IBF title in May 1987, losing on a tenth-round stoppage at the Las Vegas Hilton after doing well early on. Years before he had turned defeat into victory when, after barely losing one of the first eight rounds, he was stopped in the ninth by a so-so, 6ft 10in Californian named Mike 'The Giant' White. Douglas had out-boxed Oliver McCall and Trevor Berbick, but McCall was Tyson's sparring partner and Berbick had crumbled in two rounds in Tyson's first world title fight in 1986. No, the pre-fight form was clear, Douglas didn't have enough to handle even a half-interested Tyson.

How wrong can we be! Douglas found inspiration in tragedy and worry. His mother Lula died of hypertension and the mother of his eleven-year-old son Lamar was taken seriously ill while he was away in training camp. From the first bell Douglas found Tyson easy to hit with the jab. The weaving attacks that had been a vital part of Tyson's arsenal were replaced by a still-headed, straight-line advance. He threw single punches instead of the devastating combinations that were a mark of his greatness. And so Douglas piled up points at long range. In round five Douglas found the confidence to stand and belt Tyson with right hands that brought gasps from the crowd in the domed Korakuen Hall. At the bell they put an ice pack on Tyson's eye. As Snowell and Bright talked to him, he didn't even bother looking up. In the closing seconds of the eighth Tyson did find a punch that might have saved the title: he dumped Buster on the canvas with a perfect right uppercut. Douglas turned onto one knee, made it to his feet at nine, then took over again in the ninth. Tyson began to wobble. His left eye was swollen. In the tenth Douglas, after holding on from one last, defiant big shot, set up Tyson with an uppercut, then sent him sprawling with a four-punch burst, his gumshield flying out as he hit the floor. Tyson's last act as champion, as referee Octavio Meyran counted him out, was to attempt to cram his mouthpiece back into his mouth with his glove.

The announcements and post-fight interviews had barely finished when the WBC and WBA tried to screw Douglas out of his hard-won championship. Don King, who had just seen a huge fight between Tyson and Evander Holyfield dissolve, tried to persuade everyone who had ears that Meyran had messed up, had given Douglas a long count when he was down and that Tyson had really won by knockout in round eight. Technically, the replays showed that Douglas was down for longer than the official count of nine, but that wasn't a hanging offence. Nor was it Douglas's problem. His job was simply to get up before the referee reached ten, not take a stopwatch out of his pocket and time it himself. King wheeled out Meyran, an honourable and experienced official, to say, 'I made an error. I missed the count. I cannot explain it.' Jose Sulaiman, criticised so often in the past for his ridiculously close business relationship with King, excelled himself. The self-appointed 'Humble Servant of Boxing' said the WBC would not recognise the result and would hold a hearing ten days later. The WBA president Gilberto Mendoza said much the same thing. Only the IBF president, Bobby Lee, who ironically was to be brought down by a corruption scandal nine years later, refused to take the King line. 'Douglas is the champion because he won the fight in the ring,' said Lee. Tyson joined in. The man whose relationship with the media had been at best uneven, pleaded with them. 'You guys know me,' he said. 'You know I walk like I talk. I've never cried or bitched about anything. I knocked Buster Douglas out fair and square...'

As soon as the news of what King, the WBC and WBA were trying to do reached the celebrating Douglas team, they erupted. 'When I saw how poor his defence was, I knew all I had to do was concentrate,' said Douglas. 'What they are trying to do is a disgrace.' His manager, John Johnson, exploded: 'It's sickening to see Don King manipulating the WBC and the WBA. Buster kicked Tyson's ass. It's as simple as that. These guys can go to hell.' Two days later public outrage forced Sulaiman, Mendoza and King to backtrack. The result stood.

A lesser controversy emerged when the scorecards revealed that the judges had the fight level after nine rounds. The American, Larry Rozadilla, had it right at 88-82 for Douglas, but somehow the two Japanese judges, Ken Morita and Masakuzu Uchida, got themselves in a tangle. Uchida saw it 86-86 and even worse Morita had it 87-86 for Tyson. Fortunately, they were not a factor in the outcome, but the scoring merely increased the sour taste.

A legal wrangle then broke out when Douglas decided to defend the title against Holyfield without King, his former promoter, having any involvement. Steve Wynn, who owned the new Mirage hotel-casino on the Las Vegas Strip, won the purse bids for the fight with $32 million. King somehow picked up $4.5 million in compensation, while Donald Trump was also awarded $2.5 million. Wynn also withdrew from negotiations with Bob Arum, who had wanted to charge $2 million for his services in helping him stage the event. Wynn said, 'Arum's offensive personality convinced me he was not a suitable associate for our company.' Arum countered that Wynn had a diseased mind and a horse's ass! Douglas's gross was $24.75 million plus an agreed $100,000 bonus from the Tyson fight to be paid by King because of the terms of their contract. Most of that was taken away from him in deductions, legal fees and payoffs, but he still set himself up for life. The court settlement, perhaps crucially, said that after Wynn had promoted the Holyfield fight, Douglas must give the second defence to King. If ever a decision was likely to depress a man it was that one.

When Douglas stepped into the ring against Holyfield in October 1990 he was 14½lbs heavier at 246lbs that he had been for Tyson. That said enough. In round three Holyfield hit him with a right hand and Buster went down, and stayed down. Even his father Bill, a world-class middleweight in the 1970s, said he could have got up.

Douglas put his energy into charity work in his home city, but ate himself into obesity and, while still in his mid-thirties, collapsed into a diabetic coma. He recovered, then amazingly began working for a comeback at the same time as Tyson came out of jail from his rape sentence. In 1996 a 244lbs Douglas stopped journeyman Tony LaRosa after three rounds in Atlantic City. The story was on: a Tyson-Douglas rematch was possible. However, Holyfield got to Tyson first this time and stopped him in another huge upset in November 1996. Douglas kept working, and winning, until he was knocked out in the first round by Lou Savarese.

JACK DOYLE

Born: 31 August 1913, Cobh, Co. Cork, Ireland
Died: 13 December 1978, London, England, aged 65
Height: 6ft 5in   **Weight at peak:** 210lbs (15st)
Fights: 23   **Won:** 17   **Lost:** 6
KO percentage: 69
Rounds boxed: 51
World title fights: 0
Career span: 1932-43 (11 years)
KO wins: 16
KO defeats: 4

Jack Doyle, the heavyweight champion of the people of Ireland, if not the world, had a thunderous punch – and a glass jaw. An easy-going extrovert with an appetite for life well beyond anything boxing could offer, Doyle transcended the sport in the 1930s. Only fifteen months into his professional career, and with ten straight knockouts behind him, all inside two rounds, Doyle fought Jack Petersen for the British heavyweight title at White City Stadium in London. Such was his magnetism that the area around the famous open-air venue was gridlocked for hours. Unfortunately, as Doyle's biographer Michael Taub relates, the big man from Cork had contracted a venereal disease and was in considerable discomfort. Aside from that, his natural way of fighting was to sally forth, swing his big right hands and trust something would land sooner rather than later.

In the first round he connected with plenty of swings – most of which were low. When he repeated the offence in round two, he was disqualified. There was uproar among a crowd that some say was as large as 90,000, but the referee, one Pickles Douglas, said he had given Doyle his final warning at the end of round one, and that was that. The British Boxing Board of Control, which included Douglas among its stewards, suspended him for six months and fined him £2,740 of his £3,000 purse. Somehow they considered it within their powers to divide the remaining £260 between Doyle and his mother in Cork to be paid by the promoter at the rate of £5 a week. Doyle, understandably, was extremely annoyed. After serving his ban, during which he earned a fortune in vaudeville in Dublin, he knocked out Frank Borrington of Derbyshire in one round, and then celebrated what seems from this distance an inevitable victory in the court case against the Board of Control.

He returned to the theatre, made a movie and went to New York. He won three fights by knockout, but in his first real test was stopped in one round by Buddy Baer. Both were very young: Doyle twenty-two, Baer only twenty. Jack was knocked down three times. By then his new wife Judith (who incidentally was a former girlfriend of Buddy's big brother Max) had fainted. That was the end of Doyle's American ring enterprise. His marriage failed too and he took up with the famous movie actress, Movita. He made one more go at a career in London, did out-point the well-travelled American King Levinsky at the Empire Pool, Wembley, but then lost a ridiculous fight with Eddie Phillips at Harringay. Doyle missed with an extravagant swing, fell out of the ring and was counted out.

They made a rematch before another huge crowd at White City. Upwards of 30,000 people were locked out and twenty minutes before he was to walk to the ring Doyle serenaded the disappointed to huge applause. In the fight, Doyle was on the brink of victory after flooring Phillips twice, then was knocked out himself – all this in two minutes twenty-five seconds. That was the end apart from a couple of small fights in Dublin in 1943. As the world rejoiced at the end of the Second World War, Doyle was alone and broke. The drink took hold and he hit the bottom. Even then, his constitution was strong. It took until December 1978 for the inevitable cirrhosis of the liver to kill him.

RICHARD DUNN

Born: 19 January 1945, Leeds, England
Height: 6ft 4in   **Weight at peak:** 208lbs
Fights: 45   **Won:** 33   **Lost:** 12
KO percentage: 35
Rounds boxed: 237
World title fights: 1
Career span: 1969-77 (8 years)
KO wins: 16
KO defeats: 11

A big southpaw from the North of England, Richard Dunn had talent enough to win British and European titles – and was in the right place at the right time to gross £100,000 for challenging Muhammad Ali for the world heavyweight title in Munich in May 1976. He lasted into the fifth round against Ali and was knocked down five times but he earned respect and a measure of popularity in Britain because of the refreshing honesty of his effort. The previous year Joe Bugner, an infinitely better fighter than Dunn, was castigated for surviving fifteen rounds with Ali in the stifling heat of Kuala Lumpur. Dunn sat in his jockstrap, crying tears of disappointment in his dressing room and British sports fans knew they could have asked no more of him than he fight to his limits. 'I had a go, like I promised I would,' he said. 'I couldn't get out of the way of those right hands... I don't think I disgraced anyone. It were right hard in there.'

Dunn had been provided with the services of a hypnotist, Romark, in the lead-up to the fight, which caused great hilarity among the cynical old-stagers of the boxing scene. Dunn was no fool, but went along with it – and might even have begun to believe it. In a letter to his veteran manager, George Biddles, a week before the fight, Dunn wrote that he had a recurring dream that he stopped Ali in round eight. It wasn't to be, and some say that a puzzled Romark was heard to remark sadly, 'I must have forgotten to hypnotise his chin…'

Dunn was twenty-four when he turned professional in the summer of 1969 in a heavyweight competition organised by the legendary British promoter Jack Solomons at the World Sporting Club in London. He was knocked out in one round by Danny McAlinden. For several years he seemed to be just one of a dozen or so half-decent heavyweights who could top-up earnings from a day job (in his case as a scaffolder) with a six or eight-round bout here and there. In his youth he had made sixty-seven parachute jumps with the British Territorial Army before becoming too heavy to be safe. One of eleven children himself, he and his wife Janet had three of their own to feed: son Richard, called Rocky, and daughters Karen and Gillian. Dunn also played loose forward for a rugby league team in Halifax. His arms were tattooed with swallows and parachutes.

He won more than he lost on the way up, though the Philadelphia stylist Jimmy Young and the crude, heavy-hitting Spaniard Jose Urtain both stopped him. By 1975 he was still short of the British title. Then he contacted Biddles to see if the wise old man from Leicester could do anything for him. They agreed a deal and the transformation was remarkable: Dunn out-pointed Bunny Johnson, ironically one of Biddles's former charges, over fifteen rounds at Wembley to win the British and Commonwealth heavyweight titles, and knocked out McAlinden in two rounds in his first defence. He won the European title, too, against the lanky German Bernd August.

Biddles agreed a promotional deal with the powerful group of Harry Levene, Jarvis Astaire, Mickey Duff and Mike Barrett, and they clinched the fight with Ali. When the two fighters met before the world media, someone raised the subject of Dunn having once been a paratrooper in the British Territorial Army, presumably as an illustration of the bravery he would bring to the fight. Ali said, with a twinkle in his eye, 'A paratrooper? He'll know how to fall then…' Janet Dunn, whose brother Jim was a boxer and worked in Richard's corner, defended her man by declaring that Ali couldn't fight southpaws, which amused him enormously. 'Southpaw, northpaw, eastpaw or westpaw, I ain't worried,' said the champion. Somebody wrote that Dunn had a face that looked like Ilkley Moor on a clear day.

Biddles made a speech that sounded as if he'd had one conversation too many with Romark. 'I see myself touring luncheon clubs in southern California, I see a big parade forming at Heathrow, I see lovely motorcars heading into the countryside and at every village I see crowds cheering and people throwing flowers. Richard Dunn is world heavyweight champion…'

Duff says before the fight he asked Ali for his gloves to auction for charity at a sporting club show in London. Shortly after the Master of Ceremonies had announced Ali was 'still the heavyweight champion of the world, after two minutes forty-five seconds of round five', the great man pulled off his gloves and gave them to Duff. 'Look inside,' he said. Inside was a piece of paper, containing a sweat-stained message in Ali's own handwriting: 'Ali wins, round five.'

When Dunn returned to his hotel, British journalists applauded him. 'Give over,' he said. 'Don't be so soft.' He and Ali had dinner together. Dunn walked away with about £60,000 and what he has always remembered as 'a brilliant, brilliant night'. The following year, Bugner knocked him out in one round at Wembley to take away his British, Commonwealth and European titles. His last fight was a £10,000 payday in Johannesburg against the South African Kallie Knoetze, who beat him in five rounds.

A hotel venture didn't work out and in 1989 he was working on an oil rig when he fell forty feet from a platform and shattered both legs below the knee. It was years before he could walk even a few painful steps. He lives in Scarborough on the North Yorkshire coast. In Bradford, his birthplace, a sports centre was named after him.

E

JIMMY ELLIS

Born: 24 February 1940, Louisville, Kentucky
Full name: James Albert Ellis
Height: 6ft 1in   **Weight at peak:** 197-201lbs (14st 1lb-14st 5lbs)
Fights: 53   **Won:** 40   **Lost:** 12   **Drawn:** 1
KO percentage: 45
Rounds boxed: 341
World champion: 1968-70 (WBA)
World title fights: 3
Career span: 1961-75 (14 years)
KO wins: 24
KO defeats: 4

Jimmy Ellis, the most modest of men, was a long-time sparring partner of Muhammad Ali and emerged from the great man's shadow to hold the World Boxing Association championship.

Ellis, who began his professional career as a middleweight, was a conservative, organised boxer. While a thoroughly good and respectable man, he didn't move fans the way darker souls did. Consequently, he was never given a great deal of credit for his achievements. When he did win the WBA belt, Ali's presence remained – and Smokin' Joe Frazier confused the position further by earning the recognition of the powerful New York State Athletic Commission and their friends around the world.

After Ali's licence to box had been withdrawn in 1967, the WBA tried to find a logical successor and set up an elimination tournament. It was a good idea, but Frazier's backers decided to go their own way, with the support of the New York commission. While Frazier beat Buster Mathis for New York recognition, Ellis came out on top of the WBA 'pile'. In the quarter-final in Houston, Texas, in August 1967, he stopped Leotis Martin, who sustained a horrible gash in the mouth, in the ninth round. In the semi-final in Louisville in December 1967, Ellis out-pointed Oscar Bonavena over twelve rounds, scoring knockdowns in the fourth and tenth. Then he won the vacant WBA championship in Oakland, California, by out-thinking Jerry Quarry over fifteen dull rounds in April 1968. In his first defence in Stockholm he was considered lucky to get a fifteen-round decision over Floyd Patterson. Referee Harold Valan, the sole judge, scored for Ellis by nine rounds to six. Valan said in *Ring* magazine, 'At no time did Patterson, with so much at stake, take the initiative. Floyd backed away for fifteen rounds... Ellis kept flicking and scoring.' *Ring* magazine polled their writers, some of whom watched on television. Nat Fleischer saw it 9-6 Patterson, and overall they came out 4-2-1 in favour of the loser. For ABC, commentator Howard Cosell felt the verdict was an outrage.

Ellis's championship claim ended with a unification fight against Frazier in Madison Square Garden in February 1970. Frazier left hooked him brutally to the canvas in the fourth round and although Jimmy survived to the bell, Angelo Dundee retired him.

As an amateur he was a National Golden Gloves champion and even when they were young he and his wife Marietta (Mary) had four youngsters to feed. He worked as a cement finisher. Early in his career he was a top-class middleweight: in his fourth fight he beat Wilf Greaves on a ten-round majority decision; he lost his unbeaten record to Holley Mims, won a rematch and knocked out Rory Calhoun in one. His middleweight days ended in 1964 with points defeats by Rubin Carter, George Benton and Don Fullmer but by then he had joined Angelo Dundee in Miami and was working as Ali's sparring partner. He picked up plenty of work on Ali undercards – in Lewiston, Las Vegas, Toronto, London and Frankfurt.

After the Frazier defeat, Ellis boxed for five years. In May 1971 he out-boxed George Chuvalo in Toronto, and then collected a decent payday against Ali, who was coming back following his own defeat by Frazier. Ellis believed he could win, but was stopped in the twelfth round. Ali wasn't in his most devilish mood, which was understandable.

Ellis dropped back a level to regroup, put together a string of eight wins but then ran into the runaway truck that was Earnie Shavers in New York in June 1973 and was knocked out in the first round. That defeat seemed to shake everything out of him and he quickly deteriorated into the role of quality stepping stone. He lost decisions to Boone Kirkman, Ron Lyle and Joe Bugner and lost in nine to Frazier in, of all places, Melbourne, Australia. He retired at the age of thirty-five after he caught an accidental thumb from a sparring partner and lost much of the vision in his left eye.

In retirement he led a contented family life in Louisville, trained and managed boxers and from the mid-1980s worked for the Louisville Metropolitan Parks and Recreation Department. He mowed the grass at his local church. He helped with youth groups, senior citizens and the disabled but by the early years of the new century was suffering the effects of his career. He declined an invitation to attend the Mike Tyson-Danny Williams fight in Louisville in 2004 because he could not condone Tyson's hedonistic lifestyle.

JOE ERSKINE

Born: 26 January 1934, Cardiff, Wales
Height: 5ft 11in   **Weight at peak:** 193lbs (13st 11lbs)
Fights: 54   **Won:** 45   **Lost:** 8   **Drawn:** 1
KO percentage: 24
Rounds boxed: 415
World title fights: 0
Career span: 1954-64 (10 years)
KO wins: 13
KO defeats: 6

In his prime Joe Erskine was a beautiful technical boxer with perfect footwork and a dazzling left hand, as he demonstrated when he gave a boxing lesson to the brilliant stylist from New Orleans, Willie Pastrano, at Wembley in February 1959. The quietly spoken, modest Welshman, ABA heavyweight champion in 1953, won the vacant British title with a fifteen-round decision over Johnny Williams at the Maindy Stadium in Cardiff in August 1956. Unfortunately on the back of that his manager, Benny Jacobs, took an ill-advised match against the world-class Cuban, Nino Valdes, at Earl's Court in February 1957. It was Erskine's first fight as British champion – and he was too tense. Valdes smashed him to the canvas twice and the mismatch was stopped.

Erskine retained his title with a fifteen-round decision over Cooper and then won the Empire championship by outscoring the Jamaican Joe Bygraves but, in a European title bid, Ingemar Johansson forced him to retire after thirteen one-sided rounds in Gothenburg. Erskine took a pounding. He lost his British and Empire titles in his next fight to Brian London at White City. For six rounds Erskine was ahead, then a clash of heads in the seventh left him cut and in the eighth he went down on one knee to be counted out. He was an ex-champ at twenty-four. Although he turned it on to beat Pastrano, he was stopped by Cooper three times in British title attempts. He retired in in 1964 when Billy Walker out-worked him over ten rounds. He died of cancer in 1990, aged fifty-six.

ALFREDO EVANGELISTA

Born: 3 December 1954, Montevideo, Uruguay
Height: 6ft 1½in   **Weight at peak:** 209lbs (14st 13lbs)
Fights: 79   **Won:** 62   **Lost:** 13   **Drawn:** 4
KO percentage: 53
Rounds boxed: 469
World title fights: 2
Career span: 1975-88 (13 years)
KO wins: 42
KO defeats: 4

An aggressive, brawling Uruguayan with a powerful punch but poor technique, Alfredo Evangelista made his name by staying in with a poorly prepared, fading Muhammad Ali for fifteen rounds in Landover, Maryland, in May 1977. Ali confused and bemused Evangelista, at one point almost suspending himself from the ropes with his chin hanging out and daring the mop-haired South American to hit him. Ali stopped working for long enough in four rounds to concede them but won the rest to take a unanimous decision by margins of six and seven points. Ali had given away 3,000 tickets to local community groups, which swelled the crowd to 12,000.

Evangelista had no right to share a ring with even the declining Ali, for he had lost his previous fight, on points over eight rounds, to the Italian Lorenzo Zanon. After losing to Ali, Evangelista held the European title in three spells between 1977 and 1987. He was also selected as the opponent for Larry Holmes' first defence of the WBC crown at Caesars Palace, Las Vegas, in November 1978.

Evangelista's slow, rumbling aggression was the perfect foil for Holmes' skills and the champion outclassed him in an educated exhibition in seven rounds.

F

TOMMY FARR

Born: 12 March 1913, Clydach Vale, Tonypandy, Wales
Full name: Thomas George Paul Farr
Died: 1 March 1986, Hove, Sussex, England, aged 72
Height: 6ft   **Weight at peak:** 205lbs (14st 9lbs)
Fights: 197   **Won:** 95   **Lost:** 43   **Drawn:** 22
KO percentage: 7
World title fights: 1

Career span: 1926-53 (27 years)
KO wins: 27
KO defeats: 11

They lit bonfires on the hills above the Rhondda Valley on the night Tommy Farr fought Joe Louis for the world heavyweight title before 40,000 fans in Yankee Stadium, New York. Inside and outside the village hall in Blaenclydach thousands listened to the live radio broadcast on the BBC – and went to their beds convinced their hero was the victim of an American injustice. He wasn't, but Farr, who always admitted he lost fairly, did push Louis for the full fifteen rounds and cemented his reputation as one of the best heavyweights Britain ever produced. Mike Jacobs, who promoted Louis, rang Farr's home in 1940 to set up a rematch but Farr's wife, Monty, explained that Britain was at war and Tommy was serving in the Royal Air Force. 'He didn't seem to understand,' she said.

Farr was born in Blaenclydach, which overlooks Tonypandy, on 12 March 1913 (often wrongly given as 1914). He was one of eight children of a miner and bare-knuckle mountain fighter. Farr's mother died when he was nine. A year later Tommy's father, broken by his wife's death, became too ill to work. At thirteen, in the year of the General Strike, Tommy began boxing professionally in order to add to the family income. By fourteen he was working in the pits and survived an underground explosion within weeks of beginning the job. He stuck it for two years before considering boxing a safer option. By the time he was sixteen he was regularly fighting over ten rounds.

His breakthrough came in January 1936 at the Albert Hall, London, when he upset the former world light-heavyweight champion Tommy Loughran on a controversial ten-round decision. By then Farr was managed by the influential Ted Broadribb, who persuaded promoter Jeff Dickson to use him as an opponent for Loughran, who was the star of the show. Farr seemed to have been out-boxed but finished very strongly in the last two rounds – and received a debatable verdict that sparked sustained booing and jeering in the crowd.

Farr won the British heavyweight title by outworking the champion Ben Foord over fifteen rounds at Harringay Arena – and a month later beat former world champion Max Baer in a twelve-rounder in the same north London stadium. Farr cut Baer badly in a hectic opening round, took the heavy-punching American's big right hands, and used his jab out of his crouching style to take over. He won well. Farr, who always had a solid chin, honed his own style of box-fighting and made up for his lack of a real heavyweight punch with expert ringcraft. He did hit hard enough, however, to knock out the dangerous German Walter Neusel in three rounds in front of the German ambassador Von Ribbentrop and Max Schmeling, who was being considered as Farr's next opponent. That didn't come off. Instead, he took the boat to New York City and fought for the heavyweight championship of the world.

Although he had a frosty relationship with Broadribb, Farr's preparations went perfectly in Long Branch, New Jersey. He was trained by Tom Evans and also brought over his old conditioner Job Churchill. He ignored the American critics, who dismissed him as a bum, refused to be psyched by Louis's reputation and went the full fifteen rounds. The British Boxing Board of Control, incidentally, made themselves look stupid by refusing to recognise the contest as for the world title. They considered it a final eliminator on the grounds that Louis was not champion until he had beaten Schmeling! Farr was cut on both cheeks but never floored, although he admitted he was badly hurt by a right in the eighth. 'I felt as if a thousand red-hot needles were running down my neck,' he said. For the record the scores were all for Louis: 9-6 and 8-5 with two even from the judges and a ridiculous 13-1 with one even from 'house' referee Arthur Donovan.

After rising to such heights at the age of twenty-four, Farr had four more fights in New York and lost them all on points: to Braddock, Baer, Lou Nova and Clarence 'Red' Burman. Back in Britain he ended the career of the superb Canadian Larry Gains with a five-round win before the Second World War closed his career until financial problems forced a short-lived, unsuccessful return in 1950 at the age of thirty-seven. He worked as a columnist for the *Sunday Pictorial* newspaper, then as a salesman and a director of a paint company. He died of cancer on St David's Day, 1 March, 1986.

JESSE FERGUSON

Born: 20 March 1957, Raleigh, North Carolina
Height: 6ft 2in   **Weight at peak:** 224lbs (16st)
Fights: 44   **Won:** 26   **Lost:** 18
KO percentage: 36
Rounds boxed: 334
World title fights: 1
Career span: 1983-99 (16 years)
KO wins: 16
KO defeats: 7

Jesse Ferguson was a top-class journeyman pulled out of the pack to challenge Riddick Bowe for the world title in May 1993. Bowe had beaten Evander Holyfield in a classic battle to win the title six months earlier, had blown away the washed-up Michael Dokes in one and enjoyed a 'world tour', and again wanted an undemanding outing as a showcase in Washington DC.

Ferguson, thirty-six, had upset Ray Mercer on points three months earlier in Madison Square Garden but the victory was marred when a television microphone appeared to catch Mercer trying to persuade Jesse to throw the fight. Mercer was prosecuted but acquitted. Ferguson got himself in shape – which is more than the world champion did. It made no difference. Bowe knocked him down in the first round and put him away only seventeen seconds into the second. Though born in North Carolina, Ferguson was a Philadelphia fighter, trained by Bouie Fisher, who came to prominence later as trainer of undisputed middleweight champion Bernard Hopkins. Nicknamed Thunder or The Boogieman, Ferguson began boxing in 1983 when he was already twenty-five and in May 1985 served notice of his ability with a ten-round majority decision over James 'Buster' Douglas.

When he was chosen as opponent for the nineteen-year-old sensation Mike Tyson in Troy, New York, in February 1986, Ferguson managed to spoil his way into round six before the fight was stopped. Originally, it was announced as a disqualification, though the New York Commission amended that to a stoppage win for Tyson.

Ferguson drifted along below the top rank for years and when he was selected to challenge Bowe had lost four of his previous six. A scandalous match, in fact. Matchmaker Ron Katz said, 'If you looked up the word journeyman in a diction-ary there would be a picture of Jesse Ferguson next to it. He's a guy who goes in, does the best he can, always puts in some quality rounds and usually comes up short. But on a given night he can win a fight he isn't supposed to win.'

After losing to Bowe he won only one of his next eight, including a ter-rible performance when he folded in the first round against Frank Bruno in Birmingham in 1994. He did show pride, though, in lasting the distance with Larry Holmes, Hasim Rahman and Andrew Golota, when nobody would have cared much had he folded against any of them.

LUIS ANGEL FIRPO

Born: 11 October 1894, Junin, Buenos Aires, Argentina
Died: 7 August 1960, Buenos Aires, Argentina, aged 65
Height: 6ft 3in   **Weight at peak:** 216lbs (15st 6lbs)
Fights: 39   **Won:** 33   **Lost:** 6
KO percentage: 66
Rounds boxed: 226
World title fights: 1
Career span: 1917-1936 (19 years)
KO wins: 26
KO defeats: 3

The Wild Bull of the Pampas, Luis Firpo, had one moment of glory – when he let his big arms go like windmill sails to send Jack Dempsey crashing out of the ring in their astonishing battle at the New York Polo Grounds in September 1923. There were eleven knockdowns in three minutes fifty-seven seconds before

Firpo was counted out in round two, with Dempsey touching down in the opening seconds and roaring back to batter the Argentine to the canvas several times. Then Firpo rushed him across the ring and pounded him out of it, backwards on to the ringside press tables. Dempsey got back in, cursing, and before round two was a third of the way through had laid Firpo out face first.

Firpo was from Junin in the Buenos Aires province, the son of an Italian father and Argentine mother who took their family of four children to the capital city when Luis was nine. He fought in Argentina and Uruguay before walking across the Andes to Chile. He stayed long enough to win the South American title, but it was back in Argentina that he twice beat a washed-up Gunboat Smith. In 1922 he travelled to New York to make his fortune. His first big win there was a twelfth-round knockout of Bill Brennan and, in July 1923, Firpo bludgeoned out the forty-two-year-old former champion Jess Willard in eight rounds in Jersey City. Two months later Firpo walked out to fight Dempsey before 82,000 fans at the Polo Grounds in the second million-dollar-gate fight promoted by Tex Rickard.

On the back of his part in one of the most sensational fights of all time, he took in exhibition tours in Canada and Peru. However, though he had created a place for himself as the father of Argentine boxing, the spotlight was already dimming: he came off second best in No-Decision bouts with Harry Wills and Charley Weinert. He drifted along until Arturo Godoy beat him in three rounds in Buenos Aires in 1936.

Firpo invested the money from the Dempsey fight and made it last. He lived on an estate outside Buenos Aires until his death from a heart attack in August 1960 at the age of sixty-five. Schools, roads and even an El Salvadorian soccer team are named after him.

BOB FITZSIMMONS

Born: 26 May 1863, Helston, Cornwall
Full name: Robert James Fitzsimmons
Died: 22 October 1917, Chicago, Illinois, aged 54
Height: 5ft 11¾in   **Weight at peak:** 167lbs (11st 13lbs)
Fights: 88   **Won:** 54   **Lost:** 8   **Drawn:** 7   **No Decisions:** 19
KO percentage: 53
Rounds boxed: 356
World champion: 1897-99
World title fights: 3 (heavyweight only)
Career span: 1883-1914 (31 years)
KO wins: 47
KO defeats: 8

A spindly, pale figure with a broad back and thin legs, Bob Fitzsimmons was called 'a fighting machine on stilts' by one writer wanting to capture his rather jerky but so very effective style. Old films tend to suggest he stood tall, threw awkward-looking punches and just didn't look the way fighters should. He was also known as 'Ruby Robert' because of the rim of red hair that ran around the edge of his bald pate – and because in the sun his freckled skin burned bright pink. He was also the lightest of all the men who have held the heavyweight championship: when he defeated world champion James J. Corbett in the rarefied air of Carson City, Nevada, in March 1897, Fitzsimmons weighed only 167lbs (11st 13lbs). That is inside the super-middleweight limit today. Fitzsimmons also held the middle-weight and, late in his career, the light-heavyweight championships, and for many years was the only man to have held world titles in three weight divisions.

Fitzsimmons was born in Helston, Cornwall, and was a child when his family emigrated to New Zealand. The rest of his upbringing took place in Timaru, a coastal town on South Island. A blacksmith, he learned to box under the legendary bare-knuckle boxer Jem Mace, then moved to Australia, where it was rumoured he took a dive against Jem Hall in 1890. Years later Fitzsimmons said in his naivety he threw the fight because he was told if he didn't he wouldn't be paid. He sailed to the United States two months later.

He won his first world title, at middleweight, in New Orleans in January 1891, when he stopped Jack 'Nonpareil' Dempsey in the thirteenth round. It was a one-sided fight. Fitzsimmons retained the middleweight championship in two rounds against Dan Creedon in New Orleans in 1894 but by then was thinking about fighting Corbett for the heavyweight title. When Corbett announced his retire-ment, Fitzsimmons and Peter Maher met on the Texas bank of the Rio Grande near Langtry in 1896 to determine Gentleman Jim's successor, but when Bob blew away Maher in ninety-five seconds, Corbett decided to 'unretire'. Fitzsimmons' claim to the championship was denied.

Fitzsimmons lost a bitter, foul-filled fight with Tom Sharkey in San Francisco in December 1896 when the referee – the lawman Wyatt Earp – disqualified him for a low punch in round eight. Fitzsimmons took Earp to court, accusing him of fixing the decision, but the case was thrown out. Three months later it became irrelevant – at the age of thirty-three, Ruby Robert was world heavy-weight champion following a sensational fourteenth-round knockout of Corbett in Carson City, the gold rush town high in the Nevada mountains. In a specially erected but sparsely populated wooden arena, Fitzsimmons survived a sixth-round knockdown and an early-rounds boxing lesson to wear down Corbett with body attacks. Fitzsimmons' redoubtable wife Rose famously encouraged him, 'Hit him in the slats, Bob!' In the fourteenth he landed a short left hook to the pit of the stomach and Corbett went down for the count.

Just as his predecessor had done, Fitzsimmons exploited the heavyweight crown by hitting the vaudeville circuit. In the two years that followed he had only an exhibition knockout over a blacksmith in a town called Leadville. Finally, he agreed to defend against James J. Jeffries in Coney Island, New York, and on a summer's day in 1899 he was badly knocked out in eleven rounds by the young giant from California.

At thirty-six, Fitzsimmons might easily have retired, but felt he had more in him yet, put it about that he felt as if he had been somehow drugged in or before the bout, and in July 1902 had a rematch with Jeffries, who was now well established as an active champion. At thirty-nine, Fitzsimmons' skills were still sharp but his legs were not what they were – and he had damaged his left hand in training. For several rounds he smashed punches into Jeffries' face, ripped open cuts on his eyebrows and broke his nose, but the big man kept on coming. Finally, with his face swollen and his eyes closing, the champion found a body shot that put Fitzsimmons down for the count. That was the end of the Cornishman as a heavyweight contender but in November 1903 in San Francisco he out-pointed George Gardner, an Irishman from Massachusetts, over twenty rounds for the new-fangled light-heavyweight crown. Gardner was floored seven times.

Fitzsimmons lost the light-heavyweight title in thirteen rounds to Philadelphia Jack O'Brien in December 1905, by which time he was forty-two years old. Two years later Jack Johnson took only two rounds to knock him out and in an ill-conceived attempt to win the Australian heavyweight title in December 1909 he lost in twelve to Bill Lang.

Four-times married, Fitzsimmons was a gregarious, egotistical man who enjoyed a party and his celebrity status. He also knew his boxing, as is illustrated by a 1914 letter to the man who would eventually found and edit, for fifty years, *Ring* magazine, Nat Fleischer: 'The cavemen of the ring are extinct. Champions such as we had when I was in my prime are gone, never again to return.... Fighting, like all other sports, is reaching out along lines of improvement...You'll find as the years pass that fighting will become more and more scientific and championships will change hands on points and not on knockouts.'

Fitzsimmons died of pneumonia in Chicago at the age of fifty-four. Like so many other great champions he had lost almost all of his money. An organisation called the American Board of Boxing Control paid for his funeral and his grave and a stonemason provided his headstone free of charge.

JIM FLYNN

Born: 24 December 1879, Hoboken, New Jersey
Other names: Andrew Haymes, Andrew Chiariglione
Died: 12 April 1935, Los Angeles, aged 55
Height: 5ft 9½in   **Weight at peak:** 175-182lbs (12st 7lbs-13st)
Fights: 115   Won: 54   Lost: 49   Drawn: 18   No Decisions: 4
KO percentage: 34
Rounds boxed: 1,020

World title fights: 2
Career span: 1901-25 (24 years)
KO wins: 33
KO defeats: 20

Jim Flynn fought twice for the world heavyweight title and knocked out Jack Dempsey in one round. Nicknamed 'Fireman' because he used to work stoking the fires of rail engines, he had a reputation for being a mean-spirited, dirty fighter. Originally from Hoboken, New Jersey, but fighting mostly out of Colorado early in his career, he had done very little of note when he was picked to box Tommy Burns for the heavyweight championship in Los Angeles in October 1906. Burns stopped him in fifteen rounds. The following year he improved with an eighteenth-round knockout of the former light-heavyweight champion George Gardner and a sixth-round win over the Australian Bill Squires. However Jack Johnson, already the best heavyweight in the world, toyed with him and knocked him out in round eleven in San Francisco in November 1907.

Flynn was knocked out twice in 1908, in nine by Al Kaufman and in one by Sam Langford. He kept active but made no impression the following year (when for some reason best known to himself, Stanley Ketchel turned down $5,000 to box him in Los Angeles). In February 1910 he got the better of Langford in a ten-round No-Decision bout, recovering from being shaken up in the second and third rounds to 'win' clearly, but in a rematch the following month Langford knocked him out in the eighth. Then Flynn found a bit of form with seven consecutive knockout wins in 1911, the best of which was a tenth-round revenge win over Al Kaufman.

By July 1912 there were no obvious (white) takers for the heavyweight title and so Johnson defended against Flynn in Las Vegas, New Mexico, much to the consternation of the governor and religious groups, who denounced the event as a disgrace to the state. Flynn didn't train properly, concentrating his efforts on sharpening up his weaponry of fouls on a succession of unwitting sparring part-ners. The old middleweight champion Tommy Ryan walked out of Flynn's camp in disgust, declaring that he had no chance and was 'hog fat'. He predicted the Fireman would lose by disqualification. A 17,000-capacity arena was constructed with the Las Vegas police insisting they would escort out of the vicinity any strays, hobos or ne'er-do-wells. Around 4,000 people paid at the gate, grossing around $35,000, of which Johnson took $31,000. The promoter, Jack Curley, lost heavily. Flynn, out-boxed and cut over both eyes, could make little impression on the bigger, infinitely more talented man, but fouled and mauled his way to the ninth when he was disqualified for a blatant head butt. He was literally jumping up and down trying to ram his head into Johnson's face!

Two fights later he was knocked out in sixteen rounds by one of the new genera-tion of 'White Hopes', Luther McCarty, in Vernon, California, in December 1912. He was considered washed-up in August 1913 when Gunboat Smith knocked him out in five. Carl Morris and Fred Fulton both beat him, too. However, he injected some sudden life into his career in the backwater of Murray, Utah, in February 1917 when he upset the young Jack Dempsey in two minutes of the first round in front of around 400 fans. Dempsey was down four times, then his elder brother Bernie threw in the towel. A year later Dempsey avenged the embarrassing defeat by knocking out the by now thirty-eight-year-old Fireman in the opening session. Flynn plodded away for a little longer and still had enough left to stop the future world middleweight champion Tiger Flowers in five rounds in Mexico City in September 1923. He twice lost to an equally aged Sam Langford during the same Mexican stay. He retired in 1925.

Flynn died in Los Angeles on 12 April 1935, aged fifty-five.

ZORA FOLLEY

Born: 27 May 1932, Dallas, Texas
Died: 1972, Tucson, Arizona, aged 40
Height: 6ft 1in   **Weight at peak:** 200lbs (14st 4lbs)
Fights: 96   **Won:** 79   **Lost:** 11   **Drawn:** 6
KO percentage: 45
Rounds boxed: 672
World title fights: 1
Career span: 1953-70 (17 years)
KO wins: 44
KO defeats: 7

Family man Zora Folley was one of the best heavyweights of the late 1950s and early 1960s but had to wait until he was almost thirty-five before his world title opportunity came… against a peak Muhammad Ali.

Folley was outclassed in a one-sided fight. Ali dropped him in the fourth and knocked him out in the seventh before a modest turnout of 13,708 fans at Madison Square Garden on the snowy night of 22 March 1967. It was Ali's last fight before his suspension for refusing to be conscripted for the Vietnam War – and the first heavyweight championship fight in the Garden since Ezzard Charles beat Lee Oma sixteen years before. Folley tried but couldn't do anything with Ali and while it was right to celebrate the supremacy of a brilliant champion, it was all a little sad. At least Zora came out of it with a decent payday: fifteen per cent of gate receipts, plus $25,000 from ancillary rights. As ticket prices were high, the receipts were a Garden record for the old arena on West 49th Street in Manhattan – $244,471. That brought Folley's financial reward to $61,670, which softened the blow to his pride.

Surprisingly, judge Tony Castellano gave Folley three of the first six rounds to score the fight even, while referee Johnny Lobianco and judge Frank Forbes had it 4-2 to the champion. Whatever the mathematics, Ali looked to have the fight under control from start to finish. In the ring afterwards the beaten challenger's young son, Zora jnr, stood at his father's side crying. Ali, who had treated Folley with great respect throughout, called the boy over and consoled him by telling him his father's chance had simply come too late and there was nothing to be ashamed of. Ali himself had selected Folley as the opponent because he had read about what a good fighter he used to be and thought it right to give him the payday.

The year before, Folley's manager, Bill Swift, had said, 'If ever a guy got a raw deal in sports, it's Zora Folley. He's been one of the undeniably fine heavyweights in the world for years but... I suppose he hasn't whined enough or gotten his name in the papers enough, or been arrested enough.'

Folley, a father of nine, was a minister who built his own church. Folley was born in Dallas, Texas, on 27 May 1932, and raised in Chandler, Arizona. He lied about his age to join the Army at sixteen, and had seventy-two amateur bouts in the services. He served in the Korean War as an infantryman, was given five battle stars for his part in fighting around Pusan, Inchon and a place known simply as Bloody Ridge. 'I can't get nervous any more,' he said later. 'I left all that back there.' At one point he also suffered from frostbite after a sixteen-mile retreat and was flown to Tokyo for treatment, which was just in time to prevent gangrene.

He made his professional debut in Los Angeles in September 1953 and quickly became a quality prospect. He twice stopped Howard King, lost an early fight when he was hampered by ribs broken in sparring, and out-boxed Nino Valdes to move into world class. During the rest of the decade, Folley lost only once, on a ten-round verdict to Henry Cooper in London (subsequently avenged in a couple of rounds), and the record shows he could and should have boxed for the world championship at any time from 1959 onwards. He knocked out Pete Rademacher, the 1956 Olympic champion who, of course, boxed Floyd Patterson for the title in his pro debut. Folley took out the Olympian in four rounds in Los Angeles in July 1958. He looked unlucky to draw with Eddie Machen in a disappointing twelve-rounder before 12,000 fans at the Cow Palace in San Francisco, and unanimously out-pointed Machen in a return two years later.

When pressure was put on Cus D'Amato to allow Patterson to defend against Folley, the wily manager refused. He claimed Folley was controlled by the International Boxing Club and George Parnassus – and D'Amato would do business with neither. Swift was furious. 'Folley and I are independent of anyone, except my partner, newspaperman Al Fenn, who has a ten per cent interest in Zora,' he said. 'No one in the IBC, nor Parnassus, has any agreement with us – nor do they have any financial interest.'

Folley admitted that when Patterson was involved in his three-fight series with Ingemar Johansson from 1959 until 1961, when nobody else could get a look in, he lost heart. In July 1960 he was beaten in three rounds by Sonny Liston. His detractors can also point out that he won and lost against Doug Jones and lost on points to Ernie Terrell. That said, he out-pointed George Chuvalo, Oscar Bonavena and

Bob Foster, and drew in Germany with Karl Mildenberger. After Ali knocked him out, Brian London, Bonavena and rising Californian Mac Foster all beat him.

In the summer of 1972, two years after he retired, Zora died in an accident at a motel in Tucson. He suffered fatal head injuries in an apparent fall on the side of the swimming pool in what was described as 'horseplay' with friends.

BEN FOORD

Born: 21 January 1913, Vriede, Orange Free State, South Africa
Died: 29 September 1942, Ladysmith, South Africa, aged 29
Height: 6ft 2¾in   **Weight at peak:** 205lbs (14st 9lbs)
Fights: 59   **Won:** 40   **Lost:** 15   **Drawn:** 4
KO percentage: 37
World title fights: 0
Career span: 1932-40 (8 years)
KO wins: 22
KO defeats: 5

South African Ben Foord held the British and Empire titles and might, had he understood the need for dedication and discipline, have gone onto bigger things.

A warm, generous man from a rural background in Orange Free State and raised in Ladysmith, Natal, he was spotted by his first manager, Louis Walsh, while working as a lifeguard on the treacherous beaches around Durban. Foord learned quickly, won the South African trials for the Los Angeles Olympics of 1932, but to his disgust was not selected. The following year he moved to London to make his fortune as a professional fighter. He made a great impression with his courage in a thirteenth-round defeat by the Welshman Jack Petersen, then broke through in November 1935 when he out-pointed, somewhat luckily, Larry Gains, over twelve rounds in Leicester.

Out of the ring he had a crazy streak. For a bet, he swam the Thames at Windsor Bridge, where the currents were notoriously strong, in less than a minute. There was also a car crash, in which Walsh was seriously hurt, and a rather embarrassing court case involving a gambling debt. His brother, Stephen, said Ben saw boxing as easy money and a good way of impressing women.

In the ring he outscored former light-heavyweight champion Tommy Loughran, beat Gains again (deservedly), and won the British and Empire heavyweight titles in August 1936 with a three-round revenge win over Petersen. That night, before a 24,000 crowd at the Tigers' rugby ground in Leicester, was his peak. He lost to Walter Neusel at Harringay and his career spiralled downwards rapidly. Tommy Farr took away his British and Empire titles at Harringay Arena with a fifteen-round decision in March 1937 – and a desperate attempt to make an international impression led only to a gruesome, prolonged ninth-round stoppage defeat by Max

Baer and then a points loss to another former heavyweight king, Max Schmeling, in Hamburg.

Neusel beat him again, so did Eddie Phillips, and by the summer of 1939 he had returned to South Africa. Married with a baby daughter, he joined the army as a sergeant-training instructor based in Potchefstroom.

Foord died in 1942 when, larking about in front of his understandably nervous wife while home for the weekend, he shot himself in the face. He was only twenty-nine.

GEORGE FOREMAN

Born: 10 January 1949, Marshall, Texas
Height: 6ft 3½in   **Weight:** 1970s: 220lbs (15st 10lbs); 1990s: 250lbs (17st 12lbs)
Fights: 81   **Won:** 76   **Lost:** 5
KO percentage: 83
Rounds boxed: 349
World champion: 1973-74, 1994-1995 (WBA & IBF)
World title fights: 7
Career span: 1969-97 (28 years)
KO wins: 68
KO defeats: 1

In his youthful prime he was a menacing, robotic monster from a horror movie and in genial middle-age he was the Punchin' Preacher, as American as apple pie, a fun-loving, burger-munching role model for greybeards and baldies everywhere: George Foreman, the boxing treasure.

It was quite a transition. Foreman, from a poor home in Marshall just outside Houston, Texas, was a troubled youth who found a direction through boxing. At nineteen, he biffed his way to the Olympic Games heavyweight gold medal in Mexico City. This was the games when sprinters Tommie Smith and John Carlos outraged the American establishment with a black-gloved protest on the medal rostrum during *The Star Spangled Banner*. To the growing numbers of anti-war demonstrators and to the Civil Rights cause, they were heroes. When his turn came to have his gold medal hung around his neck Foreman, who was just grateful for his opportunities, waved a miniature Stars and Stripes.

As a professional he piled up victories, most of them without breaking sweat, until he was in a position to challenge Smokin' Joe Frazier for the championship in Kingston, Jamaica, in January 1973. His best win up to then was a third-round destruction of the Canadian George Chuvalo in Madison Square Garden in August 1970. However, the cagey Argentine veteran Gregorio Peralta had twice given him fits. Foreman won on points the first time and caught up with Goyo for a tenth-round stoppage second time around. It was a huge leap from the likes of Ted Gullick, Miguel Paez and Terry Sorrell to trading blows with Frazier, but Foreman, only twelve days after his twenty-fourth birthday, steamrollered Frazier inside two rounds. Referee Arthur Mercante waved it over as Frazier struggled to his feet after the sixth knockdown.

Financial wrangles prevented Foreman from working in the United States. In September 1973 he travelled to Tokyo and knocked out a Puerto Rican, Joe 'King' – cruelly dubbed 'Only Joking' – Roman in one round. In Caracas, Venezuela, in March 1974, he nearly decapitated Ken Norton, the former Marine who had broken Muhammad Ali's jaw the previous year. It was all over inside two rounds. Then, in the heat and chaos of Kinshasa, Zaire, Foreman was brought down to earth by Muhammad Ali's magical ring brain in October 1974. The fight was postponed for a month when Foreman was cut in sparring, and perhaps he went stale. Others said he simply believed his own publicity and refused to accept that Ali could handle his power. He had no 'plan B'. After seven rounds of whaling away, Foreman tired – and in the eighth, Ali pulled the miracle, manoeuvring swiftly off the ropes and blasting a quick combination to Foreman's head. The champion was disorientated and more right hands pitched him forward to the canvas. He rolled over but did not get up. Ali had recreated his own legend and destroyed a myth.

Foreman was out of the ring for more than a year, then had a marvellous war with Ron Lyle in Las Vegas in January 1976. Both were down twice but it was Lyle who was counted out in round five. He stopped Frazier in a rematch in June 1976, but Joe was washed-up by then. The first phase of his career ended when he was knocked down in the twelfth round and out-pointed by Jimmy Young in a title eliminator in Puerto Rico. In the shower afterwards Foreman had a 'Damascus Road' meeting with God. He gave up boxing and began to preach the Gospel on the streets. In 1981 he built the Church of the Lord Jesus Christ in Rosemary Lane, Houston, and said, 'This is the only thing I've ever done with all my heart.' He ignored boxing, didn't know a thing about it, until he was persuaded to spar with a marine champion in a public engagement. He did it for fun, but it turned a little nasty when the marine belted him on the head, and he found himself putting the serviceman in his place.

He returned to the ring, ostensibly to help his church funds, in 1987 after a break of ten years. He enjoyed himself – and astonishingly put together a run of nineteen wins before they matched him with Gerry Cooney in Atlantic City in January 1990. When critics pointed out that Foreman was slow, Archie Moore, who had trained him in his youth and was still around the camp, pointed out, 'That makes no difference. George didn't have any speed to lose.' Foreman won in two rounds. In April 1991 he challenged Evander Holyfield for the world title in Atlantic City. The crowds came out to watch him try, and most of them were on his side. At the time Holyfield was perceived as boring. Someone said watching him was as exciting as watching hairs grow on big George's shaven head.

Foreman lost to a faster, sharper, obviously younger champion but at the final bell was still standing. 'I proved forty isn't a death sentence,' he beamed.

He finished a points winner over Alex Stewart but with an eye closed. Then he lost on points to Tommy Morrison, who chose to out-box him on the outside. He seemed to be drifting into retirement, then challenged Michael Moorer in Las Vegas for the WBA and IBF versions of the title. Amazingly, wearing red shorts that echoed his glory days, he knocked out Moorer with a booming right hand in the tenth round. He was forty-five years old.

He considered himself old enough to do what he wanted by then, and not kow-tow to the whims of the ruling bodies. Accordingly, he sniffed at the WBA instruction to box Don King's veteran Tony Tucker and was stripped of the belt. Then, when he seemed to have lost to the sturdy, hard-working German Axel Schulz, in Las Vegas in April 1995, the unpredictable Nevada judges gave him a majority points win: 115-113 twice, 114-114. The IBF ordered a rematch, but George ignored them. Therefore, they stripped him as well. Instead, claiming a couple of minor titles and declaring himself the linear champion, he laboured to wins over unbeaten but unremarkable fighters in Crawford Grimsley and Lou Savarese, before dropping a much-criticised majority decision to another young pretender, Shannon Briggs, in Atlantic City in November 1997. While the judges and the New Jersey Commission were put under severe scrutiny, George took it all with a smile and at last, at the age of forty-eight, wandered off into the sunset.

He made a separate fortune by putting his name to a healthy eating grill, and for several years he continued to work as an analyst for Home Box Office, but at the end of 2003 said he was giving that up to spend more time with his family. He had eight or nine children, at least four of whom were called George!

SCOTT FRANK

Born: 30 March 1958, Oakland, New Jersey
Height: 6ft 2in   **Weight at peak:** 211lbs (15st 1lb)
Fights: 25   **Won:** 23   **Lost:** 1   **Drawn:** 1
KO percentage: 64
Rounds boxed: 131
World title fights: 1
Career span: 1978-97 (19 years)
KO wins: 16
KO defeats: 1

Untried, untested one-time amateur international Scott Frank was thrown to Larry Holmes in a championship fight at Harrah's in Atlantic City in 1983. For four rounds he was easily out-boxed but tried to make a fight of it. Then in the fifth he caught a thumb in the eye as Holmes let the punches roll with Frank backed up to the ropes

and, in agony, he dropped down, claiming a foul. Referee Tony Perez didn't want to
know about that and shortly afterwards the fight was stopped.

The Holmes camp knew what they were hiring. Frank's last four wins had
come on points. The biggest names he had beaten were the veterans Chuck
Wepner and Ron Stander. He had drawn with Renaldo Snipes.

Frank boxed only twice more after the anguish and bitterness of his title bid:
in 1987 he knocked out the notorious loser Stan 'The Animal' Johnson in one
round in Crystal City, just outside Washington DC; then, ten years later at the age
of thirty-nine, he stopped Derek Amos in five in Asbury Park, New Jersey.

JOE FRAZIER

Born: 12 January 1944, Beaufort, South Carolina
Full name: Joseph William Frazier
Height: 5ft 11½in   **Weight at peak:** 205-210lbs (14st 9lbs-15st)
Fights: 37   **Won:** 32   **Lost:** 4   **Drawn:** 1
KO percentage: 72
Rounds boxed: 214
World champion: 1968-73
World title fights: 12
Career span: 1965-81 (16 years)
KO wins: 27
KO defeats: 3

On a magical night in Madison Square Garden on 8 March 1971, Smokin' Joe
Frazier out-fought, wore down and out-pointed Muhammad Ali to prove he was
the best heavyweight in the world. He and Ali never liked each other, but they
needed and fed off each other's talents. Ali's personality and longevity as a fighter
took him to heights Frazier could not achieve and, of course, wins in their second and third epic battles. Frazier's reputation was also dented when George
Foreman trounced him so brutally to take away his world title in 1973 but he
admitted years later that once he had proved how good he was by taking away
Ali's unbeaten record, some of the hunger went out of him.

Frazier was born in Beaufort County, South Carolina. His parents worked ten
acres of dry farmland where only cotton and melons would grow. They also toiled
as hired help on the better lands of the white farmers. When he was fifteen Joe took
a greyhound bus to New York, worked in a Coca-Cola plant, in construction, did
his share of street living and moved on to Philadelphia. In 1962 he began training at
the Police Athletic League gym to lose weight. He had trained on a heavy bag as a
child, but in Philadelphia, under the guidance of Duke Dugent and Yancey Durham,
he not only shed 40lbs of blubber but made the Olympic team for Tokyo in 1964
– when Buster Mathis, who had out-pointed him in the trials, pulled out with a

broken hand. By then Joe had married his childhood sweetheart, Florence, and had set up home with her and their son Marvis. By day, he worked in a slaughterhouse.

In the semi-finals he broke his left thumb but told no one and won the gold on a 3–2 split over Hans Huber of Germany. When he returned to Philadelphia he needed two operations but worked in the gym – alongside, incidentally, world-class middleweights Bennie Briscoe, George Benton and Stan 'Kitten' Hayward. At first he failed to attract sponsors and took whatever jobs he could get – he earned $2.50 an hour with a removal firm, less as a church janitor. His pro debut in August 1965, a one-round win over Woody Goss, netted $125. After four wins, a group of businessmen formed the Cloverlay Syndicate, put him on a salary, gave him a nominal job and a solid financial deal from his fights. In September 1966, only thirteen months after his pro debut, he became world class by out-pointing Oscar Bonavena over ten rounds in New York. It was desperately close, with Frazier floored twice in the second round and eventually winning a split decision. Referee Mark Conn scored 6–4 Frazier, judge Joe Eppy had it 5–4–1 Frazier and judge Nick Gamboli saw it 5–5 in rounds, but with the edge to Bonavena on the weird countback system. In those days no extra points were given for knockdowns. If they had been, Frazier would have lost.

Two months later Frazier improved again, wearing down Eddie Machen for a tenth-round stoppage in Los Angeles. Then he beat Doug Jones in six and in July 1967 stopped George Chuvalo in four. His backers ignored the WBA's elimination tournament and instead negotiated backing from the New York State Athletic Commission for a shot at their version of the title against his old amateur rival Mathis.

In March 1968, Frazier destroyed the giant Mathis with sledgehammer left hooks in eleven rounds at the new Madison Square Garden. He destroyed Manuel Ramos of Mexico in two rounds and in December 1968 clearly out-pointed Bonavena before a disappointing crowd at the Philadelphia Spectrum. In April 1969 the no-hoper Dave Zyglewicz was blown away in a round, but in June before a 16,570 crowd at the Garden, Frazier destroyed Jerry Quarry with a stoppage on the advice of the doctor at the end of round seven. The Californian could no longer see out of his swollen right eye and could not see Frazier's left hooks coming. Afterwards Jimmy Ellis, the WBA champion, and Frazier exchanged words over the ropes to set up their unification fight.

And before 18,079 fans on the night of 16 February 1970, Frazier's rolling, relentless aggression and speed was too much for Ellis. In round four Ellis went down twice, the second time almost on the bell. He got up and wobbled back to his corner. Angelo Dundee wouldn't let him take any more.

Three weeks after Ali's comeback win over Quarry in Atlanta, Frazier defended his world title with a murderous second-round knockout of the light-heavyweight champion Bob Foster in Detroit. He was at the top of his game. The so-called Fight of the Century was made for Madison Square Garden on 8 March 1971. Ringside seats were $150, each man was guaranteed $2.5 million, and in addition to the millions who watched this amazing hour of sporting history unfold on closed-circuit screens around the world the Garden buzzed with a sell-out crowd of 20,455 that provided a gate of $1,352,952. It was the first million-dollar gate since the rematch between Joe Louis and Billy Conn a quarter of a century earlier and the fifth highest live gate in history. Ancillaries are believed to have raised the total receipts to $20 million.

Frazier was fresher, stronger, quicker and hit harder. For four rounds he worked the body to slow Ali's legs, then mostly switched his rumbling attacks to the head. Ali won rounds – the fifth and in particular the ninth, when he had Joe bleeding from the nose and mouth and rocking – but not enough of them. He hit Frazier with jabs and combinations solid enough to raise grotesque swellings on Smokin' Joe's face. The right side of Ali's jaw was also hugely swollen, even before it was further damaged by a left hook that floored him in the last round. He slumped to the canvas, but showed the instinct and heart of a champion to get up and fight on to the final bell. The turning point for Frazier was the eleventh round when he hurt Ali with a thudding left hook and the former champion had to hang on desperately, his knees dipping. At the end of the round the ringside doctor was so alarmed by Ali's body language that he examined him without the invitation of referee Arthur Mercante. The decision for Frazier was unanimous: 8-6-1 in rounds from Mercante, 11-4 from judge Bill Recht and 9-6 from Artie Aidala. Both went to hospital – and Frazier remained for six days because as well as mental and physical exhaustion he had kidney problems. Frazier said he didn't think Ali would want a rematch, but of course there were two more to come.

Smokin' Joe enjoyed a European tour with his soul band The Knockouts, had comfortable defences in mismatches with Terry Daniels and Ron Stander, then lost the title, bludgeoned to the canvas six times in two rounds by the unbeaten George Foreman in Kingston, Jamaica. Six months later Frazier floored and out-pointed Joe Bugner in a hard, competitive twelve-rounder at Earl's Court, London, but in January 1974 lost the return with Ali on points over twelve rounds in Madison Square Garden. He was badly shaken in the second round and well beaten.

A fifth-round stoppage of Jerry Quarry checked the slide (Joe Louis refereed) and then he wore down Jimmy Ellis in nine in Melbourne. The third, epic fight with Ali was in Manila on 1 October 1975. Both had gone back, but still had enough left to take each other to unbelievable limits. Ali survived Frazier's ferocity to outlast him. After the fourteenth round Eddie Futch, Frazier's chief second following the death of Yancey Durham, told his man, 'Sit down, son, it's over. Nobody will ever forget what you did here today.'

Just as they had made each other, Frazier and Ali finished each other. Neither should have boxed again. Both did. Frazier, looking nothing like the Smokin' Joe of his youth because he fought with a shaven head, was stopped in five by Foreman and quit. Against the wishes of his family he came back in December

1981, when he was nearly thirty-eight, and laboured to a ten-round draw with Floyd Cummings in Chicago. That really was the end.

In 1976 Frazier had bought the old Cloverlay gym on North Broad Street, Philadelphia and he turned to training, including his eldest son Marvis – who would go on to box Larry Holmes and Mike Tyson – and Marvis's brother Hector, as well as a nephew or two. Marvis eventually took over as head trainer – and in 2002 his sister Jacqueline Frazier-Lyde boxed Laila Ali, daughter of Muhammad, over eight rounds in Verona, New York, in a bout billed to commemmorate, or exploit, the thirtieth anniversary of that wonderful night in the Garden when Smokin' Joe fought The Greatest and won.

FRED FULTON

Born: 19 April 1891, Blue Rapids, Kansas
Died: 7 July 1973, aged 82
Height: 6ft 5in   **Weight at peak:** 215lbs (15st 5lbs)
Fights: 113   **Won:** 85   **Lost:** 18   **Drawn:** 4   **No Decisions:** 6
KO percentage: 63
Rounds boxed: 498
World title fights: 0
Career span: 1913-33 (20 years)
KO wins: 72
KO defeats: 10

In the reigns of champions Jack Johnson and Jess Willard, big Fred Fulton might have boxed for the title, had opportunities been more readily available. Billed as the Giant of the North – and more prosaically the Sepulpa Plasterer – Fulton was born in Blue Rapids, Kansas, but lived in Minnesota. In Johnson's time as champion Fulton lost twice on fouls to Carl Morris, but beat Arthur Pelkey and Jim Flynn. By then Johnson had taken the title to Europe. Then, when Willard wore the crown, the 6ft 5in Fulton used his bulk to wear down Sam Langford in 1917, and then beat Morris on a sixth-round foul in a disgraceful brawl in Canton, Ohio. The idea was that the winner should box Willard, but in effect Fulton and Morris disqualified themselves by their disregard for the rules.

He stopped Gunboat Smith and Frank Moran. However, when he took on the rapidly rising Jack Dempsey in Harrison, New Jersey, in July 1918, Fred was blown away in eighteen seconds of the opening round. And once Dempsey destroyed Willard to win the championship a year later Fulton was out of the picture altogether. Even though Fulton had a good run of form, a return was unmarketable. Harry Wills knocked Fulton out in three rounds in Newark, New Jersey, in July 1920 to end any dwindling ideas Fred might have had of boxing Dempsey.

Fulton still won more than he lost, but then shamed himself by taking part in a fixed fight in Culver City, California, in November 1924. He took a dive in thirty-five seconds against Tony Fuente – after telling his friends not to bet on him. He was arrested briefly and, while he was not jailed, the episode destroyed his reputation. Fulton died in Park Rapids, Minnesota, in July 1973, aged eighty-two.

G

LARRY GAINS

Born: 12 December 1900, Toronto, Canada
Full name: Lawrence Samuel Gaines
Died: 26 July 1983, Cologne, Germany, aged 82
Height: 6ft 1½in   **Weight at peak:** 190-200lbs (13st 8lbs-14st 4lbs)
Fights: 146   **Won:** 116   **Lost:** 23   **Drawn:** 5   **No Contests:** 2
KO percentage: 43
Rounds boxed: 1,011
World title fights: 0
Career span: 1923-42 (19 years)
KO wins: 63
KO defeats: 14

When he was in his seventies, Larry Gains released his autobiography, *The Impossible Dream*. Its title pointed the finger at the racial prejudice that prevented him, and a handful of other top-class black heavyweights, boxing for the championship of the world.

Ironically, Gains' boyhood hero was Jack Johnson, the first black heavyweight to hold the world title – and it was the volatile public reaction to Johnson's controversial six-and-a-half-year reign that made promoters reluctant to allow other black fighters to box for the championship. It was grossly unfair, of course, but the situation existed for more than two decades before Joe Louis was approved as 'proper material' and allowed the opportunity to take the title away from James J. Braddock. By then, however, it was 1937 and for generations of boxers – Sam Langford, Joe Jeannette, Harry Wills and Larry Gains the prime examples – it was too late. Even then, of twenty-five defences made over twelve years, Louis fought only two black challengers: John Henry Lewis, the light-heavyweight champion who apart from being too light was virtually blind in one eye, and Jersey Joe Walcott, who boxed him twice, after the Second World War when the sporting world as a whole was at long last beginning to open up to athletes whatever their creed or colour.

Gains's prime was between 1928 and 1932, when he lost only one – a decision to Chuck Wiggins in Buffalo – of more than forty professional fights. During his career he knocked out Max Schmeling in two rounds in Germany and out-pointed Primo Carnera in London, but he didn't get even a hint of a shot at either man once they became world champion. True, Gains only rarely boxed in the United States, which was a major tactical error, especially in the wake of his win over Carnera, but those who needed to know knew well enough who he was.

As a twelve-year-old boy in Toronto he met Jack Johnson, saw Jack Dempsey in a vaudeville show and the legendary middleweight champion Harry Greb. Gains toyed with the idea of boxing in the 1924 Olympic Games in Paris but instead turned professional in London. His debut at the Blackfriars Ring in London in June 1923 was a disaster: he was thrown in with seasoned middleweight Frank Moody and lost in five rounds. Three times in 1924 alone he was stopped – in Paris, Stockholm and Cologne – but he fought wherever he could to scrape a liv-ing. Even in these lean years he had charisma: Georges Carpentier liked him and Ernest Hemingway visited him in his dressing room.

On a Sunday afternoon in Cologne in August 1925 Gains demolished a young prospect named Max Schmeling inside two rounds. Back in North America, a sixth-round stoppage by George Godfrey in Buffalo in November 1926 suggested that, for all his skills, he didn't have the punch resistance to reach the top. This was, after all, the sixth time he had lost inside the distance. Today such a conclusion might be correct, but in those days when boxing control was at a minimum, com-munication was poor, strokes were pulled and fighters like Gains worked pretty much alone, defeats didn't have the same impact. He knocked out Soldier Jones in five rounds to win the Canadian title in February 1927 and the following year beat Godfrey in a rematch on a third-round foul (a low blow) for the 'Coloured' championship. Between 1929 and 1931 he won twenty-four consecutive fights, including a second-round knockout of Phil Scott for the British Empire title in an open-air fight before 30,000 people on the Welford Road rugby ground in Leicester, the Midlands city that was his home for several years. By then he was managed by Harry Levene, who generations later became the biggest promoter in the country.

In May 1932 he scored his famous ten-round points win over Primo Carnera at White City, London. A crowd of 62,000 turned out to watch Gains concede 70lbs to the Ambling Alp and hand him a boxing lesson. So many fans wanted to shake his hand and pat him on the back it took ten minutes for Gains to get back to his dressing room. Back in Leicester thousands gathered to see his train steam in – and the Mayor gave him an official greeting.

The adulation of ordinary folk is a fine thing but Gains needed to go on from there to a shot at the world title. With hindsight he and Levene should have taken the next boat to New York. Even when they were offered a fight with Ernie Schaaf they declined, feeling it wasn't a big enough opportunity.

In his autobiography Gains seemed to admit he was comfortable with a glamorous life in Britain: 'The 1930s were gaudy days for me. I travelled first class through life. I led my own band, the Canadian Kings of Swing, I rode to hounds, gambled a little, not always wisely, and drove a red and black Lagonda.' Eventually, the high life and the passing years caught up with him. Len Harvey took away his Empire crown on points at the Albert Hall in February 1934. After four provincial non-title wins, he retired after thirteen rounds against Harvey's successor as Empire champion, the Welshman, Jack Petersen. Although he twice lost on points to the British-based South African Ben Foord he was still good enough to deal with tough guys like the New Zealander Maurice Strickland and a whole string of small-time contenders. After losing to Foord in Leicester in March 1936, he won twenty-two in a row but when he fought Harvey for the vacant Empire championship at Harringay in March 1939 he lost again in thirteen rounds.

Two months later, sixteen years after that uncertain debut at Blackfriars Ring, Gains took a £1,000 payday against Tommy Farr in Cardiff, lost in five rounds and retired. He settled in Surrey with his wife Lisa and their four children and kept involved with the sport through the ex-boxers associations.

TONY GALENTO

Born: 12 March 1910, Orange, New Jersey
Full name: Domenick Anthony Galento
Died: July 1979, Newark, New Jersey, aged 69
Height: 5ft 9½in   **Weight at peak:** 233lbs (16st 9lbs)
Fights: 106   **Won:** 75   **Lost:** 26   **Drawn:** 5
KO percentage: 50
Rounds boxed: 636
World title fights: 1
Career span: 1928-43 (15 years)
KO wins: 53
KO defeats: 6

Fat, short, with all the finesse of a charging rhino, 'Two Ton' Tony Galento made his name in a bloody, brutal fight with Joe Louis in June 1939. Writers and fans laughed when Galento, the New Jersey bar owner who could out-drink most of his customers, was announced as the seventh challenger for the world title. Louis had blown away his previous three opponents – John Henry Lewis, Max Schmeling and Jack Roper – in the first round and there was no reason to suppose Galento would last any longer.

For years he had been no more than a crowd-pleasing, club-circuit slugger with a big punch. He had won his last eleven, but at nowhere near championship level. Galento did nothing to persuade anyone that they were wrong:

his idea of roadwork was to sit in a car smoking a fat cigar while his sparring partners got themselves in shape by plodding alongside. 'Why,' he asked reporters who came upon the scene, 'should I pay these bums all that good folding money and do all the work myself?' He didn't care a fig for boxing rankings. His stock answer to questions about what he thought about other heavyweights was, 'I'll moider da bum' – or so it was written. When one bored writer referred to the not-too-distant preference of Gene Tunney for reading Shaw, Samuel Butler and Shakespeare while in training camp, Galento frowned, thought for a moment, then said: 'Shakespeare? I ain't never hearda him. He must be one of dem European bums, Sure as hell I'll moider dat bum.'

He was managed at the time by Joe 'Yussel' Jacobs, who managed Max Schmeling. They accused Louis of carrying a metal bar in his glove the night he stopped Schmeling in one, which outraged the champion, who asked for -and got – a public retraction. Galento also managed to reach Louis by telephone to tell him he was going to be knocked out. Out of curiosity people turned out to watch Louis, as sleek, smooth and venomous a heavyweight as ever walked, take on the human beer barrel from Jersey in Yankee Stadium. Galento continued to get under the young champion's skin in the build-up – and then capped it all by bad-mouthing his wife as referee Arthur Donovan went through the introductions in the centre of the ring. When the bell rang Louis was furious, lost his temper and left himself wide open. Galento's only chance was to hit him clean and early and he did it. A left hook to the jaw shook Louis, but didn't knock him down.

By the second Louis had calmed down, sliced Galento's face from distance, cut his eyes, nose and mouth and put him down. Then, in the third as he moved in to finish it, the champion walked into the path of another big left swing and, to the astonishment of the 34,852 crowd, went down. He was shaken but not badly dazed, and took over again. In the fourth he hit Galento as hard as he hit anyone in his life and eventually Two Ton Tony went down and out. Even as Donovan completed the count, he was clinging at his legs trying to get up. When his cornermen came to lead him to his corner, he spat through bloody lips, 'Who stopped da fight? They shouldn't oughta stopped da fight.'

Legend has it that when he returned to his New Jersey bar that night, he was counting the takings when a customer kept interrupting his maths with questions about the fight. Finally, the man said, 'What's it feel like to knock Joe Louis down?' With that Galento snapped, muttered 'Like this' and flattened him with a left hook.

Galento was born in Orange, New Jersey, stood only 5ft 9½in tall, but weighed around 220lbs. He made his professional debut on his seventeenth birthday in Newark and fought for a total of fifteen years. In that time he got through nine managers, including Jack Dempsey. His run up to the Louis fight began with an eighth-round stoppage of Al Ettore in Nutley, New Jersey, in July 1937. He also knocked out Leroy Haynes, who had twice stopped the washed-up Primo

Carnera, in three rounds in Philadelphia in November 1937. He took out Nathan Mann in two, Harry Thomas in three and went into the Louis fight off a three-round knockout of Abe Feldman. Three months after losing to Louis he cashed in by fighting Lou Nova in Philadelphia. In one of the dirtiest fights imaginable, Galento battered Nova to defeat in fourteen rounds. It was his biggest win. However, in July 1940 he came off worse in a brawl with Max Baer in Jersey City, losing in eight. Legend has it that he and Joe Jacobs took the advance but planned to pull out with an invented illness, so if promoter Mike Jacobs wanted the advance back he would have to give them a return with Louis. 'So I don't train and I'm having fun,' said Galento. 'And what does that lousy Joe Jacobs do to me? He goes and dies on me and I got to go through with the fight because I don't know how to duck it. Geez, if you can't trust your manager, who can you trust?'

Then Max Baer's younger brother Buddy beat him in seven and it was all over. After a two-year break, when he did a little wrestling and had ridiculous circus acts with a kangaroo, a bear and an octopus, he did finish with a win, but it meant nothing: a one-round knockout of Herbie Katz way down in Tampa, Florida, in June 1943.

Long after the insults had faded, Galento became friendly with Louis. In the 1960s he had a stroke and diabetes, said to be a result of his drinking skills, and had a leg amputated. He died, a free spirit to the last, in Newark in July 1979 at the age of sixty-nine.

TOMMY GIBBONS

Born: 22 March 1891, St Paul, Minnesota
Died: 19 November 1960, St Paul, Minnesota, aged 69
Height: 5ft 9½in   **Weight at peak:** 175lbs (12st 7lbs)
Fights: 106   **Won:** 94   **Lost:** 5   **Drawn:** 2   **No Decisions:** 5
KO percentage: 45
Rounds boxed: 764
World title fights: 1
Career span: 1911-25 (14 years)
KO wins: 48
KO defeats: 1

Tommy Gibbons boxed Jack Dempsey for fifteen rounds for the heavyweight championship of the world and didn't get paid a cent.

This was the day boxing broke the banks of the town of Shelby, Montana – 4 July 1923, the day the Manassa Mauler and his maverick manager, Jack 'Doc' Kearns, high-tailed it out of town on the first available train with $272,000 and left the locals to pick up the pieces of perhaps the most disastrous promotion in the history of the sport.

According to Kearns, he was entertaining a lady at the Morrison Hotel in Chicago when he was troubled by a telephone call by one Loy J. Molumby, the Montana commander of the American Legion. The good businessmen of Shelby wanted to attract attention to their fast-growing town, which had doubled in size in twelve months following the discovery of oil. When they met in New York, Molumby, dumbly, asked Kearns to name his price. Kearns named $300,000, the first third on the signing of contracts, the second sixty days before the bout and the final third in the final week. Molumby pulled $100,000 in cash out of his pocket. Kearns signed, and also demanded to bring the referee, Jimmy Dougherty, known for some reason as the Baron of Lieperville. Unfortunately, Gibbons' manager, Eddie Kane, was not so ruthless. He agreed on fifty per cent of the receipts between $300,000 and $600,000 and twenty-five per cent of everything above that. The Shelby backers paid for a wooden arena that seated 40,000 people and priced the seats from $20–$50. They also paid Kearns his second $100,000. The world champion and Kearns travelled to Montana six weeks early and the Doc told local newspapermen Gibbons was the best boxer in the world, Dempsey the best fighter in the world. The winner would probably box Harry Wills, and he added, 'Right here in Shelby on Labor Day. Shelby is in a position to become the fight capital of the nation.'

Anyone who had looked at a map would have burst out laughing. Shelby is forty miles from the Canadian border. As a plane flies it is 1,000 miles from Los Angeles, 1,850 miles from New York City. It's Nowhere, USA. Kearns, Dempsey and the half-dozen travelling writers, including Damon Runyon, stayed there one night because the only places to go when the sun went down were the King Tut dance hall, which was above the grocery store, and Aunt Kate's Cathouse. The next morning they decamped to Great Falls, where Dempsey settled down with sparring partners, writers, Kearns, a dog, a bull and a wolf.

Shelby had problems raising the final $100,000 of Dempsey's contract. With a week to go, the mayor visited Kearns, explained that they had only $1,600 and asked tentatively if he might accept 50,000 sheep in place of $100,000. Kearns, who lived in an apartment in New York City and in hotels around America, declined. With a day to go, he took over the promotion in order to get his hands on the gate receipts. After a demonstration outside the arena, Kearns agreed to let people through the turnstiles for $10 each. Some pushed in anyway. Eighty per cent of the seats remained empty. Dempsey said, 'It was the roughest crowd I ever fought in front of. There were guns, whisky bottles and lariats. During the preliminaries, guys lassooed the fences and pulled them down. For the first and only time, I was more worried about getting hurt by the crowd than by the guy I was fighting.' The champion was booed, looked around for his bodyguard, Wild Bill, and couldn't see him – he was hiding beneath the ring. Gibbons boxed defensively, expertly, and must have known he was fighting for nothing. He kept Dempsey on the move, didn't do enough to win but came through fifteen rounds unscathed. 'Nailing him,' said Dempsey, 'was like trying to thread a needle in high wind.'

At the final bell the champion and the New York writers moved out fast. Kearns stayed to count the gate. It came to $80,000, ten per cent of which he handed over to government tax officials. He then bribed the local stationmaster $550 to lay on a special one-carriage train to Grand Falls. His only companion was the writer Hype Igoe, who had spent some time becalmed in a bar, and was wandering the platform playing a ukelele and singing to the moon. Several days later, the banks of Shelby, who had acted as guarantors, went broke.

Gibbons and his elder middleweight brother Mike are regarded as the best boxers produced in Minnesota. Tommy began boxing in 1911 when he was twenty and fought until 1925, when Gene Tunney stopped him after twelve rounds in New York. He had four fights with Harry Greb and Billy Miske, and boxed Georges Carpentier in a No-Decision bout in Michigan City in 1924. He also beat the middleweight champion Mick King and boxed a No Decision with light-heavyweight titleholder Battling Levinsky. When he retired from boxing, Gibbons sold insurance in St Paul for ten years to 1935, then served twenty-four years as Sheriff of Ramsey County, Minnesota. He died in November 1960, aged sixty-nine.

GEORGE GODFREY

Born: 30 March 1853, Prince Edward Island, Canada
Died: 17 October 1901, aged 48
Height: 5ft 10½in   **Weight at peak:** 175lbs (12st 7lbs)
Fights: 33   **Won:** 13   **Lost:** 6   **Drawn:** 13   **No Decisions:** 1
KO percentage: 30
Rounds boxed: 271
World title fights: 0
Career span: 1879-96 (17 years)
KO wins: 10
KO defeats: 4

Boxing has always been a rough, uncompromising business, never more so than in the 1890 fight between George Godfrey and Denver Ed Smith at Cronkeim's Theater in Hoboken, New Jersey. In the twenty-third round Godfrey landed a heavy left hand. In struggling to stay upright, Smith careered backwards to the ropes, his head smacking against the brick wall that ran along one side of the ring! He stayed on his feet but before Godfrey could land another punch the fight was stopped by referee Jere Dunn, a gambler who had served time in Sing-Sing for killing the bare-knuckle champion Jimmy Elliott. In Godfrey's next, equally gruelling fight, in San Francisco in March 1891, he lost to Jake Kilrain in forty-four rounds.

Godfrey, from Prince Edward Island, Canada, fought out of Boston. He was good but when he fought the other leading black fighter of the time, Peter

Jackson, for what was known at the time as 'the coloured heavyweight title', in San Francisco in 1888, Godfrey lost in nineteen rounds, after which he faded away.

He died on 17 October 1901, aged forty-eight.

ANDREW GOLOTA

Born: 5 January 1968, Warsaw, Poland
Height: 6ft 4in   **Weight at peak:** 244lbs (17st 6lbs)
Fights: 46   **Won:** 38   **Lost:** 6   **Drawn:** 1   **No Contests:** 1
KO percentage: 67
Rounds boxed: 201
World title fights: 3
Career span: 1992-2005 (13 years)
KO wins: 31
KO defeats: 3

An eccentric Pole who played to his own rules – and sometimes to none at all – Andrew Golota's major problem was that he failed to handle the pressure of a big fight.

Before the Communist government fell in Poland at the end of the 1980s, Golota – real name Andrzej – was a precocious talent. In 1985 he reached the final of the world junior championships then lost on a second-round retirement to Felix Savon of Cuba. He won the European junior title in 1986, boxed in the European seniors and then the Seoul Olympics. His professional break came in July 1996, when he was beating former world champion Riddick Bowe after six rounds only to be disqualified for deliberately punching low in the seventh. The result sparked a riot in Madison Square Garden. The following December Golota, who lived in Chicago, gave Bowe a pounding for eight rounds – and then, incredibly, hit him low and was thrown out again!

On the back of those sensational fights he was brought in to challenge Lennox Lewis for the WBC title in Atlantic City in October 1997. Golota froze and Lewis took him out in ninety-five seconds. Afterwards the Pole's childhood stutter returned. 'Accident,' he stammered in the dressing room. 'Too nervous, too much pressure.' He quit again, while way ahead on points, against Michael Grant in 1999, beat veterans like Tim Witherspoon, Jesse Ferguson and Orlin Norris, but then walked out after two rounds against Mike Tyson in Detroit in October 2000. Golota was floored by a right hand, got up and seemed to be doing fine, then after a row in the corner quit again. He was showered by soft drinks and debris as he strode from the arena. The result was changed to a No Contest when Tyson tested positive for marijuana and Golota, according to a Chicago doctor, had a serious injury to the neck. If he had boxed on, so the medical argument ran, he would have risked permanent damage. Not too long after that, Golota was arrested for impersonating a police officer.

Yet in 2004 a rejuvenated Golota seemed to have beaten the IBF champion Chris Byrd in Madison Square Garden. Byrd escaped with a draw and Golota, by now with Don King, went on to box the WBA champion John Ruiz. Golota floored Ruiz and, again, appeared to win, only for all three judges to vote for Ruiz. Then, in Chicago before thousands of flag-waving Polish fans, he combusted again, losing in fifty-two seconds to Lamon Brewster, the holder of the minor WBO belt.

ARTURO GODOY

Born: 10 October 1912, Iquique, Chile
Died: 27 August 1986, aged 73
Height: 5ft 11in   **Weight at peak:** 202lbs (14st 6lbs)
Fights: 120   **Won:** 89   **Lost:** 20   **Drawn:** 10   **No Contests:** 1
KO percentage: 39
World title fights: 2
Career span: 1931-51 (20 years)
KO wins: 47
KO defeats: 2

Arturo Godoy was given no more chance than anyone else against Joe Louis when they met in a heavyweight championship bout in February 1940. Yet Godoy's defensive expertise convinced judge Tommy Shortell to give him the fight by ten rounds to two with three even. Unfortunately for the Chilean, the other judge, George Lecron, and Louis's regular referee, Arthur Donovan, saw it 10-4-1 for Louis, which meant the champion retained his title on a split fifteen-round decision. Most ringside reporters felt Louis won, and that Shortell's interpretation was eccentric, though Godoy had kissed Louis on the forehead at the final bell and danced around celebrating what he thought was an upset win.

Louis was never at his best against awkward, quick fighters and Godoy, trained by Al Weill, fought him out of a crouching, crab-like stance, rushing and mauling and refusing to let him settle. Louis called the fight 'the worst I ever had'. They had a rematch four months later and Louis dominated from distance with a snappy left jab, dropped Godoy three times and won in the eighth. While the first fight in Madison Square Garden drew a so-so house of 15,657 and modest receipts of $88,491, the rematch was moved outside to Yankee Stadium, where 26,640 people turned out and paid at the turnstiles a gross $164,120.

Godoy was from Iquique, a city on the Pacific coast. His father, a fisherman, was lost at sea and Arturo worked at anything that came along: he fished, was a stevedore and he fought in street bouts, where he was noticed by a journalist who helped him find real contests. He moved to Argentina, Cuba, Spain, Brazil and Miami. He was a wanderer, an adventurer, a restless soul.

His first opponent of any note was the former light-heavyweight champion Tommy Loughran, whom he boxed three times, all in twelve-round bouts. They drew the first, Loughran won the second on points and Godoy won the third. In 1936 he fought the ancient Argentine hero Luis Angel Firpo, who was making a comeback, in Luna Park, Buenos Aires. Godoy won easily in three rounds. On the back of that he travelled to New York and drew with Leroy Haynes, Al Ettore and Maurice Strickland, but knocked out Jack Roper in seven and out-pointed Tony Galento.

After the Louis fights, he beat Gus Dorazio and Tony Musto twice and had a No Contest against Lee Savold in Chicago in March 1946 when the referee threw both men out for persistent wrestling and holding. In February 1949, at the age of thirty-six, he lost a unanimous ten-round decision to the future light-heavyweight champion Harold Johnson in Philadelphia and soon afterwards returned to Chile. He ran a restaurant, married for the second time and, according to legend, had a famous fallout with Augusto Pinochet before the latter became the infamous dictator responsible for one of the cruellest regimes in the world. Godoy died of liver cancer in August 1986 at the age of seventy-three.

Two years after his death his second wife, Marta, and his son attempted to prevent the publication of a novel loosely based on his life because they felt it made fun of him.

MICHAEL GRANT

Born: 4 August 1972, Chicago, Illinois
Height: 6ft 7in   **Weight at peak:** 250lbs (17st 12lbs)
Fights: 44   **Won:** 41   **Lost:** 3
KO percentage: 70
World title fights: 1
Career span: 1994-2005 (11 years)
KO wins: 31
KO defeats: 3

At the turn of the Millennium some critics believed Michael Grant was the next heavyweight champion of the world. Big, powerful and enthusiastic, he had stacked up thirty-one consecutive wins since his pro debut in New Jersey in 1994 and was learning fast. Yet the sign that Grant was nowhere near ready for Lewis had come in his previous fight, against Andrew Golota in Atlantic City in November 1999. Golota had had Grant down twice in the first round and ready to go, was still way ahead after nine rounds and then, bizarrely, quit in the tenth after being knocked down.

As the week of Grant's challenge to Lewis in April 2000 at Madison Square Garden progressed, the more haunted and uncertain he became. By the time of the weigh-in he seemed as if he wished he were anywhere else. It took him twenty-four attempts to find a pair of gloves to his liking. As they touched gloves before the first bell, Grant looked at the champion and said softly, 'God bless.' Lewis helped himself to an easy win, hammering Grant to the floor three times in round one then finished him in round two with a vicious right uppercut when he was illegally holding Grant's head still with his other glove.

The experience overwhelmed Grant. In his next fight he was beaten in forty-three seconds by another big-hitting manufactured fighter, Jameel McCline. By 2005 he was back on the eight-round circuit.

H

ROY HARRIS

Born: 29 June 1933, Cut-N-Shoot, Texas
Height: 6ft   **Weight at peak:** 194lbs (13st 12lbs)
Fights: 36   **Won:** 31   **Lost:** 5
KO percentage: 27
Rounds boxed: 268
World title fights: 1
Career span: 1955-61 (6 years)
KO wins: 10
KO defeats: 4

At the Staples Center in Los Angeles in the summer of 2003 an elderly man in a blue windcheater posed for photographs between the giant figures of Lennox Lewis, the world heavyweight champion, and Vitali Klitschko. Looking bemused and amused, Roy Harris looked at the towering fighters on either side of him and said, 'These boys eat better than we did!'

It was forty-five years since Harris, a homely man from Texas, had challenged Floyd Patterson for the title in the long-demolished Wrigley Field baseball park. He hadn't been around the fight scene for many years, nor to Los Angeles, and he enjoyed his few days in the spotlight. Sadly Patterson was too ill to be there, but Harris recalled the fight with great clarity.

'He whupped me,' he said. 'I ran out of energy after the third round. We didn't know anything about nutrition or diet. None of us did in those days. I was so weak in the days before the fight my sparring partners were whupping me.' Harris said he trained so hard in the Arrowhead Spring Hotel near San Bernardino that he lost too much weight. 'I trained down to 178lbs and kept on getting lighter,' he said. 'They were saying I had to put some weight on or the fight would be off. They told me to drink beer. I'd never had a drink of beer in my life, but with one week to go, I said, "I think you better bring that case of beer now."' He must have done some drinking because by the weigh-in he was back up to 194lbs!

'I got my weight back but not my strength,' he said with a disarming naivety. In the fight, which drew a crowd of 21,680 and a gate of almost a quarter-of-a-million dollars, Harris took home $50,000 after splitting half and half with his manager, Lou Viscusi, who also picked up all expenses. Al Weill, for so long the brains behind the career of Rocky Marciano, was supposed to promote it, but he was denied a licence in California after being seen in the company of mobster Frankie Carbo. Bill Rosensohn replaced him.

Harris was from the tiny community of Cut-N-Shoot, north of Houston, and Rosensohn had him make a country and western record to mark the occasion. Unfortunately Roy couldn't sing! He took it all with good grace.

In the fight he managed to put Patterson down with a left hook and a little shove in round two, but in the end he was systematically beaten: down four times and cut over both eyes. His father, 'Big' Henry Harris, who at one time was reckoned to be the best 'fist, knee, knife and club' fighter in the Big Thicket area of Texas, pulled him out after round twelve. He leaned into his son's ear and said, 'It ain't no use, boy.'

Roy boxed professionally from 1955, won the Texan title and by 1957 was high in the world rankings after points wins over Willie Pastrano, later the light-heavyweight champion, and Bob Baker from Pittsburgh. Baker said he feared for his life in front of the partisan Texan fans. 'I hit him and he went down,' said Baker. 'I knew that if he didn't get up they weren't going to let me out of that town alive. I love my wife and I love my kids, and most of all I love me. And I told the kid to get up and I'm thankful that he did.' Harris beat Pastrano on workrate in front of 10,000 fans at the Houston Coliseum, although Chris Dundee, Willie's manager, said it was a bad decision. Harris closed 1957 by out-pointing Willi Besmanoff, whose manager Jersey Jones said anywhere else but Texas they would have won. 'And if my boy could give Harris real trouble,' said Jones, for whom loyalty was never an issue worth lying for, 'then anybody can give him real trouble.'

After the Patterson fight Harris remained popular in the Houston area but in 1960 he came apart in one round against Sonny Liston. Outweighed by 17½lbs, he was floored three times. 'Liston had long arms and he hit you when you didn't think he had a right to,' said Harris. 'Because of a mix-up, I went into the ring cold. I wasn't hurt all that, I could have gone on…'

After retiring at the age of twenty-seven Harris, who had done some school-teaching, practised law, made a fortune from real estate but lost it in the financial crisis of the 1980s, and then rebuilt slowly. He and his wife had six children. 'God has been very good to me,' he said.

MARVIN HART

Born: 16 Sep 1876, Jefferson County, Kentucky

Died: 17 Sep 1931, Fern Creek, Kentucky, aged 55

Height: 5ft 11¼in   **Weight at peak:** 188-190lbs (13st 6lbs-13st 8lbs)

Fights: 48   **Won:** 32   **Lost:** 9   **Drawn:** 6   **No Decisions:** 1

KO percentage: 42

Rounds boxed: 406

World champion: 1905-06

World title fights: 2

Career span: 1899-1910 (11 years)

KO wins: 20

KO defeats: 4

Marvin Hart was briefly the world heavyweight champion after the retirement of the then-undefeated James J. Jeffries in 1905. Jeffries announced his retirement on 15 May and on 3 July Hart was matched with Jack Root, an Austro-Hungarian light-heavyweight, for the vacant championship. Jeffries added his tacit stamp of approval by agreeing to be referee.

In the rarefied air of Reno, Nevada, before a crowd of around 7,000, in heat of nearly 100 degrees, Hart recovered from a seventh-round knockdown and put away Root with a right to the heart in round twelve. Hart's win was the culmination of six years of effort – and he returned home to Louisville, Kentucky, to a hero's welcome complete with a brass band that struck up *My Old Kentucky Home* the moment he stepped from the train.

Seven months later Tommy Burns frustrated and outwitted him over twenty rounds in his first defence in Los Angeles but, paper champion or not, Hart played his part in boxing history.

Hart was from farming country in Fern Creek in Jefferson County, Kentucky, not far from Louisville. He taught himself to box in a barn, reading from a textbook how to throw punches and working away at a heavy bag for hours on his own. He earned his living as a plumber. His first fight was in Louisville in December 1899, when he was twenty-three years old, and brought him a seventh-round knockout over 'Big' Bill Schiller. He soon established himself as a local prospect, showing strength and durability to go with his knockout punch. On the way up he boxed Philadelphia Jack O'Brien, George Gardner, Joe Choynski and Gus Ruhlin. He was also awarded a dubious twenty-round decision over Jack Johnson in San Francisco. Johnson felt, in spite of a fussy (he said biased) referee, he still won more or less as he pleased. He was never the most quick-witted of boxers and the style of the awkward southpaw Mike Schreck was something he could never fathom. Schreck gave him fits in a brief No-Decision bout in his first ring appearance after losing to Burns, and knocked him out of title contention by defeating him in twenty-one rounds in May 1907. Two years later Schreck beat him in four rounds in Terre Haute, Indiana. Hart fought only once more, losing in three to Carl Morris in Oklahoma.

In retirement Marvin enjoyed life as a family man, farmer and plumber around Fern Creek, ran a bar, and stayed in touch with boxing by refereeing. He was healthy into middle age but then, after officiating at a fight in Louisville in December 1930, became ill with liver disease. He died nine months later at home, where he had spent his last months mostly in bed, the day after his fifty-fifth birthday. His headstone reads, 'A Friend of Countless Hundreds, A Clean Fighter Whose Example Will Continue To Inspire Coming Generations.'

LEROY HAYNES

Born: 11 November 1918, South Bend, Indiana
Height: 6ft   **Weight at peak:** 196lbs (14st)
Fights: 66   **Won:** 41   **Lost:** 22   **Drawn:** 3
KO percentage: 50
Rounds boxed: 396
World title fights: 0
Career span: 1930-41 (11 years)
KO wins: 33
KO defeats: 7

Leroy Haynes, nicknamed 'Black Shadow', twice stopped Primo Carnera when the former champion was in rapid decline in 1936.

In their first fight, in Haynes's adopted home of Philadelphia in March 1936, he beat the former world champion in three rounds. Two months later they fought again in Ebbets Field, Brooklyn, and Haynes outstayed a brave but outgunned Carnera and eventually half-paralysed him with two body punches in the ninth round. Primo was carried to the dressing room and taken to hospital with kidney damage.

Haynes, who was originally from South Bend, Indiana, lost a decision to Maxie Rosenbloom but, after moving to Philadelphia, he made his name with some crowd-pleasing displays, not least a ten-round points win over Ed 'Unknown' Winston in Shibe Park. They fought to a standstill.

He was out-pointed three times by Al Ettore, drew with Arturo Godoy in New York, beat Bob Olin on cuts but was pounded to dramatic three-round defeat by 'Two Ton' Tony Galento, who knocked him down three times. Elmer 'Violent' Ray out-pointed him. Haynes retired in 1941.

TOM HEENEY

Born: 18 May 1898, Kaiti, Gisborne, New Zealand
Died: 15 June 1984, Miami, Florida, aged 86
Height: 5ft 10½in   **Weight at peak:** 203lbs (14st 7lbs)
Fights: 70   **Won:** 39   **Lost:** 23   **Drawn:** 8
KO percentage: 21
Rounds boxed: 712
World title fights: 1
Career span: 1921-33 (12 years)
KO wins: 15
KO defeats: 6

Tom Heeney lost a stubborn, gritty challenge for the heavyweight championship against Gene Tunney in New York in July 1928. It was in Yankee Stadium, in the Bronx, that the curly haired, immensely strong Heeney absorbed a systematic boxing lesson from Tunney until the fight was stopped eight seconds from the end of the eleventh round.

From Kaiti in Gisborne, on the east coast of the north island of New Zealand, Heeney was born on 18 May 1898. His parents, Hugh Heeney and Eliza Coughlan, were Irish immigrants. Tom was the ninth of their ten children. After school he worked at a blacksmith's before becoming apprenticed to a local plumber. A strong swimmer, in 1918 he was awarded a Royal Humane Society of New Zealand medal for his part in the rescue of two girls off the beach at Waikanae. He and his brother Jack also played in the rugby team of the Poverty Bay and Hawke's Bay areas against the touring South African side in 1921.

Heeney held the New Zealand heavyweight title three times, but fought in Australia, South Africa and England before sailing into New York in 1927. Heeney looked what he was: a short-armed slab of brawn. His style and big heart earned him the nickname 'The Hard Rock From Down Under' and although he lost a questionable ten-round decision to Paolino Uzcudun and drew a fifteen-round return, he knocked out Jim Maloney in one, out-pointed Johnny Risko and Jack Delaney, and drew with Jack Sharkey.

By then Gene Tunney was looking around for a lucrative defence after his career-defining victories over Jack Dempsey. Heeney was the perfect foil for his classical skills. Heeney was visited in his training camp by the great former champion James J. Corbett and walked to the ring in a Maori cloak sent him from New Zealand. Tunney had already decided it would be his final contest as he had become engaged to the heiress Polly Lauder and, suitably relaxed, went on to produce what he described as the most satisfying display of his career. 'Everything clicked in unison,' he wrote in his (self-penned, not ghost-written) autobiography *A Man Must Fight* in 1933.

Heeney's effort had the majority of the 46,000 fans cheering him on. He had his moments in the first, fourth and sixth rounds but Tunney gradually wore him down. His nose bled, his face leaked blood and in the eighth his eyelid turned inside out, causing him great pain. Tunney, like the great sportsman he was, stood off and allowed the injury to be attended. By the tenth Heeney was wobbling, his face swollen, and on the bell he was knocked down heavily. His trainer, Moe Fleischer, should have retired him, but Tom came up for the eleventh and didn't go down again. The end came with him pinned on the ropes taking a steady stream of hard, accurate punches.

A week later, Heeney married Marion Estelle Dunn in Suffern, New York, and took his bride to New Zealand, where they were welcomed by huge crowds. From championship contender he quickly became a stepping stone for young men on the way up. Max Baer was one of those who stopped him – in three rounds in 1931. Heeney retired in 1933 and settled in Miami Beach, where he ran a restaurant. He became a United States citizen in time to serve in the US Navy Civil Engineer Corps in the Second World War, returned briefly to New Zealand to see his mother in 1947 but continued to live in Miami for the rest of his life. After one final trip to the land of his birth, he passed away in Miami in 1984 at the age of eighty-six.

JOE HIPP

Born: 7 December 1962, Browning, Montana
Height: 6ft 1in   **Weight at peak:** 224lbs (16st)
Fights: 49   **Won:** 42   **Lost:** 7
KO percentage: 59
Rounds boxed: 224
World title fights: 1
Career span: 1987-2003 (16 years)
KO wins: 29
KO defeats: 6

It was the dream of 'Indian' Joe Hipp to become the first Native American to win the heavyweight title.

I sat talking to him at the MGM Grand Hotel in 1995, shortly before he boxed Bruce Seldon for the WBA version of the belt. 'If I could win, it would mean so much to people,' he said. 'I have friends who live on the reservations who are top-class athletes but they have no confidence.' Sadly it didn't work out. Seldon out-boxed him and, in the tenth round, with both eyes cut and swollen to slits, Hipp turned away and referee Richard Steele stopped the fight. The southpaw from Yakima in Washington had already survived a ferocious fight with Tommy Morrison in Reno in 1992. Hipp was knocked down twice and had a broken cheekbone, while Morrison had a broken jaw and hand. They slammed away until Hipp wilted in the ninth. He also lost to Bert Cooper because after five rounds he could no longer see, while early in his career he had suffered a broken jaw in a minor fight in Carson City. His best wins were a twelve-round decision over the world-rated Alex Garcia and a split verdict over Rodolfo Marin in 1994.

Born in Browning, Montana, his first job was washing dishes at a hotel in Yakima. His early heroes included Jim Thorpe, the Indian who won two Olympic gold medals in Stockholm in 1912 only to have them taken away because he had been paid for a minor league baseball game.

LARRY HOLMES

Born: 3 November 1949, Cuthbert, Georgia
Height: 6ft 3in   **Weight at peak:** 212lbs (15st 2lbs)
Fights: 75   **Won:** 69   **Lost:** 6
KO percentage: 58
Rounds boxed: 582
World champion: 1978-85 (WBC/IBF)
World title fights: 25
Career span: 1973-2002 (29 years)
KO wins: 44
KO defeats: 1

For six years Larry Holmes was the best heavyweight in the world.

Holmes had a solid, fight-winning jab, an acute boxing brain and could dig deep to fight like a real warrior if he had to, as he did when winning the World Boxing Council title with a big final minute of a thrilling fifteen-rounder with Ken Norton in June 1978. He could upset people from time to time – his comment about Rocky Marciano not being able to carry his jockstrap, for which he later apologised, was injudicious – and could never be mistaken for one of the romantics of the game. Holmes knew boxing was about earning a living, and continued to do that even when his championship days were long gone. 'Why do you think I'm fighting?' he said once. 'The glory? You show me a man says he ain't fighting for money, I'll show you a fool. I'm not a genius, just a businessman.' In Thomas Hauser's brilliant book *The Black Lights*, Holmes said, 'Right now I got a roll of $100 bills in my pocket with a gold money clip around them. When I was a truck driver I used to carry $10 in singles wrapped in a rubber band.'

Holmes was born in Cuthbert, Georgia, and at the age of six his family piled into his uncle Willie's Chevrolet and drove north, away from the toil of sharecropping to a new life in the iron and steel city of Easton, Pennsylvania. In the 1972 Olympic trials he was disqualified for holding in the third round against Duane Bobick – and, in disgust, turned professional. It took him five years to reach the top. He learned most as Muhammad Ali's sparring partner. He was called the Black Cloud, though that later changed to the Easton Assassin. Apart from an early knockdown, during a third-round stoppage win over Kevin Isaac in Cleveland in 1973, Holmes had things pretty much his own way, and eventually emerged as a world-class boxer in his own right when he handed Earnie Shavers a boxing lesson over twelve rounds in Las Vegas in March 1978. That earned him a fight with Ken Norton for the WBC belt that had been taken off Leon Spinks and given to Norton.

After fifteen marvellous rounds at Caesars Palace Holmes won by the closest possible margin: 143–142 twice and a 143–142 vote for Norton. A rematch was an obvious thought, but did not happen. Instead Holmes exhibited his skills beautifully in breaking up and knocking out Alfredo Evangelista in seven rounds of his first defence. His second was equally tame: a seven-round stoppage of an unbeaten, outclassed Osvaldo Ocasio. He had a harder time of it when he stopped Mike Weaver in twelve, but the superbly conditioned, talented Weaver would go on to hold the WBA title for a while. A rematch with Shavers almost ended Holmes' reign early: in the seventh round Shavers put the champion down with a right hand, but Holmes got up, recovered and won in the eleventh.

Lorenzo Zanon, Leroy Jones and Scott LeDoux were no real threats, and none of them lasted past round eight. Then, in October 1980, Holmes took the fight he didn't really want – against thirty-eight-year-old Muhammad Ali. Physically Ali looked about as good as he could have been, but he had taken weight-reducing drugs to do that. He was washed-up and knew it, but still turned on the promotional style to have people believing he could perform one last miracle. In fact Ali, just a hollow shell of the great champion he was a few short years before, was out-sped, out-fought and out-punched. Angelo Dundee pulled him out at the end of round ten. For Holmes it was sad. He knew he had to beat Ali, but he also knew he hadn't beaten Ali, just an imitation of him. He also knew some people would never forgive him. Still, the business beckoned: he easily out-boxed Trevor Berbick, the Canadian-based Jamaican, and then destroyed Leon Spinks, whom he said had insulted his wife, in three rounds in Detroit in June 1981. He almost blew a multi-million dollar payday against Gerry Cooney when he walked into the path of a right hand from Renaldo Snipes in Pittsburgh. He crashed to the canvas in that seventh round, got up, was all over the place but was allowed to box on when some referees would have ruled him unable to defend himself, and made the most of his fortune by rallying to stop Snipes in round eleven.

In June 1982, Holmes won a stirring struggle with Cooney in round thirteen at Caesars Palace before 29,214 fans, who paid a record $6,239,050 at the gate. He dropped the New Yorker twice, once in the second round, and then just before the finish in the thirteenth Cooney's trainer Victor Valle ran into the ring to stop it. He peppered Randy 'Tex' Cobb with jabs and combinations for fifteen rounds but was beginning to fade. Fighters he would have stopped a couple of years before were lasting the distance. He needed the full twelve to beat Lucien Rodriguez of France, was pushed all the way by Tim Witherspoon in a very close fight, and did stop the ordinary challenger from New Jersey, Scott Frank. Then he fell out with the WBC and handed them back their title because they wouldn't sanction a defence against ten-fight novice Marvis Frazier, Joe's son. The WBC were right: Holmes won in two minutes fifty-seven seconds of the first round. He switched allegiance to the newly founded IBF and, a year after the Frazier fight, wore down James Smith for a twelfth-round stoppage. Then he broke up David Bey in ten before again being pressed all the way for fifteen rounds by Carl 'The Truth' Williams. He finished with an eye badly swollen, but still had enough to win by seven points on two cards and by just one on the third.

In September 1985 he took on the undisputed light-heavyweight champion Michael Spinks, looking for a forty-ninth win that would have equalled the unbeaten run of Rocky Marciano, but lost a bitterly disputed, unanimous fifteen-round decision. Harold Lederman and Dave Moretti both scored 143-142 and Larry Wallace had it 145-142. Both *Sports Illustrated* and the *New York Times* believed Holmes won. He let himself down when, in his anger, he made the 'Rocky Marciano couldn't carry my jockstrap' remark in front of the old champion's family. He apologised but the damage was done.

For the rematch with Spinks he earned more than $1 million and again he thought he won. This time it was a split decision that went against him: Joe Cortez scored for Holmes 144-141, but Jerry Roth (144-142) and Frank Brunette (144-141) saw Spinks as the winner. Larry was furious. For more than a year he stayed away and then, without a warm-up, boxed the electrifying Mike Tyson in a freezing cold Atlantic City Convention Hall in January 1988. In the fourth Tyson put him away, dropping him three times. It was the only time in almost thirty years as a professional fighter that Holmes was beaten inside the distance.

He kept away until 1991, then tried again. In his sixth comeback fight, and at the age of forty-two, he handed Ray Mercer, the 1988 Olympic heavyweight gold medallist, a boxing lesson over twelve rounds. That earned him a shot at Evander Holyfield, and he performed well in losing on points in Caesars Palace, Las Vegas, in June 1992. His last challenge for his old WBC belt came at the age of forty-five when he pushed Oliver McCall hard and lost a close one: 114-113, 115-114, 115-112.

After that he went through the motions, adding to the bank balance wherever it suited him, and finally retired in 2002 after handing the so-called King of the Four Rounders, the 330lbs circus act known as Butterbean, a ten-round boxing lesson. Holmes was fifty-two years old.

EVANDER HOLYFIELD

Born: 19 October 1962, Atmore, Alabama

Height: 6ft 2½in   **Weight at peak:** 215lbs (15st 5lbs)

Fights: 47   **Won:** 38   **Lost:** 7   **Drawn:** 2

KO percentage: 53

Rounds boxed: 359

World champion: 1990-92, 1993-94 (WBA & IBF), 1996-99 (WBA, IBF from 1997), 2000-01 (WBA)

World title fights: 17
Career span: 1984-2003 (19 years)
KO wins: 25
KO defeats: 2

For courage and longevity, Evander Holyfield is right up there alongside the greats. His first masterful destruction of Mike Tyson in 1996 and his first epic, losing fight with Riddick Bowe rank among the best fights of the era in any weight division, and if nothing else his twelve-round draw with Lennox Lewis will be remembered as one of the most controversial decisions in the history of the division. And, of course, the return with Tyson in June 1997 was the infamous fight in which Holyfield had a chunk of his ear bitten off.

Holyfield always had wars and had an astonishing capacity for believing that, no matter what the evidence, he could perform what a sceptical public might consider miracles. Born in Atmore, Alabama, and raised in Atlanta, Georgia, Holyfield was a marvellous amateur who had the ability to win the light-heavyweight gold medal in the Los Angeles Olympics in 1984. A punch on the break in the semi-final against Kevin Barry of New Zealand got him disqualified, and he had to make do with bronze. He won the WBA cruiserweight title with a gruelling, pulsating split decision over fifteen rounds against Dwight Muhammad Qawi in Atlanta in July 1986. Holyfield lost so much weight during the fight that only the swift intervention of his wife enabled him to get the required hospital treatment. He was in danger of suffering permanent kidney damage, said doctors. He became the first man to unify the cruiserweight division with wins over Ricky Parkey and Carlos De Leon, then moved up to heavyweight in search of the rich pickings of a Tyson fight. With the bout made, however, Tyson lost to Buster Douglas, which cost Holyfield millions of dollars. He made up for that by knocking out an under-motivated, overweight Douglas in three rounds at The Mirage in Las Vegas in October 1990.

A unanimous points win over George Foreman – two margins of seven points, one of three, which seemed too close – brought him to another attempt to box Tyson. This time it was ruined when Tyson was accused of raping Desiree Washington in Indianapolis, and then injured a rib in training. Holyfield eventually faced a substitute for a substitute, Bert Cooper, in Atlanta in November 1991, and survived the first count of his career to win in round seven. A points win over forty-two-year-old Larry Holmes did nothing for his image, but he came alive in defeat in a magnificent twelve-round war with Riddick Bowe at the Thomas and Mack Center, Las Vegas, in November 1992. After a torrid tenth, Bowe dropped Holyfield in the eleventh, rode another crisis himself and eventually won clearly: 117-110 twice, 115-112. It remains an example of heavyweight championship boxing at its best.

Holyfield retired, changed his mind, looked bad in out-pointing Alex Stewart, whom he had previously stopped, and then won the bizarre return with Bowe on a majority decision at Caesars Palace, Las Vegas, in November 1993. The fight was interrupted for twenty minutes in round seven when a paraglider, James Miller, dropped into the ropes and ring apron. Bowe's wife Judy, who was pregnant, was so upset she was ferried from ringside to hospital, his trainer Eddie Futch was also taken ill, and with hindsight, it would have been sensible to curtail the whole thing as a No Contest in round seven. However, when the dust settled, Holyfield had regained the title. Then he looked an old man as, in spite of scoring a second-round knockdown, he was out-boxed by southpaw Michael Moorer and beaten on a majority decision in April 1994. This time a heart problem was diagnosed, only for Holyfield to proclaim himself cured by an act of God later in the year. Fears for his health seemed justified when he was beaten in eight rounds by Riddick Bowe in November 1995.

Accordingly, when Holyfield, after a meaningless win over Bobby Czyz, was matched with the marauding Tyson in November 1996, it was viewed as a cynical mismatch. Holyfield had always known how to beat Tyson, but at thirty-four, with so many wars behind him, hardly anybody thought he could do it. But unlike Tyson, whose life has been in perpetual turmoil, Holyfield had a stability that gave him strength. His belief in God's will was unshakeable. His new wife, Dr Janice Itson, was a pain management specialist. 'The pain,' said Evander, 'has to be worth the prize.' And it was. He had the mental strength to keep his boxing together under intense fire, counter-punch Tyson with left hooks and fight his own fight. He gradually took over, floored the defending champion in the sixth and pummelled him to defeat in round eleven.

The rematch in June 1997 saw Holyfield the more composed, determined man during the week of the fight. Tyson cut a brooding, monosyllabic figure who looked increasingly as if he would prefer to be anywhere else. In the third round Holyfield suddenly leaped back, bounding up and down, with blood running from a tear in his right ear. Tyson, angry at a cut eye caused by a clash of heads, had bitten a chunk out of it and had spat it on to the canvas. Incredibly, referee Mills Lane did not disqualify him. Tyson could not have made the message plainer: he wanted out of the fight. To make the point doubly firm in the next clinch he bit Holyfield's left ear and this time Lane threw him out. Angry scenes in the ring followed, and in the hotel casino half an hour later shots rang out. The MGM casino was closed down, which cost the establishment a small fortune, and the public streamed out of side exits onto the Strip. I was among them. It was mayhem.

Holyfield went on to stop Moorer, who was the IBF champion, in eight rounds, and in March 1999 fought a marvellously composed Lennox Lewis in Madison Square Garden in a unification fight. Just as he had unsettled Tyson pyschologically, this time Holyfield seemed the more confused of the two pre-fight, and over the twelve rounds was clearly second best in my view from a close ringside seat. Lewis hurt and almost stopped Holyfield in the fifth, was over-cautious, and jabbed his way to what appeared to be a clear win. South African judge Stanley Christodoulou thought so too, 116-113, but amazingly Eugenia Williams of New Jersey saw it for Holyfield 115-113, including an astonishing 10-9 for Evander in round five. The third judge, Larry O'Connell of Britain, had it level 115-115, which meant it was a draw. The Lewis camp were outraged, Holyfield phlegmatic. In the return in Las Vegas in November 1999, Lewis boxed the same kind of conservative fight and once again out-jabbed Holyfield. This time the judges saw the same fight: 117-111, 116-112, 115-113. There was no real doubt, although in the months afterwards a swell of opinion grew that suggested Holyfield had won some kind of moral victory. That was a strange one. He was well beaten.

The WBA stripped Lewis for seeing no point in a third fight with Holyfield, which would have meant cutting Don King in on the deal. Evander was matched for the vacant belt against John Ruiz, a Puerto Rican from Boston. It was a paper title, but Holyfield took a close, disputed unanimous decision (114-113 twice, 116-113) to lay claim to an unprecedented fourth championship reign. He was floored and out-pointed in a rematch with Ruiz in March 2001. However, he seemed to get the better of a drawn third fight with Ruiz in Ledyard, Connecticut. Only one of sixteen ringside boxing writers thought Ruiz had won.

Holyfield staged a defiant display to beat the former champion Hasim Rahman on an eighth-round technical decision, but then lost an IBF title fight on points to Chris Byrd in Atlantic City in December 2002. He fought virtually one-armed because of a damaged shoulder. When he was floored and stopped in nine by James Toney in October 2003, the shouts for his retirement increased in volume again. Stubbornly, the forty-year-old warrior refused and said he would box on. He did, but after losing a decision to Larry Donald he suffered the indignity of having his licence taken away by the New York State Athletic Commission.

J

PETER JACKSON

Born: 3 July 1861, St Croix, West Indies
Died: 13 July 1901, Roma, Queensland, Australia, aged 40
Height: 6ft 1½in   **Weight at peak:** 192lbs (13st 10lbs)
Fights: 94   **Won:** 47   **Lost:** 3   **Drawn:** 4   **No Decisions:** 40
KO percentage: 34
Rounds boxed: 459
World title fights: 0
Career span: 1882-99 (17 years)
KO wins: 32
KO defeats: 3

If boxing had been a fair and equal sport, which of course it has never been, then almost certainly Peter Jackson would have been the heavyweight champion of the world. However, in Jackson's day brilliance as a boxer was irrelevant if one's skin was not white. And so this tall, lithe, dignified athlete was not allowed to box for the title he would have probably held for years on end.

Those who saw him were in no doubt that he would have beaten John L. Sullivan, or at least the John L. Sullivan of the late 1880s. James J. Corbett, who fought Jackson to a sixty-one-round stalemate in 1891, was convinced he had shared a ring with a genius. By the time of his autobiography, *The Roar of the Crowd*, which was published in 1925, Corbett had not changed his mind. 'That night I thought Peter Jackson was a great fighter,' he wrote. 'Six months later, still being tired from that fight, I thought him a great one. And today, after thirty-three years, as I sit on this fifteenth floor of a New York skyscraper writing this, I still maintain that he was the greatest fighter I have ever seen.'

Corbett wanted no further part of Jackson. The referee ruled a No Contest on the grounds that neither man could land a telling blow on the other, which in hindsight was an extremely harsh interpretation. Most felt a draw was the just description of the result. There most certainly had been a contest: Jackson had two broken ribs and a shoulder injury while Corbett's left forearm was fractured!

Jackson was born in Christiansted on St Croix in the Virgin Islands in 1861. Some say Peter's father followed the gold rush to Australia and then sent for his family; others say Peter snr was a gentle, stay-home family man who worked as a warehouse foreman and didn't leave the West Indies! That version suggests Peter jnr left home at sixteen, worked as a deckhand on a Danish merchant ship and settled in Sydney from 1881. Take your pick!

In July 1884 he took part in the first Australian heavyweight title fight under Queensberry Rules – and was knocked out by a body punch in the third round by Bill Farnan. He didn't lose again until he was old and sick. A rematch with Farnan was curtailed when a riot broke out. Jackson won the Australian title in 1886, beating Tom Lees over thirty rounds – and early in 1888 took the boat to San Francisco to hunt down the world champion, Sullivan. He impressed in exhibitions in boxing saloons but it took nearly six months for him to find a fight, and then it was with the man acknowledged as the best black fighter in the world, George Godfrey from Boston. He beat Godfrey with a superb display of ringcraft in San Francisco in August 1888. He moved on to defeat the 6ft 5in Californian champion, Joe McAuliffe, in twenty-four rounds without taking a meaningful punch, and then knocked out Patsy Cardiff in ten. San Francisco promoters and sponsors linked together to offer John L. Sullivan $10,000 to box Jackson but he declined. 'I have never fought a Negro, and I never shall,' blustered the champion.

Instead, Jackson travelled from coast to coast and then on to London as a guest of the National Sporting Club, whose president, Lord Lonsdale, had seen him box in San Francisco. In November 1889 he defeated Jem Smith, the English champion, in two rounds at the Pelican Club. In 1891 Peter returned to San Francisco and boxed Corbett to that famous stalemate. His training was hard but he had a weak left ankle following a bizarre incident when he had climbed a telegraph pole to avoid a mad dog, only to fall several feet when he slipped while getting down! He also had to shake off the effects of a heavy cold.

In San Francisco, Jackson had always lodged with an elderly black woman, and in 1891 her daughter, whom he loved, developed tuberculosis. Every day the fighter would carry the young woman from her bed to a verandah he had built for her in the garden. Each night, until she died, he carried her back to bed. Afterwards he paid for the mother's living expenses.

Eventually, he returned to London and won recognition as champion of the British Empire by knocking out Frank 'Paddy' Slavin in the tenth round at the National Sporting Club. Years later Slavin said Jackson destroyed him as a boxer. 'Peter, when I fought him, was unbeatable,' he said. Jackson was a country house guest of Lord Lonsdale and liked it so much he stayed five months, enjoying an affair with a Welsh girl and giving sparring exhibitions. However, he also began to display the early signs of tuberculosis and back in the USA the condition worsened. In California he was told the truth about his illness and used his remaining money to stay at a sanatorium in Nevada. Partially recovered, he took a ridiculous fight with the future world champion James J. Jeffries in 1898 to pay for his passage to Australia, where he wanted to die. He lost in three rounds, but didn't earn enough and so had to go into the ring once more, another three-round defeat by Joe Jefford in Canada.

Eventually a Canadian benefactor paid his fare to Sydney, and he died in hospital in Roma, Queensland. His grave bears the inscription 'This Was A Man'.

PHIL JACKSON

Born: 11 May 1964, Miami, Florida
Height: 6ft 1in   **Weight at peak:** 218lbs (15st 8lbs)
Fights: 58   **Won:** 44   **Lost:** 13   **No Contests:** 1
KO percentage: 65
Rounds boxed: 252
World title fights: 1
Career span: 1988-2004 (16 years)
KO wins: 38
KO defeats: 7

Phil Jackson challenged Lennox Lewis in the Convention Center on the Boardwalk in Atlantic City in May 1994 and was beaten in eight one-sided rounds. Lewis took a no-risk line, nullifying the shorter Jackson's big left hook by using his reach to dominate with his left jab, using the right only sparingly until his challenger tired.

Jackson was from the grim Overtown section of Miami. After linking up with police sergeant Pat Burns at the Gibson Park gym, he won fifty of fifty-five amateur bouts and turned pro in December 1988. He flopped in his first big test, when he lost dismally in four rounds to Razor Ruddock in Cleveland. He admitted he froze. Burns brought him back at a lower level, then gambled when offered the fight with Lewis. It didn't work out, but then Lewis turned out to be the most successful heavyweight of his generation.

The only fighter of any note Jackson beat was the long-faded Alex Stewart in a ten-rounder in 1998. He retired in 2004 after the young prospect Dominick Guinn knocked him out in twenty-three seconds in that same Boardwalk building where he challenged Lewis a decade earlier. He was forty years old.

TOMMY JACKSON

Born: 9 August 1931, Hancock, Georgia
Died: 14 February 1981, New York, aged 49
Height: 6ft 3in   **Weight at peak:** 193lbs (13st 11lbs)
Fights: 44   **Won:** 34   **Lost:** 9   **Drawn:** 1
KO percentage: 36
Rounds boxed: 319
World title fights: 1
Career span: 1952-60 (8 years)
KO wins: 16
KO defeats: 4

Immensely strong, very fit with an array of swarming, flapping punches, Tommy 'Hurricane' Jackson lost a challenge to Floyd Patterson in ten rounds for the championship at the New York Polo Grounds in July 1957. Patterson, who had beaten him on a split decision in an eliminator twelve months earlier, outclassed Jackson before a disappointing crowd of 14,458. The unerringly courageous Jackson had taken a one-sided pounding and had been knocked down three times, in rounds one, two and nine. Patterson's body punches also put the Hurricane in Meadowbrook Hospital in Long Island with damaged kidneys. The champion and his wife visited the next day. Jackson was advised to remain in hospital for a week, but checked out after forty-eight hours against doctors' wishes.

Jackson was an extrovert, eccentric character who rarely gave an interview that made any sense. Before the Patterson fight, he chuckled, 'I'd like to fight this fight for nothing, just to make the world happy. There'll be blood all over the place in the first round.' Fortunately, his long-suffering manager Lippe Breidbart negotiated him a cut that grossed him more than $60,000. He was trained by Whitey Bimstein, who tried to hone his style and even teach him how to jab properly but could never get him to remember much.

Jackson was born in Georgia and lived in New York. He made his first mark in January 1954 when he stopped former contender Rex Layne in six rounds at the Eastern Parkway Arena in Brooklyn, where he was already a crowd favourite. He lost two out of three to Jimmy Slade and was outclassed in two rounds by the Cuban, Nino Valdes. But back he came, winning his next nine, including two decisions over the rapidly fading Ezzard Charles, another stoppage of Layne, and a strange points victory over Archie McBride, who seemed to have won clearly. His phenomenal workrate brought him victory over the talented but notoriously lazy Bob Baker on a majority decision in the Garden in February 1956 and he also stopped the British heavyweight Johnny Williams in four rounds in Washington DC.

The defeat by Patterson in the eliminator set him back, but he rebounded quickly with wins over Baker and the Cuban Julio Mederos to clinch his title shot. After losing the championship bout with Patterson, Eddie Machen knocked him out in the tenth in the Cow Palace in San Francisco. He retired in 1960.

For some years Jackson shone shoes on the sidewalk outside a subway station on 168th Street and later drove a taxi, working the ghetto areas where the more established companies would not go. He died in Jamaica Hospital, Queens, in 1981 after he was mown down by a car while polishing his cab. He was forty-nine.

JOE JEANNETTE

Born: 26 August 1879, North Bergen, New Jersey
Died: 2 July 1958, Weekawken, New Jersey, aged 78
Height: 5ft 10in   **Weight at peak:** 195-200lbs (13st 13lbs-14st 4lbs)
Fights: 166   **Won:** 117   **Lost:** 20   **Drawn:** 15   **No Decisions:** 14
KO percentage: 40
Rounds boxed: 1,226
World title fights: 0
Career span: 1904-22 (18 years)
KO wins: 68
KO defeats: 2

Joe Jeannette was a stocky, iron-jawed heavyweight who fought the best in the world over the first two decades of the twentieth century but, like so many black fighters, did not get a shot at the championship.

Jeannette's epic victory over one of his major rivals, Sam McVey, in Paris in 1909 has passed into boxing folklore. The two fighters were heavily criticised for a boring twenty-round maul in February of that year – and were warned when they boxed again in April that more was expected of them. Not many fans bothered to turn out, but those who opted for other entertainment missed a blood-curdling endurance battle that was a throwback to the bare-knuckle era. For round after round McVey was on top. People lost count of the number of times he floored

Jeannette, only for Joe to keep on getting up. At the end of round sixteen, the bell saved him. A doctor at ringside gave him oxygen between rounds! After thirty rounds he was still there... and McVey began to struggle. In round thirty-nine, a big left hook put McVey down for the first time. They blasted away and by the forty-second round McVey's right eye was shut, the left was swelling and his nose was broken. At the end of the forty-ninth he couldn't go on. The fight had lasted from 11 p.m. until 2.45 a.m. with an estimated, generally agreed, total of thirty-eight knockdowns. Willie Lewis, the old welterweight who trained Jeannette, said it was four in the morning by the time they returned to their hotel – and a couple of hours later there was a bang on his door. His fighter was ready for his early morning run!

Incidentally, his name was Jennette, but the 'A' has been included for so long it seems pointless to adjust it now.

From North Bergen, New Jersey, Joe regularly boxed Jack Johnson in 1905 and 1906. Mostly they were six-round bouts, but they did have a fifteen-round battle, which Johnson won on points. They also had a ten-round draw in Portland, Maine. 'Jack Johnson was a powerful, wonderful defensive boxer, but he didn't believe in over-working or taking chances,' said Jeannette. 'If you didn't hurt him, he didn't hurt you. I boxed him eight times in two years and we could have made it eight more without anybody getting hurt.

'After he beat Tommy Burns, Johnson wouldn't give us a fight. He made the weak excuse that two Negro fighters wouldn't draw at the gate. He actually drew the colour line against members of his own race.'

Jeannette had more time for Sam Langford, whom he stopped in the eighth round in Lawrence, Massachusetts, on Christmas Day 1905 and went on to box thirteen times over the next dozen years. 'He had everything,' he said. 'He was tough, a good boxer and dangerous every second he was in there. He could take you out with a punch. I got careless with him once, in Syracuse. That was the only time.' That was in May 1916, by which time Joe was thirty-six years old. Langford knocked him out in round seven. The only other man to do that in his long career was 'Black Bill', in Philadelphia in April 1905 when Jeannette was a novice.

In Paris in March 1914, the thirty-four-year-old Jeannette boxed Georges Carpentier – and surprisingly was given a decision at the end of fifteen rounds. The general consensus was that Carpentier had won. A month later he also out-pointed the popular, all-action Australian Colin Bell over twenty rounds in London, then returned to the United States and drew with Harry Wills in New Orleans. In April 1915 he knocked out the one-time 'White Hope' Arthur Pelkey in eight rounds in Montreal.

Eventually he just got old. He retired in November 1919 at the age of forty, after a disqualification win over Bartley Madden in Bayonne, New Jersey. 'I feel the old bones creaking every time I move in there,' he said.

He was a dignified, clean-living man who set his money aside in order to provide for his wife, Adelaide, and family, and for around twenty years he trained fighters in a New Jersey gym. He also ran a car repair, limousine and car rental business in Union City until he was seventy-six. Jeannette died on 2 July 1958 at the North Hudson Hospital in Weehawken, New Jersey.

JAMES J. JEFFRIES

Born: 15 April 1875, Carroll, Ohio
Full name: James Jackson Jeffries
Died: 2 March 1953, Burbank, California, aged 77
Height: 6ft 2½in   **Weight at peak:** 206-219 lbs (14st 10lbs to 15st 9lbs)
Fights: 21   **Won:** 18   **Lost:** 1   **Drawn:** 2
KO percentage: 71
Rounds boxed: 208
World champion: 1899-1905
World title fights: 9
Career span: 1896-1910 (14 years)
KO wins: 15
KO defeats: 1

It's hard to know what to make of James J. Jeffries, who was the supreme heavyweight in the world for almost six years at the beginning of the twentieth century. He was big, strong, seemingly impervious to punishment, had the ability to intimidate opponents, could punch his considerable weight, had a stiff jab – and yet some reports suggest he had a fairly rudimentary crouching technique and was painfully easy to hit. All of these were probably true to a degree, but an examination of his record reveals an extraordinarily successful prize-fighter, who retired in his prime, undefeated, and even in old age was able to last into the fifteenth round with the ring genius of the next generation, Jack Johnson. There is no doubt that when the list of great heavyweights is drawn up, Jeffries deserves to be on it. In his youth he was probably quicker and more flexible than his bulk suggested. He could, for example, run 100 yards in a little over ten seconds and high jump almost six feet. Step forward any of the modern heavyweight champions who could do that!

He was born James Jackson Jeffries on a farm near Carroll in southern Ohio, to sternly religious, kind parents who moved the family of eight children to farmland in California because one of the boys, Tom, had a curved spine and they believed he would benefit from a warmer climate. After rudimentary schooling, Jim worked on the family farm, in tin mines and a steel plant, as a meat packer – and in the boiler works of the Santa Fe railroad in San Bernardino. He learned to box in the East Side Athletics Club in Los Angeles. He was a sparring partner for the heavyweight champion James J. Corbett – they had the same manager, William A. Brady.

In the second half of 1897, Jeffries slogged his way through a pair of twenty-round draws against Gus Ruhlin and Joe Choynski. In March 1898, he knocked out the mortally sick Peter Jackson – a fight that should never have happened – and in San Francisco two months later slugged out a twenty-round points win over Tom Sharkey. He won the heavyweight crown in Coney Island, New York, in June 1899, wearing down the veteran Cornishman Bob Fitzsimmons in eleven rounds. The last world heavyweight title fight of the nineteenth century was a return with Sharkey, this time over twenty-five rounds, again indoors at the Coney Island arena. The official film of the event was lost, but some flickering footage exists, taken by an enterprising gentleman in the crowd who hid a camera in a cigar box! The fight went the distance with Jeffries a close but deserved points winner.

For years his next fight, against Jack Finnegan in the Light Guard Armory building, Detroit, in April 1900, was omitted from the record books as insignificant. However, later research demonstrated that it was indeed a title fight, and Jeffries' fifty-five-second victory remains, at the time of writing, a record for the championship.

His come-from-behind victory over Corbett in Coney Island in May 1900 was one of the all-time ring classics. Corbett trained for six months and at thirty-three was back close to his best. For round after round he treated his old sparring partner to a boxing lesson. With three of the twenty-five rounds left, Corbett only had to stand up to win. He couldn't do it. The bruised and battered Jeffries nailed him and knocked him out in round twenty-three. It was eighteen months before his next defence: a one-sided five-rounds retirement win over Gus Ruhlin.

A rematch with Bob Fitzsimmons in San Francisco in 1902 showed yet again the worst and the best of this hulking, bear-like champion. At the start Jeffries was cut to ribbons by Fitzsimmons' precise, sharp punching – some said Fitzsimmons had plaster of Paris under his bandages – but Bob's left hand, damaged before the fight, let him down, and the Boilermaker kept charging and, with his face bleeding heavily, knocked out the old champion with a body shot in round eight.

The paucity of contenders was illustrated by the fact that the next candidate was Corbett, who was still convinced that he should have regained the title when they met three years earlier. However, by August 1903, Corbett was almost thirty-seven years old. He still had the wits and the skills to stretch Jeffries a little, but was down twice in round ten and counted out. By then Jeffries was considered invincible. Just before Christmas 1903 he had a four-round exhibition with a Canadian, Jack Monroe, who didn't do too badly – and so in August 1904 Monroe was given a chance at the title. The poor man froze and Jeffries steamrollered him in a couple of rounds. Jeffries ran out of contenders and, feeling there was no longer a point in training hard, retired to his alfalfa farm near Burbank, California, to a life of peace and quiet.

He refereed the fight that found his successor, Marvin Hart, in 1906, and seemed content that his time had come and gone. Sadly, he allowed himself to be persuaded out of retirement at the age of thirty-five by those who felt, following

Jack Johnson's victory over Tommy Burns in Sydney on Boxing Day 1908, that the title should be restored to the white race. Racial issues were fairly unapologetic in those days. Nobody thought twice about calling a black man a 'nigger' or a 'coon'. Nobody thought anything of furthering the theory that black men were weak in the belly. Physically, slavery had gone. Emotionally, it held on tight to the white American consciousness.

Jeffries, who was no more and no less than a man of his times, had ballooned to 320lbs (more than 22st) in retirement. He trained for months to shed the weight and sharpen himself up. It was nowhere near enough. When Johnson gave him a one-sided boxing lesson and stopped him in the fifteenth round in Reno in July 1910 he accepted the fact, which is more than can be said for too many Americans who reacted horribly on news of his defeat. Black workers were murdered in Georgia; two black men were killed in Little Rock, Arkansas; impromptu lynchings took place in Texas, Louisiana, Virginia, Delaware and New York City; a white man had his throat slashed in Houston; black people took over the town of Keystone, West Virginia and so on and so on. A total of nineteen people died and 251 were seriously injured. One newspaper recorded soberly, 'Most of the casualties were negroes.'

Jeffries earned a total of $192,066 from the purse plus movie rights – a fortune at the time. He later said it wasn't worth it. 'I felt as if I had every white American on my back,' he said years later. 'I would like to have met Johnson at my peak. I'm not saying I would have beaten him, but you would have seen a completely different fight.'

Jeffries, who had invested his fortune in stocks and shares, was bankrupted by the 1929 Wall Street crash. He ran a boxing gym in a barn on his farm and promoted amateur shows but, although he loved to talk boxing into his old age, he was never the same after his wife, Freda, was killed crossing a street in 1941. He was paralysed down one side by a stroke five years later, and was a month short of his seventy-eighth birthday when he died following a heart attack in 1953. He is buried in Inglewood Park cemetery outside Los Angeles.

INGEMAR JOHANSSON

Born: 16 October 1932, Gothenburg, Sweden
Height: 6ft ½in   **Weight at peak:** 194-196lbs (13st 12lbs-14st)
Fights: 28   **Won:** 26   **Lost:** 2
KO percentage: 60
Rounds boxed: 173
World champion: 1959-60
World title fights: 3
Career span: 1952-63 (11 years)
KO wins: 17
KO defeats: 2

The summer of 1959 belonged to the enigmatic Swede, Ingemar Johansson, whose seven-knockdown trouncing of Floyd Patterson in Yankee Stadium, New York, made him the first European since Primo Carnera to win the heavyweight championship. It was one of the most comprehensive batterings ever handed out in a world heavyweight championship fight. All seven knockdowns came in round three, after the first two sessions had produced nothing of note. The tape shows Patterson was 'out of it' after the first knockdown. When he got up, Floyd walked to a corner, and years later said he was under the impression he had just knocked Johansson down!

Johansson had watched Patterson's defence against Brian London in Indianapolis and said, 'I have seen what I wanted to learn.' He trained hard at Grossinger's camp in upstate New York, but was criticised for bringing his girl-friend, Birgit Lundgren, with him. Fighters in those days just didn't do that. Before he left Sweden he had a relaxed, half-hour meeting with the Prime Minister, Tage Erlander. He was managed and advised by Edwin Ahlqvist, who helped him with his investments as well as guiding his boxing career. Even before he was world champion, Johansson had a ninety per cent interest in a fishing trawler and owned a construction company. He had a suite of offices in Stockholm. Later he bought half of a small island called Galo in the Gothenburg archipelago.

For beating Patterson, he earned $81,428, plus television, radio and film rights that pushed the gross above $300,000. The promotion was plagued by difficul-ties between promoter Bill Rosensohn, Patterson's manager Cus D'Amato and his partner, Irving Kahn, who owned a closed-circuit theatre company named TelePrompTer and the St Nick's Arena in Brooklyn. Some said Rosensohn was no more than an office boy – and it's true that D'Amato and Kahn carved up the ancillary rights between them. However, Rosensohn, who said he lost $40,000 on the promotion, did hold the rights to promote Johansson... and suddenly found himself with the world heavyweight champion. He wanted to stage the mandatory rematch at Yankee Stadium in September 1959, but he was forced out of his role as head of Rosensohn Enterprises Inc. and replaced by a New York lawyer, Vincent J. Velella, who was working with Kahn and, it was implied, D'Amato. Things became so murky that the New York District Attorney, Frank Hogan, began to dig and names of Mob figures like Frankie Carbo, 'Trigger' Mike Coppola, Fat Tony Salerno and the head of the exposed, deposed International Boxing Club, James Norris, also cropped up. The New York Commission eventually barred 'a shocked and dismayed' D'Amato from holding a licence. They also suspended Rosensohn's licence for three years – so ending his interest in the sport. This whole episode delayed the rematch until the following June.

Johansson visited Hollywood, toured South America, picked up money from personal appearances and from television shows, and let the situation work itself out. He also upset some Swedes by buying a home in Switzerland for tax purposes.

The return was at the Polo Grounds, the former home of the New York Giants, with new promoters Roy Cohn, Thomas A. Bolan, Denniston Slater and Bill Fuguzy installed, alongside Vellela's closed-circuit company. Johansson wasn't unfit: he had worked out for six weeks in Montana while making a movie called *All the Young Men*, and then did his full camp at Grossinger's.

However, before an official crowd of 31,892, plus about 9,000 whom the promoters said 'climbed walls and crept through holes in the fences of the old stadium', Johansson was knocked out in the fifth round as Patterson became the first man to regain the world heavyweight championship. His left hooks were quicker than Johansson's 'Hammer of Thor' right hand. The Swede's 'Toonder' punch landed only once, in the second round, and Patterson absorbed it, then floored Ingemar with a fast left in the fifth for nine, before laying him out flat on his back, blood trickling from his nose down the side of his face and his left leg twitching as he was counted out by referee Arthur Mercante. It was ten minutes before he could leave the ring.

The decider was at the Miami Beach Convention Hall in March 1961, the promotion underwritten by Bill McDonald, who would promote the Sonny Liston-Cassius Clay fight three years later. Johansson was better prepared – and nearly regained the title when he dropped Patterson twice in the opening round. However, near the end of the round he was down briefly himself, and after that it was a wild, sloppy but close fight – until Patterson put the Swede down for the count in round six. It was the end for Ingemar in the world class.

The son of a Gothenburg stonecutter, Johansson left school at fifteen to work in the docks and as a labourer. From the age of thirteen, Ingemar trained to be a boxer but his amateur career was blighted by his disqualification in the final of the 1952 Olympics in Helsinki for 'not fighting' against the American, Ed Sanders. As a professional he was a good European champion then moved into the world class with a terrific first-round knockout of Eddie Machen in Gothenburg in September 1958. That win set him up for the sensational knockout of Patterson nine months later.

After the Patterson fights, Johansson returned to Sweden, regained the European title by knocking out Dick Richardson in eight rounds, but retired after he finished badly hurt and slumped against the ropes, a points winner but moral loser, against Brian London in Stockholm in April 1963.

He enjoyed life and his businesses, at one time in the 1970s owning a motel in Florida as well as property and luxury boats in Spain. Later he moved back to Sweden and lived on the island of Dalaro near Stockholm. He worked regularly for Scandinavian television as a boxing analyst until the late 1990s. By 2003 he was being cared for in a nursing home, suffering from Alzheimer's Disease.

JACK JOHNSON

Born: 31 March 1878, Galveston, Texas
Full name: Arthur John Johnson
Died: 10 June 1946, Raleigh, North Carolina, aged 68
Height: 6ft 1¼in   **Weight at peak:** 192-206lbs (13st 10lbs to 14st 10lbs)
Fights:127   **Won:** 91   **Lost:** 14   **Drawn:** 12   **No Decisions:** 10
KO percentage: 40
Rounds boxed: 1,065
World champion: 1908-15
World title fights: 8
Career span: 1897-1938 (41 years)
KO wins: 52
KO defeats: 7

Jack Johnson's politicised role in boxing history is obvious: he was the first black heavyweight afforded an opportunity to win the heavyweight championship – and the first to do so.

The full effect of Johnson's one-sided fourteenth-round victory over Tommy Burns in a specially constructed wooden arena at Rushcutter's Bay, Sydney, on Boxing Day 1908 is hard for us to understand almost a century on. In Johnson's time black boxers were tolerated and patronised in the lighter divisions, but excluded at heavyweight. They were also expected to rock no boats – political or sporting – and behave in a manner acceptable to the white folk who had freed their fathers and mothers from slavery. Johnson would have none of it. He strutted his stuff without apparent fear, casting a gold-toothed smile in the direction of prejudice and enjoying his habit of turning accepted norms upside down. He proved he was the best heavyweight in the world; he also enjoyed the company of, and married, white women; he raced the flashiest cars through streets with a reckless disregard for safety; he dressed expensively. He flaunted himself like a magnificent, irritating peacock.

From Galveston, Texas, Johnson was born in 1878, the son of an illiterate freed slave, Henry Johnson, and his wife Tiny, who worked hard, bought a house and the small piece of land it stood on, and raised their six children to read, write and go to the 'blacks only' school where Henry worked as janitor. Jack, whose real name was Arthur John, was regularly defended from childhood bullies by his elder sisters! After the day's classes he would help Henry sweep and clean. He took part in the infamous Battle Royals where, for the entertainment of Southern white gentlemen, black youngsters would be put into a ring to fight each other, up to eight at a time with the winner the last man standing. Occasionally, to spice things up a little, they would be blindfolded or forced to box naked. Out of this humiliation came a proud, bitter man.

Johnson was boxing professionally by his late teens. His first experience of world class brought a three-round defeat by the old contender Joe Choynski

in February 1901. After moving across to California, he out-pointed George
Gardner over twenty rounds in San Francisco – Gardner would become the
world light-heavyweight champion the following year – and then, in Los Angeles
in the space of three weeks in February 1903, he won and defended the unofficial
'black heavyweight title' by outscoring first Denver Ed Martin and then Sam
McVey. Somehow he lost a twenty-round points verdict to the tough but less
skilled Marvin Hart in San Francisco in March 1905. The referee, who was also
the promoter, Alex Greggains, gave the win to Hart, claiming Johnson held too
much. 'I always give the gamest and most aggressive man the decision,' he said.
Johnson, disgusted, left California for Philadelphia. When James J. Jeffries retired,
Hart became champion.

Tommy Burns, the 5ft 7in, 180lb Canadian, beat Hart for the championship,
and astutely avoided Johnson, who had lost only the disputed decision to Hart
and by disqualification to Joe Jeannette in six years and almost fifty fights. Ed
'Gunboat' Smith, a heavyweight contemporary, told the American writer Peter
Heller, 'Johnson used to stand flat-footed and wait for you to come in. And when
you come in, he'd rip the head off you with uppercuts, cut you all to pieces.'

Johnson followed Burns to England and then Australia in 1908, and the wearied
champion finally acknowledged the inevitability of the match. Hugh D. – nicknamed Huge Deal – McIntosh paid Burns £7,500 to sign, but was so suspicious
of Johnson that he carried lead piping wrapped in sheet music 'in case that black
bastard tries any funny business'.

Johnson played the promotional game: alongside his orthodox, rigorous training
he is said to have chased and caught a rabbit and greased pig and won a race with
a kangaroo, which then dropped dead, either of shock or old age. Burns played
the racial stereotype, declaring that Johnson had 'a yellow streak a mile wide'. The
anti-Johnson feeling, fuelled by his gregarious personality, was captured in an editorial in *The Illustrated Sporting and Dramatic News* in Sydney. 'Citizens who have
never prayed before,' it said, 'are supplicating Providence to give the white man a
strong right arm with which to belt the coon into oblivion.'

Men travelled to the stadium by boat, train, on horseback, even on foot to
watch Johnson humiliate Burns. The champion had said Johnson wouldn't take
his body punching. Johnson often exposed his body and said, 'Go on, Tommy.
Hit me here... Now here.' Burns bled from the nose and cuts around his eyes
but talked back. Johnson laughed, clinched and, as Muhammad Ali did sixty-odd
years later, chatted with ringsiders. By the fourteenth Burns was tottering and
the police stopped it after he had been knocked down. Jack London, the novelist,
wrote in the *New York Herald* that James J. Jeffries must come out of retirement to
deal with Johnson. 'Jeff, it's up to you,' he concluded. In the United States, black
Americans mostly enjoyed the result quietly. In Chicago, there was a momentary
reversal of roles as a group of black people hired a club – and white waiters to
serve them.

Johnson's next major fight was in October 1909 against the marauding, brilliant world middleweight champion Stanley Ketchel, who was too small to win, but good enough to put on a show. Ketchel was a legend around whom stories grew like weeds. They said he became a twelve-year-old hobo after the murder of his mother and father in Grand Rapids, Michigan. They said he was mad. One writer wrote, 'A face like that cannot be manufactured by make-up artists. To find such a face – search the insane asylums, or the prison death house.' Ketchel fought at the start with tears of rage streaming down his face, Johnson wearing the American flag as a belt, which drew boos from the predominantly white crowd. Johnson more or less did as he pleased as Ketchel, blood running from nose and mouth, kept up the charge. In the twelfth Johnson either got careless or, if we would believe him, played to the cameras. He took a long right hand above the left ear and went down, his right glove propping his fall. He got up without a count and Ketchel walked into a fast burst of punches, ending with a right uppercut that laid him out unconscious on his back. They found two of his teeth embedded in Johnson's right glove.

That night Ketchel and Johnson went off to play craps together in a gambling hall. A year later the middleweight was dead, shot in the back over breakfast by a farmhand, Walter A. Dipley, who believed Stanley was messing with his girl-friend. As they ferried his body back for the biggest funeral Grand Rapids had ever seen, a woman claiming to be Ketchel's fiancée, Jewell A. Bovine, tried to poison herself. By then Johnson had beaten Jim Jeffries on 4 July 1910. Jeffries had come from his Californian farm to reclaim the title for the white race, but was toyed with, cut to shreds and stopped in fifteen rounds. Johnson taunted him most of the way: 'How do you feel, Jim? How do you like it? Does it hurt, Jim?' Incredibly, Jeffries chewed gum most of the way. In round fifteen, Johnson knocked him down twice for counts of nine, and then with the count at seven in the third knockdown, his handlers raced into the ring to prevent it being said he was counted out. Semantics didn't matter. An hour earlier Johnson had walked into an arena with a specially built area at the back for ladies, through crowds who had been listening to a white band playing a selection of songs including the popular ditty *All Coons Look Alike to Me*. Now he left the ring in silence, his broad, gold-toothed grin taunting the white supremacists who still dominated a nation's thinking. The horrific riots, murders and lynchings that spread across the nation in the days that followed the fight exposed the extent of the racial tension that remained forty-four years after the abolition of slavery.

Tex Rickard, who had promoted the Johnson–Jeffries event, was reluctant to get involved with the champion again. A succession of 'White Hopes' were pro-duced but mostly cancelled each other out. Fireman Jim Flynn, well beaten by Johnson five years earlier, was offered a chance in Las Vegas, New Mexico, but fouled his way through to the ninth when his impression of an outraged goat earned him disqualification.

Johnson was living in Chicago, but in September 1912 his long-suffering wife Etta shot herself in rooms at his club, the Café de Champion. A month later he was arrested under the bizarre Mann Act, which forbade the 'transportation of women across state lines for the purpose of prostitution, debauchery or immoral purposes'. His supposed crime was to travel with a white teenager, Lucille Cameron, who had been working as a prostitute in Chicago for six months. Johnson's unpopularity and egotism had led to a witchhunt. His club was closed down and the prosecution eventually made a charge stick, not for his behaviour with Cameron, but with another woman, Belle Schreiber, who had been his mistress more than two years earlier and, accordingly, had travelled with him. Johnson, who meanwhile married Lucille Cameron and announced his intention to move into an exclusively white area of Chicago, was indicted on eleven charges from aiding prostitution to the supremely vague 'crime against nature'. After a sensational trial, he was convicted, sentenced to a year and a day in jail and fined $1,000. He fled across the Canadian border to Montreal and then to Europe.

His life became increasingly sad. His exhibitions were booed by audiences who expected more of the world heavyweight champion than an ill-conditioned man in his mid-thirties going through the motions. In June 1914 he out-boxed Frank Moran from Pittsburgh in a twenty-round title defence, but again the crowd booed the lack of action. As the German army advanced into France, Johnson left for London and then had exhibitions in Argentina and Cuba, where he finally lost the championship to the big, ponderous Jess Willard. On a racetrack outside Havana, Johnson, his waist thickened, tired in the hot sun after out-boxing Willard easily in the early stages. Willard knocked him out in the twenty-sixth round. Johnson used the photograph of him lying on his back with his forearm apparently shading his eyes from the sun as proof that he had thrown the fight, but as Willard said, 'If a man wants to throw a fight, he doesn't fight for twenty-six rounds.'

A vaudeville tour to England flopped and left him with debts and lawsuits. He was asked to leave the country, so lived in Spain until the end of the First World War and then moved to Mexico and on to the United States to serve his sentence in 1920. He did his time in Leavenworth, Kansas.

Johnson married another white woman, Irene Pineau, in 1924 and got by on his wits. He was wheeled out occasionally to talk about the heavyweight situation. Johnson and the second black world heavyweight champ, Joe Louis, did not get on. Bizarrely, Jack took to affecting a strange British upper-class accent and had a long-time speaking engagement in a seedy New York club. His driving had always been appalling and at the age of sixty-eight, in June 1946 when on the way from a personal appearance tour of Texas to New York to watch Louis box Billy Conn, his car smashed into a lamppost twenty miles north of Raleigh, North Carolina. He died in hospital a few hours later.

BATTLING JIM JOHNSON

Born: 1883, Danville, Virginia
Died: Uncertain
Height: 6ft 3in   **Weight at peak:** 225lbs (16st 1lb)
Fights: 71   **Won:** 19   **Lost:** 31   **Drawn:** 9   **No Decisions:** 12
KO percentage: 16
Rounds boxed: 663
World title fights: 1
Career span: 1910-18 (8 years)
KO wins: 12
KO defeats: 6

One of the least celebrated of all heavyweight title challengers, Battling Jim Johnson was supposed to serve as the fall-guy for world champion Jack Johnson's Christmas payday of 1913. Johnson, exiled from America and facing a jail sentence should he return, was enjoying himself in Paris. As he ran through his money rapidly, he needed to appear in the ring once in a while. He took wrestling exhibitions if it suited him – and only three weeks before defending his title against his namesake he had knocked out a wrestler, André Spoul, in two rounds of a riotous encounter. The story goes that he had injured his left arm a little but thought nothing of it – and at the Velodrome d'Hiver was in a merry mood before a twenty-round bout against a man who was tough, awkward and quick but not especially talented. For three rounds Jack staged an exhibition, then in the fourth his arm 'went'.

Battling Jim, who at 6ft 3in and around 225lbs was actually bigger than the champion, was wary. Jack was content to move around and not do much and the fans, who had paid to see a genuine 'king of the ring', booed and jeered. Some walked out in disgust, some loudly demanded their money back. In the end, in spite of Jack's technical superiority, the non-event was called off after ten rounds and a draw was announced. Doctors diagnosed a fractured bone in the champion's left arm. History now regards this shambles as the first heavyweight championship bout between two black fighters.

Battling Jim was born in Danville, Virginia, but was sometimes billed, like Jack Johnson, out of Galveston, Texas. This may have been a mistake he just let ride because it linked him to the champion. He was also said to have come from Tennessee. After beginning his career in the USA, he tried his luck in Europe. In England he scored an eleventh-round knockout over Jewey Smith, who had boxed Tommy Burns for the championship. Following his farce with Johnson, he returned home and campaigned for another four years, boxing Joe Jeannette, Sam Langford, Sam McVea and Harry Wills regularly. They were all superior fighters, though he did get a freak two-round retirement win over Wills, when Harry broke his wrist in St Louis in 1917.

His last bout was an eight-round points loss to Langford in St Louis in August 1918. One record source says he died on 1 November 1918 but the founder of *Ring* magazine, Nat Fleischer, in *Black Dynamite*, suggested that for several years after his retirement he was employed as a rubber in the Pioneer Gymnasium in New York.

DOUG JONES

Born: 27 February 1937, New York City
Height: 6ft   **Weight at peak:** 187lbs (13st 5lbs)
Fights: 41   **Won:** 30   **Lost:** 10   **Drawn:** 1
KO percentage: 48
Rounds boxed: 289
World title fights: 1
Career span: 1958-67 (9 years)
KO wins: 20
KO defeats: 3

Doug Jones almost wrecked the Cassius Clay masterplan when he gave him an unexpectedly tough ten-round fight in Madison Square Garden in 1963. Jones went down by a single point on two cards – 5-4-1 for judges Artie Aidala and Frank Forbes – although Clay was seven points up according to referee Joe Loscalzo.

The shaven-headed New Yorker troubled Clay in the first and sixth rounds and refused to fold when his legs were buckled in the ninth. At the end 18,732 fans voiced their disapproval of the verdict. There were the customary yells of 'fix' and programmes, cartons and other missiles cascaded down on the ring. A ringside poll of reporters came out 12-9-2 in Jones's favour. Not that this is necessarily a recommendation for anything...

'I didn't think any boxer could go ten with me,' said Clay. At ringside world champion Sonny Liston grinned one of his baleful smiles and said, 'I'll get locked up for murder if we're ever matched.'

Jones turned to boxing while in the US Air Force, lost three of forty amateur bouts and turned professional as a middleweight in 1958. In August 1960 Jones scored his sixteenth straight win by stopping the faded former world middle-weight champion Carl 'Bobo' Olson in six rounds in Chicago and two fights later, by then a big light-heavyweight, he conceded 17lbs to the 1956 Olympic heavyweight gold medallist Pete Rademacher and floored him four times for a fifth-round knockout in St Nick's Arena, New York. He lost his unbeaten record when Eddie Machen out-pointed him in Miami, dropped a fifteen-round deci-sion in a world light-heavyweight title challenge against Harold Johnson in Philadelphia and was out-pointed by Zora Folley.

In October 1962 Jones wrecked the unbeaten record of the young Bob Foster, knocking out the future light-heavyweight champion in the eighth round. Then he won a rematch with Folley in seven to move into contention for Liston's title... and the bout with Clay.

His reputation grew with that fight and three more wins, including a fifth-round stoppage of the one-time title challenger Tom McNeeley, suggested a rematch with Clay, by then Muhammad Ali, for the championship could be made. However, a shock points defeat to Billy Daniels spoiled things and then in Madison Square Garden in October 1964 he was knocked out in eleven rounds by George Chuvalo.

In June 1966 Jones boxed the WBA's pretender Ernie Terrell in Houston, Texas. Terrell, 22lbs heavier and around 6ins taller, out-pointed him clearly in a poor fight. The 9,346 crowd didn't like Terrell's jab-and-grab style, but it was effective and Jones couldn't do much with him. The official scores were 145-140, 146-141, 146-140, which included two points taken away from Terrell for fouls.

Jones lost his next fight on points to Thad Spencer, and in February 1967 he was steamrollered to a fifth-round defeat by the unbeaten twenty-three-year-old Smokin' Joe Frazier. He did get a cut-eye win over another unbeaten hope, Boone Kirkman, but retired when he lost the return in August 1967.

LEROY JONES

Born: 10 February 1950, Meridian, Mississippi
Height: 6ft 5in   **Weight at peak:** 254lbs (18st 2lbs)
Fights: 27   **Won:** 25   **Lost:** 1   **Drawn:** 1
KO percentage: 47
Rounds boxed: 173
World title fights: 1
Career span: 1973-82 (9 years)
KO wins: 13
KO defeats: 1

A blubbery heavyweight who was actually quite nimble and had good hand speed, Leroy Jones was unbeaten until he boxed Larry Holmes for the World Boxing Council title in 1980. Unfortunately, the thirty-year-old challenger suffered a detached retina in an eighth-round defeat — he claimed Holmes caught him with the thumb — and retired. He had outweighed the champion by more than 40lbs but hadn't won a round on any of the three cards when the fight was stopped four seconds from the end of round eight.

Born in Meridian, Mississippi, in February 1950, Jones was raised in Brooklyn, where he played college football and twice won the New York Golden Gloves. His best win was in August 1978 in Las Vegas (where he was then working as a maintenance engineer in the Holiday Inn) against future WBA champion Mike Weaver. He won a ten-round decision. In his first fight of 1979 he got off the floor to out-point Fili Moala in San Diego, but victories over Harry Terrell and Jim Beattie, neither of whom were great shakes, took him to the Holmes fight in Las Vegas in March 1980.

He had one comeback fight in Gary, Indiana, in August 1982, a second-round knockout of Jeff Shelburg, but he had put on 30lbs since the Holmes fight and clearly his enthusiasm had gone.

K

VITALI & WLADIMIR KLITSCHKO
Vitali
Born: 19 July 1971, Belovodsk, Kyrgyzstan
Height: 6ft 7½in   **Weight at peak:** 248lbs (17st 10lbs)
Fights: 37   **Won:** 35   **Lost:** 2
KO percentage: 91
Rounds boxed: 147
World champion: 2004-05
World title fights: 3
Career span: 1996-2005 (9 years)
KO wins: 34
KO defeats: 2

Wladimir
Born: 25 March 1976, Semipalatinsk, Kazakhstan
Height: 6ft 6in   **Weight at peak:** 241lbs (17st 3lbs)
Fights: 48   **Won:** 45   **Lost:** 3
KO percentage: 83
Rounds boxed: 192
World title fights: 0
Career span: 1996-2005 (9 years)
KO wins: 40
KO defeats: 3

Vitali Klitschko, and his younger brother Wladimir, were considered the 'new generation' heavyweights who would follow Lennox Lewis. For several years it was

Wladimir who was considered the heir apparent, but his challenge faltered with knockout defeats by Corrie Sanders and Lamon Brewster. Ironically, while those setbacks all but ruined Wladimir's reputation, Vitali made his in a losing fight with Lewis in Los Angeles in June 2003. Vitali had been scheduled to box Cedric Boswell, while Lewis was to have defended the WBC title against Kirk Johnson. This would then have been followed by an autumn meeting between Lewis and Klitschko. However, with a fortnight to go Johnson pulled out with a chest injury and HBO, who were bankrolling the show, pressed for Lewis and Klitschko to meet.

Lewis, who had believed he would beat Johnson without breaking sweat, was in no real shape to take on the bigger threat presented by the mechanical but fit and smart Ukrainian. And Vitali, ignoring critics who said he was too robotic and easy to hit to stand a chance, almost pulled off a sensational win. Lewis was hurt and on the ropes in round two, then cut Klitschko with a long, slashing right hand in the third. After the sixth, in which he had absorbed a terrific uppercut, Klitschko was ahead on points on all three official scorecards 58-56. However, the jagged gash on the eyelid was in a terrible state and there were other smaller cuts above and below the eye. The ringside doctor stopped the fight. Klitschko protested bitterly but the decision was understandable. Lewis was annoyed by the criticism he received but the general feeling was that the champion had been fortunate. Lewis did not exercise the rematch clause, turned down a December date and then announced his retirement in February 2004.

Meanwhile, Klitschko underwent plastic surgery on the eye, returned in December to demolish Kirk Johnson in two rounds and then in April 2004 won the vacant WBC title with an eighth-round stoppage of Corrie Sanders, the South African southpaw who had beaten Wladimir in a stunning two-round upset for the minor WBO belt the previous year. In December 2004 Vitali floored Danny Williams, the London heavyweight who had beaten Mike Tyson that summer, five times for an eighth-round win in Las Vegas.

Vitali was born in Belovodsk in what is now Kyrgyzstan, Wladimir in Semipalatinsk in Kazakhstan. Their father was a colonel in the Soviet air force, which meant the family moved around. Their mother was a teacher. It was a middle class, even privileged background. Vitali was playing chess from the age of seven – and for publicity purposes Wladimir had a game with the grandmaster Gary Kasparov. Both brothers earned PhDs in Sports Science from the University of Kiev. They make it their business to travel around the world in support of UNESCO. During the volatile Ukrainian elections of 2005, they were heavily involved in supporting the anti-Russian candidate Viktor Yushchenko, whose face was heavily scarred by poison during the campaign but who was eventually successful.

As a boy Vitali preferred kick-boxing, but at fourteen added the orthodox code to his make-up. He competed in both sports side by side, winning world kick-boxing titles then going on to a silver medal in the World Amateur Championships in 1995 and gold in the World Military Games. The Ukrainian authorities planned to take Vitali to the Atlanta Olympics at super-heavy and Wladimir at heavyweight but then a local doctor gave Vitali a 'healing substance' to treat a calf injury picked up while kick-boxing. To his astonishment, and then anger, he tested positive for a steroid. The subsequent ban meant he was out of the Olympics – and Wladimir, who had been struggling to make the heavyweight limit, went instead as the super-heavy and won the gold medal.

For their professional careers, the brothers moved to Germany and signed with Klaus Peter Kohl's Universum company. Vitali won the European title in 1998, then became WBO champion with a two-round knockout of Herbie Hide in London in June 1999. He made two defences, then lost it in strange circumstances to Michigan southpaw Chris Byrd in Berlin in April 2000. Well ahead on points, Vitali retired in his corner with a shoulder injury. HBO, who had travelled to Germany to cover the show as a part of building up the Klitschkos, were unimpressed. Vitali underwent surgery and stuck to his argument that the pain was significant and to go on could have ruined his career. He regained the European title against Timo Hoffmann in Hanover, then beat a succession of men on the fringe of world class, including long-time contender Larry Donald and former challenger Vaughn Bean.

Then came the Lewis fight that changed Vitali's career and the Sanders victory that earned him, at 6ft 7½in, the statistical record as the tallest heavyweight champion in history. 'They say my style looks ugly and clumsy but it works,' he said. 'My style is my strength.'

Wladimir won his first twenty-four fights, then on his first professional appearance in Kiev ran out of steam and was stopped in the eleventh round by American journeyman Ross Puritty in December 1998. He put that down to education about how not to let external issues distract him, beat the German Axel Schulz for the European title, and went on to avenge his brother's defeat by Chris Byrd with a one-sided decision in Cologne in October 2000 for the WBO belt. He made five successful defences against Derrick Jefferson, Charles Shufford, Frans Botha, Ray Mercer and Jameel McCline before losing in a stunning upset in two rounds to the thirty-seven-year-old South African Corrie Sanders in Hannover in March 2003.

He rebuilt and in April 2004 seemed on the brink of regaining the WBO championship when he had Lamon Brewster hurt and bewildered, only to come apart under Brewster's last desperate counterattack. He was beaten inside five rounds. It seemed a long way back from there.

KALLIE KNOETZE

Born: 24 April 1953, South Africa
Full name: Nicholas Jacobus Knoetze
Height: 6ft 1in   **Weight at peak:** 211lbs (15st 1lb)
Fights: 27   **Won:** 21   **Lost:** 6
KO percentage: 74

Rounds boxed: 121
World title fights: 0
Career span: 1976-81 (5 years)
KO wins: 20
KO defeats: 4

A big-punching, colourful heavyweight of the late 1970s and 1980s, Kallie
Knoetze was one of the most controversial sportsmen of his time. He was seen
as a walking, talking symbol of the Apartheid regime, primarily because he had
resigned from his job as a policeman following fines for assault and intimidating
witnesses. There was also the matter of the shooting and crippling of an unarmed
black youngster, Stanley Ndlovu, during a spell of civil unrest in Attridgeville. A
defensive but defiant Knoetze said he had black friends who knew he was not a
racist man. 'What happened in Attridgeville happened because I was a policeman
doing my duty,' he said. 'There was a riot on, we were being stoned, and in the
defence of law and order, I'd shoot again.'

However, when Knoetze was stopped in eight rounds of what amounted to
an eliminator for the WBA heavyweight title in Johannesburg in June 1979, the
Transvaal Post interviewed Ndlovu. 'How I wish I was there,' he said. 'I would have
kissed John Tate... I am only sorry about one thing – they stopped the fight. They
should have left Tate to punish Knoetze until he cried for mercy...

'I remember his words when he said I should drink my blood when I asked for
water... I pray all opponents remember my lost leg when they meet him.'

The *Rand Daily Mail* headlined their coverage of the fight as 'The Demise of
a Demi-God' and reported that Knoetze's Afrikaner followers 'massed along the
east-west axis leading to Mmabatho with all the arrogance and fervour of a con-
quering army'. A soldier of the supposedly independent state of Bophutatswana
(recognised only in South Africa) was injured when a gun he confiscated from a
spectator at the stadium gates went off accidentally. There were a few fights in the
stands, one man, who was drunk, broke an ankle in a fall.

Knoetze took his defeat without complaint, ploughing forward and even having Tate in some trouble before being worn down and stopped, still on his feet,
but exhausted and dazed. He was gracious in his praise of the American and
returned to a bar to dance and party the night away and lift the spirits of his fans,
one of whom had, according to the *Rand Daily Mail*, stood weeping bitterly, asking of no one in particular, 'Why did he lose? Why did he lose?'

Nicholas Jacobus Knoetze's first love had been rugby union – but his father,
Ben, talked him into boxing. He lost his first eleven amateur bouts, but improved
so much he won the South African amateur heavyweight crown in 1974 when
he was twenty-one. He and arch rival Gerrie Coetzee boxed six times as amateurs, with three wins each. He kept on playing rugby and was a good enough
flank forward to play for Northern Transvaal, but concentrated on professional

boxing after a collarbone injury. Knoetze turned professional in February 1976 at the age of twenty-two. His power was obvious: he knocked out eight of his first ten opponents, was disqualifed for repeatedly hitting Raul Gorosito low, and lost a contentious decision to Coetzee. He was down in the third but rallied and seemed to many to have won.

Knoetze won the South African title with a second-round knockout of Mike Schutte, also beat former world title challenger Richard Dunn in five, and then took out Duane Bobick in three – his finest win, as the American had lost only one of forty-one pro fights following an appearance in the Munich Olympics.

Knoetze's police problems led to protests in the United States when he made his US debut with a fourth-round win over Bill Sharkey in Miami Beach in January 1979, and then Tate exposed him so decisively in Mmbatho, which was to become Sun City, in June 1979. Three fights later he was stopped in ten by another American, Mike Koranicki, in Cape Town and then the blubbery Jimmy Abbott knocked him out in one round for the South African title. Knoetze retired after another South African, Robbie Williams, beat him in two rounds in Durban in July 1981. After leaving the police, Knoetze became a farmer. In contrast to the reserved, quietly spoken Coetzee, Knoetze was an outgoing, seemingly irrepressible figure. He was interviewed regularly once again when South Africa staged the Lennox Lewis-Hasim Rahman world heavyweight title fight in Carnival City just outside Johannesburg in April 2001.

L

BILL LANG

Born: 8 July 1883, Melbourne, Australia
Full name: William Langfranchi
Died: 1 September 1952, St Kilda, Australia, aged 69
Height: 6ft 1in   **Weight at peak:** 187lbs (13st 5lbs)
Fights: 45   **Won:** 27   **Lost:** 15   **Drawn:** 1   **No Decisions:** 2
KO percentage: 44
Rounds boxed: 438
World title fights: 1
Career span: 1905-1914 (9 years)
KO wins: 21
KO defeats: 4

If Bill Lang had no right to box for the world title against Tommy Burns in front of 19,000 Australian fans in Melbourne in September 1908, at least he gave everything he had. In fact, Lang clubbed the six-inches shorter Burns to the canvas in the second round – and the champion only just beat the count. The gritty little Canadian recovered, took over and knocked Lang out in round six.

In a nine-year career Lang also boxed Jack Johnson and Bob Fitzsimmons, both of course world heavyweight champions. Lang had only ten official fights behind him – and had won only five of those – when he boxed Johnson before a crowd estimated at up to 15,000 at a rain-soaked Richmond Racecourse, Melbourne, in March 1907. Johnson took him apart. In the second round they fell over with Lang on top, but from round four the Australian took a dizzying pounding and was floored six times in the seventh and eighth rounds. In a clinch in round nine, Lang asked Johnson, 'What round is it?' Johnson smiled and said, 'What round, Bill? Why, it's the last.' And with that he finished him off.

Lang won eleven in a row after that and then fought Burns for the championship as promoter Hugh D. McIntosh was building up the Burns-Johnson epic for Rushcutter's Bay, Sydney, on 26 December 1908, which was one of those days that changed the world. Lang's opportunity was on 2 September of that year and the Australian public seemed to respect his effort. Lang went on to earn more as a sparring partner for Johnson. He was certainly better than the china-chinned Boshter Bill Squires who challenged Burns on three occasions. Lang fought Squires four times and won all four by knockout, although once he was virtually unconscious in his corner when his brother Ernie waved smelling salts under his nose and poor Bill grabbed the bottle and drank it. He said the pain raged through his body and caused a wave of what seemed like electric shots. In panic he shot out of the corner and pounded an equally shocked Squires to defeat. Lang also boxed Fitzsimmons, by then forty-six years old, in Sydney in December 1909. Fitzsimmons, slow and old, was put away in round twelve. Sadly for Bill, the crowd, who had welcomed old Ruby Robert back to the land of his youth, booed the knockout, even though Fitzsimmons was apparently counted out while unconscious, his legs twitching as he lay. In his dressing room Fitzsimmons cried as he admitted to reporters he was too old to box any more. 'I couldn't rough it with that big, strong, husky young fellow,' he said. At another show not long afterwards Lang presented Fitzsimmons with a gold cardcase as a mark of respect and they talked long into the night at the hotel where Bob was staying.

As much as Lang listened to the old champion, he could never emulate him. Lang did box Burns in a rematch for the British Empire title in Sydney in April 1910 and lost a twenty-round decision. On a three-fight visit to London he was also disqualified for hitting Sam Langford when the great man was on the canvas after slipping over in round six at the National Sporting Club. Langford had toyed with him. Another of the great black heavyweights of the era, Sam McVey, also knocked him out easily in two rounds in Sydney in 1911. It remains a crime that men like Langford and McVey were not allowed championship bouts while less talented but white heavyweights like Lang and Squires, as well as Jem Roche and Jewey Smith, were given their chance. Lang's last win was a nineteenth-round knockout of the faded 'White Hope' Arthur Pelkey in Sydney in 1914. He retired later that year after Tom Bearcat McMahon knocked him out.

Lang's full name was William Langfranchi. Born in Melbourne, he worked as an apprentice to a blacksmith, then as a miner, where he developed his reputation as a bare-knuckle saloon brawler. When he retired from the ring he ran a hotel in Melbourne. He died at his home in the St Kilda area of the city in September 1952 at the age of sixty-nine.

SAM LANGFORD

Born: 4 March 1883, Weymouth, Nova Scotia, Canada
Died: 12 January 1956, Cambridge, Massachusetts, aged 73
Height: 5ft 8in   **Weight at peak:** 194-204lbs (13st 12lbs-14st 8lbs)
Fights: 314   **Won:** 197   **Lost:** 51   **Drawn:** 46   **No Decisions:** 20
KO percentage: 41
Rounds boxed: 2,570
World title fights: 0
Career span: 1902-26 (24 years)
KO wins: 130
KO defeats: 9

Those who saw him say Sam Langford was one of the best pound-for-pound fighters of all time, a short, barrel-chested, long-armed, thinking fighter with a vicious punch in either hand. Jack Dempsey, who won the world title in 1919 when Langford was thirty-six, said he was offered a fight with Sam a couple of years earlier. 'I think Sam Langford was the greatest fighter we ever had,' said Dempsey, in 1970. When Langford's name was mentioned, he turned him down flat. 'Not me! Goodbye!' he said. 'He was a great fighter and I didn't have the experience to fight a man like that. Even at my best I don't know whether I could have licked him or not.'

Anecdotal legends can make heroes even of rather humdrum men, but Langford really does seem to have been exceptional. A colourful, extravagant personality, he had immense confidence in his punch. Once, at the start of round six, he extended his glove in the traditional sporting gesture. 'It's not the last round,' said his opponent. 'It is for you!' said Langford. And it was. Another time he stood in the centre of the ring and addressed the crowd before the opening bell: 'You'll pardon me, gentlemen, if I make the fight short. I have a train to catch...'

Langford was Canadian, born in Weymouth, Nova Scotia. The date of birth usually accepted for him now is 4 March 1883, but nobody can be absolutely sure.

Nat Fleischer, for example, once put it at three years later. By his teens he was in Boston, where he met Joe Woodman, who owned a drugstore, ran a gym and promoted fights. The first fight on his twenty-four-year record was in Boston in 1902, when he was probably a lightweight. Such was his talent that by 1903 he was world class: there are twenty-six bouts listed for him, including the magnificent old master himself, Joe Gans, who was the world lightweight champion at the time and still around his peak at twenty-nine. Langford out-pointed Gans over fifteen rounds in Boston in December 1903. Fifteen days later Langford lost a twelve-round verdict to Jack Blackburn, who would go on to earn lasting fame as the teacher and trainer of Joe Louis. In September 1904 Langford fought a fifteen-round draw with Joe Walcott, the Barbados Demon who had lost the world welterweight title less than six months earlier. Another fifteen-rounder with Blackburn also finished in a draw. He finally beat him on points over fifteen rounds in Leiperville in August 1905. Altogether they fought six times before Langford grew too heavy.

By 1907, although only a natural middleweight, Langford was boxing heavyweights like Joe Jeannette. This was the year he was also beaten on points over fifteen rounds by Jack Johnson. Woodman put a spin on the fight to make it sound very close – and certainly Johnson wanted no part of Langford again – but according to others Jack won it easily, dropping Langford several times and busting him up quite badly. The truth may be simpler: they had similarly egotistical personalities, didn't like each other and Johnson, once he had the championship, knew a fight with Langford made no financial sense compared to the risk it involved – and he probably saw no reason to offer a man he despised a payday.

Langford often fought the same man over and over again: he boxed Joe Jeannette fourteen times and also had long series with Jim Barry, Harry Wills, Sam McVey, Jeff Clarke and Bill Tate. It was the way things were. Out of the ring, although some like the English referee Eugene Corri considered him modest and polite, he was a creature of the night, enjoyed a drink, a smoke, a bet and the company of women. Unlike Johnson, however, he was wise enough to steer clear, in public at least, of white women. He ruffled no official feathers.

Obviously he should have boxed for the world heavyweight title. Four days before Christmas 1908 in San Francisco he fought Jim Flynn, who boxed both Johnson and his predecessor, Tommy Burns, for the championship. Langford, the story goes, felt he was being underpaid. Backstage he passed Flynn's dressing room and saw a trainer cutting oranges into pieces for 'The Fireman' to suck between rounds. 'You're wasting good fruit,' said Langford, as he popped his head around the door. It was all over in the first round.

His trip to England in May 1909 increased his fame. He had crossed the Atlantic before, in 1907, and made a big impression with a one-punch knockout of Tiger Smith at the National Sporting Club, and this time he outclassed the British heavyweight champion, Iron Hague, in four. Hague, around 40lbs heavier, bowled

Langford over with a sweeping left in the second, but Langford was unhurt. He took out Hague with a clean left to the chin. Hague was astonished that a man so small could have done that to him. The NSC tried to make a world championship fight between Johnson and Langford, but the champion turned it down. Back in the United States, Langford ended his year by stopping the capable southpaw Mike Schreck in the first round in Pittsburgh.

At times, especially in No-Decision bouts, Langford went through the motions. He barely seems to have tried against Jim Flynn in Los Angeles in 1910, when newspapermen felt Flynn won. In a return the following month Langford stirred himself and knocked out 'The Fireman' in round eight. One No-Decision fight that turned into a war was against the reigning world middleweight champion Stanley Ketchel in April 1910. Ketchel had fought Johnson for the heavyweight crown six months earlier – and six months later would be shot dead over his breakfast by Walter A. Dipley in Missouri. The idea was for Ketchel and Langford to have a six-round No-Decision bout as a taster for a forty-five-round contest. Incredibly, the 'prelim' drew a gate of $18,750, a record for Philadelphia. Langford took $5,000, Ketchel almost double that. They began tamely enough, but Langford hurt Ketchel in the fourth, and the 'Michigan Assassin' swarmed all over him in the final two. By the end Langford's chest was soaked with his own blood and he was tired. Some, however, said he deliberately under-performed in a bid to nail down the big payday. Whatever the truth, the return never happened.

Back in London in 1911 he beat the Australian champion Bill Lang on a sixth-round foul – he slipped down and was struck while on the floor. In Paris he fought a twenty-round draw with Sam McVey and the pair, along with Jim Barry, took off for Australia at the end of the year. Before that Langford knocked out the former light-heavyweight champion Philadelphia Jack O'Brien in five rounds in New York. Gunboat Smith, one of the best heavyweights of the time, out-pointed Langford in Boston in November 1913. 'I beat him that time, but I never was no good after it,' said Smith. 'Every time that Langford hit me, by God, he'd break the shoelaces... I got the decision. I was tickled to death to get the hell out of there. I figured I needed a rest.' In a rematch the following year, Langford won easily in three rounds.

In 1914 he also began his long series with Harry Wills, the man who a decade later would be avoided by Jack Dempsey, or more accurately promoter Tex Rickard, because of the colour of his skin. By his mid-thirties Langford probably knew his fate would never alter. It's hard to understand how he could have lost in seven rounds to the lumbering white heavyweight Fred Fulton in Boston in 1917, but he did. The following year he was twice stopped by Harry Wills. Although those stoppages were rare, he began to lose more often, and it's possible the cataracts that eventually forced him to stop boxing were developing. Or perhaps the reality of his situation made him more cynical. He still had the punch, though: twice he knocked out one of the new generation black heavyweights, George

Godfrey, and he also beat the young Tiger Flowers, later world middleweight champion, in two rounds in Atlanta in 1922.

Bizarrely, he won the Mexican heavyweight title in 1923 by knocking out one Jim Savage in the first round in Mexico City, by which time he was around forty years old. He stayed there long enough to lose the national championship to Clem Johnson in Juarez, but beat his old rival Jim Flynn three times when both of them were old enough to know better. The last fight on his long record was in August 1926 in Drumright, Oklahoma, when he lost in one round to Brad Simmons, who would probably have been unable to hit him in his prime.

An operation on his cataracts was unsuccessful and for many years he lived in a room in Harlem. In 1944 a sports writer, Al Laney, found him – he was blind and broke, but a long way from beaten. 'I got my guitar, and a bottle of gin, and money in my pocket to buy my Christmas dinner. No millionaire in the world got more than that,' he said. Langford died in Cambridge, Massachusetts, on 12 January 1956.

ROLAND LaSTARZA

Born: 12 May 1927, Bronx, New York
Height: 6ft   **Weight at peak:** 188lbs (13st 6lbs)
Fights: 66   **Won:** 57   **Lost:** 9
KO percentage: 40
Rounds boxed: 383
World title fights: 1
Career span: 1947-61 (14 years)
KO wins: 27
KO defeats: 2

A former college student from the Bronx, Roland LaStarza gave Rocky Marciano two of his toughest fights – and some say was very unlucky not to get the decision in Madison Square Garden in March 1950. A textbook boxer with a sturdy chin – and with thirty-seven consecutive wins behind him in only three years, LaStarza dealt with Marciano's rushes calmly, and Jersey Jones, for *Ring* magazine, said, 'The split verdict in Rocky's favour did not sit at all well with most of the folks present. But it was LaStarza's own fault for making the thing even close. The chunky Bronxite had all the necessary equipment to win decisively, but he was too cautious.'

LaStarza out-boxed Marciano for three rounds, was knocked down for eight in the fourth by a right hand and came back to dominate the middle part of the fight before Marciano came on again. Both thought they had won. One judge had LaStarza ahead 5-4-1 in rounds, the other saw Marciano a 5-4-1 winner. The referee, Jack Watson, had it level at 5-5 but gave the edge to Rocky 9-6 on the strange countback system. LaStarza's manager, Jimmy 'Fats' DeAngelo, accused Al Weill, who was both Marciano's manager and matchmaker for the International Boxing Club, which ran boxing in New York, of influencing the result. When Weill tried to walk into Roland's dressing room to commiserate, DeAngelo slammed the door in his face. Weill took that personally and over the next two years avoided booking LaStarza, consigning him to working in smaller arenas in towns like Holyoke, Massachusetts, and Waterbury, Connecticut. On the only occasion Weill did book him again for the Garden, LaStarza lost a close, unanimous decision to Dan Bucceroni. After Weill had gone, they had a rematch and LaStarza floored Bucceroni five times and won on points. Out in Akron, Ohio, he lost to Fred 'Rocky' Jones, but then beat him in a return in Brooklyn before a ten-round split decision in the Garden over Rex Layne finally earned him the return with Marciano for the championship in September 1953 at the Polo Grounds.

They drew 44,562 fans, but such had been the contrast in their fortunes since the first fight Marciano was a 1-5 favourite. Few gave Roland a chance to last the distance. In the end they were right but in the early stages LaStarza out-boxed the champion. He didn't run, he stood in range and blocked the shots with his gloves and arms. Marciano also had round six taken away from him for punching low. From the seventh, though, Rocky's stamina brought him on and blood vessels in LaStarza's arms had burst, making it increasingly difficult to hold them up. He took a pounding but refused to go down until the eleventh when a right hand dropped him onto the ring apron. He got up at nine but had nothing left. The next assault had him defenceless and Ruby Goldstein stopped it. LaStarza was generous in his praise in the dressing room. He said, 'I don't hesitate to say that anybody who beats him will have to be 5,000 times better than I was tonight. Rocky's improved 100 per cent since I fought him last.'

In his next fight he travelled to London and boxed British champion Don Cockell before more than 18,000 fans at Earl's Court. LaStarza and DeAngelo were outraged by the verdict of referee Eugene Henderson for Cockell and complained bitterly to the official and to the head of the British Board of Control, J. Onslow Fane. Two American newspapermen, Barney Nagler and Bill Heinz, thought he was robbed and DeAngelo said no other American boxer should risk coming to Britain. LaStarza said bitterly, 'It's my own fault – I should have knocked the guy out. I started too late, but I'm positive I won the fight.' Most British journalists had Cockell edging it. Worse followed: in December 1954 in Cleveland, LaStarza lost a unanimous decision to Charley Norkus, who was well below the top flight, and then the erratic but heavy-hitting Cuban Julio Mederos put him down three times and knocked him out in the fifth round in Miami.

From then he boxed infrequently until 1961 when he lost a ten-round decision to Monroe Ratliff in San Francisco and retired, aged thirty-four.

SCOTT LeDOUX

Born: 27 January 1949, Crosby, Minnesota
Height: 6ft   **Weight at peak:** 222lbs (15st 12lbs)
Fights: 50   **Won:** 33   **Lost:** 13   **Drawn:** 4
KO percentage: 44
Rounds boxed: 350
World title fights: 1
Career span: 1974-83 (9 years)
KO wins: 22
KO defeats: 7

Minnesota heavyweight Scott LeDoux was strong, tough, really only fringe world class but did box for the title against Larry Holmes, who out-boxed him more or less at will in July 1980. Holmes won every round but in the sixth LeDoux was thumbed in the eye, which caused retina problems later. Leroy Jones, Earnie Shavers and Scott Frank also claimed Holmes hit them with a stray thumb in title fights. One judge, Harold Lederman, was so close he saw the punch land and called out, 'He's thumbed him!' LeDoux turned and dropped to the floor in agony. His eyelid had rolled under his eyeball. Somehow he made it through the sixth but after a stream of unanswered jabs and solid rights, the half-blind man from Minnesota was pulled out by referee Davey Pearl.

The build-up was bad-tempered as the hype over-spilled into accusations, seemingly unfounded or at least tenuous, of racist abuse. That was a shame. Perhaps the job of selling a world heavyweight championship in Bloomington, Minnesota, got a little out of hand. LeDoux always denied the slightest intention of insulting Holmes on racial grounds and said the champion deliberately twisted something out of context to make an issue of it.

As a boy in the town of Crosby, LeDoux would walk to church three miles there and back and long after his career was over he became a born-again Christian, who mixed selling real estate and insurance with some commentary for ESPN and motivational speeches. He began boxing at the University of Minnesota at Duluth and when he left in 1969 he enlisted in the army. At one point he was in line to go to Vietnam but the orders were changed at the last minute. He turned professional in Minneapolis in 1974 and built a good local following. He beat Duane Bobick's brother Rodney and former title challengers Terry Daniels and Ron Stander. When he stepped up another level he lost on points to Duane Bobick and John 'Dino' Dennis. Then he was put in far too deep against George Foreman and lost in three rounds in Utica, New York. In a return Duane Bobick knocked him out in eight. After another fight he lost, against Johnny Boudreaux, there was a post-fight melee in which LeDoux endeared himself to millions of television viewers by knocking off commentator Howard Cosell's toupee.

1. Above left: Jack Dempsey rose from the hobo jungles to become the heavyweight champion of the Jazz Age.

2. Above right: Sam Langford: stylish outside the ring and explosive in it. He was a ring legend but was never given a title shot.

3. Jack Johnson overcame persecution and racial hatred to hold the title for six and a half years – but his fifteen-round beating of old favourite James J. Jeffries sparked riots and lynchings across America.

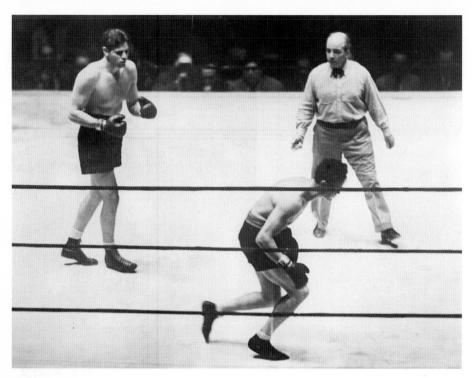

4. Buddy Baer, the bigger, younger brother of world champion Max, took less than a round to stop the cavalier Irishman Jack Doyle in 1935.

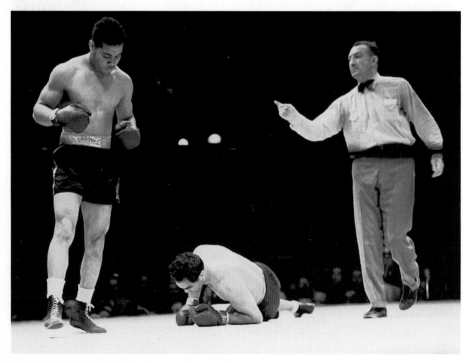

5. A fight that transcended sport. Joe Louis knocks out Max Schmeling in New York in 1938.

 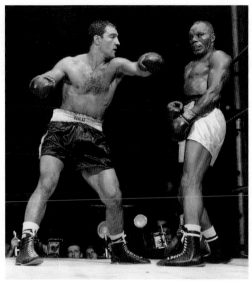

6. Above left: It's not only politicians who can do the baby-kissing routine... Joey Maxim, best known as a world light-heavyweight champ, boxed Ezzard Charles for the heavyweight title in Chicago in 1951. They fought five times in total.

7. Above right: Being knocked down and outboxed didn't discourage Rocky Marciano. Eventually he trapped Jersey Joe Walcott on the ropes and knocked him out in round thirteen in Philadelphia in 1952.

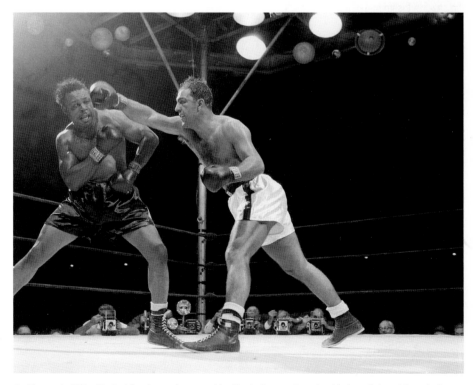

8. The end of The Rock. Marciano, down and badly shaken early, wins his last fight with a ninth-round knockout of 'Ancient' Archie Moore.

9. Above: Pete Rademacher wins the Olympic heavyweight gold medal in Melbourne in 1956. Rademacher challenged Floyd Patterson for the world title in his professional debut, lost but said he didn't regret a thing.

10. Left: Ingemar Johansson celebrates his three-round, seven-knockdown triumph over Floyd Patterson.

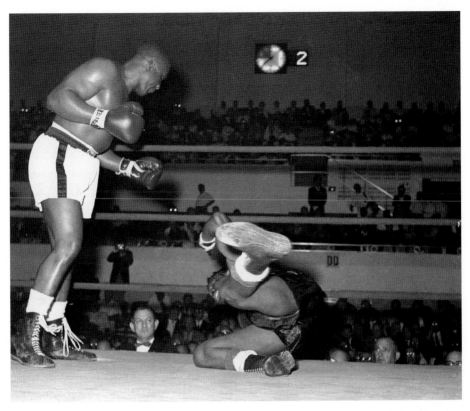

11. Champion in waiting. Sonny Liston was the best heavyweight in the world long before his one-round knockout of Floyd Patterson in 1962. Here, he takes out Howard King in Miami.

12. A cut Henry Cooper attacks Cassius Clay at Wembley in 1963. Injuries ruined both of Cooper's fights with Clay/Ali.

13. Brian London attacks against Tom McNeeley in 1963. Both challenged Floyd Patterson for the title – and lost.

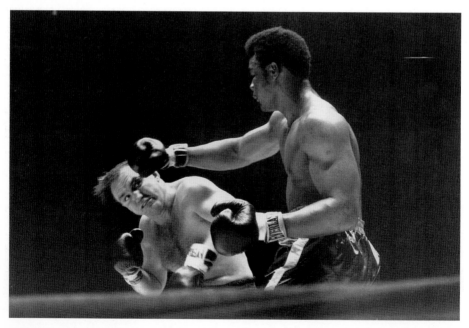

14. Chuck Wepner, the Bayonne Bleeder, takes his lumps against George Foreman in 1969. Wepner was the inspiration for the *Rocky* movies.

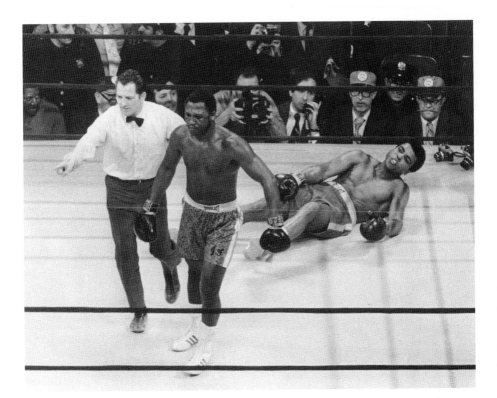

15. Joe Frazier's finest hour. Referee Arthur Mercante guides Smokin' Joe to a neutral corner as Muhammad Ali sprawls on the canvas in the fifteenth round of their epic first fight.

16. Joe 'King' Roman is on the floor when George Foreman lets an extra punch go. If referee Jay Edson had applied the letter of the law, Roman would have been world heavyweight champion by first-round disqualification. Few cared.

17. Muhammad Ali wins the astonishing Rumble in the Jungle with the supposedly invincible George Foreman in Zaire, 1974.

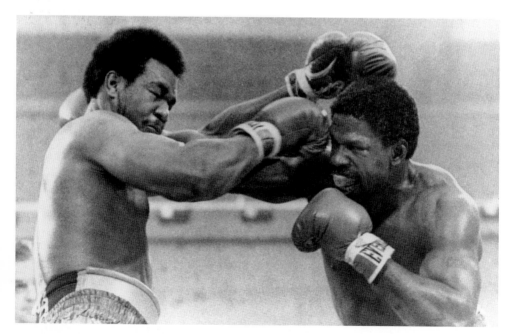

18. Ron Lyle trades with George Foreman in their sensational war in Las Vegas in 1976. Foreman was down twice but knocked out Lyle in round five.

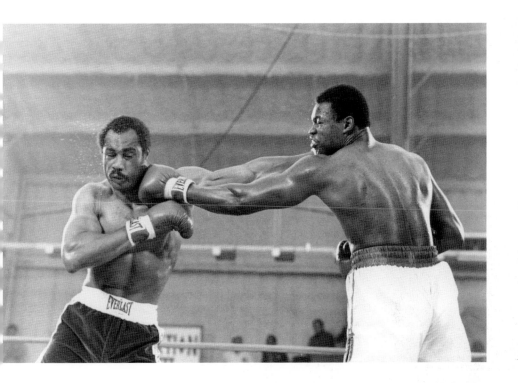

19. Above: One of the finest heavyweight title fights of the modern era. Larry Holmes (right) won the last round and, with it, the fifteen-round fight against Ken Norton.

20. Right: Larry Holmes pins Earnie Shavers in a corner as he closes in for the stoppage in round eleven of their championship fight.

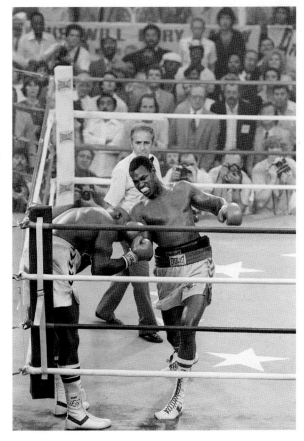

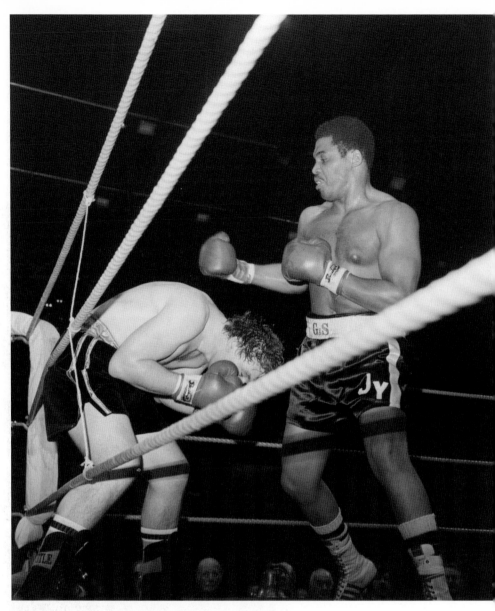

21. Jimmy Young was a slippery Philadelphia craftsman who ended George Foreman's first career and went to his grave believing he was robbed against Muhammad Ali in his only world title challenge. Here, he is too good for British champion John L. Gardner in 1979.

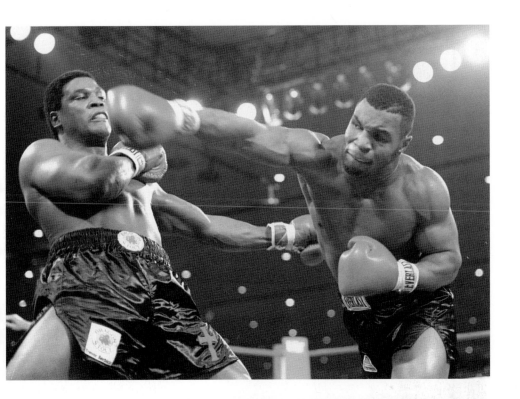

22. Above: The arrival of a new star. Twenty-year-old Mike Tyson becomes the youngest world heavyweight champion in history with a terrific two-round knockout of Trevor Berbick in Las Vegas.

23. Right: Shock of the century. The supposedly invincible 'Iron' Mike Tyson is knocked out by 42-1 underdog James 'Buster' Douglas in Tokyo.

24. One for the oldies: twenty years after losing the championship to Muhammad Ali, George Foreman knocks out Michael Moorer to regain the title at the age of forty-five.

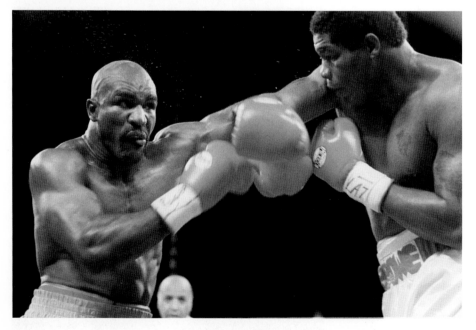

25. Riddick Bowe and Evander Holyfield had three epic battles in Las Vegas. Bowe won the magnificent first fight in 1992, a year later Holyfield won the fight infamously interrupted by a paraglider, and here they trade in the decider in 1995. Bowe recovered from a knockdown to win in round eight.

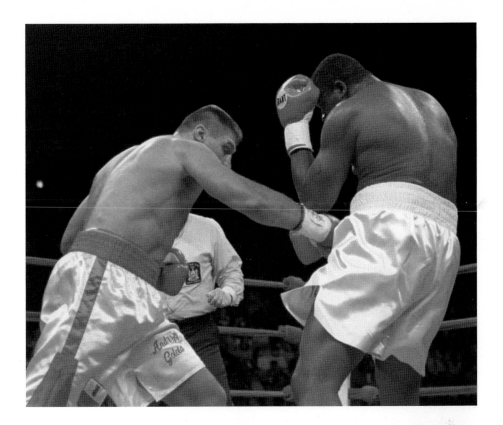

26. Above: Andrew Golota hits Riddick Bowe low in New York in 1996. Twice the notoriously erratic Pole outfought Bowe only to lose by low-blow disqualification. Bowe was never the same again.

27. Right: Tyson's disgrace. The one-time self-proclaimed 'baddest man on the planet' writes his name into heavyweight infamy by biting a lump out of Evander Holyfield's ear in Las Vegas in 1997. Tyson earned himself a $3 million fine and a licence suspension.

28. Hasim Rahman strolls away as referee Daniel Van De Wiele counts out Lennox Lewis in South Africa in 2001. Complacency played a significant role in Lewis's shock defeat – before the year was out he had regained the title by knocking out Rahman in Las Vegas.

Opposite

29. Top: Lennox Lewis said he mopped up the last misfit of his era when he knocked out Mike Tyson in the Pyramid Arena, Memphis, in 2002. American writer Michael Katz caustically declared Tyson had been buried in a pyramid by a mummy's boy – a reference to Lewis's pleasure in including his mother Violet in his team throughout his career.

30. Bottom: Vitali Klitschko was ahead on points against Lennox Lewis in 2003 when bad gashes over the left eye ruled the Ukrainian out after six rounds. Lewis never boxed again.

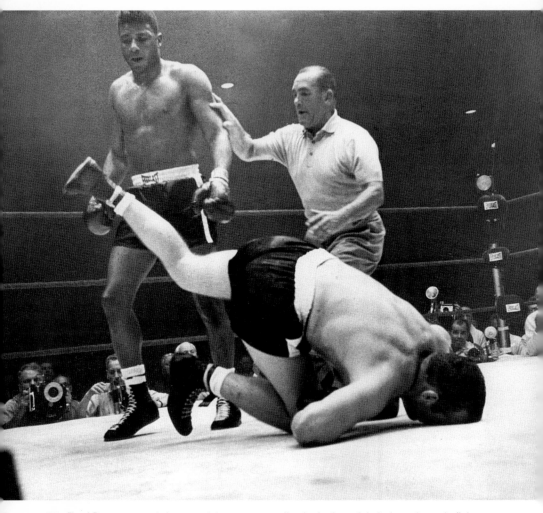

31. Floyd Patterson sends Ingemar Johansson sprawling in the last of their three dramatic fights. Patterson won in six rounds in Miami in 1961.

A ten-round draw with the 1976 Olympic light-heavyweight champion Leon Spinks marked his Las Vegas debut in October 1977 – and that was only four months before Spinks beat Muhammad Ali for the world title. There were wins but LeDoux did not quite have the ability to get past the leading contenders. He lost on points to Ron Lyle and drew with Ken Norton in 1979, and almost stopped Norton in the final round when he dropped him twice. Mike Weaver out-pointed him. Although he had won only one of his last four fights, a points win to end the unbeaten run of the Oklahoma hope Marty Monroe, he was handed the shot at Holmes in Bloomington in July 1980.

His wife Sandy had been diagnosed with skin cancer in 1979, when they had two small children. The Holmes fight gave him a payday but he found himself increasingly distracted and, though he was always fit, his interest gradually waned. In the Bahamas on the Ali-Berbick show, he was beaten in four by Greg Page. In Johannesburg he lost in eight to Gerrie Coetzee. And although he had won four in a row in North Dakota, Minnesota, Alberta and Oregon when he accepted a fight with Frank Bruno in London, he just didn't have it any more. Bruno beat him easily in three rounds at Wembley Arena in May 1983 and LeDoux said he just wasn't upset by it. That, he knew, meant he needed to retire.

His wife died in 1989. He eventually turned again to Christianity, remarried and concentrated on his varied business interests and some television work.

GUS LESNEVICH

Born: 22 February 1915, Cliffside Park, New Jersey
Died: 28 February 1964, Cliffside Park, New Jersey, aged 49
Height: 5ft 9in   **Weight at peak:** 175lbs (12st 7lbs)
Fights: 79   **Won:** 60   **Lost:** 14   **Drawn:** 5
KO percentage: 29
Rounds boxed: 610
World champion: (light-heavyweight champion 1940-48)
World title fights: 1
Career span: 1934-49 (15 years)
KO wins: 23
KO defeats: 5

Officially, according to the New York State Boxing Commission, Gus Lesnevich did not challenge Ezzard Charles for the world heavyweight title in Yankee Stadium in August 1949. Because the bout was recognised by the National Boxing Association, which was not acknowledged by the NYSBC, the state authority refused to allow the promoters to advertise the fight as a world title bout, nor even to put such a billing on the programme for the night.

History sees things a little differently, with Charles recognised as the logical

champion after his points win over Jersey Joe Walcott in Chicago two months
before he took on Lesnevich, who is therefore regarded as his first challenger.
Lesnevich, for whom this was the last of his seventy-nine professional fights, retired
after the seventh round, well beaten. From Cliffside Park, New Jersey, Lesnevich
boxed for fifteen years. He won NBA recognition as light-heavyweight champion
with a fifteen-round decision over Anton Christoforidis in New York in May 1941
and, although he had four years out of the ring during the Second World War, he
was the undisputed champion by the time he defended it with a brutal tenth-
round stoppage of Freddie Mills at Harringay Arena, London, in 1946. Mills took
away his championship in a rematch at White City, London, in July 1948.

Lesnevich died in Cliffside Park of cancer on 28 February 1964, aged only
forty-nine.

ALVIN 'BLUE' LEWIS

Born: 11 December 1942, Detroit
Height: 6ft 4in   **Weight at peak:** 220lbs (15st 10lbs)
Fights: 36   **Won:** 30   **Lost:** 6
KO percentage: 52
Rounds boxed: 208
World title fights: 0
Career span: 1966-73 (7 years)
KO wins: 19
KO defeats: 3

Best known for a 1972 non-title fight with Muhammad Ali in Croke Park, Dublin,
Al 'Blue' Lewis later took over as a trainer at the red-brick Brewster Recreation
Center on the rough east side of Detroit where the young Ray Robinson and Joe
Louis worked. Lewis gave Ali a good enough workout, climbing off the floor in
the fifth round and lasting into the eleventh.

The selling line was that Lewis had floored Ali with a body shot in sparring
– which was a rare moment of truth among the routine lies told by boxing publicists. It happened when Ali was preparing for his 1970 comeback fight with Jerry
Quarry, deliberately invited Lewis to hit him in the stomach and a shot to the ribs
put him down by the ropes. Lewis was a part of the Ali entourage for that fight
and took a delivery of a package for Muhammad in the Atlanta hotel room. It was
a decapitated chihuahua with a chilling message: 'We know how to handle black,
draft-dodging dogs in Georgia.'

One of fifteen children, Lewis was a tough guy from the streets. At seventeen
he was jailed for 20-35 years after robbing a man who later died. He did his
time in Jackson State Prison, passing some of it by boxing. He also read Sonny
Liston's story. At the end of 1965, after serving six years, he was released and by the

summer of 1966 he was boxing professionally, a big, raw-boned talent, trained at Brewster by Luther Burgess.

A second-round knockout over the clever, world-rated Argentine Eduardo Corletti in 1968 got him noticed but two defeats by Leotis Martin checked his progress and he never quite made the breakthrough. He stopped the ancient Cleveland 'Big Cat' Williams but was disqualified controversially against Oscar Bonavena in Buenos Aires. Lewis floored Bonavena three times but was thrown out for use of the head.

After that he fought Ali, who put on a show for the fans – most of whom climbed over the walls of the outdoor stadium to watch for free! Lewis tried, got up from the only knockdown, landed one or two solid punches, but by the end of the tenth his eye was closed. More importantly, it transpired Ali needed the toilet. He opened up and stopped Lewis in the eleventh. 'Man, I was just bursting!' he said to Angelo Dundee.

JOHN HENRY LEWIS

Born: 1 May 1914, Los Angeles, California
Height: 5ft 11in   **Weight at peak:** 175lbs (12st 7lbs)
Fights: 117   **Won:** 103   **Lost:** 8   **Drawn:** 6
KO percentage: 60
Rounds boxed: 788
World champion: (light-heavyweight champion 1935-39)
World title fights: 1
Career span: 1928-39 (11 years)
KO wins: 60
KO defeats: 1

John Henry Lewis was virtually blind in his left eye when he took on Joe Louis for the world heavyweight title in a desperate attempt to cash in on his decade in the professional ring.

One of the gentlemen of the sport, Lewis had been world light-heavyweight champion since October 1935 when he out-pointed Bob Olin in St Louis. As a heavyweight he had knocked out Elmer 'Violent' Ray in the twelfth round in Atlanta, and out-pointed Johnny Risko, Willie Reddish and Al Ettore. However, by the end of 1938 his sight was fading. Louis, who was his friend, knew that and agreed to give him a chance and for once promoter Mike Jacobs made a world heavyweight title fight between two black boxers. It hadn't happened for a quarter of a century, since the Jack Johnson-Jim Johnson shambles in Paris in 1913, and wouldn't happen again for ten years, until Louis boxed Jersey Joe Walcott.

John Henry's father, who was said to have been a descendant of the bare-knuckle legend Tom Molyneaux, travelled on the train from the Deep South to New York to watch. He didn't see much: persuaded by Jack Blackburn that the kindest thing to do was end it quickly, Louis floored Lewis three times and knocked him out in round one. 'I wasn't happy about that fight,' said Louis, 'but I knew John Henry was on his way out and at least he'd had the glory of a fight with the heavyweight champion – and he'd made a good dollar.'

Two months later Lewis failed his medical before a light-heavyweight defence against Dave Clark in Detroit. In his left eye he could only distinguish light from dark and could not detect the number of fingers a doctor held up eighteen inches in front of his face.

Lewis died at home in Berkeley, California, on 18 April 1974, aged fifty-nine.

LENNOX LEWIS

Born: Stratford, London, 2 September 1965
Height: 6ft 5in   **Weight at peak:** 244lbs (17st 6lbs)
Fights: 44   **Won:** 41   **Lost:** 2   **Drawn:** 1
KO percentage: 72
Rounds boxed: 225
World champion: 1993-94, 1997-2001, 2001-04
World title fights: 18
Career span: 1989-2004 (15 years)
KO wins: 32
KO defeats: 2

Lennox Lewis finally put to bed the famous old line, 'If all the British heavy-weights were laid out end to end... I wouldn't be at all surprised.' Lewis was the first British undisputed world heavyweight champion of the twentieth century... one month before it ended! He held world title belts for eleven years, avenged the only two defeats he suffered, beat every major heavyweight of his era... and had the good judgement to retire as undefeated champion. Lewis had ambition, pride and a single-minded determination and ruthlessness that set him apart. From his days as a natural athlete in high school in Canada, he built himself into one of the major sportsmen of his time.

Lewis was born in Stratford in the East End of London and was raised in West Ham. His mother, Violet, moved to Canada, took him with her for a year, but then as she was struggling financially, sent him back to live with an aunt in England until he was twelve. He rejoined her in Kitchener, Ontario, in 1977. No doubt the uncer-tainty of his upbringing and the lack of a father figure went a long way to moulding his character as a self-reliant, remote and at times even aloof man. Throughout his career, journalistic probing met with a routine smile or a stony mask, to the point where some battle-hardened hacks felt there really was nothing much there to be found. In turn this made his public relations task much harder than it was for the best of his immediate British predecessors, Frank Bruno, who was a much more outwardly emotional and open man. When Lewis returned to Britain to begin his professional career, after winning the super-heavyweight gold in a Canadian vest in Seoul in 1988, there were those who felt he wasn't really British. And in a sense, Lewis probably agreed he was a cosmopolitan figure: his roots were Jamaican, his birthplace was London and he knew enough of its streets to understand it, but by the time of his pro debut half of his life had been spent in Canada.

His decision to base himself in Britain with a little-known manager, Frank Maloney, was a surprise. As a teenager he had sparred with Razor Ruddock and Mike Tyson; in the Los Angeles Olympics he had lost a decision to the vastly more experienced Tyrell Biggs and in the Seoul final he had stopped Riddick Bowe. An American base would have seemed more natural. However, he won British, Commonwealth and European titles and established himself as a potential champion by picking apart the unbeaten Gary Mason in seven rounds , avenged his 1984 Olympic defeat against Biggs and then earned a title shot by destroying Ruddock in two sensational rounds at Earl's Court. After that he was supposed to meet the winner of the classic first fight between Bowe and Evander Holyfield in November 1992. Bowe won – but decided to give back the WBC belt rather than box Lewis.

Lewis was announced as champion by the WBC president Jose Sulaiman in December 1992 and presented with the belt at a small dinner show in a West End hotel in January 1993. His first defence was in Las Vegas four months later, when he knocked down and out-pointed the former IBF champion Tony Tucker... and ignored the overtures of Don King, who paid a huge sum to promote the fight in the first of what would be many attempts to lure him into his fold.

Lewis took time to warm up before he stopped Bruno in seven rounds on a cold, rainy night in the open air at Cardiff Arms Park in October 1993, then boxed cautiously to stop the limited but dangerous Phil Jackson in eight in Atlantic City in May 1994. Both performances were criticised. By this time Bowe had lost his part of the title back to Holyfield and his connections saw the sense in challenging Lewis but, just when it seemed that could happen, in September 1994 Oliver McCall sprung a huge upset at Wembley. McCall was a tough, hard-punching, emotionally erratic character from Chicago who had made his living as a top-ten pro and in prolonged sparring sessions with champions, especially Tyson. He knew his job, but on form alone shouldn't have won. Lewis won round one, but then his trainer, Pepe Correa, sent him out to 'knock this bum out'. Instead, Lewis walked straight into the path of a big, shut-eyed right over the top and was floored heavily. He got up, but referee Lupe Garcia didn't like the look of him and stopped the fight. Correa, who might have been sacked anyway after a tasteless pre-fight incident when he tried to present McCall with a woman's suspender belt, had to go. Emanuel Steward came in and stayed for the rest of Lewis's career. Lewis's first trainer had been the doleful, difficult John Davenport.

It took time to work his way back. He stopped Tommy Morrison in six, won a hard fight with Ray Mercer on a majority decision in New York and then had to wait while the world title situation sorted itself out. McCall lost the WBC title to Bruno, who in turn was beaten in three rounds by Tyson a year after Mike's release from jail. Lewis was the number one contender but Tyson wasn't going to meet him, and so the Lewis camp accepted step-aside money in order for Tyson to box the WBA champion, Bruce Seldon. However, in a complex series of events, the WBC stripped Tyson, who blew away Seldon in one round to 'switch sides' to the WBA. Lewis and Tyson could have met in the autumn but instead Mike chose to box the supposedly washed-up Holyfield, who then pulled off a shock win in Las Vegas in November 1996. A rematch was made – and so the WBC matched Lewis with McCall for their vacant belt in January 1997 at the Las Vegas Hilton. McCall, a recovering drug addict, shouldn't have been boxing. A cautious, suspicious Lewis moved around, out-boxing a strangely lethargic McCall, who seemed an emotional wreck. Finally, the poor man broke down in tears in the ring. Referee Mills Lane led him to his corner in an attempt to sort him out, let him box on, but then waved it off. Instead of being praised for avenging his solitary defeat, Lewis was criticised for over-caution. However, he had lost once to McCall through a stupid mistake – and how much worse it would have been if he had walked into a sudden, desperate punch from a man in the middle of a psychological breakdown?

Things got no better in the summer of 1997. Tyson was disqualified in the rematch with Holyfield for biting his ears, and then Lewis had a horrible WBC defence against the unbeaten Nigerian from London, Henry Akinwande, who was disqualified for holding in the fifth round. When Lewis needed a big performance, he produced one: a devastating ninety-five-second demolition of the dangerous Pole Andrew Golota in Atlantic City in October 1997. Golota had ended Bowe's career by handing him two sustained beatings only to be disqualified both times for low blows. He was temperamental but talented. Lewis psyched him out before the fight, then walked out and knocked him down twice.

In March 1998 Lewis was more casual against the colourful New York puncher Shannon Briggs, who was arguing that, in all the mess that developed after Bowe's deliberate division of the title, he was the rightful 'man who beat the man who beat the man'. His logic was that Bowe lost to Holyfield, who lost to Michael Moorer, who lost to George Foreman in 1994. Foreman fell out with the sanctioning bodies because he wanted to pick his own challengers and was eventually discredited. However, Foreman retired only after he lost to Briggs, who therefore claimed the linear title. Lewis walked into a big shot in the first round and was shaken but then out-punched Briggs to win in the fifth, flooring him three times. It was wildly exciting. Ironically, this time he was criticised for carelessness.

In September 1998 Lewis laboured to a twelve-round decision over the unbeaten European champion Zeljko Mavrovic in Connecticut, and then – at last – had the unification opportunity with Holyfield, who by then had beaten his old nemesis Moorer to add the IBF belt to the WBA version he had won against Tyson. Holyfield had played the religious card to the full in motivating himself against Tyson and had a tremendous certainty about him. When he fought Lewis, he couldn't do that: his marriage had disintegrated following a paternity suit from another woman. Lewis got under his skin in the pre-fight skirmishes, then in the ring seemed to out-box Holyfield with something to spare. In the fifth round Holyfield was on the brink of going down from big right hands. Yet the judges called it a draw: the South African Stan Christodoulou scored 116-113 for Lewis, but British judge Larry O'Connell saw it 115-115 and somehow the American, Eugenia Williams, gave it to Holyfield 115-113, a scorecard that included awarding him the fifth round, when he seemed on the edge of defeat. The verdict was deemed so bad the New York Commission announced an investigation. The FBI took an interest, too. The punch statistics provided a condemnation of the judges: Lewis threw 613 punches to Holyfield's 385 and landed 348 to Holyfield's 130. He outjabbed him by three to one and out-punched him by two to one. While the International Boxing Federation, which had provided Eugenia Williams (Christodoulou was appointed by the WBA and O'Connell by the WBC), was going through a bribery and corruption scandal that threatened to bring it down, the decision in the Lewis-Holyfield fight threatened to bring down the whole sport.

The rematch was in Las Vegas in November 1999 and this time, in if anything a more troublesome fight, Lewis out-pointed Holyfield on a unanimous decision. Again, his jab and long-range boxing ability was the key: he won 116-112, 117-111, 115-113. At long last he was the undisputed heavyweight champion of the world, the first born in Britain since Bob Fitzsimmons 100 years before.

Given the ridiculous nature of boxing politics, it couldn't last. Sure enough, by the time he made his first defence against Michael Grant in New York in April 2000, Lewis had been stripped by the WBA for failing to meet its number one contender... which at first was Henry Akinwande, and then was Holyfield. Lewis, not surprisingly, wanted to move on – and anyway, Grant was the WBC number one. He couldn't please everybody. In a brutally one-sided fight, Lewis knocked out Grant in two rounds after putting him down three times in the first. Grant, like so many others, was beaten before the first bell – two days before the fight I saw him sitting alone in Madison Square Garden, he was talking to himself and making little sense.

In a farewell British appearance, Lewis destroyed the South African Frans Botha in two rounds and then back in Las Vegas he handed a one-sided boxing lesson in a dull fight to a disappointing David Tua. By then Lewis was thirty-five; his body had filled out, his hair was flecked with grey, but like many a great athlete he couldn't appear to see what was happening.

In the spring of 2001 he spent time making a movie in Las Vegas and went to South Africa far too late for a defence against the Baltimore heavyweight

Hasim Rahman. He was jet-lagged, under-prepared, arrogantly over-confident. Rahman's skills were ordinary but he trained ferociously hard in Johannesburg, went in fit and sharp and in the fifth round knocked out Lewis with a right hand to the jaw. At first the beaten champion refused to believe it had happened – 'He can't knock me out,' he said in confusion, almost outrage. Seven months later a fit, fully motivated and to some extent repentant Lewis took out Rahman in the fourth round with one right hand in Las Vegas.

Lewis could have retired then, but decided he wanted to clear up a personal issue that had been on his mind for years. He should have boxed Tyson. Though nine months younger than Lewis – they would have been in the same school year – Tyson was older in life-years by decades. He was still very dangerous, especially for the first three rounds, but his great days of the late 1980s were consigned to history by a litany of crimes, social gaffes and broken marriages and relationships. Lewis was not what he was either: he had drilled himself back into shape for Rahman, but there were genuine questions over whether or not he could do that again at the age of thirty-eight. The defeats by McCall and Rahman also raised doubts over what would happen if Tyson hit him cleanly on the chin. In spite of the fact that it should have happened years before, there was still a kind of macabre interest in it, especially after Tyson had been exiled by the major American states after a bizarre, violent outburst at the press launch in New York. He attacked Lewis and in the brawl bit his leg. In the Pyramid Arena in Memphis in June 2002, Lewis contained Tyson's early burst, then broke him up and knocked him out with a right hand in round eight. Tyson said, 'I can't beat him if he fights like that. He might kill me next time.'

There was a rematch clause but there was no stomach for it. Eventually, a year later, Lewis boxed Vitali Klitschko, the big Ukrainian, in Los Angeles. Lewis should have boxed Kirk Johnson of Canada with Klitschko also on the bill to set up a showdown in the autumn, but then Johnson pulled out – and Klitschko was switched to the title challenge. The Ukrainian didn't mind. Lewis, who believed he would have beaten Johnson without breaking sweat, was in the worst physical shape of his career at 18st 4½lbs, and almost paid for it. He was rocked in round two, at times seemed virtually exhausted, and was behind on all three cards when the doctor ruled out Klitschko because of horrible damage to his left eye after round six. Lewis claimed it as a genuine win, but Klitschko had the sympathy of the fans. A date for the return was set aside for December 2003, but Lewis declined and then announced his retirement in a dignified, eloquent speech in a London hotel in February 2004.

Would he have beaten Ali, Dempsey, Marciano, Tunney, Louis? It doesn't matter – he was the best of his time and no man can be more than that.

SONNY LISTON

Born: 8 May 1932, St Francis County, Arkansas
Real name: Charles Liston
Died: 30 December 1970, Las Vegas, Nevada, aged 38
Height: 6ft 1in   **Weight at peak:** 214-218lbs (15st 4lbs-15st 8lbs)
Fights: 54   **Won:** 50   **Lost:** 4
KO percentage: 72
Rounds boxed: 272
World champion: 1962-64
World title fights: 4
Career span: 1953-70 (17 years)
KO wins: 39
KO defeats: 3

Nobody knows when Sonny Liston was born – and nobody knows when he died.

He came into this world somewhere around 1932 in the cotton fields of St Francis County, Arkansas, and he left it in the last days of 1970, alone in his house in Las Vegas, Nevada. In his seventeen-month reign as heavyweight champion of the world he was considered an unbeatable brute whose ferocious punching power was matched only by his menacing personality. Yet the meanness and violence that surrounded him always had a tragic element: he was fragile, rejected, misunderstood.

Liston's demolition of Floyd Patterson for the world title and his rapid victories over genuinely dangerous heavyweights Cleveland Williams and Nino Valdes, and wins over world-class 'ring generals' Zora Folley and Eddie Machen, demonstrated how good he was at his peak. His ring reputation was ruined by the manner of his defeats against Cassius Clay/Muhammad Ali: the first when he surrendered pitifully on his stool with a painful shoulder, the second when he folded from an innocuous looking right hand to the temple in the first round.

Liston's mother thought her son Charles was born on 8 May 1932, but at another time said it was in 1929. The confusion is understandable: he was one of twenty-five children of an Arkansas cotton-picker. In the sprawling, poor areas of farmland where he was raised, nobody bothered to register such ordinary events as births and deaths, and no government agents went looking for such confusing tasks as finding out which black child in the countryside belonged to whom and which was born when. When he left Arkansas to find his mother, who had moved to St Louis, he was registered as thirteen years old and placed in school. He was put in with the beginners because he was illiterate, and he was too humiliated and embarrassed to stay long. On the streets he became a public nuisance and eventually, in 1950, lost his liberty for a pathetic armed robbery – he and two accomplices took $37 from a store. He was sentenced to five years in jail – and liked it there. He liked the food and understood he had to pay for his crimes. 'I didn't mind prison,' he said. 'No use crying.' The chaplain at Jefferson County jail, Father Alois Stevens, managed to communicate with him and earn his trust – and also persuaded him to use his physical assets in a boxing ring: 'Sonny was just a big, ignorant, pretty nice kid. He wasn't smart-alecky but he got in little scrapes.' When he emerged in 1953 his natural talent impressed the brilliant trainer, Ray Arcel. Liston wasn't all about brute force: he always had the ability to use his left hand, as a fearsome jab or a short, impeccably timed hook. He was labelled Sonny by his first promoter, won his debut in thirty-three seconds against Don Smith in St Louis in September 1953, and set about learning his new – his first – trade. He was a volatile young man – his first manager, Monroe Harrison, said he needed someone to help him control his emotions. Some years later an acquaintance told *Sports Illustrated*, 'Sonny has the mind of a twelve-year-old child. He has no finesse, tact, whatsoever. He doesn't realise that he has to keep his name out of the paper. He's kind of mean, too. He hates policemen. They hate him.' Liston remembered St Louis all too well: 'The cops just kept grabbing me, picking me up, holding me overnight.'

In the summer of 1954 he moved to Detroit. After two decisions over John Summerlin, the second of them a split vote, he lost his unbeaten record when a slippery boxer, Marty Marshall, made him laugh with a joke and promptly broke his jaw. Liston still fought all the way and went down only on a split decision. The injury kept him out for six months. In rematches, he recovered from a knockdown to stop Marshall in six and then out-pointed him over ten rounds in Pittsburgh. However, after that third fight with Marshall he was arrested for an attack on a police officer that earned him a nine-month jail sentence.

When he resumed his career at the start of 1958 he was in Philadelphia, with his career 'guided' by the Mob: principally Frankie Carbo and Blinky Palermo. His old manager, Johnny Vitale, also continued to claim and be paid, and there was yet another 'frontman', Joseph 'Pep' Barone. Most of his money was carved up before he saw any of it. Johnny Tocco, the Las Vegas gym owner, was originally from St Louis and said even back in 1953 the Mob were involved in his career. He won eight out of eight in 1958, including two decisions over a capable fighter named Bert Whitehurst and a sixty-nine-second destruction of Wayne Bethea, who had some credentials but finished the fight with seven teeth missing. In 1959, he stopped Mike DeJohn in eight, Cleveland Williams and Nino Valdes in three each and Willi Besmanoff in seven. By then he was probably the best heavyweight in the world, but hadn't quite earned his shot. Any doubts were removed in 1960, when he stopped Howard King in eight, Williams in a return in two, Roy Harris in one, Zora Folley in three and then outscored Eddie Machen in his first experience of twelve rounds.

At that time Floyd Patterson and Ingemar Johansson were 'hogging' the title in their three-fight series, and Liston was kept waiting. Out of the ring, the Kefauver Committee investigated corruption in boxing, concentrating on the activities of the Mob and the International Boxing Club, which had controlled boxing for more than a decade from its New York headquarters. Liston was called to testify and at one point in the hearing said he had learned how to write his name but could not read the figures on a cheque, nor recognise his address.

By then Carbo was doing twenty-five years and Palermo fifteen for extortion and Liston had 'bought' his contract from Barone for $75,000, and signed first with George Katz and then Jack Nilon. In 1961 Liston boxed only twice: he knocked out Howard King in three rounds in Miami and Albert Westphal in one in Philadelphia. Finally, in September 1962, officially aged thirty, he won the world heavyweight title with a breathtaking 126-second knockout of Floyd Patterson in Comiskey Park, Chicago. He just walked out of his corner, hunted the champion down and battered him to the canvas. Perhaps the most heart-rending moment in Liston's life was his return to Philadelphia. He had rehearsed his official welcome home speech before Jack McKinney of the *Philadelphia Daily News* on the flight back and told him he wanted to visit the black neighbourhoods and churches to tell them he would do his best to be a role model. 'I want to reach them and tell them, "You don't have to worry about me disgracing you."' And he was already planning visits to orphanages and reform schools to tell youngsters, 'Don't give up on the world, good things can happen if you let them.' And then he got off the plane – and there was no welcome, beyond a few pressmen and airport staff. McKinney suggested he never got over the hurt – and the next year left the city with the cutting farewell, 'I'd rather be a lamppost in Denver than mayor of Philadelphia.' Yet a sparring partner said the police in Denver enjoyed taunting him: at one point they stopped him on twenty-five consecutive days.

A rematch with Patterson was absolutely pointless, but the clause was in the contract and Floyd meekly promised to 'last longer next time'. He did – by four seconds. That fight, in Las Vegas in July 1963, was one of the most cynical mismatches in the history of the sport.

When they gave Liston twenty-two-year-old Cassius Clay as his next challenger he couldn't take the idea seriously. He thought he would intimidate the young man, who had been Olympic light-heavyweight gold medallist in Rome, but Clay ranted and raged so much at the weigh-in that Liston thought he was mad. Clay was fined $2,500 by the Miami Commission for his unruly behaviour and a doctor pronounced him 'scared to death'. He was acting. Harold Conrad, Liston's public relations man, said Clay won the fight at the weigh-in when he answered Sonny's malevolent stare with, 'Who you looking at, you big ugly bear?'

Clay's much publicised decision to convert to Islam under the political agitators the Black Muslims had created fear and controversy, coming as it did only three months after the assassination of John F. Kennedy in Dallas. The USA was a country in emotional crisis, in political and social turmoil, and here they had a known thug defending the heavyweight championship of the world against a Black Rights activist who was reportedly turning his back on Christianity. People stayed away – and missed one of the defining moments in sport.

Liston was cut below the left eye, gave Clay the charge only to hit thin air and after three rounds looked disbelieving, old, vulnerable. After four rounds, something got into Clay's eyes and blinded him – and he told his trainer, Angelo Dundee, to cut off his gloves. He was shoved out for the next and danced out of the way of Liston's lunges until his eyes cleared. Then he began to pepper the champion again and after the sixth Sonny stayed on his stool, claiming a damaged shoulder. Doctors explained the injury, but he was disgraced because he had not gone out the way champions do. Years after Liston's death, Conrad insisted the injury was genuine and the Mob did not fix the result. He said Liston was anguished by the loss of his title and insulted by the accusations that he had thrown the fight on instructions. He trained ferociously hard for the rematch, intent on proving himself, only for it to be postponed when Clay, by then Muhammad Ali, suffered a hernia and needed surgery. Conrad and the writer Jimmy Cannon both said something went out of him with the postponement. In the fight, before only a couple of thousand people in Lewiston, Maine, Liston was dropped by a chopping right cross. Referee Jersey Joe Walcott lost control and took time getting Ali to back off. Liston got up, but the timekeeper had counted him out. Walcott hadn't, but *Ring* editor Nat Fleischer banged on the canvas to attract the referee's attention – and the fight was waved off. Sonny had lost in the first round. The fans screamed 'fix', the knockout blow was roundly dismissed as a nothing punch, and Liston was cast off into the boxing backwaters. Again, there were those who said he threw the fight.

When he returned to the ring it was in Sweden, where he won four fights in 1966 and 1967. His American return had to wait until March 1968 when he knocked out Bill McMurray in four rounds in Reno, Nevada. Even though he was officially in his mid-thirties, and with Ali in political exile, he suddenly began to look a live contender again. He knocked out all seven of his opponents that year, the best of them the competent West Coast heavyweight Henry Clark. In 1969 he had to go ten rounds to outscore Billy Joiner, but stopped George 'Scrap Iron' Johnson in seven and knocked out Sonny Moore in three. The run ended, however, when the world-rated Leotis Martin knocked him out in the ninth round in Las Vegas. His last fight was in June 1970 when he chopped Chuck Wepner to shreds for a tenth-round stoppage. Wepner, nicknamed forever the Bayonne Bleeder, needed fifty-four stitches in his face.

Liston's wife Geraldine went to visit relatives over the Christmas and New Year holiday at the end of 1970, leaving Sonny at home on his own. When she returned she found his body, which was already in a state of decomposition. For official purposes, his date of death was recorded as 30 December 1970, but nobody knew for sure. Officially he was supposed to have died of an accidental, self-administered heroin overdose, but very few believed that. Old acquaintances say he was working for some heavy 'loan sharks' in Las Vegas at the time, crossed them and was murdered. He had also, it was said, fallen out with Ash Resnick, who ran the Thunderbird Hotel. Conrad was certain he was murdered. So was Johnny Tocco. Both of them, and Geraldine, said Liston was so terrified of needles that he could never have injected himself with anything. She believed, or wanted to believe, that he had died of a heart attack.

Liston was buried in Paradise Memorial Gardens, Las Vegas, in an area called the Garden of Peace. Even there, though, peace is a rare thing: it's directly beneath the flight path of the jets taking off from McCarran International Airport.

BRIAN LONDON

Born: 19 June 1934, Hartlepool, England
Height: 6ft   **Weight at peak:** 205lbs (14st 9lbs)
Fights: 58   **Won:** 37   **Lost:** 20   **Drawn:** 1
KO percentage: 44
Rounds boxed: 360
World title fights: 2
Career span: 1955-70 (15 years)
Longest winning run: 12 (1955-56)
KO wins: 26
KO defeats: 11

Brian London boxed both Floyd Patterson and Muhammad Ali for the world title and held the British and Commonwealth championships in a fifteen-year career. Although well beaten by Patterson and outclassed by Ali, London is now remembered with affection as a crowd-pleaser from a time when Britain was blessed with several heavyweights who could fill the best indoor arenas in the country.

London's father Jack held the British title in the 1940s. The real family name was Harper and it was under that name, while on national service in the Royal Air Force, that Brian won the ABA heavyweight title in 1954. When he turned professional he used London, originally boxing out of the family home town of Hartlepool and later moving to Blackpool. He lost his unbeaten record to Henry Cooper at Earl's Court, London, in May 1956 when he was stopped in the first round, pinned in a corner by a terrific barrage of hooks. The world-class Willie Pastrano knew too much for him over ten rounds at Harringay in February 1958, but in his next fight, in June 1958, London won the British and Empire titles by knocking out Joe Erskine in the eighth round at White City. For six rounds London was out-boxed, then a crack of heads left the Welshman with a cut left eye. London took over, slamming home big punches until Erskine went down to take the count on one knee.

In September 1958 he beat Pastrano in a rematch on cuts, but then lost the titles on points to Cooper at Earl's Court in January 1959. When he was offered a shot at world champion Floyd Patterson he accepted, only to be informed by the stuffed shirts at the British Board of Control that as he was not British champion he would be refused permission to box. He went anyway, lasted into the eleventh with Patterson in Indianapolis and happily paid his fine for disobeying the board when he returned home. He had still made a handsome profit.

Before the fight Cus D'Amato, Patterson's manager, pumped things up by declaring London was faster than Rocky Marciano, 'a dangerous, two-fisted fighter, a young bull, a hot puncher, a real tiger, brave and courageous'. London had a more realistic view of his talents. Out at his training quarters at a place called Fall River Creek, he said, 'If I hadn't taken this fight I should deserve to be kicked in the backside. What can I lose? Patterson won't kill me. I am getting a £20,000 payday... I won't even talk about winning, but if I do pull it off, there's a million dollars in the kitty.' Patterson controlled a rather pedestrian fight, cut London under one eye, knocked him down in the tenth and put him away in the eleventh. Many in the 10,088 crowd booed.

London returned home, settled his account with the Board of Control and lost on a cut in seven rounds to the big Cuban Nino Valdes, but then knocked out the Olympic gold medallist Pete Rademacher in seven. An infamous European title showdown with Dick Richardson in Porthcawl in August 1960 ended in a mass brawl – London dominated the fight only to be cut by what he felt was a deliberate butt in round seven. That injury forced his retirement after the eighth, but Brian went berserk, knocked down Richardson's trainer Johnny Lewis, and the ring was suddenly full of people, including London's father and brother and around twenty policemen, who eventually managed to calm things down.

Eddie Machen stopped him in five rounds at Wembley in October 1961, cutting him around both eyes and smashing his nose, but Brian came back well again, beating Howard King in six rounds in a rain-sodden open-air show in Blackpool and outscoring Tom McNeeley. Although he lost a twelve-round decision to Ingemar Johansson in Stockholm, he had the Swede in desperate trouble at the final bell, which gave him a kind of moral victory – and persuaded the former world champion to retire. However, a return with Cooper for the British, Commonwealth and vacant European titles in Manchester in February 1964 ended in a points defeat. He lost what seemed to ringside writers an incomprehensible decision to Johnny Prescott in Liverpool in August 1964, after which London had an altercation with a fan who jumped into the ring and ran at him. Believing the man wanted to attack him, he downed him with a decisive head butt... only to find the poor chap was trying to commiserate with him over the verdict.

He had too much experience for the other rising star of the British game, Billy Walker. London out-pointed him at Wembley in March 1965 and said, rather pointedly, 'I may not have the face to launch hair-oil campaigns, but in my old age I am a hell of a good fighter.' London won nine rounds out of ten, according to Peter Wilson in the *Daily Mirror*. He lost to Thad Spencer on points, but a disqualification win over another American, Amos Johnson, was enough to earn him the world title fight with Ali at Earl's Court in August 1966. He barely landed a punch before Ali opened up with a bewildering volley of blows that left him on the canvas for the count in round three. After the fight he caught the train home to Blackpool, where the welcome-home committee on the platform consisted of a schoolboy with an autograph book.

London lost to Jerry Quarry in Los Angeles but ended 1967 with a points win over the long-time contender Zora Folley in Liverpool. The victory over Folley, won quite simply on workrate as the American spent too long doing very little, was the last of his career. After that he had six fights. He drew one against the Californian, Henry Clark, but was stopped in the other five. Jack Bodell beat him in nine, Jerry Quarry in two and in his final fight at Wembley in May 1970 he lost in five to Joe Bugner. 'Five years ago, I would have pulverised him,' said London.

In retirement London remained in Blackpool and put his money into night-clubs, which prospered. He also gave occasional after-dinner speeches and kept himself extremely fit well into late middle age. In spite of a rather gruff, blunt exterior, he had flashes of unexpected wit – most famously his glorious one-liner: 'I'm just a prawn in the game.'

TOMMY LOUGHRAN

Born: 29 November 1902, Philadelphia, Pennsylvania
Full name: Thomas Patrick Loughran
Died: 7 July 1982, Altoona, Pennsylvania, aged 79
Height: 5ft 11in   **Weight at peak:** 180lbs (12st 12lbs)
Fights: 174   Won: 113   Lost: 30   Drawn: 13   No Decisions: 8
KO percentage: 9
Rounds boxed: 1,560
World champion: (light-heavyweight champion 1927-29)
World title fights: 1
Career span: 1919-37 (18 years)
KO wins: 17
KO defeats: 2

Tommy Loughran was clever enough to feint most heavyweights into knots and use his quick hands to pepper them with light punches. If he had been heavier, or at least heavier punching, he might have gone all the way to win the championship. As it was he had to make do with being light-heavyweight champion from 1927 to 1929 and holding wins over three men who did go on to hold the biggest prize of them all: Jack Sharkey, Max Baer and James J. Braddock.

When his heavyweight title chance came it was against Primo Carnera, in Miami in March 1934. Carnera was just too big for Loughran to handle. There was a gap of 6¾in in height and 86lbs in weight – 270lbs to 184lbs. Loughran was cunning enough to smother his hair with the foulest-stinking oil he could unearth and in a clinch in the first round managed to shove his head under big Primo's nose. After that Carnera wanted to keep things at long range, which is where Loughran could survive. The points decision wasn't in doubt, but at least he managed to go the distance. In fact Loughran only failed to do that twice in a 174-fight career: when Sharkey beat him in three rounds in his heavyweight debut before 45,000 fans in Yankee Stadium in September 1929 and three years later when he lost in the second round to Steve Hamas.

He began in 1919 in his native Philadelphia, when he was only just seventeen. After suffering a bad break in his right hand he learned to rely mostly on his left. In the early 1920s he fought the great middleweight champion Harry Greb six times, all distance fights. He also had an eight-round No Decision with Gene Tunney and out-boxed both Johnny Wilson, the former middleweight champ, and Georges Carpentier, who had been the light-heavyweight holder. He also earned his keep as sparring partner for Jack Dempsey before the first Tunney fight in September 1926 and boxed on the bill, winning a six-round decision over Jimmy Delaney before the amazing crowd of 120,757 in the Sesquicentennial Stadium in Philadelphia.

When he challenged Mike McTigue for the vacant world 175lbs belt in October 1927, Loughran had won his last twenty-three fights, mostly on points. He proved too clever for McTigue as well over fifteen rounds in Madison Square Garden, although he had to survive one or two worrying moments in the final three minutes. He was a good champion: he made five successful defences, the most meaningful the fifteen-round decision he earned over James J. Braddock in Yankee Stadium, New York, in July 1929. He gave up the championship two months later to box at heavyweight. He established himself in the division in 1931 with a run of nine wins, the best of which was a ten-round decision over future champion Max Baer in New York. Two years later he also out-boxed Jack Sharkey over fifteen rounds in Philadelphia, so avenging the knockout defeat he had suffered against him in 1929. After Sharkey he out-pointed Ray Impellitiere to set up the title shot against Carnera. Apparently, he was given it when a priest, Father O'Leary, called in an unrecorded old favour from Carnera's manager Bill Duffy. After six rounds the fight was close, then Carnera drew clear. Unfortunately the fans stayed away, which meant the takings were ridiculously low. Loughran was paid only $5,000.

That seemed to knock the desire out of him. He lost his next three on points to Walter Neusel, Johnny Risko and Jose Caratolli, and drifted into life as a quality 'opponent' in world class. He retired in 1937, following a final points win over Sonny Walker in front of his old Philadelphia fans. He was thirty-four years old and had been managed from the first to the last day of his career by Joe Smith.

Loughran stayed in touch with boxing, refereed fights – including the world heavyweight championship bout in 1957 between Floyd Patterson and Pete

Rademacher in Seattle – and was a regular at Veteran Boxers Association functions. He felt the sport softened in later years and could not take seriously a situation where men he felt were mere novices were being recognised as champions. This was understandable, for it had taken him eight years and 102 fights to become light-heavyweight champion. He boxed Carnera in his 148th professional bout.

Loughran died in Altoona, Pennsylvania, on 7 July 1982, aged seventy-nine.

JOE LOUIS

Born: 13 May 1914, Lafayette, Alabama
Full name: Joseph Louis Barrow
Died: 12 April 1981, Las Vegas, Nevada, aged 66
Height: 6ft 1¾in   **Weight at peak:** 197-203lbs (14st 1lb-14st 7lbs)
Fights: 67   Won: 64   Lost: 3
KO percentage: 74
Rounds boxed: 416
World champion: 1937-49
World title fights: 27
Career span: 1934-51 (17 years)
KO wins: 50
KO defeats: 2

Joe Louis had everything. A smooth, shuffling fighting machine with a devastating left jab, marvellous, economical combinations and knockout power in both hands, he was an unrivalled master of his art during his peak years between 1937 and 1942.

Altogether Louis was champion for almost twelve years and made twenty-five defences of the championship before retiring as undefeated champion in March 1949 at the age of thirty-four. It was immensely sad that financial nightmares, mostly attributable to a draconian attitude by the Internal Revenue Services, bad advice and his own high spending, forced him into first a comeback when he didn't have a lot left, and then into the quasi-comic world of wrestling, where he is said to have damaged heart muscles, which aged him prematurely. In his later years he was also mentally ill and, for a time, a drug user. Fortunately he retained enough friends to help him through various crises and in his last years he was also given work as a greeter at Caesars Palace in Las Vegas. It shouldn't have come to that, but Louis was a humble, friendly man, who was at his happiest when mixing with ordinary people. The job suited him.

As a fighter he is forever the legendary Brown Bomber who graced the ring for those few short years before and during the Second World War. He ended the prejudice against black heavyweights that had been the legacy of Jack Johnson's tumultuous reign a quarter of a century earlier. He changed boxing techniques too and took the sport into a new era. As sporting role models go, the in-ring Louis was about as good as it gets. Those who look at tapes of Louis for the first time are often astonished by his composure and the speed and precision of his punches. He did make mistakes, could occasionally be put down, but he could turn in an instant from jabbing and counter-punching into a devastating attacking fighter There was nothing remotely wild about him. He measured everything and even the world-class opponents he fought would say that when he hit you, he hurt you.

Louis was born Joseph Louis Barrow to poor sharecroppers in the region of Lafayette, Alabama, in May 1914. When his father lost his mind, his mother set up home with a neighbour, Patrick Brooks, and they moved to Detroit. His stepfather worked for the Ford Motor Company. They were poor, but not beneath the breadline. Famously, his mother once paid for violin lessons, but instead he went to the Brewster Gym, which is still open today. Mike Tyson trained there before his October 2000 fight with Andrew Golota. Louis won the American Amateur Union light-heavyweight title and turned pro, aged twenty, with a first-round stoppage of Jack Kracken in Chicago in July 1934. His progress was meteoric. He had been a professional fighter for less than a year when he brutalised former champion Primo Carnera in six rounds in his New York debut. From being a boy who was glad to add to the family income with a merchandise cheque from his amateur bouts, in no time at all he had become rich beyond his dreams. For the Carnera fight, he grossed $60,433. Six weeks later it was more than $50,000 for a one-round demolition of a petrified Kingfish Levinsky, and then he grossed an incredible $240,833 for a classical four-round knockout of Max Baer, who had lost the heavyweight title only three months before. For the whole year his earnings came to $429,655. He was promoted by Mike Jacobs and, unusually for the time, was managed by two black businessmen, Julian Black and John Roxborough. His trainer was Jack Blackburn, who had been a world-class lightweight in the early part of the century and had served time for killing a man. Blackburn was a brilliant teacher, Louis a perfect student – most of the time.

As most young men do, he needed a salutory lesson, and it came in June 1936 when, just past his twenty-second birthday, he was nailed repeatedly by Max Schmeling's right hands and knocked out in the twelfth round. It was such a bad hammering that some critics felt he would not recover, but two months later he was back, ending the career of another former champion, Jack Sharkey, in three one-sided rounds.

Louis won the world heavyweight title in Comiskey Park, Chicago in June 1937. He was an overwhelming favourite because the general perception was that the Cinderella Man, James J. Braddock, had already had his day of glory when he upset Max Baer on a fifteen-round decision to win the championship two years earlier. Braddock had not boxed since, was thirty-one years old, and while his skills were respectable enough there was nothing about him that electrified spectators. He did better than expected, shocking Louis with a first-round knockdown, but then courageously took a hammering before being knocked out in round eight. During the fight Braddock was asked by his manager Joe Gould if he could retire him. 'If you do,' he said, 'I'll never speak to you again as long as I live.'

Louis's first challenger, the stubborn, wily Welshman Tommy Farr, lasted the full fifteen rounds in Yankee Stadium in August 1937, but it was his fourth defence, the rematch with Schmeling in June 1938, that elevated Louis to superstar stature. The twenty-four-year-old American blasted out Schmeling in two minutes four seconds in a fight that transcended sport. Schmeling was seen, unfairly, as the representative of the increasing international menace of Nazi Germany. Louis was no longer a black kid from the Detroit slums – he represented America and so, in the eyes of the fans, writers and politicians alike, all that was good and great. He had met Franklin D. Roosevelt who had told him, for the benefit of writers, 'Joe, we need muscles like yours to beat Germany.' The image of Schmeling as a Nazi, or at least a sympathiser, was portayed by writers who carried stilted, invented quotes including 'I would not take this fight if I did not believe that I, a white man, can beat a Negro.' Years later Schmeling and Louis would become lifelong friends but, in the political cauldron of 1938, both were political pawns. Well-paid pawns – Louis grossed $329,228 – but pawns nonetheless.

Louis gave his friend John Henry Lewis, the world light-heavyweight champion, a shot next. John Henry's eyesight was failing and knew he didn't have long to cash in on his career. Joe won in 149 seconds. Then he completed a third consecutive one-round win with a first-round stoppage of Los Angeles no-hoper Jack Roper in April 1939. Tony Galento, the brawling New Jersey bar owner, somehow managed to knock Louis down with a left hook, but was then cut to ribbons in four. He went down, grabbing Louis's legs as he went, blood pouring from his nose and eyes, and afterwards complained gruffly, 'They shouldn't oughta stopped the fight.'

Bob Pastor, a crafty, ringwise boxer, had stayed the full ten rounds with Louis before he won the title and deserved a shot. He did well too, lasting until the eleventh, though mostly on the run, before he was stopped. Another 'cutie', the awkward South American Arturo Godoy, stood up for the whole fifteen rounds in New York in February 1940 and somehow his sniping from a crouch impressed one judge enough for him to consider him the winner. However, the other two voted for Louis.

One writer asked, 'Have you ever seen a ghost walking?' after Johnny Paychek's challenge had lasted only two rounds, then Godoy was stopped in eight of a return and in December 1940, Mike Jacobs decided to keep Louis busy with what became known as the 'Bum of the Month' campaign. Louis always objected to that, saying his challengers were all good fighters with dreams and hopes of their own, and that they deserved respect. He stopped Al McCoy in six, Red Burman in five, Gus Dorazio in two, big Abe Simon in thirteen, Tony Musto in nine, Buddy Baer in seven and rounded up the fights with his epic thirteenth-round knockout of Billy Conn in June 1941. Conn out-boxed Louis, was ahead on points after a hard fight by the twelfth, but was taken out with two seconds left in round thirteen.

Louis boxed three more times before the Second World War interrupted his career: a sixth-round stoppage of Lou Nova, who practised yoga and claimed he had a cosmic punch; a one-round demolition of Buddy Baer and a sixth-round defeat of Abe Simon. He donated the purses from the last two fights to the Army and Navy relief funds. Years later, the hard-hearted members of the IRS suggested this was Louis's choice and therefore still had to pay tax on his income, which forced him to box when he should have been enjoying the fruits of his long career. In the war he joined up as Private Joe Louis and was employed in a public relations role on both sides of the Atlantic. He spoke to troops and gave exhibitions wherever he went, but it was 1946 before he boxed again, the long-awaited return with Billy Conn. Louis had more left and won in eight rounds.

In September 1946 he was shaken up by heavy-handed Tami Mauriello, but responded with typical venom to win in 129 seconds, then was out of the ring for fifteen months and deteriorated sharply. When he boxed again, he was knocked down twice and out-thought by Jersey Joe Walcott and was extremely fortunate to get the decision. In a rematch in June 1948 he got off the floor to knock out Walcott in the eleventh round. Nine months later he carried out a promise to his family to retire – in a deal in which the International Boxing Club paid him a $20,000 annual salary.

However, his financial troubles emerged and he had to go straight back into a title shot against the new champion, Ezzard Charles, in New York. Charles took no pleasure in beating his old hero on a wide fifteen-round decision. After that, Louis won eight times, including solid performances against fellow veterans Lee Savold and Jimmy Bivins, but then hit the end of the road when Rocky Marciano left him unconscious beneath the ropes in New York in October 1951. He was thirty-seven – and still owed the taxman half a million dollars, which continued to accrue interest until his death. Although in the 1960s the IRS agreed in view of his contribution to the country to stop pursuing him, the debt was never officially wiped out.

Louis had grossed $4,684,297.69 in his seventeen years as a professional fighter. It seems incredible that even this did not provide him with financial security for the rest of his days. He was married twice to his first wife Marva, to Rose Morgan and finally to Martha Malone-Jefferson, a lawyer who looked after him in his declining years, when he was debilitated by cocaine abuse and paranoia. He was committed to a psychiatric hospital in May 1970, worked at Caesars Palace, but continued to have relapses. He suffered a severe heart attack in 1977, after which he was confined to a wheelchair, and he died on 12 April 1981, the day after attending a world championship fight between Larry Holmes and Trevor Berbick. He is buried in Arlington Cemetery, Washington DC.

RON LYLE

Born: 12 February 1941, Dayton, Ohio
Height: 6ft 3½in   **Weight at peak:** 217lbs (15st 7lbs)
Fights: 51   **Won:** 43   **Lost:** 7   **Drawn:** 1
KO percentage: 60
Rounds boxed: 326
World title fights: 1
Career span: 1971-95 (24 years)
KO wins: 31
KO defeats: 4

Ron Lyle came as close as it gets to dying when he was knifed in a Colorado jail by a fellow inmate. A doctor pronounced him dead and began to write out the death certificate... only to see him respond and fight back when the medical officer went through the routine procedures of checking life had been extinguished. In spite of losing a total of thirty-four pints of blood and needing surgery that lasted seven hours, Lyle not only recovered but came through to box Muhammad Ali for the world title in May 1975.

Lyle was born in Dayton, Ohio, and was raised in a Denver housing project where his father, Willie, produced nineteen children. Ron ran away a lot, including one trip to Montana where he ended up in jail. His education, such as it was, was interrupted when he was sent to reform school for stealing. A year later he shot a man dead. At seventeen he was convicted of second-degree murder and incarcerated on a 15-25-year stretch in Canon City, Colorado.

Fourteen days after the surgery that saved his life, he was sentenced to ninety days in solitary confinement and a further ninety of breaking rocks in a chain gang. In his seven-and-a-half years behind bars, Lyle also discovered boxing fascinated him. One day he told a fellow prisoner, 'I'm going to be the heavyweight champion of the world.' He didn't quite make it, but he did pretty well for himself, changed his life and now works as a security guard in Las Vegas.

When he was paroled in November 1969, a businessman, Bill Daniels, took on his career, installed Chickie Ferrara and Bobby Lewis as his trainers and set him to work. He turned professional in Denver in April 1971 when he had already passed his thirtieth birthday. In his eighth fight he out-pointed the Mexican Manuel Ramos, who had once briefly challenged Joe Frazier for the championship. He knocked out men like Vicente Rondon, the former light-heavyweight title claimant, Larry Middleton and Buster Mathis.

The run ended in Madison Square Garden in February 1973 when Jerry Quarry out-boxed him over twelve rounds. So convincing was Quarry's demonstration that the Californian was given a standing ovation by most of the 16,571 fans in the house. Lyle kept looking for the big single shot – a consistent fault throughout his career – and was out-boxed and out-punched. Tony Castellano scored 10-2 Quarry, Bill Recht had it 9-2-1 and referee Waldemir Schmidt called it 7-4-1.

That lesson seemed to curb Lyle's power. Only two of his next ten fights ended inside the distance. One of those was a third-round knockout of Jurgen Blin, and he did stay in the world class with points wins over Oscar Bonavena and Jimmy Ellis in 1974, but the aura had gone. A ten-round points defeat by the quick-handed, slick Jimmy Young in Honolulu in February 1975 looked as if it had wrecked plans for him to earn his big payday against Ali. Madison Square Garden wanted the fight, but backed out. Instead, it went to the Las Vegas Convention Center – and three months after losing to Young, and still coming off that defeat, the one-time murder convict was boxing for the championship of the world. Lyle tried hard and Ali had a lazy night. Much of the way he was content to let Lyle work away as and when he raised himself. After ten rounds the challenger was in the lead on two cards and level on the third, but then Ali opened up, took over and sent him reeling with a chopping right hand. Ali pounced with a triple left hook to the head and another right that made Lyle lurch across the ring. Ali hit him at will, at one point inviting referee Ferd Hernandez to stop it, which he eventually did sixty-eight seconds into round eleven.

'I wasn't hurt,' said the disappointed challenger. 'I could have gone fifteen rounds. I don't know why the ref stopped it. This is for all the marbles and a man deserves a full chance. This is the championship, not a four-round bout.'

Ali said Lyle deserved another title shot but it didn't happen. Ron did knock out Earnie Shavers in the sixth round in Denver but at the start of 1976 he lost a sensational fight with George Foreman in the fifth round – after both had been knocked down twice. Jimmy Young out-boxed him again, but points wins over Joe Bugner and Scott LeDoux kept him on the fringe until a little-known club fighter, Lynn Ball, biffed him out in two rounds in Phoenix in December 1979. In October 1980 he was knocked out in one round by Gerry Cooney and retired.

Amazingly, after a fifteen-year break, Lyle returned to the ring in Kentucky at the age of fifty-four, won three 'nothing' fights for a few hundred dollars in clubs and then retired for good after a 'homecoming farewell' two-round knockout of one Dave Slaughter in Denver in 1995.

EDDIE MACHEN

Born: 15 July 1932, Redding, California
Full name: Edward Mills Machen
Died: 8 August 1972, San Francisco, California, aged 40
Height: 5ft 11½in   **Weight at peak:** 195lbs (13st 13lbs)
Fights: 64   **Won:** 50   **Lost:** 11   **Drawn:** 3
KO percentage: 45
Rounds boxed: 502
World title fights: 1 (WBA)
Career span: 1955-67 (12 years)
KO wins: 29
KO defeats: 3

Eddie Machen was a talented, clever counter-puncher with a stiff, accurate left jab who was in the top handful of heavyweights in the world for ten years. His one attempt at a major championship was when he was slightly past his best – and he lost on points over fifteen rounds to Ernie Terrell for the vacant World Boxing Association belt in Chicago in March 1965. The WBA had stripped Muhammad Ali – an indicator of the kind of knuckle-headed decisions we were likely to get from so-called governing bodies in the years to come – and matched Terrell and Machen for what they declared was the world championship. The awkward, 6ft 6in Terrell was too big and a little bit too fresh for Machen and won by margins of between three and six points on the three cards. Machen, like Zora Folley, should have had a chance when Floyd Patterson was champion and the title was more or less in abeyance in the early 1960s when Patterson, Ingemar Johansson and then Sonny Liston were dominant. Near the end of his career, he said, 'I've had so much heartache and dashed hopes that I sincerely wonder if it was worth it.'

From Redding in northern California, Edward Mills Machen was not the easiest of characters. The son of a postman, he left high school early after a row over the football team and said, 'I fought so much, the family decided I might as well get paid for it.' Unfortunately, before that could happen he was convicted of armed robbery in 1952 and given a three-year jail sentence. When he came out, he worked with his father, and turned professional in Sacramento in March 1955. He made his first real impression in Richmond Auditorium only six months and nine fights into his career when he knocked out Howard King in the tenth round. King was a seasoned heavyweight with twenty-five wins in thirty-six bouts at the time, but Machen handled him well. Even more impressive was a ten-round unanimous verdict he scored over the dangerous, big punching Cuban Nino Valdes in San Francisco in April 1956. In a rematch three months later he improved on that by stopping Valdes in eight rounds in Miami. After fifteen fights he had proved himself capable of operating at the highest level and he knew it. 'It may take a year, maybe less, maybe a little more,' he said, 'But I'm more than ready for what's up there now.'

In January 1957, with Rocky Marciano retired and Patterson installed as the new champion, Machen floored and out-pointed the veteran former light-heavyweight champion Joey Maxim. In a rematch in Louisville, Machen won again, followed up with wins over Bob Baker and Tommy 'Hurricane' Jackson but then, as he closed in on Patterson and his reluctant manager, Cus D'Amato, was held to a draw over twelve rounds by Zora Folley in the Cow Palace arena, San Francisco. D'Amato wriggled out of having Patterson box either of them. In frustration, Machen took a job in Sweden against Johansson and was surprisingly knocked out in one round.

Machen stayed in world class, however, into the 1960s. He was out-pointed by Floyd Patterson in Stockholm in July 1964 – Floyd was living in the Swedish capital at the time – and then at thirty-two he boxed Terrell and lost their WBA title fight. He was out-pointed by the German southpaw Karl Mildenberger in Frankfurt in February 1966, and then lost a split decision to a rough but ordinary Mexican, Manuel Ramos, in Los Angeles in June 1966. A month later he earned his last big win, by outscoring Jerry Quarry in the Olympic Auditorium, Los Angeles. In September 1966 he out-pointed the journeyman George 'Scrap Iron' Johnson for the last victory of his career. Shortly, afterwards he filed for bankruptcy.

Joe Frazier, in only his thirteenth fight, wore him down and stopped him in the tenth round in the Olympic Auditorium, and then he lost on points to Californian rival Henry Clark in Sacramento. He retired after another unbeaten youngster, Boone Kirkman from Seattle, knocked him out in three rounds in May 1967.

Machen died in strange circumstances, aged forty, in August 1972. He was found dead in the driveway of his house in San Francisco. He was under psychiatric care at the time, had taken sleeping pills and had fallen from a window. The fall had ruptured his liver and he had bled to death.

PETER MAHER

Born: 16 March 1869, Galway, Ireland
Died: 22 July 1940, Baltimore, Maryland, aged 71
Height: 5ft 11in   **Weight at peak:** 173-181lbs (12st 5lbs-12st 13lbs)
Fights: 98   **Won:** 61   **Lost:** 24   **Drawn:** 6   **No Decisions:** 7
KO percentage: 42
Rounds boxed: 336

World title fights: 0
Career span: 1888-1910 (22 years)
KO wins: 42
KO defeats: 18

Galway-born Peter Maher fought in one of the more bizarre championship fights in history. At the start of 1896, James J. Corbett had officially, if temporarily, retired and Maher was matched with Bob Fitzsimmons, whom Corbett despised, for the vacant title on 21 February. Judge Roy Bean was the instigator of the fight, which attracted the interest of both the Texan and Mexican authorities, neither of whom were keen to condone a prize-fight. Therefore, Bean brought spectators to his home town of Langtry, Texas, by hiring a train, then had a footbridge built out to a sandbar in the Rio Grande. Technically it was on the Mexican side of the river, but the Mexican police couldn't reach it. William Barclay 'Bat' Masterson, who with Wyatt Earp had cleaned up the notoriously unruly town of Dodge City, Kansas, was head of security. It was a throwback to bare-knuckle days, when fighters and fans went to extraordinary lengths to avoid the attentions of the law.

Sadly for the fans who made the arduous journey, Fitzsimmons, who had been arguing with Bean about his fee and his cut from a talked-about film of the fight, knocked out Maher with a sweeping left hand in ninety seconds of round one. The poor man whose job it was to film the fight was still tinkering with the mechanism and didn't get a single frame of the action.

Corbett was so annoyed by the result he cancelled his retirement and reclaimed the title. As tradition had it that a champion could only lose his crown in the ring, or by retiring, Fitzsimmons's claim was disallowed.

Maher was boxing in Dublin in 1888, was knocked out in two rounds by the legendary Peter Jackson in the city's Leinster Hall in December 1889 and travelled to a new life in the United States in 1891. He won a string of fights by quick knockout then lost in twelve rounds to Fitzsimmons in New Orleans in March 1892. Maher was in considerable discomfort during the latter stages, retching after swallowing blood from a gash inside his mouth.

Maher was good enough to knock out most of the men he fought, including George Godfrey and Frank 'The Harlem Coffee Cooler' Craig. Even after Fitzsimmons flattened him in one round, Maher was still good enough to stop Frank Slavin in four rounds in Madison Square Garden in June 1896 and knock out Joe Choynski in six in the Broadway Athletic Club, New York, in November 1896. A wild brawl with Tom Sharkey was called off as a draw after the police intervened after the seventh round and he drew with Gus Ruhlin in a twenty-round fight in New York in May 1899. However, in a scheduled twenty-five-round bout with middleweight champion Charles 'Kid' McCoy, Maher was outclassed. McCoy floored him three times for a fifth-round knockout at Coney Island Stadium in Brooklyn on New York's Day, 1900.

By 1902 he was washed up and he was stopped or knocked out regularly until he eventually retired in 1910. He died on 22 July 1940, aged seventy-one.

NATHAN MANN

Born: 3 May 1915, New Haven, Connecticut
Real name: Natale Menchetti
Died: 26 October 1999, aged 84
Height: 6ft   **Weight at peak:** 193lbs (13st 11lbs)
Fights: 90   **Won:** 74   **Lost:** 12   **Drawn:** 4
KO percentage: 50
Rounds boxed: 557
World title fights: 1
Career span: 1934-48 (14 years)
KO wins: 45
KO defeats: 5

Nathan Mann, real name Natale Menchetti, was a Mob-controlled heavyweight who was projected into a fight with Joe Louis for the championship at Madison Square Garden in February 1938.

Mann could punch with the right hand and started fast as Louis took a good look at him – and he even managed to hurt the champion momentarily in round two. That awoke the sleeping giant – before the end of the session Mann was on the floor for a count of nine. In round three Mann, in spite of conceding height, reach and weight, stood and traded punches, went down twice more for short counts and then for good from a left hook.

Mann was born in New Haven, Connecticut, home of Yale University. More or less from the time he turned professional at the age of eighteen in April 1934, he was controlled by Marty Krompier, who was in the direct employ of the infamous gangster Dutch Schulz. On the night of 23 October 1935, Krompier was gunned down and needed two blood transfusions to save his life. Mann was one of those who rushed to the hospital to give blood. The following night Nathan, still only twenty, knocked out George Chip in three rounds for his twenty-third win in twenty-seven professional fights. Krompier should have died, but clung to life and nine weeks later walked out of hospital in a fur coat, having steadfastly refused to give the police any information about his shooting.

In 1936 Mann out-pointed Jack Roper and in 1937 beat Arturo Godoy and Bob Pastor. How much Krompier and Schulz were able to influence those decisions is unknown, but three months after Louis knocked him out he was knocked out in two rounds by Tony Galento and the New York Commission didn't like the way he went down. They suspended his licence, probably as a matter of show, for several months.

In later years he won and lost against Al McCoy and was out-boxed in Detroit by Gus Lesnevich. He lost three years to service in the Second World War and when he emerged he confined his ring activity to Connecticut, fighting nobody of influence. He retired in 1948 following a fourth-round stoppage by Bernie Reynolds in New Haven.

Mann died in October 1999 at the age of eighty-four.

ROCKY MARCIANO

Born: 1 September 1923, Brockton, Massachusetts
Full name: Rocco Francis Marchegiano
Died: 31 August 1969, near Newton, Iowa, aged 45
Height: 5ft 10¼in   **Weight at peak:** 184-189lbs (13st 2lbs-13st 7lbs)
Fights: 49   **Won:** 49
KO percentage: 87
Rounds boxed: 240
World champion: 1952-56
World title fights: 7
Career span: 1947-56
KO wins: 43
KO defeats: 0

Rocky Marciano was a no-frills, rampaging bundle of aggression who refused to acknowledge the possibility of defeat. He wasn't the cleverest fighter of his own or any other time but he had cunning enough, could take a shot and could punch... and, of course, he is the only world heavyweight champion who won every professional fight he had.

Historically, Marciano has his critics: he was cut prone, they say; he was knocked over from time to time, he was too short, too light, didn't fight Nino Valdes; of his seven world title fights, five were against men past their prime. Well, perhaps, but a man can only beat those who are put against him and the Rock did that... forty-nine times out of forty-nine. The record shows he deserves to be recognised as one of the best heavyweights of all time. His dramatic, come-from-behind knock-out of Jersey Joe Walcott to win the title in the Municipal Stadium, Philadelphia, in September 1952 remains one of the great heavyweight championship fights.

Rocco Francis Marchegiano, the eldest of six children of Italian parents in Brockton, Massachusetts, left school at sixteen, drifted through a few jobs and was drafted into the US Army in 1943, where he began to box. On his discharge in 1946 he dug ditches for the Brockton Gas Company. In March 1947 he had a rogue professional fight under the name Rocky Mack – he knocked out Lee Epperson in Holyoke, Massachusetts – and then continued to box as an amateur, also failing a baseball trial with the Chicago Cubs. In the Golden Gloves he lost to

Coley Wallace and then a thumb injury forced him out of the 1948 US Olympic trials. When he turned professional properly, in Providence, Rhode Island, in July 1948, he had won eight of twelve amateur bouts... and of course had already chalked up win number one in his pro career.

He contacted New York fight manager Al Weill, who kept an eye on him, then brought him to the city to learn under Charley Goldman. Goldman worked long and hard on shortening his punches, increasing his leverage and improving his balance. He did some eccentric work of his own too, like throwing uppercuts underwater and throwing a football with his 'wrong' left hand to strengthen the arm. As he blazed through his first dozen opponents without having to go beyond round three, Weill signed him to a proper contract and put Goldman and Marciano's friend and 'local manager' Allie Colombo on salaries too. In 1949 he went ten rounds twice, for points wins over Don Mogard and Ted Lowry, and had a scare when Carmine Vingo, whom he knocked out in six rounds, collapsed and almost died. In New York in March 1950 former college student Roland LaStarza stretched him to the tightest of ten-round decisions. In terms of publicity, he moved on to a higher level when he finished off the career of thirty-seven-year-old Joe Louis with an eighth-round knockout at the Garden.

While Ezzard Charles and Jersey Joe Walcott were engaging in their series of fights for the championship, Rocky had to wait – but then challenged Walcott for the championship in Philadelphia before 40,379 fans on 23 September 1952. Walcott, who believed Marciano's crude style would present few problems, scored a first-round knockdown. Marciano's strength and persistence brought him into the fight from the third to the sixth, as he slowed Walcott's thirty-eight-year-old legs. Walcott rallied, took over again and was in front by two, three and four points on the cards after twelve rounds. Then in the thirteenth round Marciano suddenly closed the range and found the space for the punch he called his Suzy Q, a short, perfectly timed right that knocked the champion out on his feet. Walcott's body was suspended on the ropes for a second, then twisted and slumped down, Marciano helping it fall with a clipping left that was more a seal of satisfaction at a job done than a significant blow.

Marciano was far from being a youngster: he won the title three weeks after his twenty-ninth birthday. He was settled with wife Barbara, neither drank nor smoked, limited himself to one cup of coffee a day and trained ferociously hard. He was a mature man who knew what he wanted – and what the job demanded of him.

Walcott announced his retirement, changed his mind and took the rematch for the money. After a delay of a month because Marciano was cut in sparring, Rocky took out the thirty-nine-year-old Jersey Joe in two minutes twenty-five seconds in Chicago in May 1953. Walcott was terrible. In September 1953 in front of 44,562 fans at the New York Polo Grounds, Marciano wore down LaStarza with non-stop attacks, blasting away at his opponent's arms so persistently that he broke blood vessels in them. Rocky, always a rough fighter, surpassed himself this time with butts, elbows and punches after the bell. Referee Ruby Goldstein took the sixth away from him for a low punch. By the eleventh LaStarza had nothing left. He was cut, he went down, got up but was stopped on his feet.

Surprisingly, Marciano had trouble with old champion Charles in Yankee Stadium in June 1954. A crowd of 47,585 saw Charles box superbly, dragging up a performance out of his own peak years. Marciano bled from an injury by his left eye, but eventually his strength and persistence brought him through to a unanimous decision over fifteen rounds. In a rematch three months later Charles was down in round two, but came back to split Marciano's left nostril wide open. It was a horrible vertical gash that threatened to stop the fight, and when Rocky's left eye also went, it seemed he must lose. Knowing his time was running out, he went for broke in round eight and floored thirty-three-year-old Charles twice, the second time for the count.

In May 1955, Marciano took a softer job, fouling systematically in a tiny ring and eventually stopping the unerringly game, outgunned British challenger Don Cockell in nine rounds in the Kezar Stadium, San Francisco. His last fight was against the light-heavyweight champion, Archie Moore, who at forty-two was still good enough to dominate the 175lb division and beat good heavyweights with his masterly ring-generalship. He almost beat Marciano too, putting him down heavily in round two with a superbly timed right hand. Marciano got up but looked groggy and, crucially, referee Harry Kessler delayed the restart, holding Moore back as he tolled out an eight count that was not in the rules. Then he wiped both fighters' gloves – by which time the champion had recovered his senses. Moore couldn't find another punch to finish the fight and Marciano's strength and comparative youth took over. Moore was down in the sixth, almost out in the eighth and then finished off in round nine.

Marciano knew it was time to go, even though he was still only thirty-two. 'If an old man like Moore can give me that much trouble, it's time for me to retire,' he said, though he delayed confirmation of the decision until April 1956. He turned down repeated offers of a comeback, enjoying meeting his old fans, and made his status as undefeated champion pay well. He was a miser of the old school, hiding bundles of notes in an assortment of strange places – hotel room curtain rails, for example – and was also embarrassed when he grew bald. He wore a toupee, even in the film of his strange 'computer' fight with Muhammad Ali in 1969. Ali knocked it off for fun, but Marciano didn't see the funny side of it. Although different endings were filmed, rumour had it that he also took part only on condition that he won.

When he died, in a plane crash in Iowa the day before his forty-sixth birthday, much of his money was so well hidden his heirs never found it.

LEOTIS MARTIN

Born: 10 March 1939, Helena, Arkansas
Died: 20 November 1995, aged 56
Height: 6ft 3in   **Weight at peak:** 200lbs (14st 4lbs)
Fights: 36   **Won:** 31   **Lost:** 5
KO percentage: 52
Rounds boxed: 218
World title fights: 0
Career span: 1962-69 (7 years)
KO wins: 19
KO defeats: 2

Just when Leotis Martin was looking as if he might emerge as a world title contender at the age of thirty, he suffered a detached retina in a ninth-round knockout
win over Sonny Liston in December 1969 and was forced to retire.

Martin, a Philadelphia heavyweight born under the name Otis Lee in Arkansas
in 1939, won the National AAU middleweight title in 1961 and turned pro the
next year. He fought out of Yancey Durham's gym, where the star was the young
Smokin' Joe Frazier. Martin was involved in a ring tragedy in Philadelphia in May
1965 when he knocked out Sonny Banks in the ninth round. Banks, who had
once floored Cassius Clay, died of brain injuries. In August 1967 Martin found
Jimmy Ellis too clever in the first round of the WBA elimination tournament to
find a successor to Muhammad Ali. Martin's lip was sliced open in the first round
and by the ninth he could no longer breathe properly because so much blood was
in his mouth. The fight was stopped.

British fans old enough to remember still talk with reverence of his classic war
against Thad Spencer at the Albert Hall, London, in May 1968. Martin won in the
ninth.

Martin was out-pointed in Buenos Aires by Oscar Bonavena, but then he twice
beat Alvin 'Blue' Lewis in Detroit. The win over Liston was his fifth in succession
– and he might well have boxed for the world title had it not been for his injury.

Martin died at the age of fifty-six in November 1995.

BUSTER MATHIS

Born: 5 June 1943, Sledge, Mississippi
Died: 6 September 1995, Grand Rapids, Michigan, aged 52
Height: 6ft 3in   **Weight at peak:** 245lbs (17st 7lbs)
Fights: 34   **Won:** 30   **Lost:** 4
KO percentage: 61
Rounds boxed: 176
World title fights: 1

Career span: 1965-72 (7 years)
KO wins: 21
KO defeats: 2

In a bizarre poll in high school in Grand Rapids, Michigan, Buster Mathis was voted the boy most likely to go to jail. A huge boy with a serious inferiority complex, he lashed out with his fists too often but like so many found a direction in his life once he was steered into boxing.

Heavyweights of 300lbs were rare beings in the early 1960s, when Floyd Patterson, the world champion, weighed less than 190lbs, and initially Mathis was an object of curiosity and fascination. However, people took notice when, displaying unexpected speed and finesse, he won the US amateur title and beat Joe Frazier to earn a slot in the Olympic team for the Tokyo Games in 1964. That's when the ill luck that would dog his life hit him first. In beating Frazier he cracked a knuckle on his left hand – and the doctors wouldn't let him go. Frazier, who actually lost both of their amateur meetings, substituted and returned home a gold medal hero.

Mathis turned pro in Montreal in June 1965, just after his twenty-first birthday, and by the end of the year had a promotional deal with Madison Square Garden. They labelled him 'Two Tons of Fun' but he slimmed down as best he could and in only his sixth fight he beat Chuck Wepner in three rounds. When Frazier refused to take part in the WBA elimination tournament in 1968, the New York State Athletic Commission matched with him Mathis for their version of the championship. They met on the night the 'new Garden' was opened, alongside a world middleweight title fight between Nino Benvenuti and Emile Griffith. Publicists referred to Mathis as 'an elephant that ballet-dances, a Sherman tank that turns on a dime' and rather more prosaically, 'a master of being a step ahead of his opponent all the time'. Mathis, who was none of these things, fought with great pride and a measure of skill but Frazier's relentless attacks broke him up for an eleventh-round knockout.

The popular theory was that his bubble had burst and he had been 'found out', but Mathis came back well in the rest of 1968 with five decent wins and then began 1969 by out-pointing perennial contender George Chuvalo over twelve rounds in New York. It was the best win of his career but a hard fight. A month later he was put in with Jerry Quarry and this time lost the decision. To so many critics he remained the 'fat-man heavyweight' – and his attempts to overcome the humiliating image were not helped when his trunks split during the Quarry fight.

He didn't box at all in 1970, but after a long layoff showed heart and durability to last the full twelve rounds in a non-title fight with Muhammad Ali in Houston, Texas, in November 1971. By then he had Sugar Ray Robinson's old manager, George 'The Emperor' Gainford, in his camp.

After Ron Lyle knocked him out in seven rounds in September 1972, Mathis retired. He had lost only to Frazier, Ali, Quarry and Lyle. Buster could fight all right. His career earnings suggested he had not, shall we say, been overpaid. He took home only $22,000 of a $75,000 gross purse for his championship fight with Frazier, and his combined take-home pay from the Chuvalo and Quarry bouts was only $26,000. The one sound business move he made was to buy a house in 1968 and at least he continued to live there, although the rest of his money slipped away – some to lawyers, when he tried in vain to recover some of what he believed he was owed from his career.

Mathis said in the late 1970s, 'When you come from nothing and go where I went, you've come a long way. I never went to prison. I never got into trouble. I fooled everybody. In high school I was voted the one most likely to go to prison. I wasn't a bad kid, just a kid who wasn't smart. They said I didn't have a heart when I was fighting. What do they know about it? What do they know about what it takes to go into the ring and fight like I did?'

Mathis was undoubtedly hurt by the rejection but remained fond of the sport. He continued to live with his wife Joan and children Antonio and Buster D'Amato, whom he named after his trainer from the early years, the legendary Cus. As he aged, Mathis became severely obese. Some say he eventually scaled almost 500lbs. Obviously unfit to work, he suffered two strokes, a heart attack and kidney problems, and died when only fifty-one.

HARRY MATTHEWS

Born: 9 December 1922, Emmett, Idaho
Died: 11 March 2003, Emmett, Idaho, aged 80
Height: 5ft 11in   **Weight at peak:** 179-183lbs (12st 11lbs-13st 1lb)
Fights: 103   **Won:** 89   **Lost:** 7   **Drawn:** 7
KO percentage: 60
Rounds boxed: 584
World title fights: 0
Career span: 1937-1956 (19 years)
KO wins: 62
KO defeats: 3

Harry Matthews drove from Seattle to Chicago in 1950 to persuade Jack 'The Deacon' Hurley to manage him. Although he was never more than a blown-up light-heavy, it was a decision that took him within sight of the world heavyweight title. He was called Harry the Kid, the Pride of Seattle, even Debonair Dynamite, but Hurley referred to him as the Athlete. Briefly, in the late spring and early summer of 1952, it seemed as if he might go all the way. Matthews was unbeaten in nine years when he floored and out-pointed the established contender Rex Layne in the

Pacific Livestock Pavilion in Portland, Oregon. The importance of the match was plainly understood: 11,361 fans paid receipts of $66,581, which was a state record at the time. Matthews put Layne down in the second round and won a unanimous ten-round decision. However, two months later he travelled to Yankee Stadium in the Bronx and was badly exposed inside two rounds by Rocky Marciano before a crowd of 31,188. As good fighters tended to, Matthews out-boxed Marciano in the opening round and even rocked him with right hands early in round two. Then Marciano's big right hands began to land – and two left hooks finished the fight.

Matthews began boxing professionally in Ontario, Oregon, in 1937 when he was a fourteen-year-old featherweight. By 1941 he was a middleweight and made his name in Seattle the following year when he edged out former world championship claimant Al Hostak on a majority decision over ten rounds.

Before Marciano, the only person to stop the Kid was Eddie Booker in five rounds in San Francisco in 1943. Booker is virtually forgotten now but at the time had lost only four of around seventy fights. Matthews was in the US Army in the last years of the Second World War and resumed his career, but it meandered along until 1950 when he signed for Hurley. In March 1951 he made a classy New York debut by out-boxing and out-punching Bob Murphy over ten rounds in a Madison Square Garden thriller.

The Layne fight in Portland earned him the Marciano fight and, after taking so long to reach the top, it was as if he couldn't summon up the drive any more. He lost three times to Don Cockell, his penultimate fight was a ten-round decision over the rapidly fading Ezzard Charles in Seattle – and Matthews bowed out of the sport he had served so well in November 1956 at the age of thirty-three with a points win over Alvin Williams in Boise, Idaho.

In retirement he returned to his birthplace, Emmett, where he died in 2003 at the age of eighty.

TAMI MAURIELLO

Born: 18 September 1923, Bronx, New York
Height: 6ft   **Weight at peak:** 200lbs (14st 4lbs)
Fights: 96   **Won:** 81   **Lost:** 14   **Drawn:** 1
KO percentage: 61
Rounds boxed: 564
World title fights: 1
Career span: 1939-49 (10 years)
KO wins: 59
KO defeats: 5

Tami Mauriello rocked Joe Louis with a big, sweeping right swing in the opening exchanges of their championship bout in front of 38,494 people at Yankee

Stadium, New York, in September 1946. For a few fleeting seconds Mauriello and his backers, who included Frank Sinatra, thought they were about to pull off one of the upsets of all time, but all Tami's big punch did was stir the champion into action. He got off the ropes and overpowered Mauriello in a total of 129 seconds, dropping him three times. 'I got too goddamn careless,' said an anguished Mauriello live on the radio afterwards – and the profanity caused a bout of mass eyebrow raising among the chattering classes of America.

Mauriello had an accident as a teenager – a collision with a truck – that almost cost him his left leg. He boxed as an amateur with the Catholic Youth organisation in the Bronx and then turned professional as a fifteen-year-old welterweight in July 1939. It is said his name was actually Steve and he used the details of his brother Tami in order to get a licence.

In 1941 Mauriello twice lost fifteen-round decisions to Gus Lesnevich for the world light-heavyweight title. By the following year Mauriello was a heavyweight – and combined his career with running a bar in the Bronx. He could fight. He beat Lee Savold, Lou Nova, Tony Musto, Bruce Woodcock, Lee Oma and Red Burman, and he drew with Bob Pastor. Against that, Jimmy Bivins twice handed him a boxing lesson and he also lost a decision to Joe Baksi in the Garden. Then the Louis fight made his name and destroyed his confidence. He lost twice more to Lesnevich, still won more than he lost, but retired at thirty-six after Cesar Brion knocked him out in two rounds at St Nick's Arena in October 1949.

In retirement Mauriello's most famous moment was when he and Tony Galento played union-hired goons in Budd Schulberg's *On the Waterfront* in 1954.

ZELJKO MAVROVIC

Born: 17 February 1969, Zagreb, Croatia
Height: 6ft 3½in   **Weight at peak:** 214lbs (15st 4lbs)
Fights: 28   **Won:** 27   **Lost:** 1
KO percentage: 78
Rounds boxed: 137
World title fights: 1
Career span: 1993-98 (5 years)
KO wins: 22
KO defeats: 0

A likeable, intelligent Croatian with a Mohawk haircut, Zeljko Mavrovic was dismissed as a tomato can by cynical American journalists before his world title bid against Lennox Lewis in the Mohegan Sun complex in Connecticut in September 1998. Afterwards the critics turned on Lewis for labouring to a twelve-round unanimous decision over the supposed no-hoper.

As Mavrovic never boxed again, history cannot help determine whether they were right or wrong. Having seen Zeljko several times at close range on the way up, I believe Lewis struggled because he underestimated his boxing ability and psychological strength. Lewis won because he was the superior boxer – as Mavrovic put it, he knew better when to throw which punch – but the Croatian stayed with him and by the end the champion was close to exhaustion. Critics of the performance hold as evidence the low number of punches thrown – and they have a point. However, whatever your view on him, Mavrovic remains one of the few men who gave Lewis a tough night's work.

Born in Zagreb, Mavrovic was a talented amateur: he boxed in two Olympic Games – in Seoul in 1988 when, as a nineteen-year-old he lost on points to the eventual finalist from the host nation, Hyun-man Baek, and in Barcelona in 1992 when he was out-pointed by the American, Danell Nicholson, in his second bout. Mavrovic turned professional in Germany with Wilfried Sauerland in 1993, with an English trainer, John 'Darkie' Smith. In his sixth pro fight he stopped the veteran David Bey but the only American fighters who would travel to Europe to box rising stars were journeymen, faded stars or never-could-have-beens. Consequently, it was hard for Mavrovic to make an impression. However, he made six European title defences before challenging Lewis. He lost that 117-111, 117-112, 119-109, and when he returned to Croatia was asked to do his national service. He said some years later this was merely a promotional issue on behalf of the government, but then he fell ill with a mystery condition some attributed to his macrobiotic lifestyle.

He refused to change his way of life but lost more than 40lbs in weight. He never boxed again, but resurfaced some years later with Croatian television, working as an analyst, when Lewis boxed Mike Tyson in Memphis in 2002.

JOEY MAXIM

Born: 28 March 1922, Cleveland, Ohio
Real name: Giuseppe Antonio Berardinelli
Died: 2 June 2001, Cleveland, Ohio, aged 79
Height: 6ft 1in   **Weight at peak:** 175-180lbs (12st 7lbs-12st 12lbs)
Fights: 115   **Won:** 82   **Lost:** 29   **Drawn:** 4
KO percentage: 18
Rounds boxed: 1,052
World title fights: 1
Career span: 1941-58 (17 years)
KO wins: 21
KO defeats: 1

Joey Maxim is best known as a world light-heavyweight champion but he also boxed Ezzard Charles for the heavyweight title in Chicago in May 1951 and lost on points. Charles wore him down with body punches and won a one-sided, runaway decision. The peculiarity of the scoring system in New York at the time made the mathematics hard to fathom but the two judges saw it 85–65 and the referee, Frank Gilmer, was criticised for marking it close at 78–72. Perhaps easier to interpret is the view of *Ring* editor Nat Fleischer, who gave the champion thirteen of the fifteen rounds with one even and just one, the ninth, to Maxim. Many of the 7,226 fans booed and hissed at the end of a fight in which the challenger, once he realised he was going to lose, spoiled his way to the finish. Afterwards Maxim collapsed in the dressing room and was given oxygen as doctors tended to him for more than an hour. Yet he was back in the ring three months later as if nothing had happened, turning back a challenge for his light-heavyweight crown from Bob Murphy.

Maxim's real name was Giuseppe Antonio Berardinelli but he took his ring name because someone said his rapid jabbing style reminded them of the action of the Maxim gun. He wasn't the biggest hitter or the classiest boxer but what he did, he did exceptionally well. He could jab, his punches were accurate, his defence was tight and his chin solid. He was also managed by the legendary Jack 'Doc' Kearns, who had handled Jack Dempsey. The great American writer W.C. Heinz once said, 'His fights do not inspire enthusiasm and his style appears controlled by caution.' Nevertheless, Heinz admired him. His most famous win was when Sugar Ray Robinson attempted to take away his light-heavyweight title on a sweltering night in New York in 1952. Robinson was ahead on points but he was disorientated by heat exhaustion, floundering around the ring and was retired after the thirteenth round.

After he stopped boxing in 1958, Maxim earned a living as a taxi driver in Florida, lived in Las Vegas for twenty years, then returned to his birthplace, Cleveland, and died on 2 June 2001 at the age of seventy-nine. Incredibly, he was survived by his mother, Henrietta!

OLIVER McCALL

Born: 21 April 1965, Chicago, Illinois
Height: 6ft 2in   **Weight at peak:** 231lbs (16st 7lbs)
Fights: 48   **Won:** 40   **Lost:** 7   **Drawn:** 0   **No Contests:** 1
KO percentage: 62
Rounds boxed: 235
World champion: 1994-95 (WBC)
World title fights: 4
Career span: 1985-2003 (18 years)
KO wins: 30
KO defeats: 1

An overhand, shut-eyed right that detonated on the jaw of Lennox Lewis put Oliver McCall's name in the history books. With that one sensational punch the erratic, difficult man who called himself the Atomic Bull became World Boxing Council heavyweight champion at Wembley Arena, London, in September 1994.

McCall, from Chicago, had been working the circuit for more than eight years, and had earned regular pay as Mike Tyson's sparring partner. He had also been a hired help to Tim Witherspoon, Michael Spinks, Pinklon Thomas and, briefly, Frank Bruno. His first attempt at world class in Atlantic City in July 1989 brought him a ten-round points defeat by Buster Douglas, who then fought Tyson and of course knocked him out. McCall rolled along, winning some, losing others: he knocked out Bruce Seldon in nine rounds in Atlantic City in April 1991, out-pointed Jesse Ferguson, lost a split verdict to Tony Tucker and stopped the Italian Francesco Damiani. By the time he challenged Lewis, he had Emanuel Steward working his corner. Don King was promoting him. The one-punch win brought Oliver the title at the age of twenty-nine but already this intense father of six had problems. In time he would admit to drug and alcohol addiction. In his only successful defence he scored a surprisingly close twelve-round decision over the veteran Larry Holmes at Caesars Palace, Las Vegas, in April 1995. Then, with his problems escalating, McCall lost the title to Frank Bruno in the open air at Wembley Stadium, London, in September 1995. He seemed incredibly casual, as if he felt he could win any time he liked. When he did open up and hang some heavy shots on Bruno's chin it was too little too late and the proud, focused Englishman was already too far clear on the cards. McCall surrendered his WBC belt on scores of 117-111 twice and 115-113. On the back of that he walked away without taking the British Board of Control drug test and was, for what that was worth, disciplined.

When Tyson beat Bruno and gave back the WBC belt rather than defend it against Lewis, McCall was matched with Lewis for the vacant title at the Las Vegas Hilton in February 1997. It was one of the most bizarre world championship fights in history. McCall's drug and alcohol problems were out in the open. He had admitted first taking drugs at the age of thirteen, had spent 1996 in and out of rehabilitation units and had criminal issues to deal with over an incident in a Nashville hotel over the Christmas period in which he had allegedly thrown a Christmas tree across the lobby! Incredibly, he arrived in Las Vegas for his $3.1 million gross payday with a personal drug counsellor. He was a member of Narcotics Anonymous and Alcoholics Anonymous. McCall barely threw let alone landed a punch and eventually crumpled into tears. Lewis, puzzled, didn't go in and finish it. Referee Mills Lane asked more than once if McCall was all right, asked his trainer George Benton to persuade him to fight, then decided he was emotionally unfit to continue and led him away in the fifth round. McCall babbled something about waiting for a call from God.

After that, nobody felt like giving him another chance – and his out-of-the-ring problems led to more brushes with the police. He had one last hour in the limelight at the Mandalay Bay, Las Vegas, in November 2001 when he knocked out Henry Akinwande in the tenth round. Afterwards he offered up his best gap-toothed beam and rumbled around the media benches telling anyone who would listen, 'The Bull is back!' He wasn't.

LUTHER McCARTY

Born: 20 March 1892, Driftwood Creek, Nebraska
Died: 24 May 1913, Calgary, Canada, aged 21
Height: 6ft 4in   **Weight at peak:** 205lbs (14st 9lbs)
Fights: 25   **Won:** 20   **Lost:** 4   **Drawn:** 1
KO percentage: 64
Rounds boxed: 158
World title fights: 0
Career span: 1911-13 (2 years)
KO wins: 16
KO defeats: 1

The most tragic figure of the controversial 'White Hope' era, handsome giant Luther McCarty had charisma and talent, lived a spartan, teetotal life – but was only twenty-one when he was knocked out by a light punch in a clinch against Arthur Pelkey in Calgary, Canada, on 24 May 1913. He collapsed immediately, was carried from the ring and lay on the ground, where he died eight minutes later. A famous photograph shows a beam of light shining down through the roof of the arena belonging to the old heavyweight champion, Tommy Burns, onto McCarty's unconscious form as he was counted out. The day after the fight the stadium was burned down.

The inquest heard that McCarty had gone into the contest with Pelkey suffering from serious neck injuries after being thrown from a horse. This, it was decided, could have contributed to the brain haemorrhage that killed him. There was also the little matter of a neck injury in a fight only three weeks earlier against Frank Moran, but that, apparently, was not considered.

McCarty was from Driftwood Creek, Nebraska. He turned professional in Montana in January 1911, when he was eighteen. His manager Billy Carney was known as the Professor on the perfectly reasonable grounds that he once spent two weeks studying Law at the University of Pennsylvania. McCarty attracted attention when he knocked out Carl Morris in six rounds in Springfield, Missouri, in May 1912. He also boxed a No-Decision bout with Jess Willard, the man who would eventually dethrone Jack Johnson, in New York in August 1912. Two months later McCarty outclassed the more experienced Al Kaufman in two rounds in San Francisco. Kaufman was knocked down three times, the last time out of the ring on to the ringside press row.

In December 1912 McCarty impressed again with a sixteenth-round knockout of Fireman Jim Flynn in Vernon, California, and on New Year's Day 1913 he won the so-called 'White heavyweight championship' in eighteen rounds against Al Palzer. He seemed to closing in on Johnson when his life was cut short.

AL McCOY

Born: 22 March 1913, Winslow, Maine
Real name: Florien La Brasseur
Died: 1989, aged 76
Height: 5ft 11in   **Weight at peak:** 180lbs (12st 12lbs)
Fights: 169   **Won:** 116   **Lost:** 32   **Drawn:** 20   **No Decisions:** 1
KO percentage: 27
Rounds boxed: 1,110
World title fights: 1
Career span: 1928-1942 (14 years)
KO wins: 46
KO defeats: 5

Al McCoy was a veteran of more than 160 fights when he joined the long list of no-hopers who challenged Joe Louis. McCoy's chance came in Boston Garden in December 1940. He was rescued after five rounds because Louis, fighting at half pace, had landed enough punches to close his left eye. Not much else happened in one of the least eventful championship bouts of all.

McCoy's real name was Florien La Brasseur. Of French-Canadian extraction, he came from Maine – born in Winslow and based in Waterville if you're an expert on those hives of boxing activity – could dig a bit but had lost three of his last four fights when his 'Bum of the Month' opportunity came around. McCoy, who had been boxing since he was fifteen, once made a spurious claim to the world light-heavyweight title, which attracted backing in Canada, but his best wins were over the middleweight Lou Brouillard and the veteran Tommy Loughran. After his world title payday he boxed once, knocking out Angelo Wright in Massachusetts, then retired. He died in 1989, aged seventy-five.

TOM McNEELEY

Born: 27 February 1937, Cambridge, Massachusetts
Height: 6ft 2in   **Weight at peak:** 197lbs (14st 1lb)
Fights: 51   **Won:** 37   **Lost:** 14
KO percentage: 54
Rounds boxed: 306
World title fights: 1

Career span: 1958-66 (8 years)
KO wins: 28
KO defeats: 5

Tom McNeeley was a raw, unerringly brave heavyweight who was handpicked as Floyd Patterson's challenger for the heavyweight title in Toronto's Maple Leaf Gardens in December 1961. Patterson knocked him out with ease. It was testament to McNeeley's courage that the fight lasted into the fourth round – he had taken nine counts and had two more 'knockdowns' ruled slips, before the referee, Jersey Joe Walcott, waved it over. Along the way the twenty-four-year-old challenger from Arlington, Massachusetts, somehow managed to put Patterson down for a flash knockdown with a right hand in the fourth. Walcott called a slip, but the champion said afterwards, 'I really felt that punch, but I knew exactly what was going on when I went down.' Afterwards McNeeley's wife Nancy, a former Miss New Hampshire, leaned over the ropes to console him. He sobbed, 'Oh, honey. Oh, honey.' On the way from the ring McNeeley was in tears as he saw his father, Tom snr. He said to him, 'I tried, Dad. I really tried.'

While writers rattled out their condemnations at ringside – Red Smith, for example, called it 'a mismatch of scandalous proportions' – the Canadian crowd applauded McNeeley's courage.

Going in, McNeeley was unbeaten but untested in twenty-three fights. His best win was a third-round knockout of the Tongan Kitione Lave in Boston in March 1961. He had also out-pointed Willi Besmanoff over ten rounds and had two points wins over Utah heavyweight George Logan. Ominously, Logan had put him down twice. Otherwise, nothing. *Ring* magazine generously ranked him number ten in the world. Those who tried to justify the match talked about McNeeley's desire – always a bad sign – and Patterson's vulnerable chin. 'Patterson can be hit, can be hurt,' said McNeeley's manager, Peter Fuller, whom it was alleged had sparred with his man in private late-night sessions and, embarrassingly, had cut him slightly over the right eye. McNeeley denied it, saying he nicked a pimple by mistake. Jimmy Cannon, the New York writer, said, 'McNeeley has more glass in his chin than the United Nations building has windows.' The veteran fight manager Johnny Buckley suggested McNeeley, although 8-1 according to the bookmakers, was nearer a 1,000-1 shot. 'The match never should have been made,' he said. 'I feel sorry for him because I like him. Tom is a nice kid, a good boy. He has been rushed into this fight. I've known him a long time – hell, I used to manage his old man and made him quit the ring.'

Boxing certainly runs in the family. In 1985 Peter McNeeley, son of Tom jnr, was also given a one-off opportunity in a terrible mismatch against Mike Tyson in Las Vegas. He lasted eighty-nine seconds.

SAM McVEY

Born: 17 May 1884, Oxnard, California
Died: 23 December 1921, New York, aged 37
Height: 5ft 10½in   **Weight at peak:** 200-215lbs (14st 4lbs-15st 5lbs)
Fights: 97   **Won:** 64   **Lost:** 16   **Drawn:** 12   **No Decisions:** 5
KO percentage: 48
Rounds boxed: 977
World title fights: 0
Career span: 1902-21 (19 years)
KO wins: 47
KO defeats: 6

Short and strong, Sam McVey was one of the great black American heavy-weights of the Jack Johnson era. Tentative plans for him to box Johnson for the world championship in 1912 were ruined by financial problems – and instead 'Fireman' Jim Flynn was offered the chance in Las Vegas, New Mexico. Johnson had trounced McVey three times in 1903 and 1904, and in the third fight gave him such a pounding before knocking him out in the twentieth round that for a long time Sam was disinclined to box him again. Eight years on who knows what would have happened, but McVey deserved an opportunity.

From Oxnard, California, a town on the coast road north of Los Angeles, McVey was considered ugly, not only by the white media, but even by his own father, who gave him a silver pipe as a present, with the instruction to keep it until he saw a man who was uglier than he was! A newspaper writer suggested McVey was so awful to look at that he would scare back the rising moon.

Johnson inflicted his first defeat with a twenty-round boxing lesson in Los Angeles in February 1903. In a rematch eight months later McVey absorbed a pounding to go the distance again but lost several teeth along the way. After Johnson knocked him out in San Francisco in April 1904, McVey was beaten by Denver Ed Martin and didn't box again for more than a year. Persuaded to try again, he was so frustrated by his inability to get matches with the leading white heavyweights of the time he left for a European tour. He trounced Jewey Smith in three rounds in Paris in March 1908 – yet a month later it was Smith not McVey who challenged Tommy Burns for the heavyweight championship in the French capital. He also featured in the incredible marathon with long-time opponent Joe Jeannette in Paris in April 1908. Two months earlier McVey had outscored Jeannette in a relatively bloodless affair over twenty rounds and the French press criticised them so heavily that they agreed on a quick return – and a fight to the finish to persuade the sceptics that they were genuine. The Paris sports writers stayed away – and missed an amazing, brutal bout that was a throw-back to the bare-knuckle era in terms of endurance. Jeannette was knocked down repeatedly – reports differ as to how many times – in the first thirty-seven rounds, but refused to quit. Gradually McVey punched himself out and after three hours and twelve minutes, at the start of round fifty, he collapsed with exhaustion. He was confined to bed for two weeks.

In 1910 McVey twice fought Battling Jim Johnson, who would box Jack Johnson in a farcical heavyweight title fight three years later. The first was a fifteen-round draw, but McVey won the second in twenty-one rounds. He boxed the first of many fights against Sam Langford – a twenty-round draw in Paris in April 1911, then took the boat to England where he knocked out the South African, George 'The Boer' Rodel, in one round. He went with Langford to Australia, where they had half-a-dozen surprisingly gruelling encounters – McVey won the first, Langford the next four, then the last was a draw. On the tour Sam also knocked out another world title challenger, Bill Lang, in two rounds. In his last fight in Australia, in Melbourne, in June 1914, McVey took only four rounds to destroy one of the 'White Hope' heavyweights, Arthur Pelkey.

Back in the United States he out-pointed Harry Wills over twenty rounds. Apart from Langford on their Australian tour, nobody had beaten McVey since his marathon with Jeannette in April 1909. The championship was pretty much in limbo from the moment of Johnson's exile from America until Jess Willard, who was disinclined to defend, lost to Jack Dempsey in the summer of 1919. Would-be challengers had to be content to fight each other. After a loss to Wills in 1918, McVey took eighteen months off, had a few more 'nothing' fights and then faded away. He earned some welcome money as a sparring partner for Jack Dempsey in 1920.

Early in December 1921 he developed pneumonia and died in hospital in Harlem. McVey had no money, but Nat Fleischer said he was saved from a pauper's burial by Jack Johnson, who paid for 'a proper funeral'.

KARL MILDENBERGER

Born: 23 November 1937, Kaiserslautern, Germany
Full name: Karl Heinz Mildenberger
Height: 6ft 2¼in   **Weight at peak:** 196lbs (14st)
Fights: 62   **Won:** 53   **Lost:** 6   **Drawn:** 3
KO percentage: 30
Rounds boxed: 492
World title fights: 1
Career span: 1958-68 (10 years)
KO wins: 19
KO defeats: 4

A genial southpaw from Kaiserslautern, Karl Mildenberger was given a shot at the world championship during Muhammad Ali's 'European tour' in 1966. The great man won on a twelfth-round stoppage, but for a time the German's left-handed stance gave him something to think about. Mildenberger came forward and whacked him around the body quite effectively in the early stages. Eventually, however, Ali toyed with Mildenberger just as he did with most of his challengers of the time. When the referee, Teddy Waltham, who was also the secretary of the British Boxing Board of Control, ordered him to close his glove when punching, Ali said, 'Like this?' And promptly knocked Mildenberger down! Mildenberger was dropped three times, fought back defiantly in the ninth, but was taking punches without landing anything back when Waltham stopped it in the twelfth.

From his debut in 1958 Mildenberger was developed into an attraction, though from time to time he had the benefit of home advantage – as when in March 1961 he fought Thorner Ahsman in Berlin. After being floored three times, Mildenberger twisted Ahsman's arm in a clinch. Ahsman could not go on because his elbow was damaged and he was ruled the loser. In January 1962 Mildenberger out-pointed Pete Rademacher, the Olympic gold medallist who had fought Floyd Patterson for the world title on his pro debut. However the next month, when Mildenberger challenged Dick Richardson for the European title in Dortmund, he was knocked out in one round.

Points wins over Joe Bygraves and Joe Erskine helped him rebuild, though again, when Zora Folley seemed to beat him clearly, the German judges came up with a draw. Mildenberger also out-pointed Eddie Machen, and won and defended the European title three times. When he fought Ali he was unbeaten, officially, in five years and twenty-two contests.

Mildenberger took part in the WBA elimination tournament but lost his opening bout on points to Oscar Bonavena before an 18,000 crowd in Frankfurt in September 1967. A 1-4 favourite pre-fight, Mildenberger was knocked down four times: in rounds one, four, seven and ten, when he had the benefit of a long count. A three-knockdown, seven-rounds loss to Leotis Martin cost him more ground, and his final fight was when he lost the European title in eight rounds to Henry Cooper at Wembley in September 1968. Cooper dropped him in rounds two and seven, but in the eighth, when a clash of heads left the Englishman with a bad cut on his right eyebrow, in addition to another smaller cut on the left eye from a previous round, Mildenberger was disqualified for butting. His camp made a token protest, but it was time for him to retire anyway.

BILLY MISKE

Born: 12 April 1894, St Paul, Minnesota
Died: 1 January 1924, St Paul, Minnesota, aged 29
Height: 6ft   **Weight at peak:** 187lbs (13st 3lbs)
Fights: 107   **Won:** 69   **Lost:** 14   **Drawn:** 13   **No Decisions:** 13
KO percentage: 32
Rounds boxed: 769

World title fights: 1
Career span: 1913-23 (10 years)
KO wins: 35
KO defeats: 1

Billy Miske's legend built up around his brief challenge to Jack Dempsey for the world title in Benton Harbor on the shores of Lake Michigan in September 1920. 'I knocked him out because I loved the guy,' said Dempsey, who won seventy-three seconds into round three before a 15,000 crowd. 'He was dying of Bright's Disease. I didn't know it was as bad as it was. All I knew was that he begged me for the fight. He was broke and needed a good payday so that he could rest and regain his health... Fighters know each other's problems, hopes, tough times.'

Dempsey hurt Miske with body shots in round one, knocked him down in round two and finished him off with a right hand in the third. 'I carried Billy to his stool and nearly got sick to my stomach while the two seconds worked on him, bringing him to,' said Dempsey. Miske, according to Dempsey, took around $25,000 home to St Paul, Minnesota, but did not simply fade away and die. He had another twenty-five fights, including one on the Dempsey-Georges Carpentier undercard in the big stadium at Boyle's Thirty Acres, Jersey City, in July 1921. Miske boxed an eight-round No-Decision bout against one of Dempsey's sparring partners, Jack Renault.

He knocked out one-time contender Fred Fulton in a round and beat home city rival Tommy Gibbons on a foul in ten rounds in the main event at Madison Square Garden in October 1922, though Gibbons won the 'newspaper verdict' in a ten-round rematch in St Paul in December 1922. But a month or so after that, he was too sick to train. To provide for his wife and children for Christmas 1923 he took a fight with Bill Brennan in Omaha, Nebraska, in November. It appears Brennan didn't try before going down for the count in round four, because his $2,100 purse was confiscated and given to charity.

Miske was known as the St Paul Thunderbolt. Because boxing was not legalised in Minnesota until 1915, the previous year, when they were unbeaten novices, he and Tommy Gibbons fought a No-Decision bout across the St Croix River in Hudson, Wisconsin, in March 1914. He also boxed world champions in the lighter divisions – Harry Greb, Mike O'Dowd, Jack Dillon and Battling Levinsky. In Miske's second fight with Levinsky in Brooklyn in October 1916, his opponent's world light-heavyweight title was considered on the line. But although Miske won the newspaper decision, because the fight went its allotted ten rounds, the title could not change hands. So many of Miske's bouts were No-Decision affairs that it's hard to estimate the real level of his ability, but he also won a newspaper verdict over Carl Morris, the big heavyweight contender from the Deep South, in September 1917. Miske, who was only a light-heavy at the time, conceded 50lbs.

As a heavyweight Miske twice boxed No-Decision bouts with Dempsey but beat Gunboat Smith, Fireman Jim Flynn and Brennan. After a No-Decision bout with Levinsky in Ohio in July 1919, his illness became apparent. When he asked Dempsey for the payday he had hospital bills outstanding and a car business had failed. Miske did not tell his family the prognosis, but his manager Jack Reddy knew and so did a newspaperman, George Barton. They agreed to keep the secret and he kept the family fed and watered for another two-and-a-half years before he became too ill. For his last fight against Brennan in Omaha, he earned $2,400. Reddy wouldn't take his cut. Billy bought a piano for his wife Marie, presents for children Billy jnr, Douglas and Marie, and then fell severely ill on Christmas Day. On Boxing Day he was driven by Reddy to St Mary's Hospital in Minneapolis – he told his wife the full truth in the car – and he died on New Year's Day, 1924. He was twenty-nine.

CHARLIE MITCHELL

Born: 24 November 1861, Birmingham, England
Full name: Charles Watson Mitchell
Died: 3 April 1918, Brighton, England, aged 56
Height: 5ft 9in   **Weight at peak:** 158lbs (11st 4lbs)
Fights: 55   **Won:** 30   **Lost:** 3   **Drawn:** 14   **No Decisions:** 8
KO percentage: 18
Rounds boxed: not known
World title fights: 1 (plus 1 bare-knuckle)
Career span: 1878-94 (16 years)
KO wins: 10
KO defeats: 2

One of the fighters who lived through the cross-over period between the bare-knuckle and gloved era, Charlie Mitchell boxed for both championships – against John L. Sullivan and James J. Corbett.

From Birmingham of Irish parents, Mitchell was only a middleweight but could hit hard enough to cope with heavyweights and was clever and slick enough to out-general all but the best. He learned his trade in London boxing taverns like the White Bear in Bermondsey, the Blue Anchor and the Five Ink Horns in Shoreditch and St Giles Room in Leicester Square. He was a boxing instructor at a pub, the White Rose, and when travelling he opened a boxing school at the Palais Rubens in Antwerp.

In June 1881 Mitchell was jailed for six weeks along with opponent Jack Burke, the English welterweight champion, when the police broke up their bare-knuckle bout in the twenty-fifth round after an hour and seventeen minutes of fighting. He was still only nineteen years old. By 1883 he was in New York and only a month after law enforcers stopped a fight he was winning against Mike Cleary in the third round, he boxed the world heavyweight champion John L. Sullivan in a supposed exhibition in Madison Square Garden. Mitchell conceded around 40lbs to Sullivan but stunned him and the crowd by putting him down with a left hand in the first round. Sullivan got up and in round two battered Mitchell through the ropes. Charlie hurt his back, but fought on. In the third, after going down several times, Mitchell fell over with Sullivan landing on top of him. They both got up and wanted to carry on, but the police chief, one Clubber Williams, stopped it. Mitchell was on a forty per cent share of the gate and took away around $6,500. From that moment their rivalry intensified. In 1884 Mitchell turned up to box Sullivan in the Garden only to discover the champion was barely sober enough to walk, let alone fight!

When Sullivan came to Europe the following winter he at last agreed to box Mitchell in a bare-knuckle bout for the championship – and on the grounds of Baron Alphonse Rothschild at Apremont, near Chantilly, north of Paris, on 10 March 1888 they fought, at last, for real. The referee was the Englishman Bernard Angle, Mitchell's manager and father-in-law George 'Pony' Moore was in his corner, and in the crowd Sullivan's girlfriend, Anne Livingston, was dressed as a man because ladies were not permitted.

Mitchell was clever enough to keep out of the way of Sullivan's rushes – and gradually the ring turned into a square of churned-up mud. Sullivan sprained his right arm, and his left arm, recently broken in a fight with Patsy Cardiff, gave him pain. By the fifteenth round a chilly rain had set in. By the thirty-first round Sullivan's teeth were chattering. Mitchell just kept on moving, sniping, ignoring everyone who wanted him to stand and fight. At one point some of Baron Rothschild's gamekeepers turned up and stood watching the spectacle in astonishment. By the thirty-ninth round, after three hours and eleven minutes, Mitchell offered the draw and Sullivan accepted. Afterwards gendarmes arrested both boxers but released them on bail and left them to slip out of the country.

Mitchell was in Jake Kilrain's corner when he challenged Sullivan in the last bare-knuckle championship bout in Richburg, Mississippi, in 1889. Legend has it that he abused Sullivan verbally throughout the seventy-five rounds! Back in Britain, Mitchell boxed the great champion of the previous era, Jem Mace, in a two-minute-round gloved bout in Glasgow in February 1890. Not surprisingly, Mitchell was beating the fifty-eight-year-old 'Swaffham Gypsy' comfortably when the police called things off in round four.

When Sullivan was goaded into defending his title in 1892, he included Mitchell on the list of men he considered suitable contenders. He called him 'that bombastic sprinter, whom I would rather whip than any man in the world'. Corbett took the fight instead and dethroned Sullivan in twenty-one rounds – the first championship fight with gloves.

Mitchell's last contest of note was when he challenged Corbett in a specially built arena on the Firefield race track, six miles out of Jacksonville, Florida, in

January 1894. Bad publicity kept the crowds away and in the end only about 2,000 people paid at the gate. Mitchell had goaded Corbett with a tirade of abuse, then kept him waiting in the ring for ten minutes. When the referee, 'Honest' John Kelly, called them together, Mitchell set off with another foul-mouthed barrage. Corbett tore from his corner in a vile mood. Mitchell bust his lip with a jab and out-boxed him, but then the champion settled down, used his advantages properly and floored Mitchell three times in round two. The Englishman carried on swearing at him while on the canvas, and Corbett should have been disqualified for brushing the referee aside and hitting him again. It was all over in round three, with Mitchell down three more times. Again, if the rules had been strictly interpreted Corbett might have been thrown out – his seconds had to rush into the ring to hold him back when Charlie was floored.

'Corbett is the cleverest man I saw,' said Mitchell when he recovered. 'If he keeps his health he will never be beaten. The trouble is I got him too damn mad!'

In retirement he remained a close follower of boxing, particularly admiring the skills of the Welsh flyweight Jimmy Wilde, though at one point he was jailed for fourteen months for fracturing the skull of a policeman he had hit with his cane. He died after an illness of some months in Brighton on 3 April 1918, aged fifty-six.

GUNNER MOIR

Born: 17 April 1879 Lambeth, London, England
Real name: James Moir
Died: 12 June 1939, Sutton, Surrey, aged 60
Height: 5ft 9½in   **Weight:** 200lbs (14st 4lbs)
Fights: 27   **Won:** 15   **Lost:** 12
KO percentage: 37
Rounds boxed: 127
World title fights: 1
Career span: 1903-1913 (10 years)
KO wins: 10
KO defeats: 7

Quite why the gentlemen of the National Sporting Club in London felt Gunner Moir was capable of mounting a decent challenge against the tiny but effective world champion Tommy Burns in 1907 isn't quite clear. Apart from winning the British title with a ninth-round disqualification victory over Jack Palmer, Moir, a tattooed former soldier, had done very little of note in a four-year career.

Burns won very easily. Moir was put down early on, tottered his way through the ninth and was laid out flat in the tenth. The defeat shattered Moir's confidence and he barely won another bout. Iron Hague knocked him out in one round to relieve him of the British title in April 1909 and although he managed to knock out Bombardier Billy Wells in 1911, he retired after the rematch two years later when Wells knocked him out in the fifth.

After his retirement he became an attendant at Canterbury Music Hall, did some film work – he found a particular niche playing executioners – and died in hospital in Sutton, Surrey, in 1939, leaving a widow and six children.

MICHAEL MOORER

Born: 12 November 1967, Brooklyn, New York
Height: 6ft 2in   **Weight at peak:** 218lbs (15st 8lbs)
Fights: 52   **Won:** 47   **Lost:** 4   **Drawn:** 1
KO percentage: 71
Rounds boxed: 271
World champion: 1994 & 1996-97
World title fights: 6
Career span: 1988-2004 (16 years)
KO wins: 37
KO defeats: 3

The first southpaw to win even a piece of the heavyweight championship, Michael Moorer didn't have the best punch resistance in the world but his skills and 'wrong-way round' style, plus his share of power, made him one of the better operators of the mid-1990s.

His finest hour came in the open air and searing heat of the Caesars Palace outdoor arena in April 1994 when he recovered from a second-round knock-down to out-box an increasingly weary, some said ill, Evander Holyfield and win a majority decision. That fight was famous for the magnificent 'Gettysburg Address' delivered to a seemingly hesitant Moorer by his trainer Teddy Atlas between rounds – suitably fired up, he took over and won.

Moorer was born in Brooklyn, raised in Monessen in south-west Pennsylvania, and was taught to box by his grandfather, a former pro middleweight named Henry Smith. When he was thirteen he shaved his head to look like his hero, Marvin Hagler, but wanted to be a fireman or a policeman. Eventually, he became an international amateur and boxing for a living became an inevitability.

For his professional career, Moorer moved to Detroit and wore the famous gold trunks of the Kronk Gym run by Emanuel Steward. Only nine months after his pro debut, Moorer won the inaugural WBO light-heavyweight fight and with the Kronk certificate of authenticity behind him, people took him seriously. He was also exciting in a grim kind of way. He admitted to one interviewer a liking for guns and after one brush with the law wore a T-shirt with 'You Have The Right To Remain Violent' emblazoned across it.

Moorer held the WBO light-heavyweight title for two-and-a-half years before he put on 30lbs and moved up to heavyweight. In May 1992 he won a four-knockdown war with Smokin' Bert Cooper – two knockdowns each – to become WBO heavyweight champion, but gave the belt back, declaring boldly it was hindering his progress. Beating Holyfield should have set him up, but in his first defence in November 1994 he lost in ten rounds to the forty-five-year-old George Foreman at the MGM Grand in Las Vegas, and never recovered his reputation.

In Dortmund in June 1996 he won with a twelve-round split decision over the German, Axel Schulz, for the vacant IBF title. Disgruntled fans tossed champagne bottles into the ring – at least it was a better class of riot. Moorer was also ahead on two and behind on one card going into the twelfth round of his first defence against Frans Botha in Las Vegas, then stopped the unbeaten South African in the final session. His reign was colourless: defence number two was a forgettable majority decision over Vaughn Bean in Las Vegas in March 1997.

He lost a unification fight with Holyfield involving Evander's WBA title at the Thomas and Mack Center, Las Vegas, in November 1997. Holyfield, older but a far more upbeat fighter than the one who lost to Moorer in 1994, won convincingly. Moorer was down in round five, twice in the seventh and twice more in the eighth, after which the doctor advised ref Mitch Halpern to wave it off.

Moorer was out of the ring for three years, tried to work his way back but was blown away in thirty seconds by David Tua in Atlantic City in August 2002.

FRANK MORAN

Born: 18 March 1887, Cleveland, Ohio
Died: 1 December 1967, Los Angeles
Height: 6ft 1½in   **Weight at peak:** 199-203lbs (14st 3lbs-14st 7lbs)
Fights: 68   **Won:** 40   **Lost:** 23   **Drawn:** 3   **No decisions:** 2
KO percentage: 42
Rounds boxed: 428
World title fights: 2
Career span: 1908-22 (14 years)
KO wins: 29
KO defeats: 6

A strong, slow, red-haired heavyweight with a heavy right-hand punch he labelled Mary Ann, Frank Moran boxed both Jack Johnson and Jess Willard for the world championship – and couldn't make an impression on either. Johnson out-boxed him in Paris on 27 June 1914 – with Georges Carpentier as referee. The Willard bout was, under the New York law of the day, a No-Decision bout over ten rounds. Therefore, Moran had to knock out the former Kansas cowboy to win the title and couldn't do that. The majority of ringside newspapermen thought Willard had the better of it anyway. When Moran boxed Johnson, the champion was thirty-five years old and Paris, in those months immediately before the First World War, was the nightlife capital of Europe, conducive to pleasure rather than hard graft. It was a poor fight, a slow, listless exhibition that drifted on in front of a bored crowd of 7,000 or so in the Velodrome d'Hiver cycling arena. By the last of the twenty rounds a lot of the paying customers had already walked out in search of something more dramatic. Moran was cut over both eyes but unhurt.

The next morning a young Serb, Gavrilo Princip, changed the world forever as he stepped from a crowd in Sarajevo and shot the Archduke Ferdinand and his wife Sophie. Within weeks political crisis had spiralled into war. In the chaos that erupted across Europe, the lawyer who dealt with the finances of the Johnson-Moran bout was sent to the front and was killed within days of the war starting. Neither boxer was paid.

Moran was born in Cleveland, the son of Irish immigrant parents who moved to Pittsburgh when Frank was five. He trained as a dentist, but gave up pulling and drilling teeth. He liked knocking them out much better. He also served five years in the US Navy, working for the latter part of that time as a quartermaster on *Mayflower*, the presidential yacht. He lost on points to Gunboat Smith in a San Francisco twenty-rounder, and boxed a ten-round No Decision against Luther McCarty in New York. Three weeks later McCarty lost to Arthur Pelkey and died of a brain haemorrhage. Moran always felt the damage had begun in their fight. 'After our fight his manager put a robe around him and walked him, stiff-necked, to his hotel several blocks from the arena,' he said. Moran heard people say McCarty had damaged three discs in his neck.

Frank knocked out Al Palzer in seven rounds, lost to Johnson but returned to Europe in 1915 and landed his big, sweeping 'Mary Ann' on popular British champion Bombardier Billy Wells for a tenth-round knockout at the London Opera House. After the Willard fight, Moran was put out of the picture when big Frank Fulton beat him in three rounds in New Orleans.

Moran acted as a tough guy in several Hollywood movies and lived fairly comfortably into old age. He died at the age of eighty in December 1967.

CARL MORRIS

Born: 23 February 1887, Fulton, Kentucky
Died: 11 July 1951, Pasadena, California, aged 64
Height: 6ft 4in   **Weight at peak:** 235lbs (16st 11lbs)
Fights: 85   **Won:** 57   **Lost:** 20   **Drawn:** 3   **No Decisions:** 5
KO percentage: 45
Rounds boxed: 452

World title fights: 0
Career span: 1910-24 (14 years)
Longest winning run: 10 (1915-17)
KO wins: 38
KO defeats: 5

A lumbering part-Cherokee Indian from Kentucky, Carl Morris exploded onto the heavyweight scene within months of his professional debut in 1910, but in spite of his meteoric rise and the fact that he remained one of the better heavyweights in the world for the next half-dozen years, he never boxed for the championship.

Morris knocked out the former world champion Marvin Hart in three rounds in Sapulpa, Oklahoma, in December 1910, only three months after making his debut. It was his fifth consecutive knockout win. The 'White Hope' publicity machine suggested Morris was working on the railroad in Oklahoma when he heard the result of the Jack Johnson-James J. Jeffries fight, told a workmate, 'I'm going to be a fighter and whip the Negro,' and walked out.

In a No-Decision bout with Fireman Jim Flynn in Madison Square Garden in September 1911 Morris took a grotesque pounding for ten rounds but stayed gamely on his feet to the final bell. The referee, Charlie White, changed shirts halfway through but didn't apparently consider stopping the slaughter. Morris ploughed on, beating Flynn twice in returns, Fred Fulton and George Rodel, lost in six to Luther McCarty and on a foul to Gunboat Smith. By 1917, when at last he was being considered as a possible opponent for world champion Willard, Morris was thrown out after a disgraceful exhibition against Fulton. Newspaper reports suggested he 'violated every rule of boxing and of good sportsmanship'.

Jack Dempsey beat him three times, the last of which was a knockout after only fourteen seconds in New Orleans in December 1918. Dempsey hated Morris from the time he was employed as a youthful sparring partner for the big man. Morris had sneered at the young man's impoverished state – and Dempsey did not forget it.

Morris boxed on until 1924, by which time he was either thirty-seven or forty, depending on who you believe. He died in Pasadena, California, on 11 July 1951.

TOMMY MORRISON

Born: 2 January 1969, Jay, Oklahoma
Height: 6ft 2in   **Weight at peak:** 226lbs (16st 2lbs)
Fights: 50   **Won:** 46   **Lost:** 3   **Drawn:** 1
KO percentage: 80
Rounds boxed: 167
World title fights: 0

Career span: 1988-96 (8 years)
KO wins: 40
KO defeats: 3

For a while, Tommy Morrison was a crowd-pleasing, aggressive and big-punching heavyweight who looked as if he might, just might, threaten the supremacy of Lennox Lewis, Riddick Bowe and Evander Holyfield in the early to mid-1990s. Nicknamed 'The Duke' because he was said to be a distant relative of actor John Wayne, he was managed by Mike Tyson's old mentor Bill Cayton.

Morrison emerged from the notorious tough-man contests to become a pro fighter in his late teens. A string of quick knockouts earned him a following and in 1991 he showed he could do it against faded but knowledgeable heavyweights in James Tillis and Pinklon Thomas. However, he took a horrible pounding on the ropes from Ray Mercer in Atlantic City in 1991, when he was more or less unconscious on his feet as veteran referee Tony Perez took an age to step in. It was the kind of beating that could have finished him, but the following year Morrison overcame a broken jaw and hand to stop Joe Hipp in nine bloody rounds in Reno. His finest win was when he turned boxer for the night and outsmarted George Foreman over twelve one-sided rounds to win the minor WBO belt in June 1993.

His spell as WBO holder was chaotic. The Texan heavyweight Mike Williams walked out of his first defence and Tim Tomashek, a glorified club fighter, was literally pulled out of the ringside seats as a replacement. Morrison won easily in four. Morrison lost the WBO belt sensationally to Michael Bentt in ninety-three seconds in Tulsa, Oklahoma. His last big fight was when he was picked apart in six by Lennox Lewis, who was between championship reigns, in October 1995.

The following year he tested HIV positive and for some time, not surprisingly, appeared to struggle to come to terms with his drastically altered circumstances.

JACK MUNROE

Born: 26 June 1874, Upper Kempt Head, Boulardarie, Nova Scotia, Canada
Full name: John Alexander Munroe
Died: 13 February 1942, Toronto, Canada, aged 67
Height: 5ft 11½in   **Weight at peak:** 186lbs (13st 4lbs)
Fights: 19   **Won:** 13   **Lost:** 3   **Drawn:** 3
KO percentage: 47
Rounds boxed: 108
World title fights: 1
Career span: 1900-06 (6 years)
KO wins: 9
KO defeats: 1

Jack Munroe was pilloried for a timid performance in a world title bid against James J. Jeffries when he was thrown in way over his head and folded inside two rounds in San Francisco in August 1904. A former coal-miner from Chester, Pennsylvania, Munroe boxed a half-interested, out-of-shape Jeffries in an exhibition in Montana. Munroe caught the champion off guard with a body punch that made him go down momentarily – and the incident was blown out of proportion by writers desperate for an angle.

Munroe acquitted himself well enough in a No-Decision bout with Tom Sharkey in Philadelphia in February 1904 and was matched with Jeffries for the championship but, in the words of one writer, 'froze like a rabbit under lights'. After that his only match of any historical note was a six-round No-Decision bout with Jack Johnson in Philadelphia in June 1905. Johnson battered him without trying to finish the fight.

Munroe retired, lived in Toronto and in the First World War served in the Canadian regiment known as the Princess Pats. He preferred going over the top with a woodsman's axe to a gun, and when he got to close quarters in a trench tended to wreak havoc. He was also given a medal for crawling out into No Man's Land while injured to bring back a wounded officer.

Munroe died in February 1942 at the age of sixty-four.

TONY MUSTO

Born: 3 December 1915, Blue Island, Illinois
Died: 30 September 1994, aged 78
Height: 5ft 7½in　　　**Weight at peak:** 190lbs (13st 8lbs)
Fights: 70　　　**Won:** 36　　　**Lost:** 30　　　**Drawn:** 4
KO percentage: 18
Rounds boxed: 538
World title fights: 1
Career span: 1937-46 (9 years)
KO wins: 13
KO defeats: 9

Eminently qualified for the Bum of the Month club, Tony Musto was labelled the Blue Island Tank. At slightly less than 5ft 8in tall, his low centre of gravity and ability to take a shot helped him survive into the ninth round with a disinterested Joe Louis in a championship fight in St Louis in April 1941. Apart from a three-round win over the ancient Johnny Risko in February 1940, he had beaten nobody when he was fed to Louis. He had also lost four of his last five: to Arturo Godoy, Red Burman, Jack Walker and Eddie Blunt. The champion later said charitably, 'Tony was strictly a local boxer who was good in his steady way.'

Afterwards Musto somehow beat Jimmy Bivins on points in September 1941 and also managed to outhustle Lee Savold in Washington DC in August 1942. Savold beat him in a rematch, but the crowd often rooted for Musto because of his size and his attacking style. However, when he lost because of a dislocated jaw against Tami Mauriello in seven rounds in July 1943 it was his sixth consecutive defeat. When he retired in 1946, he had lost more than he had won. He died in 1994, aged seventy-nine.

N

WALTER NEUSEL

Born: 25 November 1907, Bochum, Germany
Died: 3 October 1964, Berlin, Germany, aged 56
Fights: 90   **Won:** 68   **Lost:** 13   **Drawn:** 9
KO percentage: 40
Rounds boxed: 727
World title fights: 0
Career span: 1930-50 (20 years)
KO wins: 36
KO defeats: 6

When Walter Neusel fought Max Schmeling in 1934, such was the popularity of both men that they drew a crowd of more than 90,000 to an outdoor arena next to Hamburg zoo. Neusel was the scourge of British rings for a while and, when he was matched with Schmeling, was just back from a six-fight stay in New York, where he had out-pointed good men in Ray Impelletiere, King Levinsky and Tommy Loughran in Madison Square Garden. Unfortunately it had been a financial disaster. When he boxed Impellitere for ten rounds, after deductions, he put in his pocket the princely sum of $3.19! His biggest gross purse in the USA was $4,000, out of which he had to pay two managers, trainers and sparring partners.

Schmeling remembered him with respect. 'He was impulsive, always on the attack, ready to go for broke any time,' he said. When they fought, Neusel's Jewish manager, Paul Damski, stayed away. He lived in Paris and had problems with the Gestapo. Schmeling counter-punched Neusel, wore him down, cut him up and stopped him at the start of round nine.

Neusel's first appearance in Britain was in 1932, his last in 1937, when he won a bitterly disputed decision over the tall New Zealand heavyweight Maurice Strickland at Wembley. He beat Jack Petersen three times, the second time drawing a crowd of more than 60,000 outdoors at Wembley Stadium in spite of thunder storms and heavy rain all day, drew with Len Harvey, out-pointed Ben Foord and lost in three rounds to Tommy Farr. He also knocked out another British heavyweight champion, Reggie Meen, and out-pointed the veteran Australian George Cook. Altogether Neusel boxed sixteen times in England. He also out-pointed Larry Gains in Paris in 1932.

Neusel held the German title twice during the Second World War and fought Schmeling a second time in Hamburg in May 1948, when both were in their forties and desperate for money. This time Neusel won on points over ten rounds. Neusel eventually retired after Conny Rux knocked him out in 1950. He died of a heart attack in Berlin in 1964, aged fifty-six.

KEN NORTON

Born: 9 August 1943, Jacksonville, Illinois
Full name: Kenneth Howard Norton
Height: 6ft 3in   **Weight at peak:** 212-220 (15st 2lbs-15st 10lbs)
Fights: 50   **Won:** 42   **Lost:** 7   **Drawn:** 1
KO percentage: 66
Rounds boxed: 324
World champion: 1978
World title fights: 3
Career span: 1967-81 (14 years)
KO wins: 33
KO defeats: 4

Ken Norton broke Muhammad Ali's jaw in San Diego in 1973 and will go to his grave believing he beat Ali for the championship in their third fight in Yankee Stadium, New York, in 1976. Norton, a muscular, long-armed former Marine, had the style to give Ali hard fights whenever they met. In his prime he was right up there with the best of his generation.

In the record books he is a world champion because of the pompous decision by Jose Sulaiman and the World Boxing Council to strip Leon Spinks in March 1978. Spinks, a month after beating Ali in one of the upsets of the century, agreed to a rematch that most fight fans wanted to see rather than defend against the number one contender, Norton. The decision to take away Spinks's crown didn't wash with anyone then, and shouldn't now, but the WBC went a step further: on 29 March 1978, they declared Norton world champion on the grounds that he had out-pointed Jimmy Young of Philadelphia over fifteen rounds – an unpopular split decision – the previous November.

In June 1978 Norton lost a magnificent fifteen-rounder with Larry Holmes and kissed his paper title goodbye after a 'reign' of just seventy-two days. Norton's reputation was made by his fights with Ali, not by the intervention of Sulaiman's championship committee.

Born in Jacksonville, Illinois, in 1943, Norton was raised in a happy, middle-class home. He was an only child. 'I was downright spoiled!' he said. He won an athletics scholarship at North East Missouri State college, but gave it up in the second year and joined the Marines in 1964. He took up boxing there and turned professional in San Diego when he was discharged in September 1967. Early on he combined his boxing purses with a job at the Ford Motor Company. Norton learned well and had only one setback in his learning years, an eighth-round stoppage by Jose Luis Garcia in Los Angeles in July 1970, when he admitted he was over-confident. His trainer, Eddie Futch, pasted the press photo of the knockout to his locker-room door, suggested the photographer had been kind enough to get his 'best side' and asked if he would listen now.

In 1970 he sparred with Ali at the Hoover Street Gym in Los Angeles, where Futch was based. Norton, according to Futch, held his own. On the back of it, Ali offered Norton $25,000 for a real fight but Futch turned it down, insisting his man wasn't ready, and instead took him to spar with Joe Frazier. In November 1972 Norton beat the Californian champion Henry Clark in nine and then fought Ali in San Diego in March 1973. He was twenty-nine years old, only a couple of years younger than Ali, but with a lot less miles on his clock. To prepare for the fight he gave up the day job and became a full-time boxer. Nobody outside his own camp gave him a chance. Howard Cosell, the ABC commentator, declared it 'the worst mismatch in boxing history, a disgrace'.

Norton prepared ferociously in the dry heat of the San Jacinto Valley, 100 miles south of Los Angeles. He shut the doors of the gym and switched off the air conditioning. He admits he had an intensity for that fight that he never found again. Norton always credits Futch with planning the tactical moves that negated Ali's left hand and speed – Futch had been in Frazier's corner for their epic fight in March 1971 and knew at close hand what was required, but Norton also possessed the necessary obsession with victory. It also helped that, with less than two weeks to go, Ali tweaked an ankle playing golf.

Ali entered the ring in a $3,000 jewel-encrusted robe given him by Elvis Presley. It had 'People's Choice' on the back. For twelve rounds they fought a close, gruelling fight. Ali's camp said he broke his jaw in the second round. Certainly, it was broken at some point, but if you listen to trainers long enough, fight-changing injuries always seem to happen in round two! At the end judge Fred Hayes had it 6-5-1 Ali but both referee Frank Rustich and judge Hal Rickards saw it 7-4-1 Norton. The one-time marine, the no-hoper, had won. Ali underwent a ninety-minute operation at Clairmont General Hospital in San Diego on the jaw, which X-rays showed had broken cleanly. Norton visited him the next day and, even though his mouth was wired shut, Ali gave him advice about handling fame and fortune. They became friends.

In the rematch in Los Angeles in September 1973, Ali overturned the result with a split-decision win. Norton knew it was desperately close and didn't argue, although Futch and his understudy Thell Torrance both felt he had done enough. The scores were 6-5-1 each way and a 7-5 for Ali. The old champion won it on the last round.

Six months later Norton, without Futch, went to Caracas, Venezuela, to challenge for the heavyweight title against George Foreman and was blown away in the second round. Norton said he was distracted by pre-fight promotional rows and by a kidnap threat to his parents, who had flown to Caracas to watch the fight. Norton, according to his trainer Bill Slayton, was very depressed in the dressing room before the fight. 'He looked at me with a frown on his face and just shook his head in disgust,' said Slayton.

The third fight with Ali was over fifteen rounds for the championship in the house that Babe built, Yankee Stadium, before 30,289 paying customers, who shelled out $2.4 million. Norton outworked Ali and believed he had done more than enough. 'Total elation... I was smiling and crying at the same time. I had accomplished the unthinkable, beaten Muhammad Ali for the heavyweight championship of the world,' he wrote in his autobiography. The judges saw it differently: Harold Lederman and Barney Smith, ringside judges, voted 8-7 Ali, and referee Arthur Mercante saw it 8-6-1 Ali. The decision was close but unanimous: Norton had lost.

He stopped Duane Bobick in one round and the Italian Lorenzo Zanon in five, and then he had trouble pinning down the crafty, quick-handed Jimmy Young in Las Vegas in November 1977, but was awarded a split decision win that was open to argument. Then came the ridiculous intervention of the WBC and his supposed 'defence' against Larry Holmes in Las Vegas in June 1978. Don King, who had no piece of Spinks or Ali, promoted it. However much the administrative nonsense confused the situation, Holmes and Norton staged a ring classic at Caesars Palace that depended on the last of the fifteen rounds. Even that raged one way then the next, a compulsive finish that had the crowd on its feet in a prolonged standing ovation. Harold Buck and Joe Swessel saw it 143-142 Holmes, Lou Tabat had it 143-142 Norton.

Such a thin margin between success and failure, between a champion and a loser. While Holmes leaped into the Caesars Palace pool still wearing his WBC belt, Norton lay, deflated, on the table in his dressing room. Holmes later paid him full tribute. They had insulted each other before and during the fight but years on Larry said, 'This was the best fight I was ever in. It was one of the best fights a lot of people saw... I learned more about what makes Ken Norton and me tick than if I had sat down and talked to him every day of the year.'

One-round defeats by Earnie Shavers and Gerry Cooney persuaded him to retire. In addition to the $16 million he had grossed in the ring, Norton appeared in the movies *Drum* and *Mandingo*. NBC also offered him a broadcasting contract for the Moscow Olympics. He formed a personal management agency but in 1986 a road accident in Los Angeles left him with brain injuries. He spent four weeks in hospital and two years in a wheelchair but by the late 1990s had recovered enough to train boxers and open a restaurant and club in California.

LOU NOVA

Born: 16 March 1915, Los Angeles
Died: 29 September 1991, aged 76
Height: 6ft 3in   **Weight at peak:** 202lbs (14st 6lbs)
Fights: 64   **Won:** 51   **Lost:** 9   **Drawn:** 4
KO percentage: 48
Rounds boxed: 453
World title fights: 1
Career span: 1936-45 (9 years)
Longest winning run: 14 (1944)
KO wins: 31
KO defeats: 5

When Lou Nova challenged Joe Louis for the championship at the New York Polo Grounds in September 1941, he claimed his study of yoga had enabled him to develop a cosmic punch. That might or might not have been the case but Louis, who as far as we know had not studied yoga, took him out in the sixth round with a down-to-earth right cross. 'I didn't like all that mysterious shit he was talking,' said Louis.

Nova's eccentricity made the fight a financial success: 56,549 paid a total of $583,711 to watch it and Louis reaped in his biggest payday, almost $200,000, since the second Schmeling fight in 1938.

Nova was no Bum of the Month: he had twice beaten Max Baer, had outpointed Tommy Farr on a split decision over fifteen rounds in Madison Square Garden and had lost a savage encounter with Tony Galento in the fourteenth round in Philadelphia. 'Lou knew how to fight,' said Ray Arcel, who worked with him in the fight and in Stillman's Gym in New York. Arcel also suggested Nova confused himself with his yoga because he only half-understood it. Farr said Lou's style was awkward: 'Nova would waltz around, content to flick and flap and make such a pretence with his long left, which he stuck straight out and kept rigid... Nova did not look tough, but he was, and dead game.'

Originally from Los Angeles, Nova was skilful enough to win the National AAU heavyweight title and made his debut in Madison Square Garden in January 1936. He was unbeaten until the veteran former light-heavyweight champion Maxie Rosenbloom outhustled him at the Legion Stadium in Hollywood in June 1938. It was his decision over Farr that projected him into the world class.

His first win over Baer, in front of 16,778 fans at Yankee Stadium, in June 1939, further increased his profile. Baer was battered and bleeding from an horrific rip in the mouth when it was stopped in the eleventh round.

After Galento brutalised him in Philadelphia, Nova took a year off, but at the start of 1941 he was far too good for talented second-rank heavyweight Pat Comiskey in a ten-round bout in the Garden, and then he stopped Baer a second time. A mismatch against Jim Robinson in Minneapolis led to the Louis fight. After Louis, he was out of the ring for eight months, then lost on a cut after eight rounds to Lee Savold in Washington DC. When Tami Mauriello knocked him out in six and Savold beat him, again on cuts, he was finished as a world-class operator. He took to the road, winning in places like La Crosse, Wisconsin, and Lincoln, Nebraska. He returned to Madison Square Garden one last time in March 1945 but Joe Baksi out-pointed him, and he retired when a rematch with Mauriello ended in a first-round defeat in Boston in June 1945.

Nova died on 29 September 1991, aged seventy-six.

O

PHILADELPHIA JACK O'BRIEN

Born: 17 January 1878, Philadelphia, Pennsylvania
Full name: James Francis Hagen
Died: 12 November 1942, New York City, aged 64
Height: 5ft 10½in   **Weight at peak:** 165lbs (11st 11lbs)
Fights: 180   **Won:** 147   **Lost:** 14   **Drawn:** 19
KO percentage: 28
Rounds boxed: 1,149
World champion: (light-heavyweight champion 1905-1907)
World title fights: 2
Career span: 1896-1912 (16 years)
KO wins: 51
KO defeats: 4

As unscrupulous as he was clever, Philadelphia Jack O'Brien was one of the mavericks of the ring. The film of his twenty-round draw with Tommy Burns for the heavyweight championship in Los Angeles in 1906 shows him twisting, running, even turning his back on the frustrated little champion. Burns appeared to win simply because he was the only one trying to fight, but referee James J. Jeffries, probably as bored as the paying customers in the Naud Junction Pavilion in Los Angeles, couldn't decide. In a return the following year, Burns won easily, again over twenty rounds.

O'Brien, whose real name was James Francis Hagen, held the light-heavyweight title after a thirteenth-round knockout of Bob Fitzsimmons but didn't defend it. He also fought Joe Choynski, Peter Maher, Joe Walcott, Marvin Hart and Mike Schreck but had a reputation for, shall we say, occasionally negotiating the conclusion of his fights.

By 1909 he was past his best. Ketchel beat him in a No-Decision ten-rounder in New York. He won only one of his last six fights, a repeat decision over the faded Schreck, and retired in 1912. O'Brien put his name to books about the scientific craft of boxing and stayed around the fight scene for thirty years, until his death in New York on 12 November 1942 at the age of sixty-four.

OSSIE OCASIO

Born: 12 August 1955, Alto Trujillo, Puerto Rico
Full name: Osvaldo Ocasio
Height: 5ft 11½in   **Weight at peak:** 207lbs (14st 11lbs)
Fights: 37   **Won:** 23   **Lost:** 13   **Drawn:** 1
KO percentage: 32
Rounds boxed: 289
World title fights: 1
Career span: 1976-92 (16 years)
KO wins: 12
KO defeats: 5

A moderately skilled Puerto Rican nicknamed 'Jaws', Ossie Ocasio had an undeserved shot at Larry Holmes for the WBC title in March 1979, was outclassed, but reinvented himself well enough to hold a cruiserweight championship three years later.

Ocasio, from a family of twenty-two children, was a little-known prospect with eleven straight wins (after only six amateur bouts) when he upset Jimmy Young with a split decision at Caesars Palace, Las Vegas. After he beat Young again in San Juan, Don King picked him out for Holmes, who outclassed him in seven rounds at the Las Vegas Hilton.

Ocasio managed a draw with Michael Dokes, but lost a return in one round and also folded tamely at Wembley against British champion John L. Gardner in March 1981.

Ocasio won the inaugural WBA cruiserweight title with a fifteen-round split decision over Robbie Williams in Johannesburg in February 1982 and held on to it until he lost a fifteen-round verdict to Piet Crous in Sun City in December 1984. He was also stopped in eleven rounds by Evander Holyfield in a WBA and

IBF cruiserweight title fight in St Tropez in August 1987. From then to the end of his career in 1992 he was a heavyweight journeyman – among those who beat him were Lennox Lewis, Ray Mercer and Tyrell Biggs.

LEE OMA

Born: 1 March 1916, Chicago
Real name: Frank Czajewski
Died: 12 December 1976, Massapequa, Long Island, New York aged 60
Height: 5ft 11in   **Weight:** 193lbs (13st 11lbs)
Fights: 93   **Won:** 62   **Lost:** 27   **Drawn:** 3
KO percentage: 30
Rounds boxed: 650
World title fights: 1
Career span: 1939-51 (12 years)
KO wins: 28
KO defeats: 17

On his day, Lee Oma was a capable operator. The trouble was you didn't know whether Oma the decent fighter or Oma the disinterested cynic was going to turn up. When he challenged Ezzard Charles for the championship in Madison Square Garden in January 1951 he was in a good run of form and was boxing as if he wanted to be there: he had lost only one of his previous seventeen contests. And he did try, before Charles's extra talent brought an end to proceedings in round ten.

Oma's real name was Frank Czajewski, but he changed it, allegedly because a ring announcer couldn't pronounce it. Oma always was erratic: early in his career he got himself suspended indefinitely in Iowa after folding in the first round against Panther Williams in Des Moines. A free-wheeling character, he was once labelled America's Bad Boy of Boxing. He changed managers frequently, spoke his mind – and made a case for himself in the world class by out-pointing Lou Nova in Detroit in July 1944. In the Garden he stopped Gus Lesnevich but lost to Jersey Joe Walcott. He was pilloried when he went over inside four rounds without trying too hard against Bruce Woodcock in London in September 1948. 'OMA AROMA!' screamed one headline.

Back in the States he came through a tragedy when an opponent, Enrico Bertola, died in Buffalo, but he twice beat Freddie Beshore and also beat Nick Barone. He still had that self-destructive streak – in May 1950 in Cincinnati he and opponent Bill Weinberg were both thrown out for clowning instead of boxing. In his first fight with the fragile but dangerous Bob Satterfield, he scored a heavy knockdown then walked in with his hands down and was flattened himself. He was saved by the bell but knocked out in the next. In the rematch he was more careful and won on points.

In retirement he dabbled in movies, was a man about town and managed night clubs. He died in Long Island, New York, at the age of sixty.

P

GREG PAGE

Born: 25 October 1958, Louisville, Kentucky
Height: 6ft 2in   **Weight at peak:** 230lbs (16st 6lbs)
Fights: 76   **Won:** 58   **Lost:** 17   **Drawn:** 1
KO percentage: 63
Rounds boxed: 420
World champion: 1984-85 (WBA)
World title fights: 3
Career span: 1979-2001 (22 years)
KO wins: 48
KO defeats: 6

Greg Page had the ability to become a major figure in the heavyweight division: as it was he became just another of the paper champions who were switched in and out of title bouts, more or less at the whim of promoter Don King, in the mid-1980s. Page held the WBA title for four months, from December 1984 until April 1985, which was a paltry reward for his talent. To some extent he had himself to blame, but it was no coincidence that so many good heavyweights lost their way in that time, either because of drug habits or just poor motivation.

In Jack Newfield's era-defining book *Only in America: The Life and Crimes of Don King*, he recalls a conversation he had with Page when Greg was on the undercard of the Mike Tyson-Razor Ruddock fight in March 1991. 'Life ain't fair, you know,' Page had said. 'Some things are better left unsaid. But my story is even worse than Tim Witherspoon's.' In the end, perhaps for reasons only he knew, Page went on boxing way, way too long – and was eventually laid low by an acute brain injury after being knocked out in a fight in Kentucky in March 2001.

A multi-titled amateur international from Louisville, Page was only twenty years old when he made his professional debut, and was world class by the time he was twenty-three. He had begun his career with Butch Lewis but famously switched to King after the promoter paid for the funeral of his father and wept at the graveside. Lewis sued King for interference in his contract and won not only a settlement from King but a percentage of Page's world title fights.

Page's world title opportunity came after Larry Holmes fell out with WBC president Jose Sulaiman and switched allegiances to the IBF. Whatever the result of Page's vacant WBC title bout with Tim Witherspoon in Las Vegas in March 1984, neither man would be recognised as the real champion while Holmes was still fighting and winning. As it was, Page, who had been neglecting his training and complaining about conditions in the King camp, lost a majority decision to Witherspoon – two judges had Tim way ahead 9–3 in rounds, with the third somehow seeing it level. Page initially announced his retirement, claiming he was sick of the sport, but changed his mind. He lost his USBA belt to David Bey, then King persuaded him to take a trip to South Africa, to the satellite state of Bophutatswana and the new gambling mecca of Sun City, to fight Gerrie Coetzee for the WBA title. Surprisingly, with the help of an inept timekeeper who allowed round eight to go on way past the three-minute mark, Page won the championship by knockout. In that brief conversation with Newfield in 1991, he said he regretted going to South Africa and that his life had been worsened by it.

Four months later, in Buffalo, New York, he lost the WBA belt over fifteen rounds to Tony Tubbs. A ten-round points defeat by James 'Buster' Douglas next time out in Atlanta put him out of the picture at the age of twenty-seven. He was a regular sparring partner for Mike Tyson when the latter left Bill Cayton for Don King, and famously put Tyson on the floor in the lead-up to the Tyson-Douglas fight in Tokyo in 1990. Page retired for a while to work as a trainer with King's fighters.

In 1996 he returned to the ring and worked the club circuit, coming to no harm against the talent-free kids who slammed away for a couple of hundred dollars in tank towns like Wentworth, North Carolina, and Chesapeake, Virginia. He was a regular in Nashville, too. When he was almost forty I saw him floored and labouring to an eight-round points win over a tough loser named Marion Wilson in Atlantic City in March 1998. It was inexpressibly sad to see him reduced to this.

Three years later he was knocked out in the tenth round by Dale Crowe in Erlanger, Kentucky. He was fortunate to survive but was maimed for life. The Kentucky Athletic Commission had neither ambulance nor paramedics at ring-side – astonishingly, this is not required under state law – and it took two calls to the emergency services before medical help arrived, twenty-two minutes after he had collapsed. Every doctor worth the name will tell you the importance of what has become known as 'the golden hour' when a patient with a brain injury must be stabilised and treated as rapidly as possible. By the time they got Page to the trauma center at the University Hospital across the stateline in Cincinnati, Ohio, he had three areas of damage on the right side of his brain. Somehow he refused to die, even though two strokes he suffered immediately after the surgery left him paralysed.

He was in hospital for four months, during which time his fiancée, Patricia Love, said he did not receive a single card, letter or communication of any sort from anyone in boxing. Gradually, as he recovered some of his faculties and worked his way through the rehabilitation programme, donations did come in, largely due to Love's persistence and the help of former middleweight Alex Ramos, who runs the Retired Boxers Foundation.

JACK PALMER

Born: 31 March 1878, Newcastle-upon-Tyne, England
Real name: Jack Liddell
Died: 13 February 1928, aged 49
Height: 5ft 10in   **Weight at peak:** 175lbs (12st 7lbs)
Fights: 41   **Won:** 23   **Lost:** 9   **Drawn:** 3   **No Decisions:** 6
KO percentage: 41
Rounds boxed: 322
World title fights: 1
Career span: 1896-1916 (20 years)
KO wins: 17
KO defeats: 6

Jack Palmer was knocked out in four rounds by Tommy Burns for the world heavyweight title at London's Wonderland Arena in February 1908. Burns insisted on being paid before he stepped into the ring and made sure he knew the exact amount of takings at the gate by having only one turnstile open – and standing on the other side counting the doubtless irritated punters as they walked through.

Palmer's real name was Jack Liddell. He was from Newcastle – born in Benwell in March 1878 – at some point worked as a miner, and held both the British middleweight and heavyweight titles. He also boxed in South Africa, including a brutal fight with the Irishman Mike Williams in Johannesburg in 1904, when he was knocked down seventeen times and counted out in round eight. Williams was also down twice and by the end could barely see.

Palmer died on 13 February 1928, aged forty-nine.

BOB PASTOR

Born: 26 January 1914, New York City
Full name: Robert E. Pasternak
Died: 26 January 1996, aged 82
Height: 5ft 11½in   **Weight at peak:** 187lbs (13st 5lbs)
Fights: 65   **Won:** 53   **Lost:** 7   **Drawn:** 5
KO percentage: 26
Rounds boxed: 511
World title fights: 1

Career span: 1935-42 (7 years)
KO wins: 17
KO defeats: 2

A light-punching but clever, well-schooled heavyweight, Bob Pastor was the man about whom Joe Louis first said, 'He can run, but he can't hide.' Pastor's negative tactics had enabled him to take a twenty-two-year-old Louis the full ten rounds in a non-title fight in Madison Square Garden in January 1937. He used his speed and the kind of boxing ability that had taken him to two National Golden Gloves titles to offset the prowling, stalking aggression of the future world champ. At the final bell, he celebrated as if it were a runaway win. He genuinely thought he had done enough and so did the crowd, for they booed the decision for half an hour. Arthur Donovan, the house referee for Louis, scored it for Joe by eight rounds to two! In his old age, Pastor was still convinced he was robbed.

'I felt like a goddamn fool trying to chase this mosquito,' said Louis. 'Chappie [his trainer, Jack Blackburn] kept telling me to try and trap him in a corner. Impossible. I never fought anyone like him... He must have run twelve miles that night.'

When they met again it was September 1939. Louis was making the eighth defence of his title and was returning home to Detroit. Pastor was expected to employ his skills and quick hands to keep the champion out, at least early on, and the fact that promoter Mike Jacobs made the fight over twenty rounds suggests he suspected Louis might need to wear Pastor down in the later stages. In fact Pastor very nearly went out in round one, when he was knocked down three times, and round two, when he was floored again. Even Pastor didn't remember how he survived because when he got up for round seven he thought it was round two. He had used his boxing instincts well, then frustrated Louis and hung in until the eleventh when he was nailed again, put down twice and knocked out.

Pastor, whose real name was Robert E. Pasternak, grew up in the Bronx. He was a star footballer at New York University. He was managed by Jimmy Johnston, who worked for Madison Square Garden, and trained by Freddie Brown, who decades later would work with Roberto Duran. By the time he boxed Louis the first time he was the New York State champion, following a seventh-round knockout of Ray Impelletiere, and had lost only once in twenty-four fights. After Louis beat him, he beat undefeated prospect Bob Nestell in Los Angeles, then lost a decision to the Mob-controlled Italian-American from Connecticut Nathan Mann in the Garden in November 1937. Pastor drew with Lou Nova in San Francisco, out-pointed Al McCoy twice, and drew with the former light-heavyweight champion 'Slapsie' Maxie Rosenbloom.

In March 1939 Pastor toyed with the New Zealander Maurice Strickland over ten rounds. He had more trouble with his shorts than he did with Strickland – they fell down twice. He went into the Louis world title fight on a roll of six wins and, three months after it, showed no ill-effects when he easily outscored Buddy Scott in Dallas. However, in September 1940, he was knocked out for the second time, in thirteen rounds by Billy Conn, who was still the world light-heavyweight champion at the time. Two wins over Los Angeles prospect Albert 'Turkey' Thompson helped him re-establish himself and he also beat Gus Lesnevich and Jimmy Bivins, and drew with Tami Mauriello. However, after he lost a return with Bivins over ten rounds in Cleveland in October 1942, he retired at the age of twenty-eight. He was a family man with two small children, Roberta and Albert, to think about.

In retirement, Pastor owned a restaurant and a sports store, then worked as a security officer at Saratoga racetrack. In his last years he was in a nursing home, confined to a wheelchair, blind in one eye and suffering from dementia, and he died on his eighty-second birthday, 26 January 1996.

WILLIE PASTRANO

Born: 27 November 1935, New Orleans, Louisiana
Died: 8 December 1997, New Orleans
Height: 5ft 11¾in   **Weight at heavyweight peak:** 187lbs (13st 5lbs)
Fights: 84   **Won:** 63   **Lost:** 13   **Drawn:** 8
KO percentage: 16
Rounds boxed: 695
World title fights: 0 (heavyweight)
Career span: 1951-65 (14 years)
KO wins: 14
KO defeats: 2

Although he eventually won his world title in the 175lb division, Willie Pastrano was a slick, cunning boxer who was too clever for most heavyweights in the world in the late 1950s. For a year from October 1957, Eddie Machen, Zora Folley and Pastrano were the top three challengers for the title according to *Ring* magazine. Patterson defended against none of them. He was trained by Angelo Dundee and managed by Chris Dundee and Whitey Esneault.

'He was a big, good-looking guy with black wavy hair, a smile like Errol Flynn and the personality to match,' said Angelo Dundee. 'Willie was a great athlete but keeping that guy in shape was a pain in the butt.' He put Pastrano on a diet of milk to help build him up – Pastrano put whisky in it.

Willie, full name Wilfred Raleigh Pastrano, went to the gym in the Vieux Carre district because other kids called him 'fatso'. By the time he was fifteen he was a professional welterweight, but after a handful of fights his age was discovered and he was suspended. After moving to Miami and teaming up with Dundee, he out-pointed the former world light-heavyweight champion Joey Maxim over ten rounds in New Orleans in June 1955. When he closed the year with another points victory over former contender Rex Layne, his potential seemed vast, even though he relied on his speed of hand and foot to outwit opponents rather than powerful punching. From 1954 until 1957, win, lose or draw, nineteen consecutive fights went the distance. After losing what Chris Dundee called a home-town decision to Roy Harris in Houston, he enjoyed a spell of popularity among British fans as he out-boxed in turn Dick Richardson, Brian London and Joe Bygraves. He cut a dash when he arrived to box Richardson at Harringay Arena in October 1957, stepping down into the English autumn rain from the plane at London Airport in canary yellow trousers and a black and white check jacket. 'When I left Miami, the sun was shining,' he said.

A rematch with London in September 1958 began a reverse in fortunes. He lost on a fifth-round cut eye after, according to Dundee, Angelo refused to remove vaseline to allow referee Jack Hart to inspect the damage, with the result that the referee, annoyed at having his authority challenged, waved the fight over. Points defeats by Joe Erskine and Amos Johnson pushed him down the heavyweight rankings and he lost his way for a while – and even retired briefly to concentrate on a health spa in Miami.

In May 1962, his interest revived, he reminded American fans of his skills by out-pointing Tom McNeeley of Boston but could only draw with 'Ancient' Archie Moore in Los Angeles. Dundee said the atmosphere in the gym was wonderful then, with Pastrano back and working alongside the young, excited Cassius Clay and the Cuban welterweight Luis Rodriguez. He beat Harold Johnson for the light-heavyweight crown in Las Vegas on a split decision in 1963 with only three weeks' notice, defended against Gregorio Peralta and Terry Downes (in Manchester) but lost it in nine rounds to Jose Torres in New York in 1965.

Within a few years Pastrano was a heroin addict. He lost his family and his home, and took until 1977 to beat it. He said, 'I have been there, to the brink of hell. Fighting drugs is the toughest thing in the world. How do you fight something punching you from inside?' He got a low-paid job as a boxing instructor with the New Orleans Police Athletic League and said, 'Every day that I wake up is a brand new life for me. I'm lucky to be here with all my marbles. Few people in this world have been where I have been and still been able to function as a human being.'

Pastrano died at the age of sixty-two in New Orleans on 8 December 1997.

FLOYD PATTERSON

Born: 4 January 1935, Waco, North Carolina
Height: 5ft 11½in   **Weight at peak:** 182-192lbs (13st-13st 10lbs)
Fights: 64   **Won:** 55   **Lost:** 8   **Drawn:** 1
KO percentage: 62
Rounds boxed: 419
World champion: 1956-59, 1960-62
World title fights: 13

Career span: 1952-72 (20 years)
KO wins: 40
KO defeats: 5

Floyd Patterson has had a bad press for almost half a century. He was the youngest world heavyweight champion in history when he knocked out 'Ancient' Archie Moore in 1956, yet was criticised for avoiding the leading contenders of his time.

He was the first man to regain the title when he knocked out Ingemar Johansson, in their rematch in 1960, but after he lost the championship second time around to Sonny Liston people laughed when he left the arena in a false beard and dark glasses in a bizarre attempt to hide. They called him Freudian Floyd. Yet this mild-mannered, honourable man was one of the best boxers of his time. Given his way, he would probably have boxed anyone – the 'avoidance' tactics were a result of the independent eccentricity of his mentor, Cus D'Amato.

The fact that he had superb boxing skills is amply demonstrated by his achievement in winning the Olympic middleweight gold medal in Helsinki in 1952 when he was only seventeen years old. Roy Harris, the Texan who challenged Patterson for the championship in 1958, told me forty-five years later in Los Angeles, 'Patterson was a great fighter. He wasn't given the credit he should have been.'

Patterson was born in Waco, North Carolina, but moved to Brooklyn with his family when he was a baby. He was timid and withdrawn, and was described as 'One of the Lost Ones' when, at the age of ten, in September 1945, he was sent to Wiltwyck School in upstate New York, which was an establishment for emotionally disturbed young people. He was regularly in trouble for truancy and minor offences and recalled, in his 1962 autobiography *Victory Over Myself*, pointing to a family photo of him taken at Bronx Zoo and telling his mother, 'I don't like that boy.'

The memories are heart-rending: 'I hated laughter because it seemed no matter what I did, everybody was always laughing at me. They'd laugh at the dirt on my face and the torn, shabby, over-sized clothes I wore and the way I couldn't read or write or answer a question in school or even talk to somebody when they talked to me. It got so that I wouldn't look anybody in the face. I'd run and hide… I got to like the darkness. There was safety in the darkness for me.' At night he would walk the streets and stand in alleyways. In daytime he would sit in cellars or movie houses or on the subway. He found a disused room near a railway station where he could hide and sleep. At Wiltwyck School he learned to make friends and smile, but his basic fears remained. D'Amato, who knew him as well as anyone, called him a stranger in the world.

After his Olympic success, he won his first thirteen professional fights before D'Amato made a mistake, putting him in against the former world light-heavyweight champion Joey Maxim, who outsmarted him over eight rounds in Brooklyn. They put that down to education – and Floyd didn't lose again for five years. He emerged as a leading contender for the title when he out-pointed Tommy Jackson over twelve rounds in June 1956, shortly after Rocky Marciano's retirement. Then he was paired with Archie Moore for the vacant title in Chicago in November 1956. Weighing only a fraction above 13st, he used his speed and youthful snap to knock out forty-two-year-old Moore in the fifth round.

The best contenders of the time were Nino Valdes, Eddie Machen and Zora Folley, but D'Amato would have nothing to do with them, just as a little later he would ignore Cleveland 'Big Cat' Williams and the formidable Sonny Liston. D'Amato hid behind the convenient cloak of anti-corruption, insisting he would not deal with the hitherto all-powerful International Boxing Club run by James Norris. The IBC was eventually brought down because of revelations about its Mob connections – and D'Amato's caution was identified as heroic.

In 1957 Patterson boxed twice: a tenth-round stoppage of Jackson and a ridiculous sixth-round knockout of Pete Rademacher, the 1956 Olympic heavy-weight champion who was making his professional debut. Even though he beat Rademacher comfortably, the fact that he had to climb off the floor to do so made him look an unworthy champion. The situation worsened in 1958 when he boxed only once against Roy Harris, the part-time schoolteacher from Cut-N-Shoot, Texas. Harris was retired by his corner after twelve rounds after going down four times – yet he, too, had his moment of success when he dropped the champion in round two.

In May 1959 Patterson knocked out Brian London in eleven one-sided rounds in Indianapolis but a month later ran into the right hand of Ingemar Johansson in Yankee Stadium, New York, and was floored seven times before the slaughter was stopped in round three. He trained ferociously for the return in June 1960, while Johansson did not, and he made history at the age of twenty-four by becoming the first man to regain the world heavyweight crown. Johansson was knocked out in round five. The image of him flat on his back with his left leg twitch-ing uncontrollably as he was counted out remains a poignant reminder of the realities of the sport. Patterson won the decider too, in six rounds, knocked out Boston outsider Tom McNeeley in four… and then finally over-ruled D'Amato and agreed to box Liston. He satisfied his sense of honour but paid a hard price: Liston blew him away in 126 seconds. Before the inevitable, pointless rematch, Patterson hardly cut a confident figure. 'I hope to last longer this time,' he said. He did – by four seconds.

Ironically, in 1964 Patterson out-pointed Eddie Machen, one of the men whom he should have boxed when he was champion. He also beat the tough Canadian George Chuvalo and earned a shot at Ali. Floyd would have no truck with the Black Muslim section of the Black Rights movement and continued to refer to Ali as Clay, and Ali, who was astute at identifying the psychological weaknesses of opponents, labelled him the Rabbit (as in stuck in the glare of society's headlights).

Patterson's effort was hampered by a back injury and Ali toyed with him before stopping him in the twelfth round in Las Vegas in November 1965. The following year Floyd travelled to London and knocked out Henry Cooper in four, but in 1967 he drew with Jerry Quarry and then lost the rematch in the elimination tournament set up by the World Boxing Association to find a successor to the exiled Ali. It was a majority decision after twelve rounds, with two knockdowns scored by the Californian proving decisive. The referee, Vern Bybee, had it even, but two judges scored by two points for Quarry.

In September 1968 Patterson challenged Jimmy Ellis for the WBA title in Stockholm and lost on points over fifteen rounds. Referee Harold Valan, the sole scoring official, gave it to Ellis by nine rounds to six, a verdict that astonished many and one that he defended in a long article in *Ring* magazine. Patterson did not box again for two years, then won nine consecutive comeback fights, the best of them a ten-round decision over Oscar Bonavena. His final fight was in September 1972 when he fought Ali, was stopped in the seventh round and retired for good.

He kept fit and in 1982 ran the New York marathon alongside old rival Johansson. He trained his adopted son Tracy Harris Patterson to two world titles in the first half of the 1990s and was then chairman of the New York State commission. Unfortunately his memory began to fail him and he retired from the job on health grounds.

JOHNNY PAYCHEK

Born: 11 June 1914, Chicago, Illinois
Died: 3 December 1988, aged 74
Height: 6ft 1in   **Weight at peak:** 187lbs (13st 5lbs)
Fights: 47   **Won:** 39   **Lost:** 7   **Drawn:** 1
KO percentage: 53
Rounds boxed: 246
World title fights: 1
Career span: 1933-41 (8 years)
KO wins: 25
KO defeats: 3

'Did you ever see a ghost walking?' wrote one reporter after Johnny Paychek's brief, dismal attempt to dethrone Joe Louis in Madison Square Garden in March 1940. He lasted only forty-four seconds into round two and looked terrified from the moment he walked into the famous arena.

Paychek was a protégé of Jack Dempsey, but even in his mid-forties the old Manassa Mauler could probably have beaten him easily. Louis put him down four times.

From Des Moines, Iowa, he turned pro under his real name of John J. Pacek at the end of 1933, when he was nineteen. He was a Midwest club fighter. At that level he could use his reach and punch sharply. He stopped the slow old veteran King Levinsky in three, but his run was snapped when Maurice Strickland out-boxed him over ten rounds. Although he did beat Strickland on points in a rematch, he had fought nobody else of note when he was thrown in with Louis.

After that flop, Paychek boxed only once, a tenth-round knockout defeat by Altus Allen in Chicago in June 1940.

He died in December 1988, aged seventy-four.

ARTHUR PELKEY

Born: 27 October 1884, Chatham, Ontario, Canada
Full name: Andrew Arthur Peltier
Died: 18 February 1921, Ford City, Ontario, Canada, aged 36
Height: 6ft 1½in   **Weight at peak:** 207lbs (14st 11lbs)
Fights: 56   **Won:** 24   **Lost:** 18   **Drawn:** 6   **No Decisions:** 8
KO percentage: 26
Rounds boxed: 395
World title fights: 0
Career span: 1910-20 (10 years)
KO wins: 15
KO defeats: 13

Arthur Pelkey never recovered from his greatest triumph, his tragic 100-second knockout of Luther McCarty for the so-called White Heavyweight Championship of the world at the Tommy Burns Arena in Calgary, Canada, in May 1913. Pelkey landed what seemed an innocuous punch in a close-quarters maul and McCarty collapsed unconscious. He was taken from the ring and died as he lay at ringside.

Both Pelkey and Burns, the promoter and former champion of the world who managed Arthur, were arrested on manslaughter charges. They were cleared but the impact on Pelkey was deep-rooted. It was more than six months before he managed to get through even a six-round exhibition bout in Los Angeles, and when he 'defended' his spurious alternative to the real title held by Jack Johnson, Pelkey was given a sustained beating by Gunboat Smith in San Francisco on New Year's Day, 1914. He lost in the fifteenth round. One wonders what made him continue to box. He was knocked out by, among others, Bill Lang, Sam McVey, Joe Jeannette, Battling Jim Johnson, Fred Fulton and Carl Morris.

Pelkey was the anglicised version of the French-Canadian name of Peltier – he was born in Chatham, Ontario, and later moved to Windsor, the town just across the stretch of water that separates Canada from Detroit. Pelkey was a raw-boned, big-jawed man who could punch, and through the early part of his career looked a genuine prospect. For two years, until the McCarty fight, he seemed to enjoy the job and fought regularly without beating anybody of serious worth. In July 1912 he did box a ten-round No-Decision bout with Jess Willard.

Even when he was on his long losing run, Pelkey seems to have tried: he lost in nineteen rounds to Lang and in thirteen rounds to Kid Norfolk, though Jack Dempsey knocked him out in one round in Denver. Pelkey retired in 1920, took a job as a police officer, but died in February 1921 aged thirty-six of encephalitis-lethargica, the brain disease known as sleeping sickness, which killed a great number of people around that time.

Q

JERRY QUARRY

Born: 15 May 1945, Bakersfield, California
Died: 3 January 1999, Los Angeles, California, aged 53
Height: 6ft   **Weight at peak:** 198lbs (14st 2lbs)
Fights: 66   **Won:** 53   **Lost:** 9   **Drawn:** 4
KO percentage: 48
Rounds boxed: 419
World title fights: 2
Career span: 1965-92 (27 years)
KO wins: 32
KO defeats: 6

Jerry Quarry was one of the nearly men of heavyweight boxing, a clever, big-hearted counter-puncher who was unfortunate to be operating in the heyday of Muhammad Ali and Joe Frazier, both of whom stopped him twice. He boxed Frazier and Jimmy Ellis for versions of the world title in the 1960s. Frazier, who was recognised as champion by the New York State Athletic Commission and their friends, stopped him in seven rounds, months after Ellis, the World Boxing Association champion, out-pointed him. A self-deprecating man with an ironic sense of humour, he said, 'I blew it against Ellis by becoming a thinker instead of a fighter. Then I fought Frazier and didn't think enough.'

He was a tough man from a tough background – he and his brothers were raised hard by his father Jack – and his nature was to take risks. His childhood and youth were littered with accidents, his boxing career was long, hard and eventually led to a terrible, premature demise. He suffered from brain damage before dying in hospital of a heart attack following pneumonia at the age of fifty-three.

The toll boxing – and life – took on Quarry should not be avoided. That accepted, in 1990 he said, 'Would I do it all over again? When I started in 1965,

I was changing Greyhound Bus tyres for a living. You damned well know I'd go back into boxing. Yes sir!' In his prime Quarry beat Floyd Patterson, Thad Spencer, Buster Mathis, Brian London, Ron Lyle and Earnie Shavers.

He was born in Bakersfield, California, on 15 May 1945, the second eldest in a family of eight children. His parents moved around California and eventually settled in Bellflower, where Jerry played for the high school football team. His elder brother James broke his arm with a baseball bat in a fight and they also boxed each other seven times in official amateur contests. Jerry also broke his hand when he hit a baseball umpire. At thirteen he survived a serious kidney illness and at sixteen broke his back when a dive at the local swimming pool went wrong.

Quarry won the 1995 National Golden Gloves heavyweight title and turned pro a week before his twentieth birthday. He was unbeaten in his first twenty fights before thirty-four-year-old Eddie Machen outwitted and outstayed him over ten rounds in Los Angeles in July 1966. The following year he out-pointed Brian London and drew with and then out-pointed former world champ Patterson. In February 1968 he knocked out Spencer in the twelfth round, but two months later lost a dreary WBA fight with Ellis over fifteen rounds in Oakland.

He worked his way back, reasserted himself by out-pointing Mathis in New York in March 1969, but lost in seven to Frazier when his right eye was swollen shut and he could no longer see the punches coming. In October 1970 he was wheeled out as the fall guy for the comeback fight of Muhammad Ali in Atlanta, Georgia. He tried hard, but a slashing right cross split open an eyebrow and the fight was stopped in round three. At least it brought him the biggest payday of his life: $338,000.

Quarry was still only twenty-four and had plenty to offer – in 1970 he won four out of four, including a trip to London where he knocked out the English southpaw Jack Bodell in the first round. An eager reporter, at a loss what to ask, enquired if Jerry had found Bodell's style awkward. 'Well,' he said thoughtfully, 'he sure fell awkward.'

The following year his rematch with Ali culminated in a seventh-round stoppage in Las Vegas. Before leaving the dressing room he had watched younger brother Mike poleaxed by a terrific left hook from world light-heavy champ Bob Foster. 'I thought he had killed my brother,' said Jerry. 'It totally destroyed everything I wanted to do.' Yet 1973 became perhaps the best year of his career: he stopped Randy Neumann in seven, out-boxed Denver's dangerous Ron Lyle over twelve, then scored early knockouts of James J. Woody and Tony Doyle before finishing off in December with a sensational first-round demolition of Earnie Shavers in New York.

On the back of that Madison Square Garden offered world champion George Foreman a million dollars or forty per cent of the house to defend against Quarry, but Foreman had managerial and legal problems and it came to nothing. Then

Quarry lost a return with Frazier in five rounds in New York in June 1974 and was out of contention. Norton too beat him in five and with surprising speed he was finished.

He retired and worked as, among other things, a bodyguard for the pop group Three Dog Night. He returned with a win in 1977 but retired again for six years. He had two comeback fights in 1983, but after the second needed sixty-two stitches in a gruesome network of cuts. Incredibly he won the fight, but the Californian Commission was very concerned about his health. He retired again. This time he sold mobile homes and beer. He looked back on his youth and said, 'I've led a *Grapes of Wrath* life.' When his brain was sharp he had written poetry, played golf, harboured ambitions of moving into television commentary and tried it once or twice. However he had also been divorced twice and had lost himself in dead-end jobs, drink and, it was also said, drugs.

Somehow he was given a licence in Colorado in 1992, but took a six-round, $1,000 pounding from a club fighter, Ron Cramner. A year later he was living on social security cheques. Three years later he couldn't tie his shoelaces or shave, had sixty per cent short-term memory loss and the temperament of a child. He was cared for by his brother James, with whom he had enjoyed those amateur contests four long decades before. James set up the Jerry Quarry Foundation to provide for his care and said, 'He's spaced out most of the time. He hallucinates. He hears voices. He cries. He gets scared, confused... He lives in a very, very small world.'

His death was, perhaps, a blessing.

R

PETE RADEMACHER

Born: 20 August 1928, Washington State
Height: 6ft 2in   **Weight at peak:** 200lbs (14st 4lbs)
Fights: 23   **Won:** 15   **Lost:** 7   **Drawn:** 1
KO percentage: 34
Rounds boxed: 166
World title fights: 1
Career span: 1957-62 (5 years)
Longest winning run: 7 (1960-61)
KO wins: 8
KO defeats: 6

One of the most ridiculous episodes in boxing history was when Cus D'Amato, manager of Floyd Patterson, accepted a $250,000 guarantee for a defence against Pete Rademacher, the 1956 Olympic heavyweight champion. 'What's weird about that?', one might ask. Well, nothing... except that Rademacher hadn't had a professional fight at the time.

After his win in the final in Melbourne over Lev Moukhine of Russia, Rademacher, who was a twenty-eight-year-old lieutenant in the US Army, said he would not turn professional. 'I'm too old for that,' he said. Once home he changed his mind, talked to the old Seattle fight manager Jack Hurley, and persuaded twenty-two businessmen to back him and make the offer to Patterson. Although he had professional boxing in his blood – his father fought as Johnny Ray – he began boxing as an undergraduate at Washington State University. He won a National AAU title in 1953, retired to work on his father's farm in Yakima, Washington, then joined the army in 1954 and came good in Melbourne. Hurley wanted to bring Rademacher along slowly, but the Olympic gold medallist wanted $10,000 to box Patterson – and got it.

The fight at Sick's Stadium, Seattle, in August 1957 had, at best, a macabre appeal. To anyone with a love of boxing history, it was a scandal. Yet in round two, when a careless Patterson went down for a two count from a clubbing right hand, a sensational result seemed possible. As it was, the champion got up, sharpened up and took control. Rademacher went down in round three, four times in the fifth and twice more in the sixth. Referee Tommy Loughran, the old light-heavyweight champion, did a tardy job but eventually waved it off with Pete down for the seventh time, with his cornermen calling out, 'That's enough, that's enough.' When the dust had settled, the wide-eyed businessmen who had backed Rademacher's folly were light in the pocket. A crowd of 19,961, well short of the necessary 25,000, paid a gross of $243,030, which didn't even cover Patterson's purse. Rademacher was unrepentant. 'I enjoyed the idea from its infancy, through its complete promotion and even to its termination,' he said. 'I have no regrets. There's nothing like starting from the top and working one's way down!'

Rademacher had beaten Zora Folley in the amateurs and so had no hesitation in accepting a rematch for his second professional outing, even though Folley by this time was a battle-hardened operator with only two defeats in forty-four fights. At the Olympic Auditorium in Los Angeles in July 1958, Folley was far too polished for Rademacher, dropped him four times and knocked him out in four rounds.

While Brian London knocked him out with a body shot in the seventh round at Wembley, Rademacher did jab and grab his way to a clear decision over George Chuvalo, but Doug Jones floored him four times and beat him in five. The forty-eight-year-old Archie Moore dropped him eight times before the massacre was stopped in the sixth round in Baltimore in October 1961.

He retired after a points win in Hawaii over Carl 'Bobo' Olson, the former middleweight champion, and became a successful businessman, operating a division of a company that traded in swimming pool equipment. Ironically, some years later, the company, on his recommendation, briefly employed Patterson. Rademacher retired a wealthy man and in 1996 he and two of his daughters carried the Olympic flame through the streets of Cleveland, Ohio, where he had lived for some years.

HASIM RAHMAN

Born: 7 November 1972, Baltimore, Maryland
Height: 6ft 2in   **Weight at peak:** 238lbs (17st)
Fights: 46   **Won:** 40   **Lost:** 5   **Drawn:** 1
KO percentage: 71
Rounds boxed: 205
World champion: 2001
World title fights: 2
Career span: 1994-2005 (11 years)
KO wins: 33
KO defeats: 3

One fight sometimes makes a man: so it was with Hasim 'The Rock' Rahman in Carnival City on the outskirts of Johannesburg on 22 April 2001. When his fight with the world champion, Lennox Lewis, was made, few gave the man from Baltimore a chance. He had previously turned almost certain victory into a tenth-round stoppage defeat by David Tua; Oleg Maskaev had knocked him out; he had beaten Corrie Sanders, but only after a brutal fight in which both had been on the canvas.

Rahman ignored all that. Managed by Stan Hoffman, promoted by the South African Cedric Kushner, he travelled early to Johannesburg and drilled himself into that old cliché, 'the best shape of his life', in the city centre gym run auto-cratically by Nic Durandt. Meanwhile Lewis interrupted training in Las Vegas to spend a couple of days playing a cameo role in the movie *Ocean's Eleven*, then flew in surprisingly – complacently – late to Johannesburg. He was jet-lagged. By fight time, some of those who had covered Lewis's career from its bright-eyed beginnings were seriously considering the possibility of an upset. Once the bell rang, the signs were plain to see: Rahman was bright, alert, getting the best out of himself. Lewis's responses were painfully slow. Lewis won three of the first four rounds on skill and ringcraft, then unravelled in the fifth: he moved back across the ring in a straight line, Rahman chased him and cracked a right hand against his jaw. Lewis crumpled to the canvas and the Belgian referee Daniel Van De Wiele counted him out.

Rahman returned to Baltimore to a hero's welcome, then switched promoters from Kushner to Don King – a deal inspired by a large amount of folding money in a hotel room in New York. Lewis had to use the legal process to enforce the rematch clause and this time it was Rahman who lost the plot: over-excited, he was said to have run along hotel corridors wanting to hammer on Lewis's door to confront him. At the Mandalay Bay in Las Vegas, a fit and vengeful Lewis knocked out Rahman with a perfect long right hand in the fourth round.

After that, Rahman was out-boxed by Evander Holyfield and lost on a technical decision when a grotesque haematoma made him look like a gargoyle in round eight; and he could only draw in a rematch with David Tua. Then, in what the WBA fondly called an Interim championship, he was out-pointed by John Ruiz.

MANUEL RAMOS

Born: 1943, Mexico
Height: 6ft 4in   **Weight at peak:** 208lbs (14st 12lbs)
Fights: 57   **Won:** 25   **Lost:** 29   **Drawn:** 3
KO percentage: 31
Rounds boxed: 368
World title fights: 1
Career span: 1963-77 (14 years)
KO wins: 18
KO defeats: 9

Manuel Ramos put his name in the history books with a brief, exciting battle with Joe Frazier for the New York State Athletic Commission version of the world title in June 1968. After being shaken early in the first round, Frazier blasted Ramos around the ring, dropped him before the end of that exciting opening session, floored him again in round two and forced him to retire in his corner at the end of it. Frazier gave him credit for the powerful right hand he landed in round one, but pronounced the tall, slow Mexican a sucker for the left hook. There were no boos from the 10,000-plus crowd in Madison Square Garden. They knew Ramos had tried and was in over his head.

Ramos, a Yaqui Indian labelled the Hard Rock of Mexico, was crude and slow. He once went eight fights without a win, though he was exciting enough to be asked back to box at the Olympic Auditorium in Los Angeles, where it is considered a sin to retreat.

His biggest wins were upset decisions over Eddie Machen and Ernie Terrell. When he was thrown in with Frazier he was on a roll of fifteen wins over two-and-a-half years, but afterwards won only four of his next twenty-eight fights before his retirement in 1977.

ELMER RAY

Born: 10 October 1910, Hasting, Florida
Died: Unknown
Height: 6ft 2in   Weight at peak: 192lbs (13st 10lbs)
Fights: 100   Won: 86   Lost: 13   Drawn: 1
KO percentage: 70
Rounds boxed: 441
World title fights: 0
Career span: 1926-49 (23 years)
KO wins: 70
KO defeats: 9

Elmer Ray was good enough to earn decisions over Jersey Joe Walcott and Ezzard Charles, but not apparently good enough to box for the world title. Nicknamed Violent, this black fighter from Florida was a 6ft 2in, 192lbs bundle of trouble, a hurtful puncher who, between 1943 and 1946, had an unbeaten run of more than fifty fights. For much of that time the championship was in abeyance with Joe Louis in the US Army, and afterwards promoter Mike Jacobs preferred the rematch with Billy Conn for the obvious commercial reasons.

Nobody could put a case for Ray as one of the major heavyweights of the century but he deserves respect. He learned the hard way: when he was young he was knocked out in three by twenty-three-year-old Walcott, and out-boxed and stopped in twelve by John Henry Lewis. But after Albert 'Turkey' Thompson knocked him out in one round in Los Angeles in 1943, Ray began his amazing run of wins that lasted more than three years. Mostly they were over ordinary fighters, but in August 1946 in Ebbetts Field, Brooklyn, he beat Lee Savold in two rounds.

In November 1946 he out-fought Walcott for a split-decision win over ten rounds in Madison Square Garden, although Walcott got the decision in a return fight in Miami four months later. Back in the Garden in July 1947, Ray out-pointed Ezzard Charles in another ten-rounder. Again, though, the return saw a reversal of the result: in Chicago Stadium in May 1948, Charles knocked him out in nine. By then Ray was past his thirty-eighth birthday.

Between January and March 1949, Ray also boxed three so-called exhibitions with Joe Louis. It was the closest Elmer came to boxing for the title.

DICK RICHARDSON

Born: 1 June 1934, Newport, Wales
Died: 14 July 1999, aged 65
Height: 6ft 2½in   Weight at peak: 200lbs (14st 4lbs)
Fights: 47   Won: 31   Lost: 14   Drawn: 2

KO percentage: 51
Rounds boxed: 276
World title fights: 0
Career span: 1954-63 (9 years)
KO wins: 24
KO defeats: 4

A rugged, rough-house heavyweight with a big punch, Dick Richardson's finest moment was a sensational knockout of German southpaw Karl Mildenberger in two minutes thirty-five seconds of the first round before 18,000 stunned fans in Dortmund in February 1962.

Richardson was raised in the Maesglas area of Newport, the son of a milkman and part-time motor cyclist on the fairground Wall of Death. His wade-in style was always popular: when Joe Erskine defied a first-round cut eye and got off the floor in the fifth to out-point him in a ten-round bout in the Maindy Stadium, Cardiff, in May 1956, they drew a crowd of 35,000.

After a facile win over Ezzard Charles, who was disqualified for holding in the second round at Harringay, Richardson was put in with Nino Valdes, the big, world-class Cuban, and lost on a corner retirement after eight rounds. Richardson was knocked down in round two and finished with his right eye closed by a huge, purple swelling.

Richardson was disqualified three times in his career, including in March 1958 in the fourth round against Cleveland 'Big Cat' Williams. Williams was supposed to box the Welshman in a return in July 1958 but refused to get out of bed to weigh in and was sent home. Bob Baker was flown in, the show postponed for a week, and Richardson responded with one of his best displays to win on points. He couldn't get past Henry Cooper, though. They fought twice, in 1958 when Henry won in five, and secondly in Richardson's final fight, in 1963, when Cooper knocked him out in the fifth again for the British and Empire titles. In their first fight Cooper was bleeding badly from a cut between the eyes and was knocked down for six in round five. Richardson, in trying to finish the fight, walked onto a left hook and was knocked out.

Erskine out-boxed Richardson again in what was billed as 'The Feud of the Year' in Porthcawl in 1959 and twice Richardson lost brawls with the notoriously rough American Mike DeJohn, who told Reg Gutteridge of the *London Evening News*, 'I never ever met anyone who could out-butt me like Dick Richardson.'

Richardson opened his first reign as European champion when he knocked out Hans Kalbfell in thirteen rounds, the German fans protesting vigorously that the finishing punch was a cheap shot on the break. He lost the title to Ingemar Johansson in eight rounds in Gothenburg. After losing the rematch with Cooper, by which time he had earned more than £200,000 in the ring, he retired. He ran a successful butcher's business in Frimley, Surrey. Richardson died of cancer at the age of sixty-five in July 1999.

JEM ROCHE

Born: 1878, Killurin, Co. Wexford, Ireland
Died: 1934, Co. Wexford, aged 56
Height: 5ft 8in   **Weight at peak:** 189lbs (13st 7lbs)
Fights: 25   **Won:** 19   **Lost:** 6
KO percentage: 60
Rounds boxed: Unknown
World title fights: 1
Career span: 1902-10 (8 years)
KO wins: 15
KO defeats: 5

Chubby Irish heavyweight Jem Roche was perhaps the worst of all the men who had a chance to fight for this strange, sometimes magnificent championship. Roche challenged Tommy Burns at the Theatre Royal in Dublin in March 1908 and was knocked out in eighty-eight seconds. Legend has it that a quick-thinking spectator ran outside, where hundreds who could not get tickets were gathered waiting for the result. 'It's terrible in there,' he said. 'They're killing each other... blood everywhere.' And he promptly sold his ticket and vanished into the throng.

Roche was born in Killurin near Kilmuckridge, County Wexford, in 1878. He had played gaelic football and worked as a blacksmith and began boxing in paid fights around 1902. By the time he boxed Burns he had won, lost and regained the Irish title but had done nothing that qualified him for a fight with Burns. Ignoring such niceties, Dublin took him to its heart and all 3,000 tickets were snapped up, while thousands more waited in the street for the signal in specially set up lights: after each round, either a red light (for Burns) or green (for Roche) would be lit to offer a guide as to who had won the session. Roche walked to the ring to *The Boys of Wexford*, Burns to *Yankee Doodle Dandy* – this was not a misguided geographical insult, for the French-Canadian also wore the Stars and Stripes around his waist.

When Roche reached the ring, it was discovered they had left his hand wraps behind. Somebody ran to the dressing room and came back, not with bandages, but a pack of lint. Once the bell rang Roche landed one punch, a left jab. Burns then knocked him out with a quick right to the chin. The Irishman got up a fraction too late to beat the count applied by Robert P. Watson, then appealed to the champion: 'Mr Burns, surely I'm not out?'

A month later Roche fought the Australian, Bill Squires, who had spent time sparring with him in the lead up to the Burns fight. Squires knocked Roche out in four rounds.

In the Rotunda Theatre, Dublin, Roche won in one round against Frank Craig, a veteran black fighter known as the Harlem Coffee Cooler, but that too was controversial. The English referee Joe Palmer remembers watching the fight. Craig floored Roche, who was given an extraordinarily long count with the referee repeatedly chivvying him to get up. When he did, he rushed Craig and knocked him out – and the ten-second count over the American is said to have lasted five seconds!

Roche's final ring outing was a sixth-round defeat by Petty Officer Matthew 'Nutty' Curran, a leading English heavyweight of the moment, in 1910. By then he had gone back to gaelic football. He was, according to a plaque erected in Wexford after his death in 1934, aged fifty-six, a simple, sporting and modest man.

LUCIEN RODRIGUEZ

Born: 13 December 1951, Casablanca, Morocco
Height: 6ft 1½in   **Weight:** 210lbs (15st)
Fights: 52   **Won:** 39   **Lost:** 12   **Drawn:** 1
KO percentage: 40
Rounds boxed: 347
World title fights: 1
Career span: 1973-86 (13 years)
KO wins: 21
KO defeats: 5

Lucien Rodriguez was disciplined enough to take Larry Holmes the full twelve rounds in a world title fight in 1983. Holmes at the time was ready to walk away from long-time promoter Don King. Larry wanted to promote himself – and when boxers do that the effect on the boxing hierarchy is usually dramatic. According to Holmes, King laughed and told him he would be boxing not Rodriguez, but Tim Witherspoon. Holmes refused.

Again, according to Holmes, WBC president Jose Sulaiman told him they would not sanction the Rodriguez fight, even though the Frenchman was European champion, a position that more often than not in those days was accompanied by a place in the WBC top ten. Then when King, who was under pressure from a federal investigation into his business dealings at the time, came up with a compromise – that Holmes box Rodriguez on his own promotion and then defend against Witherspoon on his – the WBC were suddenly happy to recognise Lucien as a bona fide challenger. After television networks CBS and ABC both declined interest in the Rodriguez fight, Holmes did a deal with NBC. It took place in Scranton, Pennsylvania, about sixty miles from Larry's home town of Easton. Unfortunately, for the principle of boxers promoting themselves, the fight was a stinker – because Rodriguez preferred the survival option from the opening bell.

He lasted the distance because he was competent, but it was a passionless performance. Holmes was slowing at thirty-three and, though he won a landslide verdict, couldn't connect with anything hard enough to arouse any real enthusiasm.

Rodriguez was born in Casablanca, Morocco – his father Francois was a French-Moroccan and his mother Maria was Italian. He worked as a meter-reader for the French Electric Company in Paris – and was still doing that when he boxed Holmes. He began boxing, at the age of nineteen, while doing his national service and won a gold medal at the World Military Games. One of his boyhood heroes was the great French middleweight from Morocco, Marcel Cerdan, and he also read everything he could find on Georges Carpentier.

He turned professional in Paris in January 1973, and was in his second spell as European champion when he fought Holmes. Not surprisingly, nobody was over-keen to see him again at world level. He earned well out of the European title but lost it to Steffen Tangstad of Norway. He retired in 1986, a year after Frank Bruno knocked him out in a round at Wembley.

JOSE ROMAN

Born: Puerto Rico

Fights: 84	**Won:** 54	**Lost:** 26	**Drawn:** 3	**No Contests:** 1

KO percentage: 32
Rounds boxed: 600
World title fights: 1
Career span: 1966-81 (15 years)
KO wins: 27
KO defeats: 11

A stricter referee than the American Jay Edson might have disqualified George Foreman in Tokyo in 1973 – and awarded Jose 'King' Roman the championship of the world. Jose, also called Joe, was smashed to the canvas three times by Foreman and on one occasion Foreman hit him again when he was on the floor. Edson took the charitable view that the punch was on its way when Roman went down. It was all over in exactly two minutes of the first round. Japanese critics were not amused. One writer called it a hoax and a travesty.

After that dramatic episode, it was back to obscurity for the Puerto Rican, who had beaten nobody of note on the way up and didn't do so on the way down. He could box quite well, but wasn't a heavy puncher – and had a tendency to lose his cool.

Roman boxed professionally from 1966, beat ordinary fighters – and lost to ordinary fighters. He beat Chuck Wepner, Manuel Ramos and Terry Daniels, but lost to Jack Bodell, Jose Urtain and Jimmy Young. He retired in 1981 after losing his last four inside the distance.

JACK ROOT

Born: 26 May 1876, Austria
Full name: Janos Ruthaly
Died: 10 June 1963, Los Angeles, California, aged 87
Height: 5ft 10in   **Weight at peak:** 171lbs (12st 3lbs)
Fights: 56   **Won:** 47   **Lost:** 3   **Drawn:** 4   **No Contests:** 2
KO percentage: 48
Rounds boxed: 300
World title fights: 1
Career span: 1897-1906 (9 years)
KO wins: 27
KO defeats: 3

Jack Root's greatest fame came as the first world light-heavyweight champion
– the division was devised by his manager, Lou Houseman – but he also contested
the world heavyweight title after James J. Jeffries retired in 1905.

Root was virtually in retirement when the offer for the heavyweight championship bout against Marvin Hart came and, in the heat and at altitude in Reno,
Nevada, was worn down. Hart, 19lbs heavier, knocked him out in the twelfth
round.

Root was born in Austria as Janos Ruthaly. He began boxing in Chicago
in 1897 as John as well as Jack Root. In 1902 he won and lost against George
Gardner, but out-pointed Hart over six rounds, a result that gave some observers
undue faith in him when they boxed again for the title. Jack won the inaugural
light-heavyweight title bout with a ten-round decision over Charles 'Kid' McCoy
in Detroit in April 1903. He lost it three months later, knocked out in the twelfth
round by his old rival Gardner, in Fort Erie, Pennsylvania.

Root died in Los Angeles on 10 June 1963, aged eighty-seven.

JACK ROPER

Born: 25 March 1904, Pontchoula, Lousiana
Full name: Cecil Byron Hammond
Died: 28 November 1966, Woodland Hills, California, aged 62
Height: 6ft   **Weight at peak:** 196-202lbs (14st-14st 6lbs)
Fights: 98   **Won:** 45   **Lost:** 43   **Drawn:** 10
KO percentage: 21
Rounds boxed: 668
World title fights: 1
Career span: 1923-40 (17 years)
KO wins: 21
KO defeats: 15

Jack Roper was thirty-five years old, working as an electrician at Warner Brothers studios and mixing boxing with bit-part acting when he was offered as a challenger to Joe Louis in Los Angeles in April 1939. Under Californian rules, even the world heavyweight championship was restricted to a maximum of ten rounds, but frankly a six-rounder would have reflected a naive optimism on the part of the matchmaker. Roper's manager, Dick Donald, felt that if a payday was on offer against Louis, his man might just as well have it as anyone else and so asked Tom Gallery, the matchmaker for the Olympic Auditorium in Los Angeles, to offer their services. Mike Jacobs, for Louis, agreed.

Roper got himself in reasonable shape at a ranch near Ojai, California, and came out punching at Wrigley Field. He did surprise Louis with a good left hook but, after two minutes twenty seconds of round one, it was Roper who was flat out with referee George Blake finishing the count. Amazingly, the farce drew a crowd of 21,675, with Louis collecting $34,413.

Roper's real name was Cecil Byron Hammond. He was born in Pontchula, Louisiana, on 25 March 1904 and followed his elder brother, who called himself Captain Bob Roper, into boxing. By 1923 Jack, having changed his name to associate himself with his brother, was fighting professionally in the Los Angeles area. Jack wasn't overly in love with boxing, but did enjoy a drink or three, which meant he wasn't always in immaculate shape.

In the mid-1920s he was twice knocked out by George Godfrey, by Harold Mays and by Jack Renault. In March 1931 he fought James J. Braddock in the Miami arena run by Madison Square Garden – and lost in sixty-eight seconds. He had already retired three times when he was fed to Louis.

Roper's biggest win was a first-round knockout of Art Lasky in Hollywood in January 1936, but in a return Lasky beat him. Roper acted in movies from the silent days through to 1952, when he played a boxer in *The Quiet Man* opposite John Wayne. His earlier credits included classics like *Angels Over Broadway* and *Never Give a Sucker an Even Break*.

Roper died of throat cancer at the Motion Picture County House and Hospital in Woodland Hills, California, on 28 November 1966. He was sixty-two years old.

GUS RUHLIN

Born: 8 January 1872, Canton, Ohio
Died: February 1912, aged 40
Height: 6ft 2in   **Weight at peak:** 200lbs (14st 4lbs)
Fights: 40   **Won:** 23   **Lost:** 9   **Drawn:** 5   **No Decisions:** 3
KO percentage: 40
Rounds boxed: 354
World title fights: 1

Career span: 1896-1910 (14 years)
KO wins: 16
KO defeats: 4

Gus Ruhlin was a strong, upright heavyweight from Akron, Ohio, who retired angrily in the fifth round against James J. Jeffries in a world title fight at the Mechanics Pavilion, San Francisco, in November 1901. He claimed Jeffries was using foul tactics and he quit after what he felt was a wrestling throw. That was a shame for, when he and Jeffries were novices, he took the future champion the full twenty rounds to a draw.

Over a ten-year career, he won two out of three battles with Tom Sharkey and knocked Bob Fitzsimmons down in the first round of their fight in New York in August 1900. Fitzsimmons got up and dropped Ruhlin four times, the last one for the count in round six. Ruhlin was carried, unconscious, to the dressing room. Earlier that year he had been employed as a 'behind closed doors' sparring partner by James J. Corbett in twenty-five-round unofficial fights to help Corbett get ready for his own challenge to Jeffries in May 1900.

Ruhlin was only forty years old when he died in 1912.

JOHN RUIZ

Born: 4 January 1972, Methuen, Massachusetts
Height: 6ft 2in   **Weight at peak:** 227lbs (16st 3lbs)
Fights: 48   **Won:** 41   **Lost:** 5   **Drawn:** 1   **No Contests:** 1
KO percentage: 58
Rounds boxed: 265
World champion: 2000-03, 2004-05 (WBA)
World title fights: 8
Career span: 1992-2005 (13 years)
KO wins: 28
KO defeats: 1

For a couple of weeks John Ruiz had the unhappy distinction of being the only heavyweight champion in history to lose his crown to a former middleweight titleholder... twice! In March 2003 he was outsmarted in a WBA title fight by the brilliant Roy Jones jnr, who had been pound-for-pound the best of his generation. However, when Jones returned to light-heavyweight, Ruiz regained control of the WBA crown – only to lose it to another one-time middleweight champ, James 'Lights Out' Toney in Madison Square Garden in April 2005.

Ruiz, beaten unanimously over twelve rounds, retired in embarrassment. Then a fortnight later came the news that Toney had tested positive for a steroid, nandrolone, which he said was in a substance used as a treatment for an arm injury.

The New York State Athletic Commission fined Toney $10,000 and banned him for a paltry ninety days. Ruiz was reinstated.

Ruiz is of Puerto Rican descent, born in Methuen, Massachusetts – on the outskirts of Boston – and raised in the suburb of Chelsea. From the age of twenty, he was guided by boisterous local manager Norman Stone. They cut contrasting figures: while Stone was prone to noisy outbursts, Ruiz lived up to his tag of the Quiet Man. He began well after an international amateur career, but had to overcome the nightmare of a nineteen-second loss to David Tua in Atlantic City in 1996. He did stop the veteran Tony Tucker in eleven, but had to wait until the WBA stripped Lennox Lewis and paired Ruiz with Evander Holyfield for the vacant title in August 2000 to reach the top. Some good judges thought he had done enough at the Paris in Las Vegas, but at the end of twelve dull rounds it was thirty-seven-year-old Holyfield who received a close (114-113 twice, 116-112) decision. Not too many cared – Lewis was the genuine champion – and in March 2001 Ruiz and Holyfield met again, this time up the Strip at the Mandalay Bay. Ruiz won handily: 116-110, 115-111, 114-111. A third fight was arranged, and this time, with most feeling Holyfield had done enough, the judges came up with a draw, which meant Ruiz kept the WBA belt.

Ruiz won on a tenth-round foul against a laboured, uninspired Kirk Johnson but then blew the title when he plodded haplessly after Jones at the Thomas and Mack Center, Las Vegas, in March 2003. Jones won 118-110, 117-111, 116-112.

Jones went back to light-heavyweight and, while the WBA sorted out the situation, Ruiz beat Hasim Rahman on points in Atlantic City. He was then reinstated as champion. He stopped Puerto Rican hope Fres Oquendo in eleven, but he was lucky to scrape a twelve-round unanimous verdict over Andrew Golota – and then came defeat against Toney and reinstatement. In December 2005, Ruiz lost the WBA title to the huge Russian, Nicolay Valuev.

S

LEE SAVOLD

Born: 22 March 1916, Marshall, Minnesota
Died: 14 May 1972, aged 56
Height: 6ft   **Weight at peak:** 198lbs (14st 2lbs)
Fights: 136   **Won:** 92   **Lost:** 39   **Drawn:** 3   **No Decisions:** 2
KO percentage: 47
Rounds boxed: 826

World title fights: 0
Career span: 1933-52 (19 years)
KO wins: 64
KO defeats: 10

Lee Savold was one of the clutch of good heavyweights briefly caught up in the process of deciding a successor to Joe Louis. His moment came in June 1950 in London when he beat Bruce Woodcock in four rounds because of a horrible, S-shaped cut. All this happened too late for the man from Minnesota to make a real impact and his claim fizzled out. Although he was a contender for Joe Louis' title by 1942, and although Louis defended his title against a host of second-rate heavyweights dubbed 'Bums of the Month', the call to Savold never came.

Born in Marshall, Minnesota, Savold was the son of a rancher of Norwegian descent. By the time he was seventeen, with the Depression years biting hard, he was in St Paul and learning the craft of boxing from the great middleweight of a generation before, Mike Gibbons. He could jab well and had a hard left hook. His early career is a muddle still, but he developed well and in 1939 moved with his wife and three children to New Jersey and linked up with veteran manager Bill Daly. To add to his boxing income he worked as a stevedore and nightclub bouncer.

Daly kept him busy by taking him on the road. They took in Sioux City, Des Moines, Cedar Rapids, Mason City, Omaha, Waterloo… wherever they could find work. He lost to Buddy Baer and Billy Conn, but ploughed on and in Washington DC in May 1942 he knocked out Lou Nova in eight rounds. Savold lost and won decisions against another of Louis's victims, Tony Musto, but found Tami Mauriello and Jimmy Bivins too clever. Although he beat Nova again in just a couple of rounds in Chicago, the Second World War intervened and he spent a few months at sea as a crewman on a merchant ship.

In 1944 he had three fights with Joe Baksi, winning the first on points and losing the decision in the other two, but out-pointed Gus Dorazio. Time seemed to have passed him by, however, and he took a job as a bartender. 'I started drinking a lot of beer and staying up late nights,' he said. 'I smoked a lot too. Then one day Daly bet me $100 that I couldn't give up cigarettes. A few days later he found me smoking cigars, which hadn't been mentioned. So he bet me $100 I couldn't stop smoking completely. When he saw me making progress he bet me another $100 I couldn't give up beer. I won all those bets.'

Trainer Tex Pelte said tea and coffee went with the cigarettes and beer – to be replaced by vitamins and healthy food – and he even began going to bed early!

In December 1948 he made his first visit to Britain since his time as a merchant seaman – and lost what was billed by Jack Solomons as an eliminator for the heavyweight title against Bruce Woodcock. It speaks volumes for the popularity of boxing in Britain at the time that when he arrived at Waterloo station in fog-bound London, he was welcomed by huge crowds, who ignored film stars Virginia Mayo and Joan Caulfield who also stepped off the train.

Before a sell-out crowd at Harringay Arena, Savold lost on a low-blow disqualification in the fourth round. He returned to London to box Woodcock eighteen months later in a bout that Solomons, with no genuine authority, called a world title fight. At White City Stadium, before a 50,000 crowd that included future Prime Minister Harold MacMillan, viscounts, dukes and members of parliament, Savold systematically took apart the British champion from Doncaster and tore open a horrible, horizontal cut on and above his left eyebrow. Blood cascaded down Woodcock's face from the gash, his nose and mouth bled too, and at the end of the fourth round he retired. Savold was presented with a world championship trophy and took out an advertisement in newspapers to thank British fans for their fairness: 'Your friendship, your warmth and your sportsmanship all helped to make me heavyweight champion of the world.'

However, Savold's claim was never accepted in the United States. He had only two more fights, the first a disappointing sixth-round knockout defeat by thirty-seven-year-old Joe Louis, the second a painful six-rounds beating by Rocky Marciano. At thirty-five, and after well over 100 fights, he decided that was enough.

Savold died of a stroke in Neptune, New Jersey, on 14 May 1972, aged fifty-six.

ERNIE SCHAAF

Born: 27 September 1908, Elizabeth, New Jersey
Full name: Ernest Frederick Schaaf
Died: 13 February 1933, New York City, aged 24
Height: 6ft 1in   **Weight at peak:** 210lbs (15st)
Fights: 94   **Won:** 72   **Lost:** 13   **Drawn:** 2   **No Decisions:** 7
KO percentage: 42
Rounds boxed: 610
World title fights: 0
Career span: 1925-33 (8 years)
KO wins: 40
KO defeats: 1

The tragedy of Ernie Schaaf is a constant reminder why the safety of boxers should be in the hands of responsible administrators and medical officers. The circumstances that surrounded the death of Schaaf at the age of twenty-four on 14 February 1933, four days after being knocked out by Primo Carnera, remain a lesson to all who would listen.

Schaaf, originally from Elizabeth, New Jersey, fought out of Boston after a spell in the navy. He could fight. He out-pointed future world heavyweight champion James J. Braddock in New York in January 1931 and also beat well-regarded contenders Jim

Maloney, Vittorio Campolo and Tuffy Griffiths. By 1932 he was on the brink of a championship fight after a win over Young Stribling. Jack Sharkey, who was shortly to become heavyweight champion, bought out his managerial contract for $78,500 and guided him with Johnny Buckley.

In his first fight for them, Schaaf boxed the New Jersey bartender and notorious ring brawler Tony Galento in the Dreamland Park arena in Newark. In the clinches Galento gave Schaaf a battering, using in particular a rabbit punch to the neck. Although Schaaf's boxing skills earned him the ten-round decision, he was exhausted and dazed afterwards. While Galento sauntered back to his bar, Schaaf did not leave his dressing room for two hours.

Seventeen days later he boxed Stanley Poreda, lost on points and looked listless. Even in winning his next three bouts, including a good one against the rugged Spaniard Paolino Uzcudun, he was still not himself. Then he boxed Max Baer in Chicago and took a horrible beating before being knocked out in the tenth round. This time he was out cold in the ring for a full minute. They got him to his dressing room but he lay there for four hours before they took him to hospital. He should not have boxed again, but two months later lost a ten-round decision to a fighter he had knocked out easily two years earlier, known as Unknown Winston. He did beat Winston in a rematch. On 6 January 1933, in a fight postponed because Schaaf had reportedly been cut badly in sparring, he defeated Poreda in six rounds. On 17 January he was admitted to hospital suffering from flu and stayed there a week.

On 10 February, eighteen days after being released from hospital, he stepped into the Madison Square Garden ring to box Primo Carnera over fifteen rounds in front of 20,000 fans, with Sharkey promising to give the winner a shot at the championship. The fight had been offered to Larry Gains, the British-based Canadian, but he had turned down the trip and so Carnera took it instead. For twelve rounds Schaaf seemed barely interested. Then in round thirteen Carnera landed what seemed a light left hook and Ernie crumpled to the canvas. Referee Billy Cavanaugh counted him out. He was carried unconscious to the dressing room, but disgruntled punters yelled 'fake' and booed in the belief that Schaaf had taken a dive. They ferried him across the street to the Polyclinic Hospital, where he regained consciousness. Dr William Walker, the New York State Athletic Commission doctor, said Ernie sat up in bed later that night and no less than four other doctors said he was out of danger. However, overnight he deteriorated and bleeding on the brain was apparent. On Monday 13 February he underwent a three-and-a-half-hour operation but died at 4 a.m. the next day.

The autopsy should have been a damning indictment of the business. It showed Schaaf had not died simply as a result of the Carnera punch but because of a general weakening of his condition, possibly because of the bout of flu he had suffered, and inflammation of the brain. Astonishingly, it was used as proof that nobody was at fault. The sport was given official permission to wash its hands of responsibility.

MAX SCHMELING

Born: 28 September 1905, Uckermark, Germany
Full name: Maximilian Adolph Otto Siegfried Schmeling
Died: 4 February 2005, Hamburg, Germany, aged 99
Height: 6ft 1in   **Weight at peak:** 188-189lbs (13st 6lbs-13st 7lbs)
Fights: 70   **Won:** 56   **Lost:** 10   **Drawn:** 4
KO percentage: 55
Rounds boxed: 472
World champion: 1930-32
World title fights: 4
Career span: 1924-48 (24 years)
KO wins: 39
KO defeats: 5

It was the fate of Max Schmeling to illustrate to the world that, no matter how hard an athlete tries, it is sometimes impossible to avoid the influence of world politics on sport. Schmeling knew, as a German in the 1930s, that his ambitions as a boxer were being railroaded by the Nazi party, but what could he do about it? He refused to sack his Jewish manager, the American Joe Jacobs, both asked for and received a personal audience with Adolf Hitler to state his case, and did his best to uphold fair play and sportsmanship, but beyond that, like most of us would, he allowed events to take their course.

In the ring he won the world heavyweight title while writhing on the canvas from a low blow by Jack Sharkey in the fourth round before almost 80,000 fans at Yankee Stadium, New York, in June 1930. Sharkey was disqualified by referee Jim Crowley, who had at first counted over Max and then consulted the ringside judges, who confirmed the blow was beneath the belt. For a time the New York State Athletic Commission, the most powerful in the world, refused to inscribe his name on the Muldoon Trophy that represented the championship at the time and his purse was withheld, but Sharkey had not argued with the disqualification and immediately after the fight a doctor had confirmed the bruising around his groin. Former champions Gene Tunney, Jack Dempsey and Tommy Burns said Schmeling's victory was legitimate.

It was more than a year before Schmeling defended against William 'Young' Stribling in a brand new stadium in Cleveland, Ohio. Max had expected a rematch with Sharkey or a fight with Dempsey, who had been boxing in exhibition tours, but the New York commission decided it would be Stribling. The 'Georgia Peach' fought – and fouled – hard, but Schmeling wore him down and stopped him with fourteen seconds left in the fifteenth and final round. The rematch with Sharkey was in the outdoor arena owned by Madison Square Garden, the Long Island Bowl, in June 1932. Franklin Roosevelt, the Governor of New York, visited his training camp, had a conversation with him in German and told him, 'I love

Germany. I know it well.' After Roosevelt became president, they exchanged letters and gifts.

The second Sharkey fight was just as controversial as the first. Schmeling appeared to out-box the American only to lose a split decision. Jacobs was furious and yelled angrily into the microphone, 'We wuz robbed. We shoulda stood in bed!' At ringside Tunney called the decision a scandal and a disaster for the sport. A writer said that, of twenty-five journalists he asked for his column, twenty-three thought Schmeling won. Max returned home and married the actress Anny Ondra, a relationship that lasted more than fifty years. Six months after the Sharkey fight, Adolf Hitler became Reich Chancellor of Germany.

Schmeling had learned his trade in Germany from the age of eighteen. At nineteen, he was beaten in two rounds by Larry Gains, but went on to become European light-heavyweight champion. He also held the German title at light-heavy and heavyweight. Once in America, victories over Johnny Risko (a ninth-round stoppage), and Paolino Uzcudun (on points) brought him to the Sharkey fight. He was world heavyweight champion at twenty-four. When he lost the Sharkey rematch he was twenty-six, still a young man. In more sensible times they would have boxed a 'decider' but instead Schmeling was made to wait six years for another title shot. In September 1932 he stopped former welter and middleweight champion Mickey Walker in eight but a shattering tenth-round defeat by Max Baer in New York in June 1933 enabled him to be avoided.

Three years later he boxed the precocious, brilliant, twenty-two-year-old Joe Louis before 40,000 fans in Yankee Stadium. Schmeling was supposed to be the stepping stone, but he had watched Louis beat the faded Uzcudun and noticed his tendency to drop his left hand when he doubled up the jab. The German began cautiously, survived a bad third round and then lured Louis onto a clean right cross in the fourth that hurt him. Another one shortly afterwards sent him staggering across the ring and a third put him down. Louis rallied in the seventh but had his knees buckled again in round eight. This time he didn't recover and in the twelfth right hands bounced off his head until one spun him around and he fell by the ropes, knocked out. Jacobs yelled at reporters, 'So what did I tell you? Didn't I tell you we'd beat him?'

There were riots in Harlem. In his hotel suite Schmeling sat, surrounded by flowers, and read telegrams of congratulations from around the world, from Marlene Dietrich, Primo Carnera, Douglas Fairbanks... and, of course, Hitler. He was flown home on the Hindenburg airship to a tumultuous welcome at Frankfurt airport. Obviously the Nazi party made the most of one of their own, even a black-haired, beetle-browed member of the Aryan race, knocking out the black American 'super-hero'. Within days he was meeting Hitler and they watched the film of the fight, which Schmeling had brought home and for which he had, astonishingly, negotiated the overseas rights. Hitler, who in a previous meeting had listened with obvious irritation as Schmeling argued in favour of keeping Jacobs, had the triumph made into a documentary, which included the full-fight footage, which was screened in cinemas throughout Germany. This was also the year of the Olympic Games in Berlin, which the Nazis used shamelessly as a propaganda tool. However, instead of boxing for the world title, Schmeling was side-stepped by champion James J. Braddock, who instead took a fantastic financial offer to fight Louis, who knocked him out. Schmeling didn't get another fight until December 1937, when he knocked out Harry Thomas in eight rounds in New York. Even Thomas would fight for the championship before Max got his opportunity! In Germany he made do with out-pointing the London-based South African Ben Foord in Hamburg, when incidentally Jacobs, surrounded by SS men, gave a Nazi salute. The world moved ever closer to war. Hitler annexed Austria. Schmeling turned down the Dagger of Honour.

When Schmeling returned to New York for the rematch with Louis, the atmosphere had changed horribly. He was now not simply a boxer, but a representative of a menacing political regime. As his ship, the *Bremen*, docked, protesters lined the harbour with placards calling him a Nazi and an Aryan Show Horse. If he left his hotel, he was taunted on the streets with mock-Nazi salutes. Hate mail arrived by the sackload. Over an unrelated issue involving heavyweight Tony Galento, Joe Jacobs was barred by the New York Commission from Schmeling's corner and his dressing room. Meanwhile, members of the American version of the Nazis, the Bund, appeared at Louis's training camp 250 miles from New York to watch him train and to laugh.

On 22 June 1938, Yankee Stadium was a seething bowl of noise. Everyone who was anyone wanted to be there: actors, politicians, old champions and new. More than 70,000 fans paid over $1 million at the gate. On the way to the ring Schmeling, surrounded by twenty-five police officers, was pelted with debris. Once the bell rang Louis attacked, found him easy to hit and took him apart with one of the most ruthless displays ever seen in a major fight. It was all over in 124 seconds. Max was down three times and was severely injured by a left hook that, as Schmeling twisted around, landed in his back. The British writer Peter Wilson wrote that the German let out an involuntary scream that 'razored through the surrounding din, half-human, half-animal'. The punch had split a vertebrae into two places.

Schmeling was in hospital for ten days, with among his few visitors a representative of the New York commission, who wanted to know the truth of the injury because they were considering withholding his purse for lack of effort! He returned to Germany on the *Bremen*, still confined to his bed, and at home was unable to leave his room for six weeks. Hitler had cabled Schmeling before the fight, addressing him as the new heavyweight champion. When the brief massacre was underway, the radio broadcast to Germany was cut off and replaced by music. His name disappeared from newspapers.

Schmeling was called up to fight in the Second World War as a paratrooper and suffered a recurrence of the back injury from the Louis fight when he landed in a vineyard on his first mission in Crete in May 1941. His injuries ended his involvement, but the photographs of him in uniform in full battle dress were published and it was announced he had been awarded the Iron Cross. He was once again a helpless propaganda tool. He recounted the absurdity of the situation when, only able to walk with the help of two canes, he was given the job of taking a wounded English prisoner to a field hospital. When they had rounded the corner out of sight of his superiors, they joined arms to support each other – the Englishman turned out to be a boxing fan and recognised him. On the way they shared an orange. He was not officially released from the army until 1943, but had spent only two days in action. It has also been recorded how he helped shelter Jewish families he knew and saved their lives.

After the war Germany was in ruins and Schmeling was as broke as most. He returned to the ring in September 1947 on his forty-second birthday. He had five fights in the comeback, but points defeats by Walter Neusel and Richard Vogt persuaded him to stop. Even so, a career that began in 1924 and ended in 1948 had lasted almost double that of the 'Thousand Year Reich'. For a while he ran farming concerns and in 1957 was awarded the German franchise for Coca-Cola, and in that single move regained his wealth. He sought out Joe Louis again in the USA and they became close friends. As Louis's health and finances deteriorated, Schmeling was pleased to be able to help.

Schmeling retired to his home at Hollenstadt near Hamburg, remaining healthy until the Christmas holidays of 2004 when he caught a heavy cold. He failed to shake it off and he died, aged ninety-nine, on 4 February 2005.

MIKE SCHRECK

Born: August 1880, Hamilton, Ohio
Died: Unknown
Height: 5ft 8½in   **Weight at peak:** 185lbs (13st 3lbs)
Fights: 111   **Won:** 66   **Lost:** 18   **Drawn:** 24   **No Contests:** 3
KO percentage: 28
Rounds boxed: 870
World title fights: 0
Career span: 1899-1916 (17 years)
KO wins: 39
KO defeats: 6

Although he didn't box for the title, awkward southpaw Mike Schreck had the beating of two world champions, Marvin Hart and Tommy Burns. He outpointed Burns twice in Detroit before the little Canadian had become champion and twice stopped Hart after Marvin had lost his crown. The promoters of his first major bout with Hart, in Tonopah, Nevada, on 30 May 1907, pronounced it a world title fight. However, Hart had lost the championship to Burns fifteen months before that, so that was nonsense.

Schreck was from a family of German immigrants who settled in the area of Hamilton, north of Cincinnati, in the middle of the nineteenth century. He lived in the village of Sycamore with his wife Ruth and, from 1901, their daughter, also called Ruth. In the 1900 census the nineteen-year-old, newly married Schreck gave his occupation as pugilist and declared he had been employed in the occupation for five years. By then he had already out-pointed Burns twice in Detroit, in November 1902 and January 1903, though the circumstances of their first meeting are somewhat vague.

In April 1905 Schreck wore down and stopped the former light-heavyweight champion George Gardner in the twentieth round in Salt Lake City and although he lost a twenty-round decision to the world-class middleweight Jack Twin Sullivan in Los Angeles, he remained a leading contender for the heavyweight championship.

Schreck was small at 5ft 8in but a handful: hard to hit and harder to hurt – and of course, he fought 'the wrong way round'. In May 1907 he won a war with Hart in the twenty-first round. Hart had broken his wrist in training but boxed anyway and from the sixth round was one-handed. Schreck ground him down, rode out a terrific onslaught in round eighteen and then bombarded the exhausted former champion in the twenty-first until the sponge was thrown in. Neither man was the same again.

In his next fight Schreck was knocked out for the first time in his life by Al Kaufman in San Francisco. Hart detoriated even more rapidly and in July 1909 Schreck beat him in four. Hart's jaw was broken.

Schreck seemed to be losing interest. When he lost in two rounds to Sam Langford he was so far out of shape the police considered it a farce and stopped the fight. By 1910 he no longer put 'pugilist' on his census form – he was earning his main living as a fireman.

AXEL SCHULZ

Born: 9 November 1968, Bad Saarow, East Germany
Height: 6ft 3in   **Weight at peak:** 221lbs (15st 11lbs)
Fights: 32   **Won:** 26   **Lost:** 4   **Drawn:** 1   **No Contests:** 1
KO percentage: 34
Rounds boxed: 236
World title fights: 3
Career span: 1990-99 (9 years)
KO wins: 11
KO defeats: 1

'Should have' and 'would have' are constant companions in boxing's strange, uneven world. There are those who believe Axel Schulz should have been crowned heavy-weight champion of the world in Las Vegas on 22 April 1995 – and would have been had the judges been watching the fight that the vast majority in the Grand Garden arena saw. Schulz seemed to out-box a lethargic, forty-six-year-old George Foreman over twelve not entirely impressive rounds. But at the end Keith McDonald and Jerry Roth both had Foreman winning 115-113 with Chuck Giampa scoring it level 114-114. Foreman claimed the German ran, but he didn't: he moved around the slow, achingly old champion and picked him off. When Foreman landed, Schulz came straight back. Foreman won rounds but not, it seemed, the fight.

'I looked like a junkyard dog, he looked like Elvis Presley,' said George, who had grossed $10 million to his challenger's $350,000. 'A rematch? Never. I will never fight that kid again. He can go back where he came from and stay there.'

In the federal racketeering trial that exposed IBF president Bobby Lee as cor-rupt and led to his imprisonment, Schulz's promoter Wilfried Sauerland testified that he was asked to pay Lee $100,000 to secure a return. 'I had no alternative but to pay because otherwise there was no chance of Axel getting the rematch,' added Sauerland, who said he passed the money in cash to another promoter, Cedric Kushner, who acted as intermediary. Kushner paid it to IBF official Doug Beavers, who admitted he took $25,000, gave Lee's son Robert $50,000 for himself and his father and then gave another IBF member, Bill Brennan, the remaining $25,000. The IBF ordered the return. Foreman refused and was stripped. So it goes.

Schulz's luck stayed out. The IBF matched him for the vacant title against Frans Botha in Stuttgart, but he was outsmarted over twelve rounds. Botha won a unanimous decision, then was stripped when he tested positive for steroids. Then, again for the vacant title, Schulz lost a split decision to Michael Moorer in Dortmund in June 1996. He retired after losing in eight rounds to the younger, bigger, fresher Wladimir Klitschko.

From Frankfurt-Oder on the border with Poland, Schulz grew up in the spar-tan East German system in the 1980s. He turned pro in October 1990 following unification, managed by Sauerland and trained by the 1968 Olympic gold medal-list Manfred Wolke.

BRUCE SELDON

Born: 30 January 1967, Atlantic City, New Jersey
Height: 6ft 1½in   **Weight at peak:** 230lbs (16st 6lbs)
Fights: 40   **Won:** 35   **Lost:** 5
KO percentage: 77
Rounds boxed: 170
World champion: 1995-96 (WBA)
World title fights: 3

Career span: 1988-2004 (16 years)
KO wins: 31
KO defeats: 4

He held the WBA title briefly, so Bruce Seldon's name will never be erased from the record books. However, Seldon seemed to spend his life battling a lack of direction and what seemed to be an enormous lack of confidence. Like many who suffer from this difficulty, he sometimes over-compensated and appeared flashy and flamboyant. He called himself the Atlantic City Express.

Seldon was a street-kid who once, when asked about his childhood ambitions, said, 'I didn't have any dreams. I was wild. Just living day by day. Striving and surviving.' When he was six, he was mown down by a car but got away with nine stitches in his head. By his late teens he was in jail for street crimes. When he came out, he boxed and made a name for himself by winning his first eighteen fights, including a tenth-round stoppage of former contender David Bey. The wheels came off when he lost decisively in nine rounds to Oliver McCall in Atlantic City in April 1991. In his next fight, he was knocked out in one by Riddick Bowe.

Although one veteran, Tony Tubbs, out-boxed him, he beat others in Jesse Ferguson and Greg Page, and in April 1995 Don King engineered him a shot at the vacant WBA title against Tony Tucker. Seldon won when Tucker was forced to retire after round seven because his eyes were swollen almost shut. Seldon inflicted similar damage on his first challenger Joe Hipp, a Native American southpaw, in Las Vegas in August 1995, but didn't fight for a year after that. Some would say he didn't fight on the night of 7 September 1996 either: Mike Tyson steamrollered him to defeat in 109 seconds, the knockout coming from a punch that most said at best 'parted Seldon's hair'. The general feeling was that he was completely intimidated and overawed.

He was unpromoteable and then, in 1998, admitted under a plea bargain to endangering the welfare of a child, a fifteen-year-old girl he had picked up in Atlantic City, smoked marijuana with and taken supposedly provocative photographs of. More serious charges of sexual assault and drugs and weapons offences were dropped. He was jailed for a day short of a year, placed on probation for five years and ordered to sign the convicted sex offender register. 'I'm terribly sorry,' he told the court. 'I'm not a bad person. I didn't mean any of this.'

In 2004, at the age of thirty-seven, Seldon tried a comeback but it didn't work out.

JACK SHARKEY

Born: 26 Oct 1902, Binghamton, New York
Full name: Joseph Paul Zukauskas
Died: 17 Aug 1994, Epping, New Hampshire, aged 91

Height: 6ft   **Weight at peak:** 197-205lbs (14st 1lb–14st 9lbs)

Fights: 55   **Won:** 38   **Lost:** 14   **Drawn:** 3

KO percentage: 25

Rounds boxed: 463

World champion: 1932-33

World title fights: 3

Career span: 1924-36 (12 years)

KO wins: 14

KO defeats: 4

Jack Sharkey was never quite forgiven for losing the world heavyweight title when Primo Carnera knocked him out with a big uppercut in the sixth round at the Long Island Bowl in June 1933. Put simply, few believed Sharkey could lose to Carnera 'on the level' and therefore explained away the shock by suggesting it was a fixed fight. Carnera being Italian, with known Mob connections... well, people only had to raise an eyebrow.

Sharkey's protests meant nothing. He had out-pointed Carnera comfortably over fifteen rounds in Brooklyn back in October 1931 and shouldn't have had any trouble second time around. 'Don't they understand that the big bum just got better?' said Sharkey. 'I didn't give the guy credit he might improve...' That didn't wash, nor did his supposed vision of his protégé Ernie Schaaf, who had been killed four months earlier in a fight with Carnera. His doubters also pointed to a bad joke he made when he won the championship on a controversial split decision over Max Schmeling in June 1932. Asked how much the championship was worth, he said, 'Oh, about twenty-five bucks. Maybe fifty if I knew a guy who ran a pawn shop.' Even his wife, Dorothy, had her doubts. In old age he was still complaining and insisting he was innocent. 'Why would I lose?' he said. 'Boxing was my business. I was enjoying being champion of the world. There was a lot of money to be made defending it.'

Now that made sense. If ever there was a champion who was careful and shrewd with his money it was Sharkey. Before each fight, he took his paycheque to the bank and by the time he arrived home it had been credited to his account. He was a family man for whom boxing was strictly work. He didn't knock it, but neither did he hang around with boxing people after working hours.

Sharkey was born Joseph Paul Cukoschay, which was sometimes altered to Zukauskas, in Binghamton, a small town in upstate New York, on 26 October 1902. His parents were Lithuanian and there was a community of Lithuanians in Binghamton. 'When the Lithuanians fought, they fought to kill. And my favourite occupation was breathing,' he said. At fifteen he left home after being turned down as too young for the US Navy. He lived rough in New York, worked where he could and as he crossed the Brooklyn Bridge one day he decided to try the navy again. By then he was seventeen, was accepted and joined the 'Banana Fleet' that worked the Caribbean. He learned to box in the navy. The month he left the service, January 1924, he made his professional debut under the name Jack Sharkey (an amalgam of Jack Dempsey and Tom Sharkey, the turn of the century sailor-turned-heavyweight).

He married Dorothy that summer and they lived in Chestnut Hill, Boston, until 1952 when they moved into her childhood home in Epping, New Hampshire. In the ring things were not so easy. For a couple of years he looked, at best, second rate. In 1926, though, he won nine out of nine, including a ten-round decision over George Godfrey and a thirteenth-round disqualification over Harry Wills, the big black heavyweight who had been waiting for years for a shot at Dempsey for the title. Sharkey admitted Harry was past his best. In 1927 he was too fast and sharp for Dempsey for six rounds in New York. Unfortunately for Sharkey, in the seventh Dempsey hit him low with a left hook. Sharkey amateurishly turned to the referee to complain and was knocked out by a left hook to the chin. Nobody had any sympathy. 'Protect yourself at all times' was often the referee's last line of advice then as it is today. Financially, it was a huge fight, the fourth of Tex Rickard's five million-dollar gates, with 75,000 people in Yankee Stadium paying $1,083,733.

He had the talent but he had a temper too, which hampered his progress. 'Half the time I didn't know what the hell I was doing anyway,' he told American writer Pete Heller in the early 1970s. 'If I got bad decisions I'd go in a tantrum, might look like I was crying. They called me crybaby, they called me the Lispin' Lith, the Garrulous Gob, the Weeping Warrior,' he said.

When he should have gone on to nail down a fight with Gene Tunney he could only draw with Tom Heeney, who challenged Tunney instead. In 1930, Sharkey was matched with Schmeling for the vacant title, but was disqualified for a low punch in the fourth round. A fifteen-round draw with Mickey Walker didn't help his case, but then he knew far too much for Carnera, and in June 1932 beat Schmeling over fifteen rounds to earn a split decision win that most felt was a bad verdict. Sharkey didn't. The referee, Gunboat Smith, said Schmeling finished strongly but had been out-boxed over the first two-thirds of the fight. It was twelve months before he defended – and then he lost in that upset to Carnera. Sharkey blamed ring rust for his sloppy, tentative performance and said he just didn't see the knockout blow. The criticism and the disappointment hurt – and points defeats by King Levinsky and Tommy Loughran persuaded him to retire for two years. In his comeback he won four fights then took a retirement payday against Joe Louis in New York in August 1936. Sharkey's ambition had gone. Louis took him out in three rounds.

Sharkey did a little refereeing, ran a couple of bars and when he and Dorothy moved to New Hampshire he became one of the leading fly-fishermen in the United States. His wife died in 1973, but he stayed on in the house, watched over as he grew old by his daughter. He had fourteen grandchildren and ten great-grandchildren.

When Jack Dempsey died in 1983, the old man smiled and said, 'So I finally beat the bastard...' He lived to be ninety-one, dying on 17 August 1994.

TOM SHARKEY

Born: 26 November 1873, Dundalk, Ireland
Died: 17 April 1953, San Francisco, aged 79
Height: 5ft 8½in   **Weight at peak:** 185lbs (13st 3lbs)
Fights: 54   **Won:** 41   **Lost:** 7   **Drawn:** 5   **No Decisions:** 2
KO percentage: 68
Rounds boxed: 267
World title fights: 1
Career span: 1893-1904 (11 years)
KO wins: 37
KO defeats: 3

A stocky former sailor with a ship tattooed on his barrel chest, Tom Sharkey fought James J. Jeffries over twenty-five rounds in the last world heavyweight title fight of the nineteenth century. In the Coney Island Athletic Club arena in Brooklyn, New York, Sharkey conceded 32lbs to the great champion but slogged it out with him all the way to the end. He didn't win, but he cemented his place in boxing history with a typically uncompromising performance.

A rough fighter in tough days, Sharkey fought Bob Fitzsimmons in the celebrated December 1896 contest refereed by Wyatt Earp, the lawman who had cleaned up Dodge City and Tombstone. In the eighth round Earp disqualified Fitzsimmons for an illegal punch with Sharkey having been knocked out. It looked like a perfectly good left hook to the chin, but Earp decided it was a foul – and that was that. He walked over to Sharkey, who was still on the canvas, and declared him the winner. Earp's legendary integrity was questioned, in particular as the purse had been $10,000 winner takes all. Fitzsimmons talked darkly of a sub-plot that demanded he not be allowed to win and years afterwards Bat Masterson, one of Earp's sidekicks, said the fight was fixed.

Before the first bell, incidentally, there was a delay when Earp was politely asked to take off his black frock coat and his gun-belt, including the famous .45 Special that had taken care of business at the OK Corral. He didn't want to, but complied.

Sharkey was from Dundalk, Ireland, born in November 1873. His first fights were when he was a twenty-year-old sailor in Hawaii in 1893. When he left the navy he settled in California. After his win over Fitzsimmons, Sharkey had a strange contest with Peter Maher in New York that was curtailed as a draw after seven rounds. They brawled on after the bell to end the round and in the melee Sailor Tom belted one of Maher's seconds as well. The police broke it up and everyone went home, or at least out into the New York night. The law enforcers also intervened in a fight between Sharkey and another rough, world-class heavy-weight, Joe Choynski, that had descended into a festival of fouls in San Francisco.

In March 1898, before Jeffries became world champion, Sharkey lost on points to him over twenty rounds in San Francisco. He knocked out Gus Ruhlin in one round, beat Corbett on a ninth-round foul, and put away the great middleweight Charles 'Kid' McCoy in the tenth. That brought him to the twenty-five-round championship battle with Jeffries, some film of which exists taken by a spectator near the back of the arena, who had a camera in a box.

Sharkey retired in 1904. In later years he and Jeffries were great friends. Tom died in April 1953, aged seventy-nine.

EARNIE SHAVERS

Born: 31 August 1945, Garland, Alabama
Height: 6ft 1in   **Weight at peak:** 211lbs (15st 1lb)
Fights: 88   **Won:** 73   **Lost:** 14   **Drawn:** 1
KO percentage: 76
Rounds boxed: 365
World title fights: 2
Career span: 1969-95 (26 years)
KO wins: 67
KO defeats: 7

One of the heaviest-hitting heavyweights of them all, Earnie Shavers came within one punch of knocking out Larry Holmes and winning the world title.

Shavers detonated his big right hand on the jaw of the defending World Boxing Council champion in the seventh round at Caesars Palace, Las Vegas, in September 1979. Holmes went down badly hurt, but got up, somehow avoided getting tagged again and clung on to reach the end of the round. Holmes admit-ted in his autobiography that in the interval both of his trainers, Richie Giachetti and Freddie Brown, broke ammonia capsules under his nose to bring his senses back. He went on to win in round eleven.

Two years earlier Shavers had chased and harried a thirty-five-year-old, worn out Muhammad Ali for fifteen rounds in Madison Square Garden. He thought he had won but lost a unanimous decision, 9-6 on the cards of judges Tony Castellano and Eva Shain, the first woman to judge a world title fight, and 9-5-1 according to referee Johnny LoBianco. Among the 14,613 crowd were Henry Kissinger and Joe Di Maggio. Afterwards Garden matchmaker Teddy Brenner said Ali would not box again in the great arena: 'I want you to remember him as he is now, not how he is likely to end up if he carries on boxing.' An exhausted Ali, who had exploited Shavers's slow feet to steal rounds rather than dominate them, said, 'I don't believe I want to fight any more. Wouldn't I be wise to get out of this? I'm so sore all over even the light hurts.' Shavers earned $300,000 to Ali's $3 million.

Shavers was born in Garland, Alabama, a hamlet off Route 65 between Montgomery and Mobile, the fifth of ten children of a farm worker. As a boy he picked cotton to help his mother and father and nine brothers and sisters. 'We didn't have many material things but we didn't have a rough childhood,' he said. 'We looked forward to walking through the woods in the fall and gathering hickory nuts or blackberries and at Christmas there was plenty of turkey and apple pie and corn cob fights in the barn.' They travelled north to Warren, Ohio, after one of their number was accused of stealing a mule. He played football at high school, was offered an athletics scholarship but took jobs as a railroad track-man, as a fireman in a steel foundry and as a splicer in a rubber factory. Married with a family, he didn't lace on a pair of boxing gloves until he was twenty-three, but won the National AAU heavyweight title in San Diego in April 1969 and turned pro. He, manager Blackie Genaro and trainer Frank Luca travelled where they could to get fights. He created waves in 1973 with first-round victories over Jimmy Young in Philadelphia and then Jimmy Ellis in New York. He was suddenly in the title frame, but in December 1973 Jerry Quarry stopped him in one round in the Garden, which, for a time, wrecked his confidence.

When he was knocked out in six by Ron Lyle in Denver in September 1975 it looked as if he would fall short of the top, but this family man with five daughters had won eight of his last nine when he boxed Ali. After that he was soundly outboxed by Holmes in an eliminator over twelve rounds, but then resurrected his career with a stunning, brutal first-round demolition of Ken Norton at the Las Vegas Hilton in March 1979. That earned him the rematch with Holmes, when he so nearly landed the championship.

He faded away slowly, retiring and coming back over the years until 1995, when he was fifty years old. James Tillis, who got off the floor to outspeed the thirty-seven-year-old Shavers, described the knockdown: 'He hit me, man, and knocked me face down... I was in the land of make-believe, I heard saxophones, trombones... I saw little blue rats, and they was smokin' cigars and drinkin' whisky.'

In the 1990s Shavers, by then remarried, settled in Liverpool, England, and was a popular addition to the British boxing scene, where he was in demand for after-dinner speaking engagements and public appearances.

ABE SIMON

Born: 1913, Richmond Hill, Long Island, New York
Died: 24 October 1969, Queens, New York, aged 56
Height: 6ft 4in   **Weight at peak:** 254-255lbs (18st 2lbs-18st 3lbs)
Fights: 49   **Won:** 38   **Lost:** 10   **Drawn:** 1
KO percentage: 55

Rounds boxed: 258
World title fights: 2
Career span: 1935-42 (7 years)
KO wins: 27
KO defeats: 4

Abe Simon, a strapping, big-jawed giant from Long Island, New York, gave Joe
Louis one of his most demanding heavyweight championship battles in March
1941. Nobody gave Simon much of a chance – the bookies offered 20-1 against
him winning and even that seemed miserly – not least because Louis was appear-
ing before 19,000 of his home-city fans in Detroit's Olympia Stadium. Even
worse, Simon was coming off a defeat – on points over ten rounds to Big Jim
Thompson in Baltimore seven weeks earlier.

    Simon's promoter Jimmy Johnston hired the old champion Jack Johnson, who
was not popular with the Louis camp, to help prepare Abe for his biggest night.
Johnston made a lot of noise, which helped sell tickets, but on the last day of sparring Simon broke a bone in his right hand. This helped turn him from slugger to
boxer and, after being knocked down by a right hand to the jaw in the opening
thirty seconds, surprisingly he used his left lead to keep the champion thinking
for round after round. At 6ft 4in and 250lbs, Simon was a big target but he held
himself together mentally and physically whenever the 'Brown Bomber' opened
up. Then, in the thirteenth, Louis dipped past Simon's jab and went to work.
Simon was down twice for nine, then one more big left hook sent him into the
ropes, where he grabbed the top strand and turned to stare out into the crowd.
Louis held back as referee Sam Hennessey jumped in to stop the fight eighty
seconds into the round. The fight, incidentally, had been scheduled for twenty
rounds and not the usual fifteen.

    He had done well enough to earn a rematch twelve months later. This time it
was in Madison Square Garden. By then America was at war, Louis had signed
up for the army and at a fund-raising event in the Garden he had told the crowd,
'We'll win – because we're on God's side.' Around $55,000 of the proceeds went
to the Army Relief Fund, Louis's sparring sessions drew crowds of around 2,000,
but he was without his trainer, Jack Blackburn, who was desperately ill with
pneumonia in a Chicago hospital.

    Before the opening bell, Under-Secretary of War Robert Patterson gave a
speech in which he praised Louis as a fine soldier and truly great champion. Once
the bout began it was one-sided. Simon was down in the second, saved by the bell
in the fifth and knocked out by the first punches of the sixth.

    Abe Simon was born in Richmond Hill, Long Island, and went to John Adams
High School in New York City, where he met the great champion Gene Tunney
at a prize-giving. They talked, Simon said he wanted to be a boxer and Tunney
gave him an introduction to his old manager and trainer Jimmy Bronson. His

football teacher at school had also tipped off a millionaire businessman, Jock Whitney, about Simon's physical potential and he signed him to a promotional contract. Whitney and a partner, Tom Hitchcock, gave Abe a wage of $35 a week to enable him to train full time. Simon marched through the preliminary ranks, knocking almost everyone out, but lost his unbeaten record to Max Baer's brother, Buddy. After winning the first two rounds, Simon walked into the path of an overhand right in the third and, although he stayed on his feet, was swaying help-lessly with his hands by his side as the referee saved him. After working his way back, Simon knocked out a twenty-six-year-old Jersey Joe Walcott in the sixth round in Newark, New Jersey.

The second Louis fight left him with pains in the head and back and, after an examination by a clinical neurologist, Dr S. Phillip Goodhart, Simon was per-suaded to retire by his wife Rita. Fortunately, he came to no lasting harm. He went on to act in several movies, including *On the Waterfront, Never Love a Stranger* and *Requiem for a Heavyweight*. He also earned a living in the public relations department of the Roosevelt Raceway, but at fifty-six he died of a heart attack in Meadowbank Hospital, New York, on 24 October 1969.

GUNBOAT SMITH

Born: 17 February 1887, Philadelphia
Real name: Edward Smyth
Died: 6 August 1974, Leesburg, Florida, aged 87
Height: 6ft 2in   **Weight at peak:** 185lbs (13st 3lbs)
Fights: 145   **Won:** 75   **Lost:** 43   **Drawn:** 13   **No Decisions:** 14
KO percentage: 27
Rounds boxed: 1,076
World title fights: 0
Career span: 1906-21 (15 years)
KO wins: 40
KO defeats: 12

Even if some of the more bigoted critics of the day called Gunboat Smith the heavyweight champion of the world, he knew that however much anybody else liked to believe otherwise, Jack Johnson was champion until he was beaten... and they never fought. Gunboat – a nickname he acquired in the US Navy when an orderly gave him a pair of oversized shoes – had a big punch in his rather wild right hand that he often seemed to swing from the floor.

Born Edward J. Smyth, he was raised in Philadelphia orphanages until he was nine when he was hired out as a farm labourer because he was big enough to do a day's work. At sixteen he walked out. 'All I had on was a shirt, pants and a cap. I walked right off the farm and I kept on walking,' he said. Later he worked in Erie, Pennsylvania, as a railroad fireman. At twenty-two he joined the navy, then on his release became a prize-fighter. He broke through to the top rank in 1913, when he had twenty-eight fights, including twenty-round decisions over Jess Willard and Frank Moran, a twelve-round points win over Sam Langford and knockouts of George Godfrey, Bombardier Billy Wells and Fireman Jim Flynn. Against Wells he was out-boxed and had his nose broken in the first round, then floored the Englishman three times in the second. Of Willard, he said, 'I had to look twice to see all of him he was so big.' After hitting Willard with his best shots in the first four rounds, he won a hard, bloody fight by staying away. Willard finished with his ear half ripped off.

On New Year's Day, 1914, he won the 'white heavyweight championship of the world' with a fifteenth-round knockout of the French-Canadian Arthur Pelkey in Daly City, California. Six months later he lost his claim when disqualified at London Olympia against Georges Carpentier. He landed a punch after the Frenchman had touched down on all fours. Gunboat was disgusted by the decision, saying he had tried to pull the blow and that it had only glanced off Carpentier's head. Three months later he was knocked out by Sam Langford and admits something left him then. He boxed on for another seven years, but was knocked out by Jack Dempsey in December 1918, and also lost inside the distance to Fred Fulton, Luis Angel Firpo, Harry Wills and Harry Greb.

In retirement he worked on Wall Street as a runner, acted in silent films, worked in security at Madison Square Garden and Yankee Stadium and refereed the second fight between Max Schmeling and Jack Sharkey, in 1932, when he awarded Sharkey a controversial verdict. He lived in Brooklyn. Gunboat died while visiting relatives in Leesburg, Florida, in 1974, aged eighty-seven. He left a widow, Helen, whom he had married just before the Carpentier fight sixty years before.

JAMES SMITH

Born: 3 April 1953, Magnolia, North Carolina
Height: 6ft 4in   **Weight at peak:** 230lbs (16st 6lbs)
Fights: 62   **Won:** 44   **Lost:** 17   **Drawn:** 1
KO percentage: 51
Rounds boxed: 370
World champion: 1986-87 (WBA)
World title fights: 3
Career span: 1981-99 (18 years)
KO wins: 32
KO defeats: 7

'Bonecrusher' Smith was one of the surprise champions of the 1980s. He was training for a routine fight with Mitchell Green when he got a call to box Tim Witherspoon for the WBA title in Madison Square Garden on 12 December

1986. Tony Tubbs, the original choice, had pulled out with injury. For Smith, in his early thirties with a career that was treading water, it was a godsend. His chances of success were multiplied by Witherspoon's backroom problems with promoter Don King. Witherspoon threatened to pull out of the fight and only went through with it after the WBA said he would be stripped of the belt if he didn't. Smith nailed him before he had settled, knocked him down three times and stopped him in two minutes twelve seconds of the opening round. According to the computer statistics, Witherspoon threw only eleven punches, which must make it one of the tamest defences of a championship ever made.

It set up a meeting between Smith and the new young WBC champion, twenty-year-old Mike Tyson. Smith's 6ft 4in, 230lb frame and obvious punching power made it interesting. Unfortunately, after talking a big fight, Bonecrusher chose to defend and grab his way through a laborious twelve-rounder. He did land a right hand in a surprise attack in the last half-minute that registered with Tyson, but it was far too little far too late. Tyson won 120-106 and 119-107 twice. Smith was jeered but was unrepentant. He said, 'I kept grabbing him to try to break his concentration. Sure I fought to survive. Wouldn't you?'

Smith was from Magnolia, South Carolina, a town of 2,500 without a single traffic light. He was the first college graduate to win a version of the heavyweight championship, having obtained a degree in business administration from Shaw University in Raleigh, North Carolina. During a spell in the US army from 1976-78 he joined the boxing team and earned his Bonecrusher nickname. 'I crushed a few bones, broke a few noses, fractured a few ribs,' he said. After that he worked as a prison guard and counsellor, married a teacher, raised two children and toyed with boxing. Eventually in 1981 he took a professional fight as a late substitute against the former amateur international James Broad and was stopped in four rounds.

By 1984, when he travelled to London to take on unbeaten Frank Bruno at Wembley, he was trained by former welter and middleweight champion Emile Griffith. Out-boxed by Bruno for nine rounds, he suddenly caught the Englishman with big punches in the last round and knocked him out. Six months later he was thrown in as a challenger to thirty-five-year-old Larry Holmes, who just knew more than he did, cut him up and stopped him in the twelfth round in Las Vegas.

After losing to Tyson he gradually faded out of contention. In London in 1994 he was not allowed to box Henry Akinwande because of a brain scan difficulty, but he lost on points to Axel Schulz in Germany and in a ridiculous spectacle boxed forty-eight-year-old Joe Bugner in a fight in Australia that was laughably billed for the vacant World Boxing Federation heavyweight championship. The fight had hardly began when Smith's shoulder came out.

He retired in 1999 after an equally ridiculous rematch with forty-nine-year-old Holmes. Bonecrusher was stopped in eight rounds.

JEWEY SMITH

Born: Believed to be 7 January 1884, Spitalfields, London
Real name: Possibly Joseph Smith
Died: details unavailable, believed to be in USA
Height: 5ft 8½in   **Weight at peak:** 185lbs (13st 3lbs)
Fights: Record unavailable
KO percentage: Unavailable
Rounds boxed: Unknown
World title fights: 1
Career span: Retired 1913
KO wins: Unknown
KO defeats: Unknown

The squat, red-haired Jewey Smith, whose origins are unclear but who is believed to have been South African, fought world champion Tommy Burns in Paris in April 1908. Other champions might be criticised for taking on soft challengers, but Burns topped them all. Only twenty-six days before he challenged Burns, the Parisian fans had seen Smith knocked out in three rounds by Sam McVey. Burns could have defended against McVey but instead selected Smith. In a 1924 book, his trainer Jack Goodwin said Smith's roadwork before he boxed Burns consisted of laps around a billiard hall – the inside, that is! His fee is also said to have been £25 plus expenses for two, including the boat and train from London, where he was living at the time.

Apparently after four rounds of carrying Smith, Burns knocked him down in the fifth. At that point a photographer's flash gun set light to some flags and streamers hanging from the balcony, someone yelled 'Fire!' and the fans in the Neuilly Bowling Palace dashed for the exits. Smith clambered to his feet and Burns knocked him out, jumped through the ropes and left the referee, Dr Phelan, to complete the formality of the count. By the time 'ten' had been tolled, the flames had died out without causing any problem, but Phelan, Smith and Goodwin were just about the only people left in the building!

RENALDO SNIPES

Born: 15 August 1956, Houston, Texas
Height: 6ft 2½in   **Weight at peak:** 216lbs (15st 6lbs)
Fights: 48   **Won:** 39   **Lost:** 8   **Drawn:** 1
KO percentage: 45
Rounds boxed: 335
World title fights: 1
Career span: 1978-93 (15 years)
KO wins: 22
KO defeats: 2

When Larry Holmes walked into the path of a right hand from unfancied challenger Renaldo Snipes in the seventh round of what up to that point had been a fairly routine defence of the World Boxing Council belt, boxing history stood still, which is more than can be said for Holmes, who crashed down in a heap. He got up at six, lurched into a corner and hit his head on the post, turned himself around and was allowed to go on by referee Rudy Ortega. Snipes went for the finish but Holmes avoided his attempts to finish it, fought back and took over again.

Referee Ortega's decision to stop the fight in the eleventh, with Snipes taking punches but not anywhere near as hurt as Holmes had been, was contentious. Holmes admitted he was relieved – Snipes had been seen as a warm-up for the hugely lucrative fight with Gerry Cooney.

Out of the ring Snipes was a smart, intelligent man, born in Houston and living in Yonkers, New York. He had won twenty-two in a row by the time he challenged Holmes, including decisions over Eddie Mustafa Muhammad and, controversially, Gerrie Coetzee. After losing to Holmes, he was held to a draw by Scott Frank in Atlantic City and then dropped out of contention by losing four of his next five. His career drifted on until 1993 when he was stopped in the tenth round by the unbeaten Cuban Jorge Luis Gonzalez.

Snipes was rarely heard of in boxing circles after that but, following the World Trade Center disaster of 11 September 2001, he was among the volunteers who spent the following days manning the relief zones, serving food and helping workers.

LEON SPINKS

Born: 11 July 1953, St Louis, Missouri
Height: 6ft 1in   **Weight at peak:** 197lbs (14st 1lb)
Fights: 46   Won: 26   Lost: 17   Drawn: 3
KO percentage: 30
Rounds boxed: 323
World champion: 1978
World title fights: 3
Career span: 1977-95 (18 years)
KO wins: 14
KO defeats: 9

Too much happened to Leon Spinks too soon... but at least it happened – and he's there in the history books as a man who won the world title by dethroning Muhammad Ali in Las Vegas in February 1978. After the bruising fifteen-rounder against Earnie Shavers the previous September, it seemed Ali's team knew he needed nursing, that the legs that had already produced miracles nobody had the right to expect had almost run out of miles. Even his most devoted fans knew he should have retired after the ferocious third fight with Joe Frazier in Manila in October 1975. Even given Ali's decline, a match with Spinks, who had won the Olympic light-heavyweight gold medal in Montreal in 1976 and had a professional record of six wins and a draw, seemed to be reducing the championship to a trinket.

Leon had promise, of course, but a man who could only draw with Minnesota heavyweight Scott LeDoux and who needed the full ten rounds to beat the mediocre Italian Alfio Righetti surely had no place in a world championship contest? Spinks didn't care about that. The twenty-four-year-old from the poverty-racked St Louis housing projects did nothing exceptional, but kept the pressure going. He was bright enough to know even a thirty-six-year-old Ali would out-box him if he stood off, and so he worked hard – and harder still. Ali, as he had done for years, fought in bursts. His power had gone and he needed all of his showmanship to convince judges that he was still working hard enough to win rounds. Now against a young, persistent man-child in Spinks, he grew wearier than ever.

It wasn't a spectacular fight, but neither was it a bad one. The closeness of it kept it interesting. Would the judges somehow baulk at giving the championship to a novice? Would Ali's charisma persuade them to slide off the fence on his side? After fifteen rounds judge Art Lurie saw it 143-142 Ali, but Harold Buck and Lou Tabat were in no doubt. They scored for Spinks 144-141, 145-140, respectively – that's 9-6 and 10-5 in rounds.

Spinks, who weighed only 3lbs when he was born prematurely, was raised by his mother Kay, who read to her seven children every night from the Bible. She fed them with the help of a monthly welfare cheque. As a child Leon often fainted because of low blood pressure. Whereas most boys in the Pruitt-Igoe housing project got involved in street crimes, Leon and his brother Michael were under lock and key unless they were at school. Eventually they took to boxing. Sometimes, too, they fought each other. 'We fought like madmen, almost to kill,' said Michael. 'We were always mad about something. I thought I was the toughest in the house... I thought I was real good, then one day my sister busted my nose!' Leon said, 'I was the nicest kid on the block. It was a mean block but I was the nicest kid on it.'

Their personalities were contrasting: Leon was extrovert, Michael introvert. Leon spoke as the words came, Michael thought about everything. And so it was in the ring: Leon the spontaneous, combustible talent, Michael the methodical, slow burner. It doesn't take a genius to work out that it was always going to be Leon who would rise like a comet and pass just as fast, while Michael would achieve his successes more slowly and enjoy them for longer. Physically, Leon was light – only a bantamweight when he began boxing in the Capri Gym at the age of fourteen – but he learned well enough to handle himself on the street. His education was minimal and he was virtually illiterate when he joined the US Marines. 'All my friends were in jail or dead and I knew I'd end up the same way, so I joined the marines,' he said. 'I worked in supplies.' After a bronze in the 1974 world championships and a silver at the Pan-American Games, he won the light-heavyweight gold in the Montreal Olympics, beating the Cuban favourite Sixto Soria on a third-round stoppage in he final. Michael was gold medallist at middleweight.

Bob Arum paid Spinks $10,000 for his pro debut in Las Vegas in January 1977, and thirteen months later he was the champion of the world. 'I don't think this whole thing seemed real to me until a couple of days later,' he said. 'I was alone in the hotel room... I had beaten one of the great fighters of all time. I got so filled up, I began to cry. I bawled and I couldn't stop.' By the time he beat Ali, Spinks was already a father of two boys. Leon had been world champion for five days when his third son, Cory, was born (Cory would go on to win the world welterweight title in 2003). He returned to St Louis – and the party began. Years later, he said he was too naive in expecting his own people to be glad for him. He didn't understand he would be sacrificed on a huge bonfire of jealousy. He accepted gifts. It seemed every time he got into his car, he had a run-in with the police. He drove up a one-way street the wrong way. He had no licence. His photo was in the local paper... in handcuffs. In between the two fights the World Boxing Council stripped Spinks for agreeing to the Ali rematch rather than fighting Ken Norton – if anyone deserved the courtesy of a return it was Ali. It was a bizarre, stupid decision, which not only made the WBC look foolish but divided the championship and therefore did the sport a disservice.

The return in the vast Superdome in New Orleans drew a huge crowd of 63,350 and smashed the record for gate receipts at a heavyweight championship that had stood since the return between Gene Tunney and Jack Dempsey in Chicago in 1927. Ali and Spinks grossed $4,806,675. This time Ali danced, his legs didn't fail him, and Spinks, in nowhere near as good shape as he had been just seven months before, trailed after the great man, mostly hitting thin air. More than anything, Spinks seemed confused. After fifteen rounds, Ali had won by a long way: 10-4-1 twice and 11-4 on the judges' cards. Angelo Dundee responded to suggestions that it had been a sloppy fight by beaming, 'It was beautifully sloppy. It was gorgeous sloppy, wonderful sloppy.' In the Spinks corner, it was chaos. Sam Solomon told George Benton they would alternate with Michael Spinks in giving Leon advice. After five rounds Benton walked out in disgust. Art Rendon, who had worked with Spinks in the Marines, joined in. At one point, even his accountant Marshall Warren had his say. Before the fight, according to *Sports Illustrated*, they had left Leon's protective cup in the hotel room. Solomon asked someone to go and fetch it, and the man came back with a drinking cup. They had to borrow one from an undercard fighter.

Of his two purses for the Ali fights, $320,000 for the first and $3.75 million for the second, Spinks paid an estranged but still contracted manager Mitt Barnes more than $900,000.

It was all over. In his next fight Spinks was blown away in one round by Gerrie Coetzee in Monte Carlo. After working his way back he was thrown to WBC champion Larry Holmes in Detroit in June 1981 and was outclassed in three. He gave the cruiserweight division a try but the WBA champion Dwight Muhammad Qawi trounced him in six rounds in Reno in March 1986. Two years later Leon's licence was taken away after a pathetic first-round defeat by Tony Morrison, a club fighter, in Connecticut. He returned to the ring in 1991 and was eventually persuaded to stop after another defeat in St Louis in December 1995, when he was forty-two years old.

MICHAEL SPINKS

Born: 13 July 1956, St Louis, Missouri
Height: 6ft 2½in   **Weight at peak:** 200lbs (14st 4lbs)
Fights: 32   **Won:** 31   **Lost:** 1
KO percentage: 65
Rounds boxed: 225
World champion: 1985-86
World title fights: 4
Career span: 1977-88 (11 years)
KO wins: 21
KO defeats: 1

Michael Spinks won the Olympic middleweight gold medal in Montreal in 1976, put his professional career on the back burner for a while as brother Leon shot to fame then imploded, then won the WBA light-heavyweight title with a fifteen-round decision over Eddie Mustafa Muhammad in Las Vegas in 1981. He unified the division two years later by out-pointing Dwight Muhammad Qawi in Atlantic City and won a total of eleven world 175lbs championship bouts before moving up in September 1985 to challenge Larry Holmes for the heavyweight crown. Holmes had won forty-eight in a row – and a win over Spinks would have equalled the unbeaten run of Rocky Marciano, who won his forty-ninth fight, against Archie Moore, forty years before to the day.

Spinks ruined the celebrations with a unanimous fifteen-round decision at the Riviera Hotel in Las Vegas, a verdict that left Holmes fuming but made Spinks the IBF champion. 'I don't want to be arrogant or disrespectful,' said Michael. 'Larry Holmes was a great heavyweight champion... I didn't take the fight to be another number on Larry's list.'

There had to be a rematch – and in April 1986 Holmes's frustration increased as Spinks won a fifteen-round split decision at the Las Vegas Hilton. Most agreed with an extremely aggrieved Holmes that he was unlucky. Spinks had a jerky style and threw long punches from unexpected angles but could fight. As a light-heavyweight his right hand was powerful – publicists called it the 'Spinks Jinx'

– though against Holmes it was his twisting, awkward technique that worked for him. Holmes admitted in the first fight he didn't throw enough right hands but felt his jab had won it, but Harold Lederman, Dave Moretti and Larry Wallace all had Spinks in front. Spinks grossed $2 million for the second fight with Holmes, then cashed in with comfortable wins over Steffen Tangstad and Gerry Cooney, but was stripped of the IBF belt for taking the latter fight against the instructions of the sanctioning body, who wanted him to box Tony Tucker. Amazingly, Spinks was an underdog against Cooney. Even Michael's mother didn't seem to think he could win. Before the fight she yelled at promoter Ronald 'Butch' Lewis that she would sue him if her son was seriously injured. He destroyed Cooney with a sustained, accurate barrage, including two knockdowns, in round five.

Spinks was exiled, unrecognised by any of the governing bodies, but Lewis knew they only had to wait to cash in. Eventually, after Mike Tyson had cleaned up the division, Spinks became the logical opponent. And in June 1988 Tyson produced perhaps his most intimidating performance of them all, marauding through Spinks in only ninety-one seconds. Spinks insisted he had not been afraid, but he fought as if he was. Tyson put him down for the first time in his career, then laid him out flat on his back with a short, devastating right hand. The emotional hurt was tempered by the fact that by the time he had paid everyone off it was estimated he took home around $5 million – and he did not box again.

As a boy Michael had been under Leon's shadow: 'Leon was always winning, I was always losing. He had pride in what he was doing. It made me proud too.' Now he had already seen his elder brother go on too long – and blow his money. Michael had also had a bellyful of adversity, including the death of his fiancée, Sandy, with whom he had a daughter, Michelle. He walked away to take care of the rest of his life.

BILL SQUIRES

Born: 25 June 1879, Narrabri, New South Wales, Australia
Died: 1 September 1962, aged 83
Height: 5ft 10½in   **Weight at peak:** 183lbs (13st 1lb)
Fights: 33   **Won:** 20   **Lost:** 11   **Drawn:** 0   **No Decisions:** 2
KO percentage: 45
Rounds boxed: 198
World title fights: 3
Career span: 1902-16 (14 years)
KO wins: 15
KO defeats: 10

Australian heavyweight 'Boshter' Bill Squires was knocked out three times by Tommy Burns in world title fights. Squires was a man of few words. When, on his way up, a writer asked him a complicated question about his ring technique, he looked blankly at him and said, 'I just 'its 'em.' After losing in one round to Burns in their first fight in Colma, California, on 4 July 1907, he told the gathered ranks of pressmen, 'I got a bloody good lickin' and I'm goin' 'ome.' Squires was a big puncher with a glass jaw. He had slow feet and a leaky defence.

When they boxed for the second time in Paris in June 1908, Squires had just knocked out the blubbery Irishman Jem Roche in Dublin. He believed in himself again. In the fourth round Boshter Bill hurt Burns badly and the champion was saved by the bell. However, Burns came back, took over and in the eighth left Squires unconscious for ten minutes. A supreme optimist, Squires declared himself delighted with his improvement on their first fight and said, 'I'm startin' to feel like my old self...'

Two months later they boxed again in Sydney as promoter Hugh D. McIntosh built up Burns' defence in Rushcutter's Bay against Jack Johnson, which would take place in December 1908. In front of 16,000 fans, the biggest crowd on record for a prize-fight in Australia up to that time, McIntosh is said to have asked Burns to carry Squires. After ten rounds the Australian was actually ahead on points, but then Burns opened up and in the thirteenth an exhausted Squires was down and out.

Boshter Bill was born on a sheep station at Edgeroi near Narrabri in New South Wales in 1879. He was a sheep shearer, timber cutter, cook and railway labourer. He also boxed and eventually he impressed Melbourne racetrack owner John Wren enough to be signed to a contract. Squires won the Australian title with a third-round knockout of Tim Murphy in April 1906. Six months later, on the morning of the Melbourne Cup and at the Ascot track, about 15,000 people saw Squires beat Peter Kling in three. Before he set sail to fight Burns for the first time, he took forty-six seconds to knock out another Australian title challenger, Mike Williams. After losing that first fight to Burns, and even though he was given those two other chances, Squires fell apart. He lost nine of his next ten.

In the late 1940s Squires took an interest in the world-class middleweight Dave Sands, who was killed in a car crash at the height of his fame. Old Boshter lived to be eighty-two. He died on 1 September 1962.

RON STANDER

Born: 17 October 1944, Fort Jackson, South Carolina
Height: 5ft 11in   **Weight at peak:** 218lbs (15st 8lbs)
Fights: 61   **Won:** 37   **Lost:** 21   **Drawn:** 3
KO percentage: 45
Rounds boxed: 347
World title fights: 1
Career span: 1969-82 (13 years)
KO wins: 28
KO defeats: 9

A rugged, brawling heavyweight from Omaha, Nebraska, Ron Stander gave world heavyweight champion Joe Frazier an honest fight before losing after four rounds in May 1972. At the time it was ridiculed as a mismatch, and it was, but the film shows that Stander could fight a little bit better than most and had a huge heart as well as a stout chin. Sure, Frazier was well below his best – and would lose the title in his next fight to George Foreman, but Stander didn't come out of the experience that badly. Eight years on, Stander remembered the Frazier fight with a grin. 'I hit him with a hell of a right hand,' he said. 'I stepped back and waited for him to fall... only he never did.'

Stander was a popular, honest fighter, and 9,863 of his Nebraska fans turned out in the Omaha Civic Auditorium to see him try to do the 'impossible'. He wasn't intimidated: he winked at Frazier as referee Zach Clayton went through the preliminaries. That big right hand he landed was in the first round. Frazier then went about the grim task of chopping Stander to pieces. Ron refused to quit, refused to go down, but his eyes were cut so badly he needed seventeen stitches, his nose was broken and one eye was shut. The doctor, Jack Lewis, stopped it. 'I'm sorry I let people down,' he said. 'I couldn't see very good in that last round. I hope everybody realises that.' The next day his wife's view of the fight was published on the wires. 'You don't take a Volkswagen into the Indianapolis 500 unless you know a shortcut,' said Darlene Stander. They split up soon after.

Ron began boxing in 1967 when he wandered into the Foxhole Bar in Omaha, where they had a 12ft boxing ring in a back room. He watched the fighters train, then said he would like to do that too. Once trainer Leonard Hawkins sorted out his balance and gave him the basics, he slugged his way to the 1969 National Golden Gloves final. In only his tenth pro fight he won a toe-to-toe war with Earnie Shavers on a fifth-round stoppage – and you didn't beat Shavers if you couldn't handle yourself. Manuel Ramos, who had boxed Frazier for the New York version of the title, spoiled his 100 per cent record by holding him to a draw over ten rounds in Omaha in September 1970, but in April 1971 he out-fought the veteran Thad Spencer, who at one time looked championship material. When he challenged Frazier, he was still training at the Foxhole. He was persuaded to go to Boston for better sparring but one of them, Joe Young, broke his nose. Frazier had been tempted to Omaha with a $250,000 guarantee and $10,000 of the gate receipts going to Smokin' Joe's favourite charity, the fight against sickle-cell anaemia. Stander's nose went in round two. His trainer told him, 'Don't worry. Your nose is a long way from your heart.' Stander was hurt by the lack of respect he got for his effort, but lost two out of three in 1973: he admits he was depressed, with his marriage gone and two children to see when he could.

Stander bought a bar in Council Bluffs, the town where he lived just across the Iowa stateline from Omaha, sold it after three years and took jobs in construction. He drove a truck. He slid into the role of journeyman, though he did demolish Terry Daniels, who had boxed Frazier before him, in one round in Omaha in

November 1975. 'The press had always linked us together, said neither of us ever deserved a shot at Frazier,' he said. 'I figured that if I whipped Daniels, they'd realise I was better than him.' Then the defeats began to pile up: Scott LeDoux beat him on points, Ken Norton beat him in five, Gerrie Coetzee in eight, Boone Kirkman in seven. By the late 1970s he wasn't bothering to train, picking up pay-days where he could to pay his bills.

After retiring, he refereed some local bouts and was on the books of the International Boxing Federation as a judge. He remarried, had two more children and settled into a steady day job.

YOUNG STRIBLING

Born: 26 December 1904, Bainbridge, Georgia
Full name: William Lawrence Stribling
Died: 3 October 1933, Macon, Georgia, aged 28
Height: 6ft 1in   **Weight at peak:** 185lbs (13st 3lbs)
Fights: 288   **Won:** 233   **Lost:** 14   **Drawn:** 15   **No Decisions:** 26
KO percentage: 44
Rounds boxed: 2,043
World title fights: (heavyweight) 1
Career span: 1921-33 (12 years)
KO wins: 127
KO defeats: 1

Young Stribling, the strapping, handsome slugger known as the Georgia Peach, had something of the comic strip hero about him: managed by his father, trained by his mother, he was a professional fighter at sixteen, fought his way to a world title shot, had an incredible 288 fights in a dozen years – and was dead at twenty-eight, leaving a widow and a newborn child. Ed Danforth, a tremendous sports writer from the American South who knew him well, said, 'He did not under-stand fear at all. It just did not exist in his world. Whether he was fighting with gloves, riding a motorcycle, driving his racing automobile or flying a plane, he was utterly confident.'

From Macon, Georgia, Stribling began his paid career as a featherweight, fighting mostly in Macon and Atlanta. In his debut year, 1921, he had twenty-five fights. The following year he had thirty-four! And so it went on, almost without respite. Obviously Stribling learned how to defend himself, could hold and spoil when he needed to and was seemingly impervious to punish-ment when he did have to take it. Mostly, though, he dished it out. In October 1923, when he was still only eighteen, he seemed to have won the world light-heavyweight title against Mike McTigue in Columbus, Georgia. After their ten-round bout referee Harry Ertle appeared to give Stribling the decision, but an hour later said the intimidating atmosphere in the arena forced him to do that. He claimed his life had been threatened – and even said the promoter, one Major John Paul Jones, who was supposed to be a pillar of the community, told him he was being watched wherever he went. Ertle, once safe, altered his verdict to a draw. Stribling challenged McTigue again in Newark in March 1924 but the twelve-round contest ended in a No Decision under the New Jersey rules, and once again the peripatetic Georgia Peach shrugged his shoulders and took to the road. Less than a fortnight later he fought and won in Wisconsin. In March 1925 Stribling scored a ten-round decision over the stylish and elusive Tommy Loughran in San Francisco. He fought his way to another crack at the light-heavyweight championship in June 1926. By then it was held by Paul Berlanbach. After fifteen rounds in Yankee Stadium, New York, Stribling came up on the short end of the decision again, fading down the stretch.

Stribling was involved in a bizarre bout in Portland, Oregon, when opponent Harry Dillon retired in his corner after seven rounds. The referee ignored that and forced poor Dillon to box on. Stribling carried him the rest of the way. By 1928 he was a heavyweight – and the great promoter, Tex Rickard, matched him with Jack Sharkey in a title eliminator in Miami in February 1929. Rickard died of peritonitis a few weeks before the fight. Stribling lost on points after knocking the future champion down in the first round and hurting him in the fourth. At the end of 1929 Stribling enjoyed a brief European tour, which included two allegedly fixed fights with Primo Carnera. Carnera was disqualified in the first, Stribling in the return.

He eventually challenged Max Schmeling for the world heavyweight title in the Municipal Stadium, Cleveland, in July 1931. Stribling fought hard and well, but the impressive German wore him down, knocked him over with a vicious right hand and stopped him with only fourteen seconds left in the fifteenth and final round.

His last fight was the first allowed officially by law in Houston in September 1933 when he out-pointed Maxie Rosenbloom, the reigning world light-heavyweight champion, in a ten-round over-the-weight match that drew more than 10,000 fans. Nine days later the *Macon Telegraph* carried photographs of the city's favourite sporting son holding up his newborn third child, Guerry Boone Stribling. The same day Stribling crashed his motorbike three miles outside the Macon town limits on the Forsyth Road on the way home after a round of golf. He was ferried in a passing milk truck to the same hospital that accommodated his wife and child. His ankle was amputated. Telegrams of encouragement poured in – and he refused to sleep, telling doctors, 'If I've got to face this thing, I want to face it with my eyes open.' He died as the sun rose on 3 October 1933.

JOHN L. SULLIVAN

Born: 15 October 1858, Roxbury, Massachusetts
Full name: John Lawrence Sullivan
Died: 2 February 1918, Abingdon, Massachusetts, aged 59
Height: 5ft 10½in   **Weight at peak:** 182lbs (13st)
Fights: 44   **Won:** 40   **Lost:** 1   **Drawn:** 3
KO percentage: 79
Rounds boxed: 267
World title fights: 1 (gloves)
Career span: 1879-92 (13 years)
KO wins: 35
KO defeats: 1

They had to dynamite the frozen ground in order to bury John L. Sullivan in Massachusetts in February 1918 – and how the Boston Strong Boy would have loved that! Throughout his extraordinary life, Sullivan liked to provide a show, whether it be showering the adoring crowds with dollar bills from an upstairs hotel room, offering to 'lick any sonofabitch in the house' while carousing, or establishing his extravagant reputation as the saviour of boxing in the nineteenth century. Before Sullivan came along, prize-fighting was a shambolic, shadowy sport populated by ne'er-do-wells and colourless 'professors' of the art and craft. It grabbed a headline or two only when somebody died or was maimed. With the advent of Sullivan, the son of Irish immigrants born in Roxbury, Massachusetts, all that changed. His fights captured the public imagination and, with a combination of brilliance and bluster, he emerged as one of the great sportsmen of the century. Sullivan's parents, of course, wanted something different for him, something altogether quieter, more respectable: his mother would have liked it particularly if he had become a priest!

At twenty-three, he was bare-knuckle heavyweight champion of the world after a savage, one-sided win over Paddy Ryan in Mississippi City in February 1892. Ryan, who was knocked out in nine rounds lasting only ten minutes, said when Sullivan hit him with the first big punch 'it felt as if a telegraph pole had been shoved against me sideways'. He was fast, he knew instinctively how to fight and as the great ones do he assimilated technical niceties along the way. The popular modern image is of Sullivan as a slow, unsubtle brawler but that does not fit the facts. The man was unbeatable in his prime – and the rest of the boxing world knew it.

The sensitivity of the laws of the day made prize-fighting promotions difficult to organise in the 1880s and, particularly in New York and its surrounds, Sullivan had to be content with diluted 'exhibitions' under the humourless eye of the local law-enforcers. Nevertheless, he made a point every so often, as when a New Zealand Maori, Herbert Slade, was considered a threat. Sullivan intimidated him and smashed him to defeat in three rounds before a 10,000 crowd in Madison Square Garden, New York. These were the cross-over years when the 'gloved' championship did not exist but was becoming acknowledged as the acceptable alternative to the bare-knuckle fights to the finish.

Paddy Ryan, short of cash, asked Sullivan to give him work as a sparring partner and a couple of paydays as an opponent. John L. magnanimously obliged – and beat him in a round in New York in 1885 and in three in San Francisco in 1886. As his drinking got the better of him he was accused of anti-social behaviour – and domestic violence – and editors, instead of applauding, sharpened their pencils. There were still plenty of back-slappers ready to shake his hand and accept his generosity at the bar, but his fortunes had turned. He was deeply affected by the death of his two-year-old son, then he broke his arm in a six-round 'nothing' fight with Patsy Cardiff. In March 1888 he defended his title against the English middleweight Charlie Mitchell in a bare-knuckle contest in the teeming rain in fields near Chantilly, north of Paris, on ground owned by Baron Rothschild. After thirty-nine inconclusive rounds spread over more than three hours they were barely able to stand because of the conditions and agreed to call it a draw. When he boxed, again in a bare-knuckle contest, the honest family man Jake Kilrain, there were many who wished him beaten. That fight on 8 July 1889, was the last of the great bare-knuckle contests.

The fight followers assembled in New Orleans and caught a train that eventually stopped in Mississippi on land owned by a gentleman named Colonel Charles W. Rich. They called the place after him – Richburg. In stifling heat Sullivan and Kilrain battled for seventy-five rounds. Sullivan vomited but fought on. Kilrain drank whisky to numb the pain between rounds, which cannot have helped him as he began to dehydrate – and eventually Kilrain's head rolled on his shoulders. A doctor warned his corner that if they sent him up for round seventy-six he would die, and so the sponge was tossed up in surrender.

Sullivan refused to box the great black boxer Peter Jackson, took to the stage, and was out of the ring for more than three years. When he came back against James J. Corbett, a former bank clerk from San Francisco, in New Orleans in September 1892 he was almost thirty-four, hog fat and greying at the temples. Corbett toyed with him, then knocked him out in round twenty-one. 'Surely everybody will be heartily thankful that John L. Sullivan has met his match at last,' thundered the leader writer for the *Daily Chronicle*. 'He is a bully of the worst kind.'

Sullivan, his ring career ended, gave up alcohol, divorced his long-estranged wife and remarried, and was declared bankrupt. Occasionally he wrote, or at least dictated to ghost writers, pieces for newspapers on major fights, such as the 1910 heavyweight championship contest in Reno between Jack Johnson and Jim Jeffries. He died in Abingdon, Massachusetts, at fifty-nine.

T

STEFFEN TANGSTAD

Born: 22 June 1959, Toensberg, Norway
Height: 6ft 2in   **Weight at peak:** 215lbs (15st 5lbs)
Fights: 28   **Won:** 24   **Lost:** 2   **Drawn:** 2
KO percentage: 50
Rounds boxed: 156
World title fights: 1
Career span: 1980-86 (6 years)
KO wins: 14
KO defeats: 2

A capable, organised Norwegian, Steffen Tangstad held the European title twice in the 1980s and capped his career by challenging Michael Spinks for the IBF heavyweight title in 1986. He was rescued in the fourth round by referee Richard Steele and, like so many fighters who have lost relatively quickly on the biggest night of their careers, believed the stoppage premature. That said, he walked away from the sport at the age of twenty-seven and went on to a successful career as a television executive in Scandinavia.

JOHN TATE

Born: 29 January 1955, Marion County, Arkansas
Died: 9 April 1998, Tennessee, aged 43
Height: 6ft 4in   **Weight at peak:** 240lbs (17st 2lbs)
Fights: 37   **Won:** 34   **Lost:** 3
KO percentage: 62
Rounds boxed: 198
World champion: 1979-80 (WBA)
World title fights: 2
Career span: 1977-88 (11 years)
KO wins: 23
KO defeats: 2

Big John Tate could have been one of the dreamers in a Steinbeck novel of rural America, a simple, uneducated giant of a man, who could fight but whose uncomplicated nature was always likely to leave him vulnerable.

Tate succeeded Muhammad Ali as World Boxing Association champion in

October 1979 – Ali retired after regaining the championship from Leon Spinks – and to do it boxed Gerrie Coetzee in Pretoria, ignoring the international ostracisation of the South Africans because of the Apartheid regime.

He was born in Marion City, Arkansas, the second of eleven children. His parents divorced when he was young, shortly after they had moved to West Memphis, on the Arkansas bank of the Mississippi. While in hospital recovering from a stab wound to a shoulder, Tate was persuaded by a local minister to go to a gym. Months later he reached the 1975 National Golden Gloves final in Knoxville, stayed on and made the city his home. For a while he lived in a room not much bigger than a cupboard at the gym of manager Jerry 'Ace' Miller and earned a living driving a truck. A year later he made it to the Montreal Olympics but was demolished in the first round of the semi-final by the Cuban genius Teofilo Stevenson.

The fight that brought his professional career alive was a one-round stoppage of Duane Bobick, the red-haired puncher from Minnesota who had represented the USA in the 1972 Olympics. From there Tate took his first trip to South Africa, to Mmbatho, in June 1979 where he stopped the former policeman Kallie Knoetze in eight rounds before a packed house of 40,000 fans in the Independence Stadium. The *Transvaal Post* celebrated Tate's win with an editorial entitled 'Thank You, Big John'. Tate showed how little he knew of the realities of life in the republic and told the *Johannesburg Citizen*, 'I'd like to have a South African home and fight here.'

He went back to Tennessee for a month, then returned to a luxury camp outside Johannesburg to prepare for his battle for the vacant WBA crown with Gerrie Coetzee who, unlike Knoetze, was popular with black South Africans. This time it was staged before a vast, predominantly white 81,000 crowd including Prime Minister P.W. Botha at the Loftus Versfeld Stadium in Pretoria. It was a dull fight, but Tate outworked Coetzee to win a unanimous fifteen-round decision: 147-142, 148-145, 147-144. Even before the announcement the South Africans, Botha included, were filing out of the stadium without waiting to applaud the winner. Twenty miles away in Soweto, people were dancing in the street the moment they heard the result. Leslie Sehume, a journalist, said, 'It was complete bedlam. The celebrations went on all night but fortunately were very good-humoured. There was no violence or vandalism and nobody got hurt.'

The African Boxing Union, in a statement from the Zambian capital Lusaka, condemned the fight and said they no longer recognised the WBA. President Joseph Fofe said, 'We in Africa do not like a man who goes to South Africa. And anybody who shakes hands with a South African in sport is also a racist.'

Tate took the WBA title home to Knoxville for his first defence against Mike Weaver in March 1980. Weaver wrecked the party by knocking him out with only forty-five seconds left in the fifteenth round. Going into that last session, Tate was in front on all three scorecards by between three and five points. He only had to stand up to win. He couldn't.

Three months later in Montreal, on the undercard of the first epic battle between Ray Leonard and Roberto Duran, Tate lost on a ninth-round knockout to Trevor Berbick. He returned to Tennessee and drifted along on the road-to-nowhere circuit. His last appearance was when he travelled to London in March 1988 and boxed at York Hall, Bethnal Green, where the British heavyweight Noel Quarless out-pointed him in a close fight over ten rounds. Later he spent time in jail for petty theft and minor assault. He was more or less a down-and-out. When he died following a car crash at the age of forty-three on a Tennessee highway in April 1998 cocaine was found in his system. The postmortem revealed he had died of a stroke caused by a tumour at the base of his skull.

ERNIE TERRELL

Born: 4 April 1939, Inverness, Mississippi
Height: 6ft 6in   **Weight at peak:** 206-212lbs (14st 10lbs-15st 2lbs)
Fights: 55   **Won:** 46   **Lost:** 9
KO percentage: 38
Rounds boxed: 376
World champion: 1965-67 (WBA)
World title fights: 1
Career span: 1957-73 (16 years)
KO wins: 21
KO defeats: 2

Ernie Terrell was the victim of one of Muhammad Ali's cruellest performances. For almost the whole of their one-sided fifteen-round fight in the gigantic Houston Astrodome in February 1967, Ali taunted and belittled the 6ft 6in contender from Chicago. Terrell's 'crime' was both personal and professional: he insisted on calling Ali by his old 'Christian slave' name Cassius Clay – and had been recognised as champion by the World Boxing Association for almost two years (The WBA had refused to recognise the Ali-Liston rematch). By defeating him, Ali removed any opposition, however eccentric, to his reputation as the best heavyweight of his generation.

The truth about the Terrell fight has tended to be obscured by the general mood of sentimentality towards Ali that began with his political exile, was carried on by the change in American public opinion over the Vietnam War and extended by the 'romance' of his performances against George Foreman, Joe Frazier and, in their second fight, Leon Spinks. The truth is that, for many palates, Ali went too far in the Terrell fight. Verbal abuse could and should have been stamped out by Harry Kessler, the so-called 'millionaire referee', but way beyond that Ali fouled Terrell with a viciousness that should not be forgotten, nor excused.

The *Daily Express* in London blasted the champion with the headline 'Shameful, Clay – this was inhuman', while the London *Evening Standard's* front-page headline read 'Ugly, Venomous and Sickening'. Terrell did his share of rabbit-punching, mauling and wrestling – but Ali was way out of order when he grabbed Terrell in a headlock and rubbed his eye against the top rope. He used the thumb in round six and choked him in the clinches. Ali also spat at Terrell's feet and sneered at him, 'What's my name?' British writer Peter Wilson said Kessler 'failed in almost every function that I think constitutes the critical duty of a responsible official. He never checked Clay, who for at least half the fight was taunting, jeering, sneering, reviling and blackguarding the man he had sworn to torture and humiliate. Above all, he failed to stop a fight that was no longer a contest or a sporting occasion after the end of the eleventh round.'

In the thirteenth round Ali landed thirty punches without reply, but still Kessler stood back. At the end Kessler and judge Ernie Taylor scored 148-137 Ali, and judge Jimmy Webb saw it 148-133. Terrell, who finished with both eyes swollen virtually shut and a long cut over his right eye, said, 'Clay sure fights dirty.' Terrell was examined by a Houston eye specialist and flown to a Philadelphia hospital. His trainer, Sam Soloman, worried that the damage might be permanent and his manager, George Hamid, asked the Texas Boxing Commission to review a film of the fight and take action if they believed Ali was guilty of deliberate and dangerous fouls. He was, but nothing came of it. Hamid, incidentally, owned the steel pier in Atlantic City.

Terrell was born in Inverness, Mississippi, the son of a farmer and sixth in a family of ten children. When he was a baby they moved to the rough south side of Chicago where, as Ernie said, 'You either fought or you stayed in the house.' He won the vacant WBA title with a dour fifteen-round decision over Eddie Machen in Chicago in March 1965, defended that minor belt twice with points defeats of George Chuvalo and Doug Jones, and then lost to Ali in February 1967.

Understandably, after the Ali fight he was never the same again. He lost decisions in his next two fights to Thad Spencer and Manuel Ramos and retired for three years. In the early 1970s eleven straight wins brought him to the fringes of world class again, but a one-round knockout by Jeff Merritt in 1973 convinced him to retire permanently at the age of thirty-four.

From the 1960s Terrell combined boxing with singing with his group The Heavyweights, which included his brothers J.C. and Leonard and his sister Velma, and in retirement promoted his own shows in the Chicago area for many years.

HARRY THOMAS

Born: 17 December 1910, Eagle Bend, Indiana
Full name: Henry Pontius
Height: 6ft   **Weight at peak:** 196lbs (14st)
Fights: 49   **Won:** 33   **Lost:** 14   **Drawn:** 2
KO percentage: 57
Rounds boxed: 246

World title fights: 1
Career span: 1932-39 (7 years)
KO wins: 28
KO defeats: 3

From Eagle Bend, Minnesota, Harry Thomas fought Max Schmeling in 1937 at Madison Square Garden and was knocked out in eight rounds. A couple of wins over the marvellously modest Ed 'Unknown' Winston and a points defeat to Jimmy Adamick were enough to earn him a championship bout with Joe Louis in Chicago Stadium in April 1938. It was one of many soft touches Louis had in those early years of his reign: Thomas lasted into the fifth.

After Louis, he was finished. He lost his next three, including a third-round stoppage by Tony Galento, returned to Minnesota to win his last fight in January 1939 over Dick Daniels and retired at the age of twenty-eight. His real name was Henry Pontius.

PINKLON THOMAS

Born: 10 February 1958, Pontiac, Michigan
Height: 6ft 3in   **Weight at peak:** 218lbs (15st 8lbs)
Fights: 51   **Won:** 43   **Lost:** 7   **Drawn:** 1
KO percentage: 66
Rounds boxed: 288
World champion: 1984-86 (WBC)
World title fights: 4
Career span: 1978-93 (15 years)
KO wins: 34
KO defeats: 5

Pinklon Thomas was one of the champions promoted by Don King in the chaotic, unstable 1980s when heavyweights of substance were diminished by the noise and political weight of King and the self-interest of the three sanctioning bodies of the era, the World Boxing Council, the World Boxing Association and the International Boxing Federation.

The WBA was formed in August 1962 and the WBC in January 1963, both in a bid to bring some order and administrative shape to a sport clouded by Mob involvement. They took the rest of the decade to establish themselves, the 1970s to grow – and then all but ruined the sport in the 1980s, when they were joined by the IBF after Bob Lee had led a breakaway group from the WBA.

Thomas was both a beneficiary and a victim of these troubled times. He did have talent enough to win a WBC title, not least because of his promotional tie with King and King's close working relationship with the governing body and its president, Jose Sulaiman, but he will always be regarded by historians as a minor champion. As a youngster he had to kick a serious drug habit – 'I stuck a needle in my arm and I shot stuff up my nose' – and when his career was finished he dedicated himself to working with those who were struggling to cope with addiction and recovery. One man he took an interest in was a wayward teenager in Florida, the future light-heavyweight champion Antonio Tarver, whom he trained for a while.

Thomas, from Pontiac, Michigan, was just another workaday prospect with hand problems – he broke them five times – until he signed for King. In August 1984 he out-pointed a lethargic Tim Witherspoon over twelve ordinary rounds in the Riviera Hotel, Las Vegas, to become WBC champion. He made one defence, an eighth-round stoppage of Mike Weaver in Las Vegas in June 1985, then lost a close unanimous verdict to Trevor Berbick, again in Las Vegas, in March 1986. The judges saw it 115-113 twice and 115-114 for Berbick. It was close enough for a return but Thomas had to wait his turn, which came when Mike Tyson was WBC and WBA champion, at the Vegas Hilton in May 1987. Thomas boxed well for a while then was taken out by a brutal combination in the sixth round.

He was out of the ring for more than eighteen months, then lost in seven to Evander Holyfield in Atlantic City in December 1988. Riddick Bowe stopped him in eight, Tommy Morrison in one.

Thomas took a job in a centre for drug-free living in Florida, working with habitual criminals and ghetto kids, and at one time trained and motivated businessmen.

DAVID TUA

Born: 21 November 1972, Aopo, Western Samoa
Height: 5ft 10in   **Weight at peak:** 232lbs (16st 8lbs)
Fights: 47   **Won:** 43   **Lost:** 3   **Drawn:** 1
KO percentage: 80
Rounds boxed: 216
World title fights: 1
Career span: 1992-2005 (13 years)
KO wins: 38
KO defeats: 0

David Tua could punch, especially with the left hook, but he was too small to make an impression when he challenged Lennox Lewis for the title in Las Vegas in November 2000. Tua knew his only chance was to get inside and let his punches go but Lewis out-boxed him at will to stroll home 119-110, 118-110, 117-111.

Tua was a bronze medallist at the Barcelona Olympics in 1992. Born in Western Samoa and raised in New Zealand, he was the first Polynesian athlete to win an

Olympic medal in any sport. Tua's biggest early career win was a nineteen-second demolition of John Ruiz in Atlantic City in March 1996. A twelfth-round stoppage of his Olympic conqueror, David Izon – and an eleventh-round win over Oleg Maskaev rubber-stamped him as a potential champion. When he fought Lennox Lewis for the world title he had won his last ten fights, including a come-from-behind tenth-round stoppage of Hasim Rahman.

After losing to Lewis, Tua showed he could still punch his weight when he blasted out the former champion Michael Moorer in thirty seconds in Atlantic City in August 2002. However, Chris Byrd had beaten him on points and, after a twelve-round draw in a poor rematch with Rahman, Tua hit managerial trouble and was sidelined for two years. When he came back in 2005 he was still only thirty-two, but the impetus seemed to have gone from his career.

TONY TUBBS

Born: 15 February 1958, Cincinnati, Ohio
Height: 6ft 3in   **Weight at peak:** 230lbs (16st 6lbs)
Fights: 55   **Won:** 43   **Lost:** 10   **No Contests:** 2
KO percentage: 43
Rounds boxed: 343
World champion: 1985-86 (WBA)
World title fights: 3
Career span: 1980-2003 (23 years)
KO wins: 24
KO defeats: 5

Tony Tubbs has spent most of his life trying to recapture something that left him so long ago.

'The hardest thing to get back is the will,' he said in a newspaper interview when attempting yet another comeback at the age of forty-two. His mother Leola, for so many years his biggest fan, didn't want him to box any more, but Tony was just out of prison after serving time for selling crack cocaine and needed something to provide a routine in the day-to-day struggle with his addiction. Leola was in no doubt that the shock of being jailed had prevented his slide. 'Sometimes the Lord has to sit us down and get our attention,' she said.

In his prime Tubbs was a big but quick and skilful heavyweight who, had he been blessed with the work ethic to go with his talent, could have been stunningly good. For nine months, from April 1985 until January 1986, Tubbs held the World Boxing Association heavyweight title. He won it with a fifteen-round unanimous decision over another frustrated talent, Greg Page, and lost it in his first defence on a majority decision to Tim Witherspoon. There should have been so much more.

Tubbs was born and raised in Cincinnati, Ohio, one of nine children. At high school he learned to box at the St Mark's church gym. He won a National AAU title, boxed for the USA in international tournaments and as a twenty-year-old amateur sparred with Muhammad Ali. He had a chance of going to the Moscow Olympics, but President Jimmy Carter withdrew the United States from the games in a protest against the Russian invasion of Afghanistan. As a professional, he took his record to 21-0 by out-boxing James 'Bonecrusher' Smith over ten rounds in Las Vegas in March 1985. Like the rest of the heavyweights in contention he was controlled by Don King – and like so many of them, his time as a champion was brief, in his case just nine months.

In March 1988 he travelled to Tokyo to challenge Mike Tyson for the undisputed heavyweight title – Tyson was still at his marauding peak. A week before the fight Tubbs's trainer, Richie Giachetti, walked out. 'I can't be connected with a guy who doesn't want to work,' he said. 'Tony has all the talent in the world but he doesn't want to get up in the morning. And he's out at night.' Tyson destroyed him inside two rounds.

In November 1989 his darker problems became evident. After out-boxing Orlin Norris in Santa Monica, the old hippy coastal resort outside Los Angeles, Tubbs tested positive for cocaine. His last really good performance was in a very close ten-round bout with Riddick Bowe in Atlantic City in April 1991. There were plenty of good judges who felt the young, unbeaten Bowe was fortunate to get the decision – and most vocal of all was Leola Tubbs, who shouted angrily at ringside, 'They robbed my boy, they robbed my boy...' The drug addiction took its toll and he became increasingly vulnerable. Both Lionel Butler and Jimmy Ellis (not the old WBA champion) beat him in a round. He had a result reversed because of another drug test failure in October 1994 when he boxed William Morris in Auburn Hills, Michigan.

As a top-class force he was finished but, after serving his jail sentence, he returned, in his forties with his brother Nate looking after him, and appeared occasionally on low-key promotions.

TONY TUCKER

Born: 27 December 1958, Grand Rapids, Michigan
Height: 6ft 5in   **Weight at peak:** 222lbs (15st 12lbs)
Fights: 66   **Won:** 58   **Lost:** 7   **Drawn:** 0   **No Contests:** 1
KO percentage: 72
Rounds boxed: 322
World champion: 1987
World title fights: 4
Career span: 1980-98 (18 years)
KO wins: 48
KO defeats: 3

Tony Tucker's sixty-three-day reign as IBF champion champion is submerged beneath the Mike Tyson story. In another era, the big man from Grand Rapids, Michigan, might have rated more than a footnote in the history of the championship. As it was, he was reduced to the role of bit-player supreme.

He won IBF recognition with a come-from-behind, tenth-round stoppage of a disappointing Buster Douglas in April 1987. He enjoyed an official reception in his home town, then returned to training – and lost a unification fight with Mike Tyson almost before he had become accustomed to being at the top. His dour, stubborn resistance to Tyson at the Las Vegas Hilton in August 1987 was a performance filled with character and pride, but any real chance of his actually winning disappeared eleven days before the fight when he damaged his right hand in sparring.

Out of the ring it was chaos: Tucker had an army of investors, backers and advisers behind him – and suddenly realised there were so many people waiting with their hands out that he was boxing Tyson for virtually nothing. In the end, after deductions, he took home $28,500 for fighting the self-proclaimed 'baddest man on the planet' for twelve long rounds.

In the fight, he hurt Tyson with a left uppercut early on, but then broke the right hand and more or less 'old-manned' his way through the rest of it. He lost by margins of between five and eight points but made a point to himself if nobody else. He proved what he was to believe always: that for all the hype Tyson wasn't anything to get worked up about, wasn't anything he couldn't have been himself. It's the way hard luck stories sometimes are.

In those days Tucker was trained in Detroit by Emanuel Steward and an old-timer, Luther Burgess, who had fought the great world featherweight champion Willie Pep in the 1940s. Cedric Kushner promoted him and Bob Tucker, his father, managed him. After the Tyson fight, the team broke up. Tucker had been boxing since he was nine, had been a good all-round athlete in high school, had won the light-heavyweight gold medal in the 1979 Pan-American Games and even as a young man had a calm, controlled authority in a ring. After the Tyson fight he was out of the ring for two years. He was crushed, broken, dismayed. Eventually he became a born-again Christian, signed with King, and in May 1993 boxed Lennox Lewis for the WBC title at the Thomas and Mack Center in Las Vegas. Lewis knocked him down for the first time in his life, but he fought bravely to go the full twelve rounds. Tucker's next opportunity was for the vacant WBA belt against Bruce Seldon in Las Vegas in April 1995, but he was behind on points with both eyes badly swollen when Mills Lane waved it off at the end of round seven.

Two years later he found the speed and accuracy of Herbie Hide too much in a WBO bout. Tucker, whose chin was once so reliable, was down three times before it was stopped in round two. There was one more high-level fight, an eleventh-round stoppage by John Ruiz in 1998. He did go out on a win against a club fighter, Billy Wright, in Mississippi, but then a medical in Las Vegas revealed retinal damage and he was forced to retire.

He moved to Florida. The religious side of his life that was prominent in the early 1990s seemed to have quietened; two marriages had failed; he had two daughters but was struggling to maintain contact. He hoped he might train fighters.

GENE TUNNEY

Born: 25 May 1897, New York City
Full name: James Joseph Tunney
Died: 7 Nov 1978, Greenwich, Connecticut, aged 81
Height: 6ft ½in   **Weight at peak:** 189-192lbs (13st 7lbs-13st 10lbs)
Fights: 84   **Won:** 77   **Lost:** 1   **Drawn:** 3   **No decisions:** 3
KO percentage: 54
Rounds boxed: 587
World champion: 1926-29
World title fights: 3
Career span: 1915-28 (13 years)
KO wins: 45
KO defeats: 0

An elegant, meticulously controlled boxer, Gene Tunney's reputation rests largely on his two points victories over a faded Jack Dempsey in their million-dollar classics in 1926 and 1927. This is to some extent unfair because Tunney may well have beaten Dempsey at his peak. He lost only once in thirteen years and eighty-three fights – to the marvellous middleweight Harry Greb, whom he subsequently beat. However, Tunney's rather remote, cerebral attitude was in direct contrast to the open-hearted approach of Dempsey – and, having made his fortune, he retired too soon to earn more than respect.

That said, his dreams came true. An unassuming boy from a modest working-class family in New York City, he went on to become one of the most famous men in the world. He could be a touch priggish and affected. One day writers arrived in camp to find him reading Shakespeare. Another time it would be Samuel Butler's *The Way of all Flesh*, or W. Somerset Maugham. He corresponded with George Bernard Shaw, preferred the company of F. Scott Fitzgerald and Ernest Hemingway to other boxers, and had a private audience with the Prince of Wales in London. When he fought Dempsey for the first time in Philadelphia, he flew there in a stunt plane – a decision that caused promoter Tex Rickard to explode with anger at the risk he had taken. Rickard was right – the pilot was lost in fog over the Pocono mountains for an hour and Tunney was airsick all the way! Yet he could box with a smoothness and ease that is incredibly rare, especially in a heavyweight, where so much rests on power.

Born in New York City, the son of a longshoreman, he was christened James Joseph Tunney. He was raised in Greenwich Village, Manhattan, from the time he was three months old, stayed in school until he was old enough to work as a stenographer for a steamship company and in the evenings studied law at New York University. In the early days he boxed largely for fun and to keep fit. However, he supplemented his income with professional contests from the age of eighteen and then took time out to enlist in the US Marine Corps in May 1918, travelling to Europe for what turned out to be the closing weeks of the First World War.

A broken left hand cost him the first half of 1921, but his reputation increased and he stopped Soldier Jones of Canada in seven rounds on the undercard of Dempsey's world championship defence against Georges Carpentier in the Boyle's Thirty Acres arena in Jersey City. He returned to ringside and crouched down to watch Dempsey destroy the Frenchman. He was disappointed with his own performance, but more importantly learned about Dempsey at close range.

That single pro defeat against Greb, who outslugged him over fifteen rounds for the American light-heavyweight championship, was in New York in May 1922. Greb, one of the greatest pound-for-pound fighters who ever lived, gave him the kind of one-sided hammering that can finish a man. Tunney's nose was broken and he was gashed over both eyes; he collapsed on the way from the ring and had to be carried to the dressing room. He stayed in bed for a week. He fought Greb four times more and by their last encounter, in St Paul, Minnesota, in March 1925, Tunney was just too big for the middleweight champion and is said to have carried him out of respect through the later stages of their ten-round No Decision bout.

Tunney also out-boxed Tommy Loughran and stopped Georges Carpentier after fourteen rounds, flooring him four times in the tenth yet, because of a contractual wrangle and a prior agreement to guarantee Carpentier $45,000, Tunney was eventually paid a paltry $3,000. The lesson stuck in his mind.

On a sweltering day in New York in June 1925 he out-boxed and out-punched another contender, Tommy Gibbons, for a twelfth-round stoppage, a performance that confirmed him as a legitimate challenger for Dempsey's title. Dempsey sent him a telegram of congratulations. Eventually, after long negotiations, Rickard preferred Tunney as challenger to the veteran black heavyweight Harry Wills. Dempsey had not boxed for three years by the time they stepped into the ring at the Sesquicentennial Stadium, Philadelphia, on a rainy night in September 1926. Tunney boxed beautifully, outjabbing the plodding champion over ten rounds before that fantastic crowd of 120,757, who paid what was then a record gate of $1,895,733. Tunney's cut was $200,000. For the rematch at Soldier Field, Chicago, in September 1927, Tunney's purse was just short of $1 million. He gave Rickard a cheque for the balance – $9,555 – and accepted one in return for the round million. This was the infamous Battle of the Long Count, which attracted 104,953 fans and grossed an incredible $2,658,660.

Tunney out-boxed Dempsey behind his left lead, using his feet, until the seventh when Dempsey knocked him into the ropes. Tunney bounced off them into the path of a left hook that floored him. He was dazed but had the brains to understand when referee Dave Barry took time to force the fired-up Dempsey back to a neutral corner before picking up the count. It wasn't Tunney's problem that the referee took fourteen seconds to reach the count of nine. He got up, used his speed and ringcraft to avoid Dempsey's follow-up attacks and then took over again. Around the United States ten men died listening to the radio broadcast – half of them during round seven! In the eighth Gene knocked Dempsey down and by the end was an overwhelming winner. The era of the Manassa Mauler was over... but Tunney was already moving on. He agreed to defend against Tom Heeney, the New Zealand Rock, in Yankee Stadium, New York, in July 1928, stopped him comprehensively in eleven rounds and then walked away from the sport.

Rickard died of peritonitis early in 1929 before the Wall Street crash ruined so many of the fortunes made in perhaps the craziest decade of the century and the Depression set in. Tunney married Mary Josephine 'Polly' Lauder, in Rome and toured Europe. He had to endure lawsuits lodged by another woman, who claimed he had promised marriage to her, and a boxing promoter, who said he was entitled to a percentage of Gene's fortune. He won both cases but attempted to live quietly in society after that. He wrote his own autobiography, *A Man Must Fight*, in 1933, another book, *Arms for the Living*, in 1941, and was at various times involved in banking, coal mining, timber, a razor blade company and the rubber industry. He was director of athletics and physical fitness in the US Navy in the Second World War, had homes in Connecticut and Maine, and was a friend of several presidents. However, while one of his sons, John, became a US senator, his youngest child and only daughter Joan was convicted of murdering her husband at their home in Buckinghamshire, England, in 1970, judged to be insane and committed to Broadmoor. The old champion was broken by it – and died, aged eighty-one, in Greenwich, Connecticut, on 7 November 1978.

MIKE TYSON

Born: 30 June 1966, Brooklyn, New York
Height: 5ft 11in   **Weight at peak:** 219lbs (15st 9lbs)
Fights: 58   **Won:** 50   **Lost:** 6   **No Contests:** 2
KO percentage: 75
Rounds boxed: 216
World champion: 1986-90, 1996
World title fights: 16
Career span: 1985-2005 (20 years)
KO wins: 44
KO defeats: 5

At his best Mike Tyson was so young, so intimidating, such a fast and accurate puncher that it seemed he could be one of the great world champions. And, of course, he lost control of himself so violently that not only did he blow the championship he once treasured when he was only twenty-three, he spent his mid-twenties in an Indiana jail cell following a conviction for raping a beauty pageant contestant. For good or bad, Tyson's personality overshadowed his era. He compelled as he repelled. Even before he became the youngest world heavy-weight champion in history when he unhinged the legs of Trevor Berbick at the Las Vegas Hilton in November 1986, Tyson had turned off sponsors and advertis-ers with an ill-advised comment about attempting to drive the tip of the nose of Jesse Ferguson into the base of his brain. It was, as if, even then, Tyson saw himself as only partial reality: a cartoon creation of his mentors Cus D'Amato and Jim Jacobs that had only some distant base on truth.

At his best Tyson was frighteningly good but he remained a haunted, mystify-ing individual who could never shake off the psychological chains of his bleak upbringing in the Bedford–Stuyvesant ghetto of Brooklyn. The evidence appears to be that he was a sensitive child in a psychologically abusive environment – a boy with a high-pitched voice who was initially intimidated by his elders – and who then turned wild as a way of coping. It may, or may not, have been the case that he lost his temper with a bully who had torn off the head of one of his pigeons. This traumatic event may have been the demonstration he needed to learn the arts of intimidation and violence. Tyson's life is filled with truths, half-truths and downright untruths.

What is beyond dispute is that he was sent to the Tryon School for juvenile delinquents in upstate New York and 'rescued' from there when he was taught the rudiments of boxing by a former professional, Bobby Stewart, who in turn alerted D'Amato to what he had found. D'Amato, whose career had peaked with the previous youngest heavyweight champion Floyd Patterson, considered him-self a Svengali, a teacher for life as much as a boxing coach. Perhaps that is why he could work best with the impressionable and young. D'Amato brought Tyson to his home in Catskill. While Tyson became a ferocious, phenomenal machine, a man before his time, it also appears D'Amato lost perspective: in his obsession with producing a champion he spoiled the boy and mis-shaped the man. Tyson learned early on that he could do pretty much what he wanted and someone, somewhere would bail him out. Teddy Atlas famously put a gun to Tyson's head after hearing the boxer had paid unwelcome attention to an underage girl. D'Amato sent Atlas packing, but did little or nothing to admonish his star.

Tyson turned professional at eighteen after losing two decisions to Henry Tillman in the Olympic trials of 1984. His early pro opponents were hand-picked but he blew them all away. One opponent protested about his first-round stoppage, insist-ing to the referee, 'I want to fight.' The ref helped him to his corner, telling him, 'Fight? You can't even walk!' Tyson was a dynamic alternative to the listless line of under-motivated champions linked to Don King. Tyson was not, on the way up, linked to King because Jacobs and his business partner Bill Cayton would not countenance it. Even though D'Amato died in 1985, Tyson seemed unstoppable.

Tyson was still only twenty years old when he destroyed Berbick in two rounds, then took only nine months to unify the division. James 'Bonecrusher' Smith, the WBA champion, clutched and mauled his way through twelve rounds as Tyson won a lop-sided decision in a dull fight in March 1987. Pinklon Thomas, a former WBC holder, was taken out with a stunning combination in six rounds and then in August 1987 Tyson beat a negative but gritty Tony Tucker, the IBF champion, on points to complete the unification. Two months later he destroyed the 1984 Olympic super-heavyweight gold medallist Tyrell Biggs in seven rounds. Tyson, acting out his part as 'the Baddest Man on the Planet', said Biggs squealed like a girl from body punches.

In the freezing cold of Atlantic City in January 1988, Tyson knocked out thirty-eight-year-old Larry Holmes, who was coming back after two years out. Two months later he cut down Tony Tubbs, in two rounds in Tokyo. While he was there, Jim Jacobs died of leukaemia. Tyson, who had not realised the extent of his illness, was bereft. Don King famously cut a figure of great despair at the funeral. Tyson, who did not like the formal, remote Cayton, began to lean on King. He hooked up with an old friend from his schooldays, Rory Holloway, and another man associated with King, John Horne. Tyson also married an actress, Robin Givens, whose baggage included her mother, Ruth Roper. These people gradually replaced his old 'D'Amato' team in his life: Kevin Rooney, Steve Lott and Matt Baransky, who had trained and organised him from the start.

By the summer of 1988 the turmoil was threatening to engulf Tyson, yet he held it together to produce what many still consider his finest performance, the ninety-one-second demolition of the unbeaten former champion Michael Spinks. Tyson was brutal, ruthless, the total machine and so accurate that Spinks couldn't react and was taken out. Years later, Tyson said, 'Once I see fear in their eyes, that's it. It's over.'

Givens, who had humiliated him on a national talk show by explaining what she considered his psychological and social deficiencies, filed for divorce. Astonishingly, in November 1988, after a fight with Frank Bruno had been postponed, he was baptised at a Christian church in King's home city of Cleveland, Ohio. Tyson also fired Rooney. Cayton was at first inched and then shoved out of Tyson's career. Aaron Snowell, who had been in Tim Witherspoon's entourage, replaced Rooney. Tyson fought Bruno in Las Vegas in February 1989 and, after putting the big Englishman down with his first real attack, was shaken for the first time in his career by a left hook. He did not box well, but overwhelmed Bruno in five rounds. In July 1989 one big left hook accounted for Carl Williams, who protested the stoppage.

King arranged a return to Tokyo for him to box James 'Buster' Douglas, with a huge fight against number one contender Evander Holyfield to follow. Tyson, it is said, didn't want to bother with Douglas and wanted to box Holyfield – and paid an enormous price for his cynical complacency. Douglas hit Tyson with jabs and right hands all night long. Tyson put him down with an uppercut at the end of the eighth, Douglas got up as referee Octavio Meyran reached nine, and came back to take out Tyson with a four-punch volley in round ten. The effect was devastating. It showed all the ordinary heavyweights in the world that if a man hung in with Tyson long enough he could be beaten. That remained the case for the rest of his career. King was apopleptic. At first he and WBC president Sulaiman, with the WBA boss Gilberto Mendoza in tow, tried to persuade the world Tyson had actually won because Douglas was given a long count in round eight, but they had to back down when the full tide of public opinion began to hit them.

Tyson, who knew better than anyone he had let down not only himself but his legacy, kicked his heels with one-round wins over Henry Tillman, who had beaten him in the Olympic trials six years earlier, and Alex Stewart. Meanwhile, Douglas lost the championship to Holyfield. Tyson beat Donovan 'Razor' Ruddock in seven rounds then, because Ruddock protested the stoppage, fought him again and won on points.

The Holyfield fight was finally arranged for the autumn of 1991, but was scuppered when Desiree Washington, a beauty parade contestant, accused him of rape. In early 1992 he was convicted and sentenced to ten years for rape and deviate sexual conduct plus confinement. He served three. By the time Tyson walked out of jail in Indiana in March 1995 he had converted to Islam but he had not left King. Horne and Holloway resumed their positions in his life. He married again, won a facile comeback against no-hoper Peter McNeeley in August 1995, then in December he pulled out a single-punch finish to beat Buster Mathis in round three after looking shockingly bad for the first two. This brought him a chance to win the WBC title, by then in the hands of his old victim, Frank Bruno. In March 1996 at the MGM Grand, Las Vegas, Tyson walked through Bruno in three rounds and knelt and kissed the canvas. He was genuinely moved. Still only twenty-nine, he looked like a man who had found redemption.

Under WBC rules Tyson was supposed to defend next against his number one contender Lennox Lewis, but that match didn't suit King, who preferred to control both corners of the ring. He was the promotional master of the heavyweight division again – and Lewis was out of his reach. In the 'old days' Sulaiman might have helped King out but life had moved on: Lewis and his team knew their legal rights. King, if he wanted Tyson to avoid the big Briton, had to pay him off. So it was that Lewis received a summer bonus in 1996 and Tyson, instead of defending the WBC belt, was offered an alternative: a match with the King-promoted WBA champion Bruce Seldon. If he were going to do that he need not have paid Lewis step-aside money, but that was typical of the chaos that surrounded him. He beat Seldon in one round with a punch that did not appear to land cleanly, and was stripped by the WBC.

Two months later Tyson took on the by-now supposedly washed-up Holyfield in a fight that should have happened six years earlier. After the Bruno and Seldon wins, it seemed Tyson was back, with Lewis as his only real rival... then in a sensational upset in November 1996, Holyfield contained Tyson early on, floored him with a left hook in round six and stopped him in the eleventh. The rematch, in June 1997, two days before Tyson's thirty-first birthday, was one of the most notorious moments in heavyweight history. After two rounds Tyson was cut by a head clash, frustrated – and then amazingly, in a clinch, bit a chunk out of Holyfield's right ear and spat it out onto the canvas. Holyfield bounded back in pain. Referee Mills Lane should have disqualified Tyson but dithered. In the next clinch Tyson dipped his head and chewed Holyfield's left ear. This time, after a delay, Lane threw Tyson out. The ring seemed to fill with bodies. Tyson wanted to fight on, and when he had been led away accused Lane of failing to protect him from Holyfield's deliberate use of the head. Most onlookers felt he had simply fouled his way out of the fight to save himself another beating. The Nevada State Athletic Commission suspended his licence, a ban that was respected by the member states of the Association of Boxing Commissions.

In his layoff Tyson discovered business irregularities that prevailed during his time under Don King's promotional care and left him, lodging a lawsuit for $100 million. Under new manager Shelly Finkel, Tyson reapplied for his licence, but by then was facing another jail term for a road rage incident involving an attack on two middle-aged men. He admitted to undergoing psychological therapy and was under a prescription drug to control his mood swings. The Nevada relicensing hearing also revealed the financial hole he was in: he owed the Internal Revenue Service $18 million and appeared to have gone through $135 million with apparently only a hazy grasp of where it had gone.

When he boxed again in January 1999, Tyson looked terrible against the South African, Frans Botha, who said he was actually thinking of what he would say at the press conference when he was knocked out. He went back to jail for several months for the road rage attack, then emerged to box former cruiserweight champ Orlin Norris at the MGM Grand. At the end of round one he refused to stop boxing and knocked Norris down with a late punch. Norris aggravated an old knee injury and could not go on. Tyson should have been disqualified. Referee Richard Steele took away two points, the normal penalty for a deliberate foul, but after discussion with Nevada officials, it was ruled a No Contest. A two-fight British excursion in 2000 brought quick wins over Julius Francis and Lou Savarese, but he disgraced himself again by refusing to stop fighting after the Savarese mismatch was stopped after thirty-eight seconds. Referee John Coyle was knocked down as he tried to maintain order, with Tyson attempting to reach around him and go on punching. Afterwards he offered a stream-of-consciousness interview that included an insistence that he wanted to eat Lennox Lewis's children. Tyson did not attend the media conference, leaving an aide to insist,

'Mike loves children.' 'How does he prefer them,' called out one hack. 'Grilled or fried?'

From then on it was a career on the drift. Very sad, very strange. In Detroit before he boxed Andrew Golota, Tyson was happiest when he gave a media work-out at the Brewster gym where Joe Louis and Ray Robinson trained. The next day he snapped when a reporter asked a seemingly innocuous question. After the weigh-in he said it would be his retirement fight. 'I don't want to do this anymore,' he said. The notoriously unpredictable Golota got off the floor from a right hand, but then quit in his corner after round two. After all that, Tyson tested positive for marijuana. The Michigan Commission gave him a meaningless fine and the briefest of bans. He was out of the ring for a year, then ground out a six-round win over Brian Nielsen, a happy-go-lucky Dane in Copenhagen. Nielsen sauntered to the ring to the Monty Python classic *Always Look on the Bright Side of Life*. A disinterested Tyson scaled an all-time high of 239¾lbs.

At the start of 2002 the world title fight with Lewis, which should have hap-pened six years earlier, was planned for Las Vegas in April, but Tyson bit a chunk out of Lewis's leg in a crazy brawl at the press conference to launch proceed-ings in New York in January. The Nevada Commission refused to licence him. Eventually the fight settled on Memphis in June and Tyson failed miserably. Lewis hit him repeatedly with jabs and knocked him out with a huge right hand in round eight. Tyson, so belligerent beforehand, thanked him for the opportunity. On the way out, he said, 'I might just fade into oblivion. I'm just fortunate Lewis didn't kill me. I don't know if I can ever beat him if he fights like that.'

There was a rematch clause but few had the stomach for it. The full extent of Tyson's financial difficulties were also revealed. He had grossed $17.5 million for boxing Lewis, but by then his second wife, Monica Turner, had left him and he still had massive debts. His spending was still out of control. He had got through more than $37 million in the three years between 1995, when he left prison, and 1998, including $6 million on cars and motorbikes, $4.5 million on legal fees, $1.3 million on 'household expenses', $7.7 million on 'cash and per-sonal expenses', $748,000 on lawn care, $411,000 on his pigeons and large cats, $239,000 on pagers and mobile phones – and only $228,000 on child support.

In February 2003 he returned to Memphis for a bizarre mismatch with Clifford Etienne that lasted forty-nine seconds. Tyson had a new tattoo that covered most of the left side of his face. It was his final win. In Louisville, Kentucky, in the Freedom Hall where Muhammad Ali had made his pro debut forty-odd years earlier, Tyson was knocked out in four rounds by the English heavyweight Danny Williams.

Finally, in June 2005, approaching his thirty-ninth birthday, he retired after six pathetic rounds against the 19st Irish giant, Kevin McBride. It was a terrible way to go.

PAOLINO UZCUDUN

Born: 3 May 1899, Regil, Spain
Died: 5 July 1985, Spain aged 86
Height: 5ft 10½in   **Weight at peak:** 230lbs (16st 6lbs)
Fights: 70   **Won:** 51   **Lost:** 16   **Drawn:** 3
KO percentage: 48
Rounds boxed: 523
World title fights: 1
Career span: 1923-35 (12 years)
KO wins: 34
KO defeats: 1

It was a long way from the northern Spanish town of Regil to Madison Square Garden but the man they called The Basque Woodchopper made the trip.

Uzcudun also challenged the gigantic Primo Carnera for the championship in front of a crowd estimated at 55,000 outdoors in the Piazza di Sienna in Rome, as Mussolini tried to make political capital out of the big Italian hero. Uzcudun stayed with Carnera for the full fifteen rounds. He lost the decision, but fought with customary pride. That was their second meeting: before a 75,000 crowd in Barcelona three years earlier he had lost to Carnera over ten rounds. 'Primo was too tall and had too much reach on me,' said Uzcudun. 'I couldn't get close enough to him to do any damage.'

Uzcudun was boxing in Paris in 1924 when American writer Bob Ripley cabled the great promoter Tex Rickard to tell him he had just seen a Basque heavyweight who was a certain world champion. Rickard cabled back, 'Have the manager get in touch with me. What's a Basque?' Paolino, who was already the Spanish champion, won his American debut by knocking out the British heavyweight Frank Goddard in six rounds. Back in Barcelona he out-pointed Erminio Spalla over fifteen rounds for the European title.

'I had a lot of natural strength,' he once said. 'And I chopped trees. Once, I spent eight months in the mountains at a woodchopping camp where I would do nothing but chop trees, eat and sleep.' Nat Fleischer described Uzcudun's defence as 'turtle-like, head drawn down between his shoulders, perpetually covering up, and making it a difficult matter to get a direct shot at his jaw'.

In 1927 he scored a ten-round points win over another stocky, short-armed battler, the New Zealander Tom Heeney. Off the back of that he knocked out the ageing Harry Wills with a left hook in the fourth round at Ebbetts Field, Brooklyn. At one point Rickard wanted to match Uzcudun with Dempsey in a world title eliminator, and had him photographed with a case containing six axes. He was supposed to have told reporters, 'This is a strange country. I have to be prepared.' However, he and Rickard could not agree terms and, coincidentally or not, he was eliminated from the picture when he was disqualified against the Canadian Jack Delaney before 30,000 fans in Yankee Stadium.

His next big American fight was a fifteen-round points defeat by Max Schmeling at Yankee Stadium in June 1929. Schmeling counter-punched him and cut him up so badly that Paolino could hardly stand at the end. The general estimate was that Uzcudun won two of the fifteen rounds. A gruelling points win over Otto von Porat at the Garden brought him back and, after defeats by Risko and Carnera, he outslugged Max Baer over twenty rounds in Reno, Nevada, in July 1931. Jack Dempsey refereed. At the end Uzcudun had enough left to perform a couple of ungainly cartwheels in celebration. Baer thought he won, but Dempsey said Uzcudun outstayed him. It was also known that Dempsey disapproved of Baer's late-night habits in Reno, then one of the nightlife capitals of the West. Baer proposed marriage to the actress Dorothy Dunbar before the fight.

Uzcudun regained the European title by out-pointing Pierre Charles of Belgium over fifteen rounds in Madrid in May 1933 and, following a defeat of the South African Don McCorkindale, got the call to challenge Carnera in Rome. He lost – and was declining. Very lucky to draw with Max Schmeling in Barcelona, he lost a dull rematch in Berlin, and then travelled back to the United States for a retirement payday of $19,000 against Joe Louis in the Garden in December 1935. Louis knocked him down with a right hand in the fourth round that drove a tooth through his lip. Two more blows and referee Arthur Donovan waved it off.

Uzcudun invested his ring earnings well and although never vastly wealthy was able to pay for a university education for his son. He lived into old age, venerated as one of his nation's sporting legends. He died at the age of eighty-six in July 1985.

NINO VALDES

Born: 5 December 1924, Havana, Cuba
Height: 6ft 4in   **Weight at peak:** 205lbs (14st 9lbs)
Fights: 69   **Won:** 48   **Lost:** 18   **Drawn:** 2   **No Contests:** 1
KO percentage: 52
Rounds boxed: 452
World title fights: 0

Career span: 1941-59 (18 years)
KO wins: 36
KO defeats: 5

Cuban heavyweight Nino Valdes should have challenged Rocky Marciano, but didn't. He should have challenged Floyd Patterson, but didn't. It might have helped if his manager Bobby Gleason had got along with the all-powerful International Boxing Club boss Jim Norris, but he didn't.

Valdes also blamed himself. He told a story that Al Weill, Marciano's manager, came to see him and offered him the fight – for a pittance. Nino was so incensed he picked up a chair and threatened to break it over his head!

As a child he worked on a sugar plantation, which made him phenomenally strong. However, opportunities in the Second World War years were restricted and in truth the first decade of his career, from 1941, can be set aside as a prolonged apprenticeship carried out in Cuba or, occasionally, in Florida. He did box exhibitions three times with Joe Louis but in the third of those he was knocked out in the first round. By 1952 he was in New York, with Gleason managing him. He was erratic but showed how dangerous he was by out-boxing and out-fighting former champion Ezzard Charles over ten rounds in Miami. 'Valdes caught me on the worst night of my entire career and gave me a licking,' said Charles. *Ring* magazine ranked him the number one contender. Maybe he wasn't quite ready for world champion Rocky Marciano, but it is ironic that Marciano chose to fight Charles, not the big Cuban, twice in 1954 – and perhaps significant that when the match was made the supposedly perfect *Ring* editor Nat Fleischer dropped Valdes to number two and elevated Charles, whom he had beaten, to number one.

Valdes won eleven in a row, avenging an early career defeat against Archie McBride and knocking out Tommy 'Hurricane' Jackson in two rounds in New York. He was unbeaten through 1954 and into 1955, then lost to Archie Moore in front of 10,800 fans in Cashman Field, Las Vegas. It was a gruelling if not particularly spectacular fight, with both hurt in round three, and both losing a round because of fouls. The big Cuban dominated the twelfth then faded over the last three. Referee Jim Braddock scored the fight for the light-heavyweight champ by three points, in rounds eight to five with two even. Valdes finished with his left eye shut, Moore with his nose bloody, his lip and left eye swollen.

Doc Kearns, in the time-honoured way of the movers and shakers of boxing, had a piece of both men, but knew he could do business with Weill with Moore and not with Valdes. Kearns had also brought in Braddock as referee, but against the argument of malpractice is the possibility that Archie had the ring-cunning and generalship, as well as the toughness when he wanted to use it, to outwit Valdes, who for all his power wasn't quick-thinking. Valdes went through a terrible spell, as if his belief had gone, losing six out of eight fights. Bob Satterfield, Bob Baker, Zora Folley and Eddie Machen all beat him. However, he regained his ambition in Britain. He demolished Don Cockell, another who had been given a shot at Marciano, in three rounds at White City, London, in September 1955. They promised him a world title fight after that but nothing happened. He also took out Dick Richardson in eight, Joe Erskine in one and in the final fight of his eighteen-year career beat Brian London on a cut in seven.

Valdes had far more right to a championship shot than the first four challengers D'Amato brought in for Patterson: Tommy Jackson, Pete Rademacher, Roy Harris and Brian London. Gleason was still trying his best to nail down D'Amato and, after Nino bombed out the West Coast stylist Pat McMurtry in one round at Madison Square Garden, Bobby labelled Valdes 'the unofficial but true champion'.

Then in 1959, after almost two decades as a boxer, he went home to Cuba to celebrate the arrival of Fidel Castro in Havana and the end of the Batista regime on New Year's Day, and partied rather too much. He returned fat and out of shape – and Charley Powell, a part-timer who played football for the San Francisco 49ers, stopped him in the eighth. Valdes was exhausted. His title claims ended when he was demolished in three by Sonny Liston in August 1959.

In the late 1980s Valdes was living in New York and suffering from diabetes. He died on 3 June 2001 at the age of seventy-six.

PAT VALENTINO

Born: 25 January 1920, San Francisco, California
Height: 6ft   **Weight at peak:** 185lbs (13st 3lbs)
Fights: 57   **Won:** 42   **Lost:** 11   **Drawn:** 4
KO percentage: 35
Rounds boxed: 471
World title fights: 1
Career span: 1940-49 (9 years)
KO wins: 20
KO defeats: 3

A popular San Francisco slugger, Pat Valentino was half-blinded when he challenged Ezzard Charles for the championship at the Cow Palace in October 1949. Charles, too talented anyway, beat him in eight rounds. Valentino had torn a retina against local rival Tony Bosnich – and hadn't been able to close his left fist since he shot himself in the hand while on wartime service as a coastguard, but this long-haired high school dropout from the France Street area of the city could sell tickets. It was the first heavyweight championship in the area since Jack Johnson fought Stanley Ketchel. Somehow Valentino passed the Californian commission eye test. 'I could read through the part of my eye that wasn't ripped,' he said. 'I just didn't let it bother me. I wanted the title.'

After growing up as one of eight children of a shopkeeper in the Depression, Valentino boxed professionally from 1940. He was competent at his level, although not much of a puncher, and had a couple of home-town draws with Joey Maxim but twice lost to Jimmy Bivins. Wins over Freddie Beshore, Bosnich and an old rival Albert 'Turkey' Thompson were enough to clinch him the Charles fight. A crowd of 19,590 turned out to watch. He tried to get inside and work the body, did well in rounds two and three, but after that the champion was too slick, skilful and sharp punching for him. Rather ominously, after seven rounds Valentino was ahead on two of the three official cards. Then a right hand dropped him for the count thirty-five seconds into round eight.

'I just lived from fight to fight,' he told San Francisco writer Jack Fiske. 'I was given only four-and-a-half weeks and I wasn't really ready. Charles was a great fighter but I was surprised how easy he was to hit in the body.'

Two weeks after the Charles fight he lost the sight in his right eye. He still went ahead with an exhibition against Joe Louis in Chicago in December 1949 – again he passed the eye test by reading with his good eye and crossing his hands to fool the doctors. He says the Louis job was a real fight that he lost in eight rounds.

In retirement he sold beer and later on moved to Los Angeles and worked on the assembly line at Lockheed Aircraft. Eventually he moved back to San Francisco, where he worked in a restauraunt in Fisherman's Wharf.

NICOLAY VALUEV

Born: 21 August 1973, St Petersburg, Russia
Height: 7ft 2in   **Weight at peak:** 324lbs (23st 2lbs)
Fights: 44   **Won:** 43   **Lost:** 0   **Drawn:** 0   **No Contests:** 1
KO percentage: 70
Rounds boxed: 188
World champion: 2005-
Career span: 13 years
KO wins: 31
KO defeats: 0

In the 1930s they had the Ambling Alp, Primo Carnera... seventy years on came the Beast from the East, the 7ft 2in, 23st Nicolay Valuev.

In December 2005 Valuev edged out John Ruiz on a majority points decision over twelve laborious rounds in the Max Schmeling Halle, Berlin, to become the biggest man to hold a version of the championship. The belt he strapped around his substantial waist was provided by the WBA. Ruiz angrily disputed the verdict, but what's new in boxing? Valuev had home advantage, the fight was close, the rest is history. Pre-fight, Ruiz found the big man hugely amusing. 'I can't miss him,' he said. 'He's got a head the size of a Volkswagen.'

For Valuev, from St Petersburg, it stretched his unbeaten run to forty-four fights – and proved that he deserved to be taken seriously as a boxer. There were still the rival champions to take on: Vitali Klitschko had retired because of injuries to be replaced as WBC champion by Hasim Rahman; the clever but colourless southpaw Chris Byrd held the IBF belt and Lamon Brewster, who had managed to come from the brink of defeat to stop Wladimir Klitschko, held the WBO title. But while Ruiz wailed that the verdict was a disgrace, Valuev expressed grim satisfaction at a job well done – and very few at ringside felt there was much in it. Nobody outside the Ruiz camp screamed robbery.

Valuev grew up under the old Soviet regime and was originally ushered towards a life in basketball, but that didn't work out. He also tried to make it as a discus thrower before settling on boxing. To make his name he boxed in Australia, Japan, Germany, the Czech Republic, Russia, Ukraine, South Korea, Belarus, England and the USA.

In the future his size and brooding expression might make him a perfect Bond movie villain, but as a new 'world' champion, as we moved into 2006, it looked as if there was a fortune for him to make inside the ring.

W

JERSEY JOE WALCOTT

Born: 31 January 1914, Merchantville, New Jersey
Full name: Arnold Raymond Cream
Died: 26 February 1994, Camden, New Jersey, aged 80
Height: 6ft   **Weight at peak:** 194-197lbs (13st 12lbs-14st 1lb)
Fights: 72   **Won:** 53   **Lost:** 18   **Drawn:** 1
KO percentage: 45
Rounds boxed: 485
World champion: 1951-52
World title fights: 8
Career span: 1930-53 (23 years)
KO wins: 33
KO defeats: 6

Sometimes nice guys do win... eventually. Arnold Raymond Cream, alias Jersey Joe Walcott, had to wait many years, had to overcome the immense disappointment of being robbed against Joe Louis, but when he was five months past his thirty-seventh birthday he achieved the unlikeliest of ambitions: he won the heavyweight championship of the world at the fifth attempt.

Walcott was considered such an outsider that when the result of his seventh-round knockout of Ezzard Charles in Forbes Field, Pittsburgh, in July 1951 went across the wires, one British sportswriter rang his desk to tell them they had got it the wrong way round! Yet the left hook Walcott found to knock out Charles fifty-five seconds into round seven was one of the sweetest, most perfect punches anyone ever threw in a world title fight.

While some felt the result marked a new low point for boxing, on the grounds that Walcott was an old man whose genuine limits had long been exposed, others celebrated his persistence. Sentimentalists loved it. And his was an incredible story, beginning in Merchantville, New Jersey, in January 1914.

By adolescence, following the death of his father, he was selling newspapers, delivering groceries and working in a soup factory to provide for his mother, brothers and sisters. By nineteen he was married and living in Camden, New Jersey, just across the stateline from Philadelphia. In lean times he claimed $9.50 a week relief. He worked as a hod carrier on a building site, as a garbage collector and, eventually, in the war years, as a longshoreman in the suddenly overstretched shipyards. He developed a shuffling, smart defensive boxing style after coaching sessions from a cousin, Jeff Clark, who was called the Joplin Ghost because of his defensive brilliance. Jack Blackburn, who had been a world-class lightweight and earned lasting fame as the trainer of Joe Louis, taught him for a while too.

Walcott threw his punches correctly and knew instinctively about balance and timing. He was good. Of course, he was also black, which meant the pay was poor. For his professional debut, when he took the name Joe Walcott in honour of the old welterweight champion, he earned $7.50 for a first-round knockout of one Cowboy Wallace in Vineland, New Jersey, in September 1930.

When he was twenty he was seriously ill with typhoid, recovered and returned to the ring, but in those troubled days of the 1930s he repeatedly retired to find steadier work, only to drift back because, wherever he turned, there was never enough to provide anything more than the basics for wife Lydia and their six children. Early in his career he suffered a body shot knockout, he said, because he was so weak from hunger he couldn't get up. When he boxed in Camden in November 1935 (a seventh-round win over Roxie Allen), the real Joe Walcott asked to see him and said, 'As you're using my name, can you get me into the show?' And afterwards he gave him his blessing: 'There have been a lot of bums who have called themselves Joe Walcott. You're all right, boy. I'm glad you've got my name.'

In a sparring session with Joe Louis he put the Brown Bomber on the floor, something he said made him always believe he could beat him. He also knocked out Phil Johnson, whose son Harold was later light-heavyweight champion. In fact, Walcott was around the business so long he knocked out Harold as well!

In 1937 Walcott beat Elmer 'Violent' Ray, another dangerous black heavyweight who once got some publicity for wrestling an alligator, but one or two decisions went against him and his career drifted. In 1940 he was beaten in six rounds by the giant Abe Simon in Newark, and he retired.

In the winter of 1944 Felix Bocchicchio visited his home to ask him to be a part of a series of shows he was planning to re-establish boxing in Camden. Walcott pointed at an empty coalbin and told him, 'Mister, if you can keep that bin full for me I will fight for you.' Bocchicchio kept his word: in 1945, Jersey Joe had nine paydays, and moved into world class by out-pointing the bigger, stronger Joe Baksi over ten rounds. In Cleveland in February 1946, he out-pointed Jimmy Bivins and three months later he beat Lee Oma. Even when he suffered a dip in form and dropped decisions to Joey Maxim and Elmer Ray, it was only a temporary blip. In the old days he would have retired, but Bocchicchio negotiated rematches and in January 1947 Walcott beat Maxim. In March he beat Ray. By then the soft life had aged world champion Louis. When Mike Jacobs looked around for a contender, he saw what he wanted to see in Walcott: a man even older than the champ. They made the fight for Madison Square Garden on 5 December 1947 and that fifteen-round fight remains one of the most contentious in the history of the championship.

Walcott told writers, 'I've had to do a lot of things to earn a living. I was on a garbage truck and I've cleaned cess pools. But I kept my life clean. I'm just as decent a man as Louis ever was. It's just that the breaks didn't come my way. What's there to be afraid of?'

He knocked Louis down with a right hand in round one, then again with an uppercut in the fourth. Louis survived a follow-up assault and trudged forward for the rest of the fight as Walcott wheeled around him, spearing him on the move. Perhaps conscious of the thirteenth-round knockout suffered by Billy Conn in 1941, when he seemed well ahead, Jersey Joe boxed cautiously over the last three rounds. At the final bell, Louis seemed to know he had lost: he tried to leave the ring before the announcement but trainer Manny Seamon stopped him. Then came the judges' cards: referee Ruby Goldstein gave it to Walcott by one point, but the judges Frank Forbes and Marty Monroe had Louis in front by two and three points respectively. As the boos rang around the arena, Louis turned to Walcott and said, 'I'm sorry, Joe.'

The rematch was signed within days and in June 1948, in Yankee Stadium, they drew 42,667 people who paid $841,739 to watch Louis drag himself back from the brink again. Walcott dropped him in round three, then took to boxing on the move as Louis shuffled slowly in. In the tenth the referee lectured them to provide more action – and four seconds from the end of round eleven, Louis found the punches to retain his title. After Louis retired, Walcott was matched with Charles for National Boxing Association recognition, but lost a dull fight on points. He fought where he could, travelling if he had to: he knocked out Olle Tandberg in

Sweden, and in Germany beat Hein Ten Hoff (inevitably nicknamed by cynics Nine Ten Out!). Ironically, it was after a points defeat by Rex Layne in New York in November 1950 that he was given a rematch with Charles in Detroit in March 1951. Again it was a dull fight. Again he lost it. Yet someone suggested a third meeting in July in Pittsburgh – and astonishingly, Walcott found the left hook that changed his life. 'I have worked twenty-one years for this night,' he said. 'I read my Bible before I fight. I prayed between every round. I asked God to help me.'

Walcott defended the title successfully once... against Charles on a fifteen-round decision in Philadelphia in June 1952. Then the unbeaten, big ticket seller from Massachusetts, Rocky Marciano, took away his title with a thirteenth-round knockout in Philadelphia in September 1952. Yet again, Walcott was on top early. He put Marciano down and in the early stages gave him a boxing lesson. Yet Marciano's youth and strength eventually slowed those thirty-eight-year-old legs, and a perfect right hand left him senseless, his body slumping down the ropes to the canvas. When he came to, he couldn't believe it. In the way of the times Walcott was given a return, but the will had gone. The fight was postponed for a month, until May 1953, and then Walcott lasted only 145 seconds, putting up only minimal resistance.

When he retired he worked in the juvenile division of the Camden Police Department. In his spare time he helped youngsters learn to box and taught Sunday school. By 1965 he was assistant director of public safety in Camden. He also refereed the second Muhammad Ali-Sonny Liston fight and late in his life he was appointed head of the New Jersey State Athletic Commission.

In the early 1990s, when able to walk only with the aid of two sticks following a nasty fall, he was introduced by ring announcer Michael Buffer with the words: 'Ladies and gentlemen, he was so great they named an entire state after him... Jersey Joe Walcott!' I looked at the old man, smiling broadly, and saw history and legend standing there as the fans in the Atlantic City Convention Centre hooted their approval.

He died at the age of eighty on 25 February 1994.

BILLY WALKER

Born: 3 March 1939, London, England
Height: 6ft 1in   **Weight at peak:** 192lbs (13st 10lbs)
Fights: 31   Won: 21   Lost: 8   Drawn: 2
KO percentage: 51
Rounds boxed: 174
World title fights: 0
Career span: 1962-69 (7 years)
KO wins: 16
KO defeats: 5

One of the biggest crowd-pleasers to grace a British ring over the past fifty years, Billy Walker gave honesty, dedication and blood in a bid to become a champion. It didn't happen for him but nobody could fault his effort.

Walker exploded on to the scene in 1961 when, on BBC television, he knocked out the American giant Cornelius Perry at Wembley as England trounced the USA 10-0. He turned professional in a blaze of publicity on a three-fight deal for £10,000, an unheard-of sum at the time. From the beginning, Walker invested his money in restaurants, a taxi firm, a garage and other ventures, and after his retirement from the ring in 1969 he lived for many years in the Channel Islands.

Walker had two popular fights with Johnny Prescott of Birmingham in 1963. He stopped Prescott in the tenth round in the first, but lost the return on points. He beat the veterans Joe Bygraves and Joe Erskine but lost on points to Brian London and Eduardo Corletti, the clever Argentine heavyweight who was popular in British rings at the time.

His two championship bids came in 1967. He lost in eight rounds to Karl Mildenberger in a European title fight – and in six rounds on cuts to Henry Cooper for the British and Empire crowns. Walker did beat the American, Thad Spencer, at Wembley in November 1968 but retired after Derbyshire southpaw Jack Bodell out-boxed and out-fought him before a packed house at Wembley in March 1969.

MIKE WEAVER

Born: 14 June 1952, Gatesville, Texas
Height: 6ft 1in   **Weight at peak:** 210lbs (15st)
Fights: 60   **Won:** 41   **Lost:** 18   **Drawn:** 1
KO percentage: 46
Rounds boxed: 386
World champion: 1980-82, WBA
World title fights: 7
Career span: 1972-2000 (28 years)
KO wins: 28
KO defeats: 12

Nicknamed Hercules, the muscular Mike Weaver was a heavyweight claimant in the early 1980s, when Larry Holmes was acknowledged as the world number one. Weaver, originally from Gatesville, Texas, and based in Los Angeles, fought Holmes for the World Boxing Council title in New York in June 1979 and was stopped in the twelfth round.

He then caused a shock by knocking out the World Boxing Association champion John Tate in the fifteenth round in Knoxville, Tennessee in March 1980. Obviously, that win coming only nine months after the Holmes defeat meant he remained in Larry's shadow, but he was a good fighter. He ignored the apartheid situation in South Africa, travelling to Sun City in October 1980 and retaining his title with a thirteenth-round knockout of pre-fight favourite Gerrie Coetzee, but in 1981 boxed only once, out-pointing James Tillis in Rosemont near Chicago.

Weaver's loss of the title to Michael Dokes in Las Vegas in December 1982 was controversial. He was hurt but didn't seem unduly distressed when referee Joey Curtis waved the fight off after only sixty-three seconds. The crowd at Caesars Palace yelled 'Fix, fix, fix' and, harshly, 'Don King sucks'. The great promoter has been blamed for many things but he could hardly be guilty of ruining his own show!

In the return in May 1983 the judges came up with a fifteen-round draw. Two years later, with King controlling the division, Weaver was given a shot at the WBC title, then held by Pinklon Thomas, but was stopped in the eighth round.

Weaver's success was attributable to hard work and persistence. He lost three of his first four professional fights – and the Olympic silver medallist from 1972, Duane Bobick, beat Weaver in seven rounds in San Diego in July 1974. Nobody at the time would have believed that Weaver and not Bobick would have gone on to hold a version of the championship and compete in seven title fights.

CHUCK WEPNER

Born: 26 February 1939, New York City
Height: 6ft 5in   **Weight at peak:** 225lbs (16st 1lb)
Fights: 51   **Won:** 35   **Lost:** 14   **Drawn:** 2
KO percentage: 33
Rounds boxed: 362
World title fights: 1
Career span: 1964-78 (14 years)
KO wins: 17
KO defeats: 9

Chuck Wepner's heroic stand against Muhammad Ali in Cleveland Coliseum in 1975 inspired the *Rocky* movies. A strong, rough, brawler type known as the Bayonne Bleeder because he cut so freely and so copiously, Wepner provided for his wife and three small children by working as a beer salesman in New Jersey.

Chuck was managed by Al Braverman, who worked for Don King, who promoted the Ali fight. Wepner was delighted, whatever the niceties of the politics. 'This is my shot at the pie in the sky, the brass ring, the heavyweight championship of the world,' he said. 'I'll be like a man fighting for his life. I've never been one of the Marquess of Queensberry's biggest supporters. Ali will have to be ready to take on a beast. My fight plan will be the worst kept secret since Watergate. I'm going to waste the man. I'll hit him from the top of his head to his shoe tops with anything and everything.'

Before he left the hotel room for the arena, he gave his wife a new negligee and promised her, 'Tonight, honey, you will be sleeping with the heavyweight champion of the world.' Hours later he returned, his face a bruised, swollen mass and threw his kit bag into the corner of the room. His wife, sitting in her new nightwear, said, 'Well, is Muhammad coming here, or am I going to his place?'

Wepner was even mistakenly accredited with a ninth-round knockdown when referee Tony Perez didn't see that Chuck was standing on Ali's foot when he hit him in the chest. As usual, he bled from cuts around both eyes, and soaked up systematic punishment from a champion who seemed to be listless and tired much of the way. In the fifteenth round Ali went for the finish and Wepner slumped to the canvas without really taking any particular punch. He got up, but his eyes were glazed and Perez stopped it only nineteen seconds before the final bell.

Wepner, a Marine in his youth, had a slugging style that made him popular, but he seemed strictly club fighter material. He was fed to George Foreman in only George's fourth pro fight. Foreman won in three rounds. Wepner did out-point Manuel Ramos, the Mexican who had boxed for Joe Frazier's world title, but then was thrown to Sonny Liston at the Jersey Armory in June 1970. It was Liston's last fight, but he was still way too good for Wepner, who knew it only too well. 'After the fifth round I was target practice,' he said. 'One eye closed, broken nose, broken left cheekbone...' The referee, Barney Felix, wanted to stop it after the eighth but went through the motions of asking how many fingers he was holding up. Braverman had Wepner by the shoulders in the corner and tapped him three times. 'Three!' said Chuck. Felix let him go on to the tenth before calling it off. Even then, Wepner moaned, 'He was getting tired of beating the shit out of me...'

Braverman became the manager after his predecessor, Gary Garafola, was jailed. Garafola had previously been acquitted of the murder of the light-heavyweight Frankie DePaula.

After losing to Liston, Wepner went to London and lost on cuts in three rounds to Joe Bugner. British referees knew a hole in the head when they saw one.

The best result of Wepner's career was a decision over Ernie Terrell in Atlantic City in June 1973. Referee Harold Valan, the sole scoring judge who years earlier had been just about the only man in the house who thought Jimmy Ellis beat Floyd Patterson in Sweden, gave it to Wepner by two points, but all but one of the ringside pressmen had Terrell winning. *Ring* scored 9–3 Terrell, whose manager, George Hamid, said, 'The man never landed a decent punch on Ernie. This was the worst decision I have seen in any sport.' New Jersey commissioner Abe Greene said he thought Terrell won, but added, 'What can be done about it? I can't do anything.'

By the time he was given the Ali fight, Wepner was on a roll of eight wins, most recently an eleventh-round stoppage of Terry Hinke in Salt Lake City. After losing to Ali, Wepner had three easy wins, then lost in six rounds to unbeaten Duane Bobick in October 1976. Wepner's nose was broken again and he had cuts below and above the left eye when it was stopped. He boxed on until he lost the New Jersey title to Scott Frank on a twelve-round decision in Totowa in September 1978, by which time he was thirty-nine years old.

In 1986 Wepner was jailed for drug possession but the experience changed his life. He moved away from his old acquaintances and found he could make a living through motivational speaking engagements. He preached the virtues of 'desire, confidence, perseverance and just stick-to-it-ness', and liked to say, 'Ya gotta go the distance...'

JESS WILLARD

Born: 29 December 1881, Pottawatomie County, Kansas
Died: 15 December 1968, Los Angeles, aged 86
Height: 6ft 6¼in   **Weight at peak:** 225-230lbs (16st 1lb-16st 6lbs)
Fights: 35   **Won:** 28   **Lost:** 6   **Drawn:** 1
KO percentage: 60
Rounds boxed: 273
World champion: 1915-19
World title fights: 3
Career span: 1911-23 (12 years)
KO wins: 21
KO defeats: 3

Jess Willard was a strapping, raw-boned cowboy-turned-fighter who was in the right place at the right time – Havana, Cuba, 5 April 1915.

It was there that this 6ft 6¼in, 230lb giant outlasted a tired, fat, demoralised Jack Johnson to win the world heavyweight championship on a twenty-sixth-round knockout. In later years Johnson, one of the supreme champions in history, took to claiming that he dived in return for his safe passage back to the United States, where he was wanted on criminal charges. As evidence he produced the photograph of him lying on his back, his forearm shielding his eyes from the sun, as referee Jack Welch counted him out. Some of the more gullible bought it but, as the modest, stunningly ordinary and straightforward Willard pointed out, a man doesn't wait twenty-six rounds to take a dive. The truth appears to be that early in the fight even a thirty-seven-year-old Johnson out-boxed Willard easily, but lacked the snap and weight in his punches to make much impression on a strong, very game challenger. As the fight wore on, Johnson tired and Willard gradually took over and then knocked him out.

Willard was born at the end of 1881 in Kansas on the lands of the Pottawatomi nation. Whether or not Jess had any native American blood is unclear, but certainly he grew up alongside them, rode and hunted with them. In his twenties he married his wife Hattie, earned his living breaking in and trading horses, and ran a wagon train. Boxing didn't appear to have entered his mind until he was around twenty-nine years old. He was resilient and reasonably powerful, but slow of foot, big-legged and cumbersome. He developed a modest reputation in Oklahoma but when he boxed in Springfield, Missouri, in October 1911, he quit in the fifth round of a fight with Joe Cox after taking a right to the head. He pulled the referee between them and walked out of the ring!

He moved on to Chicago, leaving his business interests in Kansas in abeyance, and learned a better technique from a former heavyweight, Charles Cutler. As well as a capacity to learn, he showed he did have heart. He fought well in No-Decision bouts against other 'White Hopes', Arthur Pelkey and Luther McCarty. In 1913 his progress was checked by a twenty-round points defeat by Ed 'Gunboat' Smith in San Francisco, and a tragic bout in which an opponent, William 'Bull' Young, died after Willard knocked him out in the eleventh round in Vernon, California. He had doubts about the morality of the sport after Young's death – Jess was cleared of manslaughter charges – but eventually boxed on.

Willard wasn't a devastating puncher – he wore men down with his strength and persistence. He was unique among all the heavyweight champions of the world for, in his entire thirty-five-fight career, he didn't register a single first-round knockout. Before he fought Johnson he was inactive for a year, during which time he somehow managed to sell off seventy-five per cent of his earnings to managers, trainers and hangers-on.

Once he was champion Willard invested the money he did get in a travelling Cowboy circus, then sold the horses to the Government for the war effort. In between circus appearances he defended the championship in Madison Square Garden, New York, in a boring ten-round No Decision with Frank Moran of Pittsburgh. Then, apart from a few low-key exhibitions, he showed scant interest in the championship, preferring well-paid appearances in circus acts and silent movies. Finally, Tex Rickard tempted him back to the ring with an offer of $100,000 to box Jack Dempsey in a specially constructed ring on the shores of Maumee Bay, an inlet of Lake Erie outside Toledo, Ohio on 4 July 1919. By now shorn of most of his back-slappers, Willard knew he would keep most of the money, but at thirty-seven couldn't shift the bulk. The best he could manage was 245lbs. In spite of his inactivity and modest talents, his reputation masked the truth in the eyes of the general public. To so many he was still the fabled giant who knocked out Jack Johnson. He believed in his own hype. The night before he told writer Grantland Rice he would knock out Dempsey with an uppercut.

The fact was that it was Dempsey who was the more experienced – and infinitely superior – fighter. Dempsey had been working the hobo jungles since he was a boy, hit ferociously hard, and knew how to fight. Nobody could fault Willard's courage – he got up from seven knockdowns in round one and fought on through the pain even with multiple fractures of his cheek and with two teeth knocked out. He stayed on his stool after round three, during which some in the crowd were crying out, 'Stop it!' When a journalist went to his corner in search of a fast quote, Willard was repeating over and again, softly to himself, 'I have a farm in Kansas and $100,000... I have a farm in Kansas and $100,000.'

Ironically, as Johnson had done before him, Willard tried to explain away his defeat. 'I have it on good authority that Dempsey's bandages were hardened,' he said many years later. Yet his chief second, Walt Monoghan, oversaw Dempsey's hands being wrapped in the dressing room and then the gloves put on in the ring.

Willard retired to California, but had an idea to open a supermarket-style store in Hollywood and decided to finance it by boxing again. He knocked out Floyd Johnson in eleven rounds in May 1923 in New York, but then, for a purse of $125,000, he lost in eight to Luis Firpo in July and retired for good at the age of forty-one. He remained in the Los Angeles area for the rest of his life, was a respected family man and enjoyed a variety of business interests. He died in the Lutheran hospital in Los Angeles on 15 December 1968, aged eighty-six.

CARL WILLIAMS

Born: 11 November 1959, Jamaica, New York
Height: 6ft 4in   **Weight at peak:** 213-218 lbs (15st 3lbs-15st 8lbs)
Fights: 40   **Won:** 30   **Lost:** 10
KO percentage: 52
Rounds boxed: 241
World title fights: 2
Career span: 1982-97 (15 years)
KO wins: 21
KO defeats: 5

Carl Williams, who called himself 'The Truth', fought twice for the world title in the 1980s: as a relative unknown he gave Larry Holmes a gruelling fifteen-rounder in 1985 and four years on he was taken out in ninety-three seconds by Mike Tyson. Williams was also unwittingly responsible for one of the better wise-cracks of his era. Posing with Don King for promotional photos, one jaundiced hack said, 'That's the nearest to the truth Don's ever been!'

Williams, from New York, learned his trade in novice bouts in the small Felt Forum arena in Madison Square Garden. He broke into the world class in his sixteenth bout when he recovered from a shocking start – knocked down twice in the first round – to win a wide ten-round decision over James Tillis in Atlantic City. That was enough for him to be picked as Holmes's forty-eighth opponent. Williams, with nothing to lose, fought above expectations and even managed to close Holmes's right eye, but lost.

It was a twelve-round decision over Trevor Berbick that earned him his shot at Tyson in Atlantic City in July 1989. Little more than a minute had gone when

Tyson crashed a left hook against Williams' jaw and he went down in a heap. He got up, but referee Randy Neumann waved it over.

CLEVELAND WILLIAMS

Born: 30 June 1933, Griffin, Georgia
Died: 3 September 1999, Houston, Texas, aged 66
Height: 6ft 3in   **Weight at peak:** 210lbs (15st)
Fights: 92   **Won:** 78   **Lost:** 13   **Drawn:** 1
KO percentage: 63
Rounds boxed: 471
World title fights: 1
Career span: 1951-72 (21 years)
KO wins: 58
KO defeats: 8

It's a shame that the man they called the Big Cat should be remembered as the fall guy in what most see as Muhammad Ali's most ruthless, punch-perfect performance.

Ali was brilliant, certainly, but when Cleveland Williams fought him for the world title before 35,460 mostly Texan fans at Houston Astrodome in November 1966, he was thirty-three years old – and still had a bullet in his belly from a police shooting. Williams was shot in the stomach from a .357 magnum in the hands of Texas State Highway Patrol officer Dale Witten in November 1964. Witten stopped the fighter in his car because he was driving too fast on a highway known as Jack Rabbit Road and arrested him on suspicion of drink-driving. Witten said they scuffled briefly and the gun went off accidentally. Williams said he tried to talk Witten out of arresting him but was alarmed to find he was being taken not to Houston but to a place called Tomball.

'That didn't sound too good for a coloured man to get into,' he said. 'I told him I didn't want to go. He reached for his holster and I pulled his hand down and the next thing I knew I felt funny inside... all burning up.' The bullet ripped through his intestines and bladder and lodged in his hip joint. It also damaged nerves that controlled the use of his left leg. Tommy Cleboski, a homicide officer who arrived a few minutes later, said Williams' stomach was grotesquely swollen as he thrashed around on the ground: 'I didn't think he'd live to make the ambulance,' he added. The doctor who operated on him said the Magnum was fired from such close range it might as well have been a deer rifle. Cleboski went with the ambulance and told a hospital orderly when they arrived, 'You got a million dollars worth of fighter here. For God's sake, do something.'

The Cat 'died' on the operating table four times, had a kidney removed, but lived. Local fighters Mark Tessman, Tod Herring and Dave Birch were among those who raced to the hospital to give blood. The blood in his body was replaced three times.

Given the desperate state of his health that winter – he lost 60lbs in weight – it's incredible that he boxed again, let alone fought for the championship, but when he returned in February 1966, it was with a first-round knockout. The opponent, 'Big' Ben Black of Chicago, didn't mean much, but 7,500 people in the Sam Houston Coliseum shouted themselves hoarse. A month later Williams outpointed Mel Turnbow, and a month after that he went ten rounds again to beat Sonny Moore. A third-round knockout of the same Tod Herring who had given him life-saving blood completed the rehabilitation.

Meanwhile a Texan court gave him, for aggravated assault on the police officer who shot him, thirty days in jail.

Williams trained for the Ali fight on the 2,000-acre cattle ranch of his oil magnate manager Hugh Benbow. He said, 'If there's one thing I'm not, it's an old man.' Maybe he wasn't, but in the seven minutes and eight seconds that followed the opening bell, he became one. The Williams camp felt Ali would run, use his speed and not want to take on a man who had won sixty-five of seventy-one fights and knocked out fifty-one of his victims. As he would do years later against George Foreman, Ali contradicted the established logic and, after dancing and jabbing for one round, 'out-punched the puncher'. In round two a chopping right hand knocked Williams down for a count of two. Another one floored him for six – and drove his teeth through his mouthpiece into his lower lip. At the end of the round a ferocious attack left Cleveland flat on his back and although he was saved by the bell, his corner should have retired him. Instead they broke ammonia capsules under his nose and sent him out again. He tried but an almost casually venomous barrage of blows put him over again. He got up but was being hit at will and Harry Kessler waved the slaughter over. In the dressing room Benbow swore at him. 'All the ballyhoo scared him to death,' said the manager.

As Williams walked out of the arena, supported on one side by his wife Irene and on the other by his father-in-law, a clergyman, he was still dazed. Mrs Williams told reporters quietly, 'This will just make our life happier. He won't fight no more.' However, although Williams grossed around $160,000 he had taxes and debts to pay – and they held up his money. 'I wanted to do something for my mother, my kids,' he said. 'I ended up fighting for nothing.' He couldn't keep up the payments on his mortgage – and after working on a building site, decided to box again.

Williams was born of African-American and Cherokee heritage in Griffin, Georgia, in 1933. By the time he was eight he was working the fields behind the family mule. By the time he was fourteen he was having an unofficial professional fight here and there. At eighteen, in 1951, his career was official. By 1954 he was on the fringe of world class... then was beaten in three rounds by the erratic but heavy-punching Bob Satterfield. When he returned in 1956 he was living in Houston, where he spent the rest of his life. When he travelled to London to box Dick Richardson he pulled out and went home because he said he had received a message from God. Like Nino Valdes, he should have boxed world champion

Floyd Patterson but was ignored, and like Valdes he was blown out of the picture by Sonny Liston, who knocked him out twice, in 1959 and in 1960.

Williams came back and in April 1962 defeated future WBA champion Ernie Terrell in seven rounds. He couldn't squeeze past the wily Eddie Machen though, and was fortunate to get a draw. Terrell out-boxed him over ten rounds in a rematch in April 1963, but Wiliams stayed in the frame... until his altercation with Officer Witten.

From the late 1970s Williams suffered from diabetes and also had problems with his remaining kidney. He was on his way home from a dialysis session at hospital on 14 September 1999 when he was hit by a car and killed. He was sixty-six.

HARRY WILLS

Born: 15 May 1889, New Orleans, Louisiana
Died: 21 December 1958, New York aged 69
Height: 6ft 4in   **Weight at peak:** 220lbs (15st 10lbs)
Fights: 102   **Won:** 77   **Lost:** 9   **Drawn:** 3   **No Decisions:** 13
KO percentage: 47
Rounds boxed: 607
World title fights: 0
Career span: 1910-32 (22 years)
KO wins: 48
KO defeats: 4

Harry Wills, known as 'The Panther', was kept away from a championship fight because of the colour of his skin. It was part racial prejudice, part plain business rationale, for Tex Rickard and 'white' America remembered all too clearly the riots that scandalised the country following Jack Johnson's one-sided demolition of James J. Jeffries in Reno in 1910. Even though Wills was his own man and, had he won the title, would have lived his own life, not a replica of Johnson's, Rickard feared a premature end to the era of the million-dollar gates. Jack Dempsey was Rickard's golden goose and he saw no point in committing business suicide by risking him losing to a black man from the Deep South. Therefore, although Dempsey himself was happy to box Wills – and indeed signed to do so in 1922 – Rickard kept finding ways of avoiding the fight.

Once, Dempsey's lawyers even paid Harry $50,000 in compensation. Nat Fleischer, who edited *Ring*, pressed Wills's case in only the third issue of the magazine. Even when William Muldoon, the New York State Athletic Commission head, declared that Dempsey would not box again in New York unless it was against Wills, his words turned out to be bluster. In 1923, Muldoon allowed Rickard to promote Dempsey's defence against Luis Angel Firpo at the Polo Grounds. Under pressure, Rickard finally agreed to promote a Dempsey-Wills fight but by that time the champion was making movies in Hollywood with his new wife Estelle

Taylor and then took himself off on a prolonged European holiday. By then Wills was in his thirties and may well have lost to Dempsey anyway. But it remains one of the sad chronicles of boxing history that he was refused the chance to try.

Wills was born in the dock area of New Orleans in 1889, although during his career he often knocked two or three years off his age. He worked on the docks as soon as he was able to be of use. By 1914 he was a world-class heavyweight, competing well against the best black fighters of his time: Joe Jeannette, Sam Langford, Jeff Clarke and Sam McVey. Surprisingly, Fleischer's description of Wills's style suggests a rather crude fighter instead of the lithe, elegant athlete of legend. 'His favourite method of operation was to close in on an opponent, grab and hold him with his left hand, and club away with his right to the head and body,' wrote Fleischer. In July 1920, Wills knocked out one-time contender Fred Fulton with body punches in three rounds in Newark, with Dempsey at ringside, and the following year polished off the faded Gunboat Smith in one. Between 1917 and 1922 he was unbeaten in thirty-six bouts. After a freak disqualification loss to Tate, he added another fifteen fights without a defeat before at the age of thirty-seven he was handed down a one-sided pounding by future world champ Jack Sharkey in Ebbets Field, Brooklyn, in October 1926.

While he was waiting for Dempsey in 1924, he took on Luis Angel Firpo in a twelve-round No-Decision contest before a 70,000 crowd at Boyle's Thirty Acres in Jersey City. Unlike Firpo's two-round, eleven-knockdown war with Dempsey, this one went the full distance, but Wills was superior, according to Fleischer, and won at least ten of the twelve rounds. Immediately afterwards Firpo was arrested on suspicion of having brought a female manicurist with him from Argentina for immoral purposes and having perjured himself on his immigration forms. The charges didn't stick.

Wills invested the money from his ring earnings into several properties in Harlem, including a block that housed thirty-two families, which gave him financial security when he retired. Throughout his life he remained a fitness fanatic, sleeping only four or five hours a night, walking twelve miles a day and insisting on fasting for one month out of every year. In later life he developed diabetes, which was the primary cause of his death in New York four days before Christmas, 1958, when he was sixty-nine.

TIM WITHERSPOON

Born: 27 December 1957, Philadelphia, Pennsylvania
Height: 6ft 3½in   **Weight at peak:** 220lbs (15st 10lbs)
Fights: 69   **Won:** 55   **Lost:** 13   **Drawn:** 1
KO percentage: 55
Rounds boxed: 425
World champion: 1984 (WBC) 1986 (WBA)

World title fights: 6
Career span: 1979-2003 (24 years)
KO wins: 38
KO defeats: 4

'Terrible'Tim Witherspoon twice held versions of the world title during the 'forgotten era' of the mid-1980s when the championship seemed a fluid, unsubstantial prize. He also took promoter Don King and his son Carl to court and won a $1 million settlement over his claim that he had been financially exploited.

Witherspoon was a twenty-five-year-old near-novice when he had a nothing-to-lose challenge with Larry Holmes for the WBC title in Las Vegas in May 1983. Holmes beat him on points at the Dunes Hotel (which was later blown up for a movie scene) but there were those who considered the champion lucky to squeeze home on a split decision. Witherspoon was strong, fresh and talented and staggered the champion in round nine.

From the streets of Philadelphia, Witherspoon had only a handful of amateur contests, played tight end in the football team at Lincoln University, Missouri, and briefly worked as a waiter. His father, Charley, was a truck driver, his mother Shirley worked in a doctors' surgery. He was a sparring partner for Muhammad Ali and Matthew Saad Muhammad and earned his chance against Holmes with a ten-round decision over Renaldo Snipes in Las Vegas in June 1982. By then he was hooked up with King, who had bought his contract from his original manager, Mark Stewart. King installed his son Carl as Witherspoon's manager.

Witherspoon stopped James Tillis in a round and then in March 1984, with Holmes now recognised by the IBF, Witherspoon beat another King-promoted fighter, Greg Page, on a twelve-round majority decision to become WBC champion. Before he won the title Witherspoon told the *New York Times*, 'It's like we're racehorses. They race us until we drop and then they shoot us. And if we win, they tie a blue ribbon around our neck.'

In Jack Newfield's celebrated book *Only in America: The Life and Crimes of Don King*, he also quoted Witherspoon as saying, 'Before the fight Don told me that if I didn't get knocked out, he would make sure I won the decision. He said if I'm standing at the end, I'll win.' According to Newfield, Witherspoon's contracted purse was $250,000. He received $44,640.

His reign lasted five months. After rebelling in King's training camp in Ohio, he lost to Pinklon Thomas at the Riviera, Las Vegas, in August 1984. He left King, then changed his mind and returned. Still only twenty-six, he came back well with a string of wins, including a unanimous decision over Bonecrusher Smith, and then won the WBA belt in Atlanta, Georgia, in January 1986 with a fifteen-round majority decision over Tony Tubbs. Witherspoon, however, failed the dope test, coming up positive for marijuana. King somehow persuaded the WBA not to strip him of the title. Witherspoon, who admitted the offence, had lost interest and let his weight balloon between fights. He was seven pounds heavier for his first defence against Frank Bruno at Wembley Stadium than he had been for Tubbs, and 15lbs heavier than he had been for the Holmes fight of three years before. He also earned a take-home cheque of only $90,094. He was too good for Bruno, whose earnest effort folded in the eleventh round.

Witherspoon was in no psychological condition to defend his WBA title in Madison Square Garden in December 1986. He was matched with Tubbs, with the winner to box Tyson the following March. However, Tubbs pulled out, Bonecrusher Smith came in, and Witherspoon, his mind anywhere but in the arena, was nailed early, floored three times and stopped in the opening round. 'I didn't care,' he said. 'Losing meant Don was out of my life, and that was all I wanted.' Two days later, the New York Commission announced Witherspoon had failed the dope test, then later revealed that they had made a mistake. The FBI looked at the fight, at the New York Commission and at the Kings' operation.

Although he boxed for another seventeen years, he was not given another championship opportunity. In spite of the King court settlement in 1992, which provided him with $1 million in three instalments, he was his own walking disaster area. He blew the money and in his mid-forties was still scuffling away with third-raters before, at last, turning to training fighters.

BRUCE WOODCOCK

Born: 18 January 1921, Doncaster, England
Died: 21 December 1997, Doncaster, aged 76
Height: 6ft   **Weight at peak:** 188-190lbs (13st 6lbs-13st 8lbs)
Fights: 39   **Won:** 35   **Lost:** 4
KO percentage: 76
Rounds boxed: 199
World title fights: 0
Career span: 1942-50 (8 years)
KO wins: 30
KO defeats: 4

Britain's boxing hero of the years immediately following the Second World War, Bruce Woodcock was a decent boxer with a fair dig, but wasn't good enough to survive in the highest class.

Woodcock went to New York to make his American debut in Madison Square Garden against Tami Mauriello and, after being stunned by a clash of heads, was knocked out in the fifth round. Immensely popular, one of his best wins was when he wore down the world light-heavyweight champion Gus Lesnevich for an eighth-round stoppage before a sellout crowd at Harringay Arena in September 1946. However, Woodcock was badly hurt in a seven-rounds mauling by Joe Baksi at Harringay in April 1947. A right had almost had Bruce out in round one and, when it was all over, his left eye was seriously damaged. With hindsight he should have been taken straight to hospital. Instead, he was driven home to Yorkshire.

When the eye showed no improvement, he went to the hospital where doctors discovered he was in danger of going blind and operated. He lay still in hospital for a month. 'I had a detached retina,' he said. 'A specialist told me I must never box again, but what could I do? I had a young family and it was the only way I knew of making money.' He returned to the ring in September 1948 with an effortless four-round knockout of a reluctant Lee Oma. That led, eventually, to a fourteenth-round win over the reigning world light-heavyweight champion Freddie Mills before a 46,000 crowd at White City, London.

In June 1950, promoter Jack Solomons declared a fight between Woodcock and Lee Savold was a world heavyweight title fight following the retirement, fifteen months earlier, of Joe Louis. Solomons canvassed and received support from the British Boxing Board of Control and from the New York State Commission. Woodcock had won a previous fight on a low-blow disqualification. Solomons was foiled when Savold won because of a dreadful, curving cut above Woodcock's left eye that curtailed the fight in the fourth round. This time the crowd was estimated at 60,000. Woodcock retired when his one good eye was swollen shut against Jack Gardner and he quit the ring.

Eventually he did go blind in that left eye, and lost interest in boxing, but he remained a down-to-earth, honest man who preferred a quiet, homely existence to the bright lights. He died on 21 December 1997 aged seventy-six.

Y

JIMMY YOUNG

Born: 16 November 1948, Philadelphia
Died: 20 February 2005, Philadlephia, aged 56
Height: 6ft 2in   **Weight at peak:** 211lbs (15st 1lb)
Fights: 56   **Won:** 34   **Lost:** 19   **Drawn:** 2   **No Contests:** 1
KO percentage: 19
Rounds boxed: 437
World title fights: 1
Career span: 1969-88 (19 years)
KO wins: 11
KO defeats: 2

A slick operator from Philadelphia, Jimmy Young always believed he should have been the heavyweight champion of the world in 1976. Young ducked, dived and messed around the ageing Muhammad Ali for fifteen rounds at the Capital Centre in Landover, Maryland, and at the end had no doubts he had won.

The judges disagreed: as far as they were concerned it was Ali who had won with something to spare: in rounds one scored 11-4 for the champion, another 10-3-2, and only the third made it close at 7-5-3. There were plenty of critics at ringside who thought it was a bad call – including Dick Young of the *New York Times* who had his namesake winning eleven rounds! There were more among the paid attendance of 12,472 and among those watching on live coast-to-coast television who thought Ali lost. Ali said, 'I just didn't have it. Maybe I was out too late last night!'

It is fair to assume Ali's mind was not properly attuned to the Young fight. Before it he had been invited to the White House, where he had talked with President Gerald Ford at a state banquet for King Hussein of Jordan – an astonishing turnaround in events given his stand against the Vietnam War a decade earlier.

Young, a blue-collar fighter from Philadelphia, had worked his way into the world class from a day job as a welder. He turned professional to make a little extra money because his wife Barbara was expecting their second daughter. Under trainer Bob Brown at Joe Frazier's North Broad Street gym, he turned into an expert counter-puncher with a good jab. Exciting he was not. Effective he certainly was. He sparred with Joe Frazier and Ken Norton as he learned – and once picked up $50 for an exhibition with Ali. There were disappointments: a ten-round points defeat by Randy Neumann, a one-round knockout by Shavers, a draw in London against Billy Aird. Should we think it was all bad, when he lost to Shavers he was visited in his dressing room by Diana Ross and the Supremes, who wanted to check he was all right.

He did return to England, where his style was admired, to beat Richard Dunn in eight and out-point the Reading heavyweight Les Stevens, and a return with Shavers ended in a draw. In February 1975 in Honolulu, Young decisively outboxed Ron Lyle over ten rounds. Three months later it was Lyle who challenged Ali. Young won two more bouts, then signed for Don King. And, as if by a miracle, following a ten-round win over Jose Roman in San Juan, the Ali fight materialised. Even in defeat he was suddenly hot. In November 1976 he beat Lyle again, over twelve rounds in San Francisco, and then in March 1977 he ended the (first) career of George Foreman by outsmarting him in another twelve-rounder in Puerto Rico. Young rounded off a tremendous display of ringcraft by knocking Foreman down in the last round and won 118-111, 116-112 and a ridiculously close 115-114.

In a fight recognised as a final eliminator for the WBC title at Caesars Palace, Las Vegas, in November 1977, Young lost a fifteen-round split decision to Norton, who was then awarded the WBC belt when Leon Spinks refused to defend against him the following year. Young won 144-142 on one judge's card, but the others both saw it 147-143 for Norton. That disappointment took something out of Young and he lost his way in a fog of depression: he was smoking cigarettes, drinking beer and eventually became addicted to cocaine.

He lost to Ossie Ocasio and Michael Dokes and, although he did return to London and drag up some of his old enthusiasm to out-box John L. Gardner, he was blown out of the picture when Gerry Cooney stopped him in four rounds in Atlantic City in 1980.

Following his retirement in the late 1980s he worked where he could at whatever manual labour he could find. His memory was sharp into his fifties and his marriage, which began when he and his wife were teenagers, remained intact. Young died of a heart attack in Hahnemann University Hospital, Philadelphia, on 20 February 2005. He was fifty-six.

Z

LORENZO ZANON

Born: 10 September 1951, Noverdrate, Italy
Height: 6ft 2in   **Weight at peak:** 210lbs (15st)
Fights: 36   **Won:** 27   **Lost:** 6   **Drawn:** 3
KO percentage: 25
Rounds boxed: 235
World title fights: 1
Career span: 1973-81 (8 years)
KO wins: 9
KO defeats: 5

The clever but fragile Italian Lorenzo Zanon lost in six rounds to Larry Holmes for the WBC title at Caesars Palace, Las Vegas, in February 1980. In his only previous fights outside Europe, Zanon had lost in five rounds to Ken Norton and in nine to Jerry Quarry. He could box, but he tended to unravel under serious pressure.

Zanon had beaten Alfredo Evangelista in Turin to win the European heavyweight title in April 1979, but was way out of his depth when he was thrown to Holmes. He retired two years later.

DAVE ZYGLEWICZ

Born: 21 September 1943, Troy, New York
Height: 5ft 10in   **Weight at peak:** 190lbs (13st 8lbs)
Fights: 36   **Won:** 31   **Lost:** 4   **Drawn:** 1
KO Percentage: 44
Rounds boxed: 215
World title fights: 1
Career span: 1965-82 (17 years)
KO wins: 16
KO defeats: 2

Dave Zyglewicz had ninety-six seconds of fame – the time it took Smokin' Joe Frazier to knock him out in in their world heavyweight title fight in Houston in April 1969. Afterwards the gags came thick and fast. 'He shoulda zigged instead of zagged,' said one. 'He tried to confuse Joe with his name,' said another. So who was Dave Zyglewicz, rarely heard of before that night and certainly not after it?

Originally from Watervliet, New York, as a teenager he turned down a college football scholarship to join the navy, where he began to box. When he left the service he followed up an advertisement for young heavyweights placed by Texan manager Hugh Benbow. He won a regional Golden Gloves title and as a pro earned himself a reputation as an all-action if raw heavyweight slugger. One writer got carried away and called him a new Rocky Marciano.

By the time they matched him with Frazier he had won twenty-eight of twenty-nine bouts, the sole defeat on points over ten rounds against Sam Waytt in Los Angeles in April 1968. Fighting Frazier was a ridiculous gamble, but maybe Benbow decided Zyglewicz couldn't fight much, would be knocked out by somebody and therefore might as well get well paid for it. He walked in, his gloves low, and was dropped by a left hook. A look of astonishment and pain seemed to freeze him, but he got up at six and tore in again. Frazier switched to the body, then poleaxed him with a left hook to the jaw.

If you are interested in purchasing other books published by Tempus,
or in case you have difficulty finding any Tempus books in your local bookshop,
you can also place orders directly through our website

www.tempus-publishing.com